LUCIFER RISING

T0151186

LUCIFER RISING

Gavin Baddeley

PLEXUS, LONDON

All rights reserved including the right
of reproduction in whole or in part in any form
Copyright © 2016, 2006, 1999 by Gavin Baddeley
Published by Plexus Publishing Limited
The Studio, Hillgate Place
18-20 Balham Hill
London SW12 9ER

British Library Cataloguing in Publication Data
A catalogue record for this book is available from the British
Library

ISBN 978-0-85965-547-7

Cover design by Coco Balderrama
Book design by Mitchell Associates
Cover painting by Diabolus Rex
Printed in Great Britain by Bell & Bain Ltd, Glasgow

CONTENTS

Part Three - The Satanic Millenium

ACKNOWLEDGEMENTS

There are numerous individuals whose input, in various ways, made this book easier to write: My editor, Paul Woods, who turned my profane rantings into something approximating English with grace under pressure. My lodger and drinking partner Jason, who put up with the frequently bizarre moods and strange smells this book inspired. To my own Marquise de Merteuil, and a dangerous liaison that I will forever remember as 'beyond my control'. Kat, who continues to enchant and infuriate me just like a woman should, after many years. MacBee, who was often the only voice of sanity I'd hear for weeks. My parents, without whose Original Sin none of this would have been possible. And a reluctant salute is also due to the Evil Green Fairy. You people have a lot to answer for . . .

I'd also like to thank all of my interview subjects for sharing their time and views – whether incisive or insane – and giving readers a break from my voice. Those (anti-)heroes of the Church of Satan, Nick Bougas and Peter Gilmore, were particularly generous in providing unique photographs. Salvation Films, Hallam Foster of *Kerrang!* and Kip Trevor of Black Widow all provided essential pictures at the last minute. Stefano Piselli of Glittering Images deserves a definite tip of the hat, as do the doyen of cinema esoterica, Pete Tombs and Cathal Tohill. Jonathan at Midian, Ben at Caduceus and Michael at Delectus all deserve credit – both for providing me with rare artwork and for running such excellent book dealerships. They also deserve your custom. Stuart Ness of Luna Press also made himself invaluable in checking some points of information.

All other picture credits are acknowledged in the following rogues' gallery: Dover Books; British Film Institute; Cambridge University Library; Fortean Picture Library; History Today; Stadische Galerie Im Lenbachhaus, Munich; Wide World Photos; Paul A. Woods; Edwin Pouncey; Jordi Bernet/Glittering Images; Kinema Collection; Mark Weiss/LGI; Sandy Robertson; David Austen; Sister N'aama; News of the World/Alpha; Jonathan Self; Holland Photo Agencies; Mercury Records; Witchfynde; Metal Blade Records; Quorthon; Retna; Press Association Library; Topham Picture Library; Jay Blakesberg; Mute Records; Visionary Video; Kat; Paul Douglas Valentine; Christos Beest; Paul Douglas Valentine; Roadrunner Records; Timothy Patrick Butler; Dreamtime; Carl Abrahamsson; Fetish 23; Thomas Thorn; Lee Barrett; Osmose Productions; Michael Moynihan; Music for Nations; Misanthropy Records; Hollywood Records; Paul Ledney; Vincent Crowley; Cradle of Filth; Kerry Bolton; Luciferian Light Group; Suzan Moore/All Action; 3DO; Coop; Vivienne Maricevic/Gotherotica; Diabolus Rex.

As for the 'no thanks' section: there were numerous people who wasted my time, got on my nerves or just stood in my light while I was thrashing out my little opus. I'd like to say you know who you are, but most of you aren't even that self-aware.

See you in Hell, gentlemen!

INTRODUCTION

'Please Allow Me To Introduce Myself ...'

Satanism sells. Hot blood, forbidden sex, strange powers. It's a tempting cocktail. If anybody tries to sell you Satanism, always check out their agenda. Nobody launches themselves into territory like this without some kind of axe to grind.

Most books about Satanism fit into one of three categories. The first category are written by Christians – full of half-truths and straight bullshit – to massage the faith of the pious. These books can be quite amusing, but are no more valid than a history of the Passover written by a PLO member.

The second category are 'true crime' exposés. About halfway through, the authors of these potboilers tend to run out of murderous Devil-worshippers and rope in any lurid crime with a tenuous religious link. This leaves us in the curious position of having to accept various maverick Christian criminals as somehow 'Satanic'. The portrayal of Satanism as an international murder club demonstrates the authors' very loose grasp of the facts.

The third category are quick-buck efforts written by journalists or professional hacks. Feigning authority, these sensationalist 'studies' rely almost exclusively on information gleaned from the previous two categories. Don't get me wrong – avarice and sloth may be fine attributes, but the other five deadly sins rate much more highly as spectator sports.

So where does my contribution fit into all this? Since I started researching this book, some years back, I've thrown in my lot with the unholy opposition. I'm now a Devil's advocate, a card-carrying Satanist, an ordained Reverend (though I prefer the title 'Irreverend') of the Church of Satan. My book will obviously reflect this. Don't go thinking, however, that my perspective has been distorted by Satanism. Rather, it became apparent long ago that my sympathy for the Devil was predetermined by the perspective I already held. But don't worry either about me setting out to convert you – as this book will show, it just doesn't work that way.

Similarly, don't expect any whitewash. Satanism is a 'warts and all' approach to existence, a determination to explore extremes of both light and dark. Interviews in Parts Two and Three of this book have been left as intact as space allows, to air the conflicting voices on the Satanic scene. Dissent is an important aspect of the demonic – and besides, if Satanists can't make use of a little bad press, then who can?

The Devil's attitude is an irreverent one – flippancy may set the tone, but I challenge anyone to accuse me of bad research on that account. I did not write this book to win friends, but I haven't set out to give mindless offence either. (If, on the other hand, your reaction provokes some independent thought, I'm happy to take credit for that.)

Regardless of what sanctimonious Christians, or their smug equivalents in the humanist camp, might have you believe, Satanism is neither trivial nor tainted with some moral radiation that makes it too dangerous to contemplate. Inasmuch as the Western world is still a Christian culture, Satanism is the archetypal counterculture. It's a vital but neglected aspect of our past, present and – most importantly – the future ...

PART I

THE HISTORY OF SATANISM

THE SATANIC TRADITION

A Brief History of Satanism

ehind the accepted history of our civilisation – of great leaders and mass movements, of politics and progress – there is an alternative history, a shadow tradition. It is an oft-neglected world full of villains and vice, scoundrels and sorcerers, with an impact upon our culture out of proportion with the numbers of people involved. And much of that impact – in contrast with the catalogue of torture, rape and murder committed by those crusading on the side of 'good' – has been positive. This is the history of the dark side of Western culture: the Satanic tradition.

The beginning of our story takes us back four millennia, when the seeds of our culture were first cast across the arid plains of the Middle East. Incredibly, the prophecies and primitive laws first voiced by the forefathers of the Jewish race still echo in the law courts, schools, government buildings and temples of our modern world. The Old Testament, the first part of *The Bible*, describes how the Jews made a covenant or pact with the god Jehovah, often dubbed simply 'God'. Jehovah is a god of total power whose religion will tolerate no competition. He is a dictator deity, a jealous tyrant who treats His creation with the same petulant cruelty as a spoilt brat treats a box of long-suffering toys.

With a God as savage and spiteful as Jehovah there is little space for a Devil, and so the God of the Jews happily takes responsibility for both good and evil. The word 'Satan', in the original Hebrew, means only 'opponent' or 'accuser' – numerous holy figures, even Jehovah Himself, are referred to as 'Satans' in the Old Testament. The Jewish Devil, inasmuch as He exists at all, is a folkloric figure rather than a theological entity. He is a minion of God rather than his opponent, a servant charged with testing mortals. Those creatures who do defy Jehovah – like Leviathan or Moloch – are merely walk-on parts to be toppled by the Almighty in bouts of divine machismo, like the gallery of monsters conjured by Japanese film-makers to be destroyed by Godzilla.

Even the serpent in the Garden of Eden – who tempts Adam and Eve to 'Original Sin' – does not become a manifestation of evil ('that Ancient Serpent', as Satan is sometimes known) until later. This change occurs with the advent of Christianity, which promotes Satan from a mischievous servant of God to His implacable opponent.

Christianity was codified in the first century A.D. in the New Testament, an unofficial sequel to the first book of *The Bible* with tacked-on accounts of the life of an obscure Jewish cult leader named Jesus. One of a host of dubious prophets and crazy gurus who plagued the

Eastern provinces of the Roman Empire, Jesus claimed to be the son of Jehovah. In the fashion common to modern brainwashing cults, Jesus also demanded that his followers abandon their worldly goods and family to join his crackpot crew. After his execution as an heretical subversive, however, the Jesus cult began taking off.

Most Jews were anticipating a warlike Messiah ('anointed one') who would free them from domination by Rome. Jesus, who spent most of his time fighting imaginary demons, most certainly did not fit the bill, so the Jesus cult rejected their Jewish heritage and threw in their lot with Rome. But the Romans were unenthusiastic to begin with, and there was a practical aspect to their subsequent persecution of the Jesus cult. It was as if the Moonies or Jehovah's Witnesses had tried to set themselves up as the official state religion of the USA. The Roman Empire had thrived by absorbing, rather than destroying, the cultures they conquered, welcoming foreign gods into their temples as part of a policy of conquest by integration.

The Christians could not stomach this. Their God was supreme, and all other deities – initially regarded as hollow superstitions – began to be portrayed by their theologians as actively evil, demonic. This doctrine, demonisation, defined the totalitarian nature of the Christian creed. These demons required a leader, and so Satan was reborn not just as an adversary, but as *the* Adversary. Myths began to grow up around this new Prince of Darkness, cribbed from fanciful reinterpretations of existing doctrine and the ravings of Christian hermits driven half-mad by isolation in the desert.

Early heretical Christian documents known as the Apocryphal Gospels – written between the periods of the Old and New Testaments – claimed that the Devil was once leader of the Watcher angels. These angels were commanded by God to watch over mankind, but they pitied mortal men and lusted after mortal women. For teaching forbidden knowledge and copulating with their charges (in theological terms, the equivalent of a shepherd disgracing himself with his

Satan's power is first suggested in the New Testament, when He tempts Jesus with mastery of the kingdoms of the world – implying He has them all in His possession

flock) these disobedient angels were cast from Heaven to become the denizens of Hell, whilst their children became demons and monsters. Satan – or Semjaza, as He is known here – is the leader of these disobedient angels.

Another more widely-accepted version of the same story has Satan trying to claim God's throne before loyal angels cast Him and his co-conspirators into darkness. Traditionally, the question of whether one personally regards Satan's act as one of treachery or bravery is the definition of an individual's loyalties in the war between darkness and light. Significantly, however, many traditions state that, before His fall from grace, Satan was known as Lucifer: derived from the Latin 'light-bringer'.

This associates Satan with Prometheus, a Greco-Roman Titan (another race of semi-divine giants born from the cross-breeding of gods and mortals) who was the light-bringer in classical mythology. Prometheus pitied humanity in its squalor and ignorance, and so stole fire from the gods to ease Man's suffering. Enraged, the king of the gods punished his impertinence by chaining him to a rock where an eagle pecked out his liver for all eternity.

In Christian mythology, Satan, in the form of a serpent, offers the first humans an apple of wisdom, and is punished by being exiled to Hell. To the pagans Prometheus was a noble figure, his theft a selfless sacrifice. In contrast, Christians longed for the blissful ignorance of the Garden of Eden, regarding the fallen Lucifer as the epitome of evil for tempting humanity with enlightenment. Christianity preached of rewards in the next life, fearing knowledge and pleasure in this world, regarding rebellion as the ultimate sin. It was a cult of ignorance, obedience and abstinence. Over many hundreds of years, a philosophy would develop in direct opposition – dedicated to curiosity, independence and pleasure. These are the roots of Satanism.

Christianity, in common with many cults, was an apocalyptic sect that awaited the end of the world with glee. The last book of *The Bible*, 'Revelations', predicts the imminent cataclysm with such deranged imagery and colourful characters that some commentators have wondered if its author had imbibed psychoactive drugs. The Great Beast, the Whore of Babylon and the Antichrist all struggle for space in a psychedelic narrative wherein the author promises the imminent Apocalypse will bring Satan's minions (all non-Christians) their just desserts (eternal torment). As creeds of universal love go, Christianity is pretty mean-spirited.

But, though the early Christians never got their Apocalypse, they did win their spiritual war when, in the fourth century, an embattled Roman Empire adopted Christianity as the state religion. The short-term benefits were obvious: Christianity appealed to the oppressed, promising them great reward in the afterlife; it also appealed to the oppressor, demanding the downtrodden obeyed their superiors if they wished to enjoy those rewards. The glories of a classical world built on pagan pragmatism were eroded, then destroyed, by Christian intolerance. As the Roman Empire fell, in one of history's many dark ironies the Catholic Church set itself up in its place. Imperial purple was the uniform colour for the Church leaders' new robes, Latin their sacred tongue, Rome their headquarters.

However, while this new Roman Catholic Church could steal the superficial glories of the empire they had destroyed, they could not begin to emulate the culture, comfort or security that Imperial Rome had provided to its citizens. The end of the world had failed to arrive on schedule, but the Four Horsemen of the Apocalypse – War, Death, Famine and Plague – still characterised the medieval era, when the Christian creed held Europe in its thrall. The Middle Ages had arrived, and with them an era of cultural depression, a millennium of darkness, squalor and misery.

The Western European Catholic ('universal') Church and Eastern Orthodox ('straight thinking') Church, who had divided the Roman Empire between them, did not have it all their own way. Some Christians were interpreting *The Bible* in ways that did not suit the new totalitarian Church authorities, and were duly condemned as 'heretics' (derived from the Greek for 'those who make a choice'). This condemnation, which began as hot air, soon translated into burning flesh as the Christian religion made the smooth transition from persecuted to persecutor.

Most significant among these early heretics were the Gnostics, who believed that there were two equally-powerful gods – one 'good', the other 'evil'. Some thought the evil God was the one described in the Old Testament, the creator of this world, while the benevolent God described in the New Testament was his foe. In Gnostic doctrine, only pure spirit was 'good'. All matter, including the human body, was 'evil', and humankind was made up of spirits trapped in prisons of flesh. Widely suppressed with increasing severity, Gnosticism began to take on a variety of increasingly dark and exotic forms. Some Gnostics believed that, as all flesh was evil, it did not matter what use it was put to – in this sense, carnal excess could even be seen as redemptive, as with cults like the third-century Carpocratians, who indulged in ritualised orgies. Others, like the Cainite sect of the fourth century, reasoned that if the Old Testament God was evil, then His opponents must be good – therefore revering Old Testament villains like Cain, who proved his virtue in combat by murdering his brother, Abel. It's tempting to regard these early movements as the first Satanic sects, but the attitude of most Gnostics – that the flesh was inherently evil – was just as pathological as that of their pleasure-hating Catholic oppressors.

This is perhaps best demonstrated by the Cathar sects. The first of these, the Bogomils, was formed in the Balkans during the tenth century. The Bogomils believed Man was created when Satan vomited into an empty human vessel – a vivid illustration of their unhealthy attitude to their own bodies. Their holymen preached against sexual reproduction, leading some to adopt anal sex as a non-procreative alternative, and so the word 'buggery' was derived from 'Bogomil'. The Bogomils heavily influenced another Cathar sect, the Albigensians, who, by the end of the twelfth century, had become so successful that they dominated Southern France with their own clergymen and churches. The Catholic Church simply would not tolerate this kind of competition and, in 1208, launched a brutal crusade against the Albigensians.

The Church's sixteen-year-long campaign of massacres destroyed the Cathars, forcing Gnosticism underground. The ensuing centuries saw a bewildering series of legends grow up around this strange, doomed faith. Some have suggested Gnostic roots for the mysterious Luciferian cult that appears

Lucifer was described as half-bathed in light and half-swathed in darkness by His followers in the Luciferian cult – suggesting the Gnostic idea of a god embracing both good and evil.

to have thrived secretly in thirteenth- and fourteenth-century Germany. They believed that Lucifer – described as a curious, cadaverous figure whose body glowed during their subterranean rites – had been unjustly cast from Heaven by a treacherous God, and honoured Him in orgiastic ceremonies that also featured cats as objects of worship.

One other medieval cult has generated more fanciful theories than the Cathars and Luciferians combined. The Order of the Knights Templar was founded in 1118 to protect Christian pilgrims visiting Jerusalem, combining the military skills of a trained warrior with the pious dedication of a monk. Feared by their heathen foe and revered by their Christian brethren, the Templars rose from poverty-stricken obscurity to become one of the wealthiest, most powerful institutions in Europe. Their fall from grace was just as dramatic when, in 1314, King Philip I of France smashed the Order with a campaign of mass arrests. Philip claimed that, beneath their pious exteriors, these warrior monks were in fact an international Devil-worshipping cult and many of their number, including their Grand Master Jacques de Molay, were burnt alive for their alleged crimes.

Modern historical convention largely regards the Templars as victims of a cynical frame-up, but this has more to do with intellectual fads than hard evidence. Prominent charges against the Templars included anal sex and spitting on the cross, leading some to believe the Order were secret guardians of the Gnostic tradition (Gnostics regarded the cross as a false symbol, believing that Jesus – a spirit with no body – could not have been crucified).

One recurring feature in Templar confessions was the worship of a devil named Baphomet – variously described as a severed head, a curious idol with four faces, or, much later, a leering, goatish figure, Baphomet may have been the mummified head of the Templars' founder, a Gnostic idol, or even some kind of ritual prop. The mystery remains, but the term 'Baphomet' has become an integral part of Satanic terminology, and few occult groups are able to resist evoking the Templars as their historical predecessors.

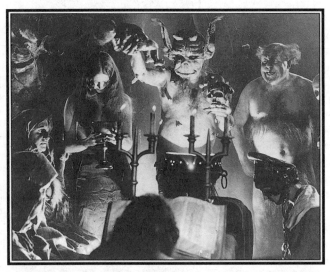

The medieval sabbat was an orgiastic, celebration parodying the solemnity of Christian worship. This early version of the Black Mass is depicted in the classic film Häxan (Witchcraft throughout the Ages – 1922.)

The bloodlust of the medieval Church was far from sated by the persecution of such alleged heretics. In the 1480s, with full papal backing, two monks named Jakob Sprenger and Heinrich Kramer issued a practical witch-hunting manual entitled *Malleus Maleficarum* ('The Hammer of Witches'), describing how to identify witches and force confessions from them under torture before consigning them to the flames. Previously, witchcraft was officially regarded as a delusion, but *Malleus Maleficarum* helped trigger an international campaign of witch-hunts that lasted over two centuries and claimed upwards of a quarter-of-a-million lives in the most brutal circumstances.

The history of witchcraft is swathed in controversy. Did the witch-cult truly exist? And, if it did, did it consist of isolated, eccentric old women, or was it a coherent international movement? And who, or what, did this cult worship? Self-styled early-twentieth century witch-hunter Montague Summers described the witch-cult as an underground conspiracy of 'heretics and anarchists', agreeing with the 'experts' of the period that they were dedicated to destroying the Church and 'turning the world upside down' in the name of their master, Satan. Numerous accounts survive of weird meetings, known as Sabbats, where the witches feasted, took drugs, danced wildly, copulated and cursed their enemies. Today, many historians deny any such rites ever took place, and cast the witch-hunters as sadistic maniacs who butchered innocents. (Indeed, the term 'witch-hunt' now generally denotes the persecution of an innocent by fanatically-unjust authorities.)

Other modern theorists maintain that the witch-cult was a benevolent religion that worshipped ancient nature gods, ancestors of the modern Wiccans – but this has little more than wishful thinking and romanticism to support it. Several more substantial historical accounts refer to Satan with such titles as 'the God of the Serfs': the Middle Ages were desperate times for the peasantry, and, if the Christian clergy supported the nobility, where else could the desperate and downtrodden turn but to the Devil? The witch-cult, therefore, may have been a creed of social rebellion based upon orgiastic revels, drug abuse and the deliberate adoption of heretical symbols, with the witches' Sabbat as a kind of medieval hippie festival.

Certainly, the medieval peasantry regarded the Devil in a very different way to the medieval Church. The grinning gargoyles that leered from church roofs, the slapstick demons that peopled the 'mystery' plays put on by rural villagers, and the Devil who appears in the folk tales of the day – all suggest a view of Satan among ordinary working folk that was sympathetic to Christianity's supposedly terrifying, hateful anti-hero. Almost every primitive culture has had a mythical character – often generically referred to as the 'trickster' – who is a morally-ambivalent figure of fun. Mischievous, horny, creative, lazy, foolish and wise, the trickster embodied the anarchic human spirit. Satan may have been an unusually savage and perverse trickster, but in such grim times it's not surprising that some peasants turned to such a volatile patron when faced with oppression by the clergy and nobility.

It wasn't only the peasantry who made resort to the demonic in times of need. In 1440 the French Baron Gilles de Rais, once one of the most wealthy and powerful men in Europe, was executed for conjuring devils. This wasn't the only charge laid against this licentious warlord, also convicted of the wholesale sexual abuse and murder of dozens – even hundreds – of children. Twentieth-century Christian myth-mongers have highlighted the crimes of Gilles de Rais as an early example of Satanic ritual child abuse. In fact, de Rais was a medieval serial killer, his vile crimes motivated by pathological sexual impulses and chronic alcohol abuse rather than any Satanic conviction. Indeed, evidence reveals Baron Gilles as a fervent Christian – it was almost certainly the internal conflict between his own homosexual urges and the demands of his faith that twisted his libido into such a monstrously sadistic form.

Gilles de Rais was certainly involved in black magic, but this was largely separate from his recreational crimes against children. On the one occasion he made use of the remains of a victim in a magical rite, the Baron was seized by remorse and, uniquely for him, gave the corpse a Christian burial. Like all good Christians, Gilles de Rais was more concerned with his own immortal soul than the actual physical suffering of those around him.

De Rais employed sorcerers as part of his staff when his extravagant lifestyle threatened to bankrupt him. Sorcery and science were, at that time, close bedfellows. In fact, as recently as the eighteenth century, such black arts as alchemy, necromancy and astrology were regarded by many intellectuals as valid areas of scientific study. Then, just as now, many involved in pioneering research were motivated by avarice, with fast-buck schemes a favourite occupation among the scholars and sorcerers of the Middle Ages and Renaissance.

Gilles de Rais employed a number of such characters to discover the alchemical secret of creating gold from base metal. It was generally believed that the darker the magic, the higher the risk – and the higher the risk, the higher the potential reward. The most Satanic of sciences was therefore the invocation of devils, the most dangerous and rewarding of all the dark arts. The sorcerers employed by Gilles de Rais were part of a loose underground of travelling scholars who plied their wares secretly across medieval and Renaissance Europe. Operating outside the authority of the Church-controlled universities, these maverick academics were equally at home translating Greek, brewing strange medicines or confounding their clients with conjuring tricks.

As far as the Church was concerned these men had made pacts with Satan, and, in many cases, they were right. Christian authorities forbade research into the mysteries of the universe as blasphemy. Anybody whose greed or curiosity led them to ignore these warnings had, knowingly or not, thrown in their lot with the forces of darkness. Few of these cerebral heretics were as prominent as Faust – the sixteenth-century European wanderer who reputedly 'called the Devil his brother-in-law'. Faust entered popular folklore via the genre of 'Faustbooks', relating how the rogue sorceror/scientist made a pact with a devil named Mephistopheles (meaning 'flees from the light') in return for pleasure and knowledge, a deal which eventually leads to his spectacular downfall and damnation. Early versions of the story were Christian morality tales, but later versions turned the roguish doctor into an anti-hero whose doomed quest was seen as understandable, or even noble. Prominent among these sympathetic treatments were the 1592 play *Doctor Faustus*, by the hell-raising English atheist Christopher Marlowe, and the 1808 poetic dramatisation *Faust*, by the mystically-inclined German romantic Johann Wolfgang von Goethe.

Medieval serial killer Gilles de Rais is remembered every year at a pageant recreating his life and crimes, at his old castle in Machecoul, France.

Of all the rituals of black magic none are as notorious as the Black Mass. At its most basic level, the Black Mass is a mockery of the orthodox Catholic Mass that substitutes the erotic and the profane for its sacred elements. Whores replace the ordained clergy, the holy altar is a naked woman, the communion wafer is blessed by insertion into her vagina. Other forms of the Black Mass had more specific roles, attempting to harness the holy power of the Mass for unholy ends. Many, if not most, sorcerers had clerical backgrounds, believing the Mass was the most inherently powerful of all Christian ceremonies – just as, outside the Church, there was an underground of sorcerous scholars, within it existed a number of maverick priests who would subvert the Mass in return for money or favours.

It was just such a Black Mass priest, the French cleric Father Guiborg, who stood trial in 1678 alongside a notorious sorceress named Catherine Monvoisin, accused of the attempted murder of Louis XIV by magic. The case was a scandal of epic proportions, involving allegations of illicit abortions, child sacrifice and poisoning, all implicating people within Louis' court. When it became clear that the King's beautiful mistress, the Marquise de Montespan, was also heavily involved (perhaps even serving as the naked altar in one ceremony), Louis decided to draw a veil over events and proceedings were halted. Nevertheless, the macabre episode is dramatic evidence not only that the Black Mass was more than myth, but that it was employed secretly at the highest levels of European society.

Not all practitioners of the Black Mass were as cynical and bloodthirsty as Monvoisin and her acolytes (evidence suggests even here that accusations of child sacrifice actually related to ritual use of aborted foetuses). Other groups existed at this time whose parodies of holy rites were more satirical, if no less heartfelt. An informal network of Hellfire Clubs thrived in Britain during the eighteenth century, dedicated to debauchery and blasphemy. With members drawn from the cream of the political, artistic and literary establishments, they became sufficiently scandalous to inspire a number of Acts of Parliament aimed at their suppression. Historians have been inclined to dismiss the Hellfire Clubs as nothing more than riotous drinking societies, but the significance of many of the nation's most powerful and brilliant men dedicating themselves to Satan is difficult to ignore. That they did so

with laughter on their lips, and a drink in their hands, does not diminish the gesture so much as place them more firmly in the Satanic tradition.

The inspiration for the Hellfire Clubs did not come exclusively from sorcerous sources, but also drew heavily from profane literature – such as *Gargantua*, an unusual work combining folklore, satire, coarse humour and light-hearted philosophy, written in the sixteenth century by a renegade monk named Francois Rabelais. One section of the book concerns a monk who, as reward for bravery in battle, has an abbey built for him that he names Thelema. Like any monastic abbey it is a place of seclusion, but in other respects it's an 'anti-abbey', dedicated to the pleasures of the flesh. Only the brightest, most beautiful and best are permitted within its walls, and its motto is 'Fait Ce Que Vouldras' ('Do What You Will').

One of the last and best known of the Hellfire Clubs was founded in emulation of the Abbey of Thelema, taking on its distinctive motto. This club was known as the Order of Saint Francis, with headquarters in Medmenham Abbey near London and on its founder Sir Francis Dashwood's estate in Buckinghamshire. The Order finally collapsed in the 1760s due to internal conflicts between members over the pressing political issue of the day, the demand for increasing

The Marquis de Sade has influenced generations of deviant philosophers since his death in 1814. This blasphemous orgy scene from his novel Justine *is often mistakenly identified as the first literary record of the Black Mass.*

independence by Britain's American colonies. It's a measure of the club's distinguished membership, however, that it contained prominent politicians from both sides of the debate.

Sir (Saint) Francis was a close personal friend of Benjamin Franklin, the leading spokesman for the colonists in London, and one of the most important figures in founding the independent United States of America. Franklin was a frequent guest at Dashwood's home, and it's tempting to imagine the fate of the American colonies – destined to become the world's most powerful nation – being discussed at a smoky Hellfire Club meeting over fine wines and whores. (This may explain why the American Constitution, partially written by Franklin, made such a revolutionary separation between Church and State.) Anton LaVey, the twentieth century's foremost Satanist, claimed in typically bombastic fashion: 'If people knew of the role the Hell Fire Club played in Benjamin Franklin's structuring of America, it could suggest changes like: "One Nation Under Satan", or "United Satanic America".'

One of the most important figures in the development of Satanic aesthetics and philosophy was a relative of Sir Francis Dashwood, the seventeenth-century English poet John Milton. Milton's masterpiece is *Paradise Lost*, written in 1667, which retells the legends of Man and Satan's fall from grace in a form which could be understood by the common reader. It's more than a literary milestone, contributing a great deal to what is commonly believed about the Devil and his minions – more, in fact, than *The Bible* itself. Most importantly, in Milton's poem Satan achieves a certain dark magnificence, becoming the archetypal anti-hero whose doomed rebellion is the act of a noble, if flawed character, His position most famously expressed in the line 'Better to reign in Hell, than serve in Heav'n.'

Just how and why Milton, a fervently pious man, created such a powerful and attractive Satan is something of a literary mystery. Another English poet, William Blake, offers one of the best-known solutions: 'The reason Milton wrote in fetters when he wrote of Angels & God, and at liberty when of Devils & Hell, is because he was a true Poet and of the Devil's party without knowing it.' Born in 1757, when Sir Francis Dashwood's Hellfire Club was at the height of its influence, Blake was an artist, poet, mystic and epitome of the theory of a thin line between genius and insanity. (The young Blake communed naked in a tree with angels, deriving his vivid poetic style from the visions and prophecies that inspired him.)

It seems strange that the author of 'Jerusalem', still one of the most popular hymns sung in English churches, should belong to the Satanic tradition. But belong he does. In 1900, the Irish playwright George Bernard Shaw wrote *The Devil's Disciple*, a play which features as its noble anti-hero Dick Dudgeon, a fervent philosophical Satanist willing to sacrifice his life for his principles. Shaw observed: 'A century ago William Blake was, like Dick Dudgeon, an avowed Diabolonian: he called his angels devils and his devils angels. His devil is a Redeemer. Let those who have praised my originality in conceiving Dick Dudgeon's strange religion read Blake's *Marriage of Heaven and Hell*, and I shall be fortunate if they do not rail at me for being a plagiarist . . .'

Blake is often regarded as a pioneer of the Romantic movement. Today the term conjures images of willowy fops pressing flowers in flowing, loose-sleeved shirts, but in reality these young men were wild-eyed radicals whose antics led a more restrained poet of the day to label them 'the Satanic School'. Sex and drugs and poetry were the fuel that inspired the fashionable rebel of the early nineteenth century.

'I feel confident that I should have been a rebel Angel had the opportunity been mine,' opined the poet John Keats. The club-footed womaniser Lord Byron observed in his *Miscellaneous Thoughts* that, 'The Devil was the first o' the name / From whom the race of rebels came.' 'Nothing can exceed the energy or magnificence of the character of Satan as expressed in *Paradise Lost*,' wrote his contemporary Percy Bysshe Shelley, in many ways the most thoughtful of the Romantics. Shelley, who was expelled from Oxford University in 1811 for his anti-Christian beliefs, also had a strong demonic vein running through much of his own work.

While the Romantics flirted with Satan, by the end of the nineteenth century a literary movement appeared that positively adored Him. The Decadents were poets, painters and authors who championed extremes of sensation over common sense or convention, their quest taking them to the brothels, opium dens and morgues of the world's most fashionable and exotic cities. Inevitably, Satanism is a prominent theme in the work of these artists.

Most notorious among them is the foppish Isidore Ducasse, better known under his penname of the Comte de Lautreamont. De Lautreamont was absorbed by strongly Satanic ideas about religion and human existence, potently expressed in his masterpiece, the bizarre 1868 epic *The Songs of Maldoror*, which combines nauseating horror and delirious absurdity in a surreal story of a war with God.

The French poet Charles Baudelaire is often regarded as the quintessential Decadent. He once declared 'all literature is the consequence of sin', and the evidence for this is explicit in his work. In the poem, 'Epigraph for a Condemned Book', Baudelaire addresses readers of his most Satanic works, *The Flowers of Evil*, advising them to 'Just throw it out! unless you've learned / Your rhetoric in Satan's school / You will not understand a word, / You'll think I am hysterical.' Indeed, the poetry contained in Baudelaire's masterpiece does appeal to the Satanic spirit with its blend of beauty and decay, balancing a passion for life with a constant awareness of the proximity of death.

The sad-eyed American alcoholic author Edgar Allan Poe had a profound influence on the Decadents – particularly Baudelaire, who translated some of his short stories into French. While there's nothing obviously Satanic about Poe (though his morbid stories and poems were filled with doomed love, insanity and disease) his 1829 poem 'Alone' is a demonic hymn to alienation, one of the major themes of 20th century Satanism: 'From childhood's hour ... I have not seen / As others saw – I could not bring / My passions from a common spring ...'

The artistic world of the late nineteenth century maintained a burgeoning interest in the occult that also centred on Paris, capital city of decadence. The most significant figure of nineteenth-century sorcery was Eliphas Lévi, whose shadow still falls across the history of the occult. In 1856 he published his magnum opus *Dogme et rituel de la haute magie*, (translated as *Transcendental Magic*), quickly building a reputation as Europe's foremost authority on the magical arts. While

One of the first 'Satanic conspiracy' hoaxes was perpetrated by **The Devil in the Nineteenth Century.** *This illustration from the book, 'Lucifer', depicts the devil as an archetypal 1890's dandy.*

outwardly a devoted Christian, a more careful reading of Lévi's works implies he thought Christianity was all well and good for the masses, but that more enlightened souls were entitled to probe deeper. There's a definite ambivalence about Lévi's relationship with Satan – sometimes he roundly denounces the Prince of Darkness, at others he suggests that Satan is potentially a useful or even positive force.

Since the Middle Ages, sorcerers had worked with a bewildering patchwork of ideas borrowed from dozens of different sources and cultures. It was Lévi who first pulled that patchwork together, creating the discipline we now call 'occultism' by mixing Jewish mysticism, Renaissance card games and speculative eighteenth-century science. Subsequently, Lévi's books were period best-sellers, introducing magic to the drawing rooms and coffee-houses of Europe.

During this period, Christianity was also coming under sustained attack from other angles. Among the most significant figures in this assault (albeit a reluctant one) was the English scientist Charles Darwin. The 1859 publication of his *Origin of the Species* sent shockwaves through the foundations of every church in the western world. Darwin's theories shattered Christian fairy stories of Creation and revealed man for what he truly is: an animal. He observed once, in a letter to a friend, 'What a book a devil's chaplain might write on the clumsy, wasteful, blundering, low and horrible cruel works of nature!' If there was a hand shaping Creation, it was not the benevolent touch of a loving God, but a callous and cruel fist. Another important voice in this anti-Christian chorus was the German philosopher Friedrich Nietzsche, who famously declared 'God is dead!' and titled one of his most important works *The Antichrist*. Nietzsche combined poetry and pragmatism in his ridicule of Christianity, which he described as a 'slave religion'. As a radical individualist, Nietzsche believed that creative, talented individuals were of prime, almost mystical importance, in comparison with the cowardly, resentful, expendable mass of humanity. Nietzsche's central idea – his 'master-slave' morality, that transcended the traditional Christian morality of good and evil – was to gain impetus after his death in 1900. It influenced a wide range of people: most infamously, Adolf Hitler – though his patronage sits distinctly at odds with Nietzsche's insistence that he preferred the Jews, as cultural outsiders, to his own dull countrymen – but also the twentieth century's international Satanic community.

In his interpretation of The Temptation of Saint Anthony, *Belgian artist Felicien Rops – one of the most shamelessly Satanic members of the Decadent movement – presents a classic hybrid of the sacred and the erotic.*

Another important anti-Christian figure of the late nineteenth century was the American writer Samuel L. Clemens, better known by his penname of Mark Twain. Many would be surprised to find Twain – author of the wholesome, much-loved *Adventures of Tom Sawyer* and *Huckleberry Finn* – credited as a Satanic thinker, but his own sentiments bear it out. As Twain once wrote in an essay, 'I have always felt friendly towards Satan. Of course that is ancestral; it must be in the blood.' As his life progressed, Twain became increasingly bitter towards Christianity and its brutal, stupid God. His last work was a story entitled 'The Mysterious Stranger', which he reworked several times on account of its importance to him. The stranger of the title is possibly Satan, or at least a relative of His, and the tale relates how He gives a gang of boys a brutal lesson in the futility of life and the cruelty of their Creator.

Twain dedicated much of the last years of his life to satirical pastiches and attacks upon *The Bible*, God, and Christianity in general. In 1906, four years before his death, he wrote to a friend, 'To-morrow I mean to dictate a chapter which will get my heirs and assigns burnt alive if they venture to print it this side of 2006 A.D. – which I judge they won't . . . The edition of A.D. 2006 will make a stir when it comes out. I shall be hovering around taking notice, along with other dead pals. You are invited.'

Twain's pessimistic estimate of how long it would be before the world was ready for his blasphemous work was an overestimate – but only by eleven years (the full anthology of his heretical final thoughts was issued in 1995, entitled *The Bible According to Mark Twain*). It appeared at the end of a century when America had come to dominate the world. It would be nice to believe, however fanciful the idea, that America's best-loved writer was somehow 'hovering around taking notice', as the world entered a new Satanic era.

A New Aeon

he magical orders and mystical fraternities of the nineteenth century endured into the new era. In an age lit by electric light, shadows remained on the fringes of radical Freemasonry, the arts and established religion. From these shadows emerged a colourful cavalcade of rogue mystics and maverick messiahs.

None of these dark stars shone as brightly as Aleister Crowley. Crowley, the self-styled 'Great Beast', declared himself the 'magical child' (via a kind of mystical adoption scheme) of Eliphas Lévi, the French magus who dominated nineteenth-century occultism. Often referred to as 'the father of modern Satanism', many of his present-day followers take great exception to any suggestion that Crowley was a Satanist at all.

The Great Beast was born in England as Edward Alexander Crowley in 1875, to a moderately wealthy Warwickshire brewing family. His parents were members of the Plymouth Brethren, an austere Christian sect dedicated to self-denial and discipline. Young Edward had a great affection for his pious but eccentric father, but, when he was only twelve, his father died and the boy's care fell into the hands of his priggish mother and bigoted uncle, both of whom he despised. Crowley was sent to a Plymouth Brethren school in Cambridge, remembering his time there as 'a boyhood in Hell'.

In order to toughen himself up, to face the school's harsh physical discipline and the cruelty of fellow pupils, Crowley took up mountaineering. Not long afterwards, he discovered the orgasmic peaks of sex – seducing the maid while his mother was at church. Characteristically, he became an accomplished if unorthodox mountaineer, and incorporated his fierce libido into the personal philosophies he developed later.

His mother took to calling Crowley 'the Great Beast 666', after the devilish monster of the Book of Revelations. Taking the invective as a compliment, the youthful Edward revelled in his mother's sanctimonious alarm. Meanwhile, any remnant of Christian belief was lashed out of him by the school cane and his mother's sharp tongue. Crowley led a rakish existence at Trinity College, Cambridge, where he read exhaustively in everything but his prescribed studies, wrote poetry and womanised tirelessly. Inherently egotistical, Crowley bemoaned, 'The stupidity of having had to waste uncounted priceless hours in chasing what ought to have been brought to the back door every evening with the milk!' – these essential dairy products were the sexual favours of women.

It was at this time that Crowley, convinced of impending greatness, adopted the Celtic version of his middle name, Aleister, believing it somehow more conducive to a life of achievement. Without bothering to graduate from Cambridge, he then set out to tour Europe.

Having toyed with magic and mystical philosophies during his studies, young Crowley hoped to slake his ravening thirst for forbidden knowledge. None of the secret societies or esoteric orders he encountered in his travels impressed him – until he met a chemist named Julian Baker in a German tavern. Baker introduced Crowley to the Hermetic Order of the Golden Dawn – which, at that time, was rumoured to count among its ranks some of the more interesting literary figures of the late nineteenth century (in descending order of probability): the Irish poet W. B. Yeats, horror authors Arthur Machen and Algernon Blackwood, Sax Rohmer (creator of 'yellow peril' Dr Fu Manchu), and Bram Stoker (author of *Dracula*).

The young Aleister Crowley – black magician, mountaineer, poet, prophet, poseur and sexual athlete.

In 1898 Crowley was initiated into the Golden Dawn by its founder, the influential but eccentric occultist S. L. MacGregor Mathers. (Yeats later derided him as 'half lunatic, half knave', while the impoverished but egomaniacal Mathers' proudest boast was that, 'There is no part of me that is not of the gods.') The Golden Dawn was a system of magical knowledge, welded together by Mathers from the traditions of ancient Jewish, medieval and Renaissance sorcery. It also owed much to Theosophy, as pioneered by a remarkable Russian mystic named Helena Blavatsky. In many ways a precursor to today's New Age movement, the Theosophical Society – which survives into the present day in a more pedestrian form – took a novel mixture of Eastern mystical philosophies and glued them all together with candy-floss and bullshit.

The part of Theosophy which most appealed to Mathers was the idea of 'the Masters': benevolent supermen, or demigods, who used Blavatsky as their spokeswoman on earth. Mathers worked them into his own system as the 'Secret Chiefs' – the hidden masters of the Golden Dawn, who only communicated via him. Cynics won't be surprised to learn that these exalted entities promptly declared Mathers the 'Supreme Magus', demanding that all members of the Golden Dawn sign an oath of obedience to him. The Order, whose sorcerous rituals were supposedly aimed toward gaining power and enlightenment, subsequently became a semi-bureaucratic series of ranks and grades.

As with any serious occultist, the young Crowley kept a careful balance between open-mindedness and scepticism. He cottoned on quickly that the way to achieve genuine occult power was not to accept the myth-making of others, but to mythologise oneself.

Crowley developed an occult philosophy he called 'Thelema' – a cross between ego, will and charisma, qualities that the Great Beast possessed by the bucketful. Harking back to Francois Rabelais' sixteenth-century tale *Gargantua,* Crowley – like Sir Francis Dashwood, with his Abbey of Medmenham – longed to create an Abbey of Thélème wherein a society of 'anti-monks' could thrive, insulated from the dull masses.

His progress through the order of the Golden Dawn was rapid, under his new magical title Perdurabo (meaning 'I will endure'). However, many members objected to Crowley's increasingly scandalous lifestyle – experimenting with drugs, rutting like a ram with partners of both sexes – and arrogant manner. However, as long as Crowley idolised the decidedly seedy Mathers, he in return protected the promising young initiate from the Order's hostility.

Then, in 1900, Mathers went to Paris, and in his absence Crowley's enemies fell upon him. Yeats was the leader of a rebel faction who declared the *enfant terrible* morally unsuitable for rising to the next grade. Mathers rallied behind his protégé. Bitter duels of magic ensued, with curses hurled and demons supposedly conjured, as well as blackmail and common-or-garden violence (Crowley hired bouncers to forcibly remove his enemies from the Order's HQ).

Perdurabo did not endure, and the Order collapsed into disarray. In the final act of his involvement, Crowley fell out with his erstwhile guru and claimed that black magic was very literally invoked against him. He alleged that Mathers summoned a middle-aged vampiress called 'Mrs M_', who confronted Crowley at a friend's house where, transformed into a beautiful young girl, she subjected him to a near-fatal seduction. According to Crowley's account, he repelled her with his mystic forces, whereupon:

'She writhed back from me, and again approached me even more beautiful than she had been before. She was battling for her life now, and no longer for the blood of her victim. The odour of man seemed to fill her whole subtle form with feline agility. One step nearer and then she sprang at me and with an obscene word sought to press her scarlet lips to mine. As she did so I caught and held her at arm's length and then smote the sorceress with her own current of evil. A bluish-green light seemed to play round the head of the vampire, and then the flaxen hair turned the colour of muddy snow, and the fair skin wrinkled, and her eyes dulled and became pewter dappled with the dregs of wine. The girl of twenty had gone; before me stood a hag of 60. With dribbling curses she hobbled from the room.'

Crowley, evidently disillusioned by such remarkable experiences, used his inheritance to begin travelling again. He visited Mexico, Ceylon, India and Burma, indulging his great passions, mountaineering and sex, while absorbing as much local religious and mystical tradition as he could. The Great Beast immersed himself in the many gods of Hinduism, the sublime lethargy of the Tao, the serenity of yoga, and the beautiful emptiness of Buddhism – wherein the adherent seeks to eliminate self and become one with the greater universe, achieving the true peace of Nirvana (benign oblivion) and escaping life's horrors.

In 1903 Crowley returned to Britain, married a dim but beautiful high-society girl named Rose and went on an extended honeymoon. While visiting Cairo, he conducted a magical experiment for his new wife's entertainment; as if possessed, she suddenly declared, 'They are waiting for you.' 'They' were interpreted as being an Egyptian god, Horus, who apparently had a personal message for Crowley.

Crowley asked his wife a number of esoteric questions, to which she answered each correctly – the likelihood of which he calculated as being 21,168,000 to one against the odds (hardly flattering to young Rose). Convinced he was indeed speaking to a deity, Crowley obeyed his wife's instructions to prepare to receive dictation at his desk. There, he claimed, he was visited for the first time by his guardian angel, an entity named Aiwass, who dictated to him the first chapters of *The Book of the Law*.

Crowley's *Book of the Law* sees the world as governed by a series of ages, or aeons. The previous aeon was the age of the Egyptian goddess Isis, a time of maternal power. The current aeon is the age of the resurrected god, seen by the Egyptians as Osiris, the Greeks as Dionysus and the Christians as Jesus Christ. But this age is coming to an end, and will be replaced by the aeon of Horus, the Crowned and Conquering Child. In this new age, the only moral commandment will be, 'Do what thou wilt shall be the whole of the law' – carried down the centuries like a Chinese whisper, the maxim decreed all would discover their true selves and behave accordingly. But to reach this golden age, the world must first endure an orgy of barbarism and terror.

The Great Beast. Familiar occultic symbols in this portrait include the eye of Horus (in pyramid) and the psychic cross, symbol of Thee Temple ov Psychic Youth. Portrait by Graham Wain.

The Book of the Law foretold that Crowley would be the herald of this new age: he was, as his mother had told him, the Great Beast 666, who watches as the world collapses. But rather than the end of the world – as *The Bible* insists – the Apocalypse would bring about a new world of joy, freedom and truth.

Even the egomaniac Crowley wondered if anyone could swallow all of this wholesale, so Armageddon was temporarily put on hold. In the ensuing years, he began the Order of the Silver Star, an intended successor to the Golden Dawn, and became involved with a German-based movement called the Order of the Eastern Templars – better known as the Ordo Templi Orientis, or OTO. With its roots in renegade masonic lodges, the OTO traced its origins back to the Knights Templar, and persists in dozens of variations to the present day.

Crowley's entry into the OTO came about when its leader, German spy Theodor Ruess, accused him of publishing some of their greatest secrets in his (perhaps aptly-titled) 1912 *Book of Lies*. When Crowley protested he had been told no such secrets, Ruess concluded he must have some natural aptitude for magic, initiated him under the name Baphomet (the demonic severed head allegedly adored by the Templars though it's now associated with the Satanic symbol of the goat's head), and set him to establishing an OTO lodge in Britain.

The OTO secrets Crowley stumbled upon were of a sexual nature – the mystic powers contained within human sperm, a power enhanced by its mixing with female love juices upon orgasm. The central power of the cosmos, it seems, definitely originated with a Big Bang. This appealed to Crowley, ever eager to experiment sexually. (The Golden Dawn never explored this avenue – Mathers had a distaste for sex which seems phobic, and probably never consummated his marriage.) As with many magical philosophies, the OTO believed everything in the universe was connected – if the individual effected significant change in mind or self, this caused wider change through a kind of cosmic domino effect. As the profoundest physical experience is that of sexual orgasm, it therefore followed that sexual energies mirrored the most powerful energies of the universe.

By this time *The Book of the Law* had been reprinted, and Crowley now dedicated himself to fulfilling its prophecies. In 1920 he established his Abbey of Thélème, in a ramshackle, rural Sicilian farmhouse. Somewhere between a cult commune and a hippie retreat, the Abbey witnessed countless magical experiments that – away from the prying eyes of polite society – took some decidedly oppressive and downright deranged turns. Perhaps the most notorious legend insists that one ritual required a female disciple to copulate with a goat, which then had its throat cut. Things came to a head in 1923 when a young visitor named Raoul Loveday died, and Crowley was subjected to a campaign of pious slander by the popular press. He had already attracted attention the previous year with his semi-autobiographical novel *Diary of a Drug Fiend*, which the British press labelled 'a book for burning'. After the death at the Abbey they went wild, printing lurid suggestions of human sacrifice (in reality, Loveday probably died of a fever caught from drinking tainted water). Following this pillorying, Crowley was expelled from Sicily by the dictator Mussolini, who probably decided there was only room for one dangerous megalomaniac in Italy.

In 1925, Crowley was invited to Germany to become the international head of the OTO. The Great Beast was at the height of his powers. In the years that followed he self-consciously evolved the religion of Thelema, as set down in *The Book of the Law*, and wrote further books designed to make his magical philosophies accessible, such as *Magick in Theory and Practice* (1929), *The Book of Thoth* (1944) and *Magick Without Tears* (1945).

Whereas in lesser men an insatiable appetite for sex and drugs might prove a distraction, to Crowley they were an integral part of his evangelical process. However, not even his seemingly invincible constitution could sustain this intense lifestyle forever. During the 1930s the Great Beast's health went into serious decline, and his finances, which had been shaky for a long

An unflattering image of the drug-addled Crowley adorns an album sleeve by spoof Satanic rockers Upsidedown Cross.

time, teetered on the abyss. Crowley became a parasite on the funds of his disciples. He also went through a brief period trying to revive his fortunes in the law courts, suing for libel in 1934 over uncomplimentary remarks about the Cefalau period in former acolyte Nina Hamnett's autobiography *The Laughing Torso*. It was a farce, Crowley's reputation having been destroyed by British and American tabloids ('the king of depravities' and 'a man we'd like to hang' being two descriptions from *John Bull*). The most ludicrous moment in the trial came when counsel asked if Crowley called himself 'the Beast 666', to which he responded, '"The Beast 666" means merely "sunlight". You may call me "Little Sunshine".' He was in court again the following year, this time to declare himself bankrupt. His legendary vitality exhausted, the Great Beast spent most of the 1940s at rest homes and hotels along England's South Coast. Chronically addicted to heroin, which he claimed he'd first been prescribed for chronic asthma, he died, in relative obscurity, at the appropriately gothic-sounding Netherwood rest home in Hastings, on 1 December 1947. His last words, legend has it, were 'I am perplexed.'

To the casual observer, Crowley is a bewildering patchwork of different personae (indeed, one of his favourite hobbies was pretending, on his travels, to be some Persian Prince or Scottish Laird – a mystical Walter Mitty).

He was a macho, mountaineering mystic determined to test every fibre of his intellectual, physical and moral being, to endurance and beyond; a perverse, parasitic poet and painter, desperate to escape into the decadent fantasies he created. The Great Beast was also a traditional English gentleman, who allowed his rakehell tendencies to swallow him whole, and a classic sorcerer – an erudite rogue who swung between priest and conman. But was he ever truly a Satanist?

None of the various orders and lodges he belonged to, or led, saw themselves as inherently Satanic. This was, however, an aspect of magic that Crowley enjoyed immensely – he frequently invoked demons throughout his career, with a brazen indifference as to whether his magic was considered 'black' or 'white'. On the other hand, this demonic current was often all but eclipsed by his Eastern influences, while Satanism is specifically linked with the Western 'cult of the individual' – the idea that individuality, not group identity, is sacred. The Satanic spirit is in a persistent state of conflict with the universe – it constantly seeks knowledge and experience, in order to imprint itself upon its surroundings. It's these same spiritual rough edges that Oriental mystics wish to file off, in order to reach 'enlightenment'.

Modern magus Kenneth Anger (right) and sexologist Alfred Kinsey explore Crowley's Abbey of Thélème at Cefalu. Anger made a 1955 documentary film about restoring the building.

Crowley's 'Do what thou wilt' can be read as a maxim for Satanic libertinism, as well as a command to discover the true self. However, his Abbey of Thélème became a nightmarish laboratory for spiritual experimentation and mind-control games – such psychic self-laceration being severely at odds with the purer pleasures of, say, the Hellfire Club's Medmenham Abbey.

Popular myth insists upon sex and drugs as an integral part of modern Satanism, and Crowley was certainly influential in making sex central to much modern ritual magic. However, sexual activity in Satanic ritual is a pure celebration of the carnal over the spiritual – an end in itself, rather than a meditative exercise to enable 'enlightenment'. Many modern Satanists are also disdainful of drugs, believing they make the individual physically weak and cloud his mind – to them, Crowley's almost supernatural diet of narcotics was the Great Beast's greatest flaw.

Still, Crowley's self-indulgence remains the key to understanding this curious man. For anyone who doesn't believe magic has any power or use, it's a profitable exercise to look at a picture of Crowley – a faintly malevolent Buddha of a man – and consider how many beautiful and respected women he bedded. (Crowley attributed his sexual magnetism to a lotion he rubbed upon his shaven head – apparently also attracting horses, which would neigh at him and follow him up the street.)

It seems Crowley could only feed his appetites if he turned them into 'sacraments'. To his modern followers, their guru instructs them in the sacred rites of love and the exploration of inner space – while a less charitable interpretation is that the Great Beast never really shook his rigid Christian upbringing, and could not enjoy 'sin' for its own sake. To turn the worst of Christian sins into a sacred act was less the endorsement of a new faith than a blasphemy against the religion that scarred his infancy.

Remove Christianity – or anti-Christianity – and Crowley stops making sense. Just as he treasured the title of the Great Beast 666, he also insisted on calling his many mistresses 'Scarlet Women' – after the monstrous whore in 'Revelations' who personifies Christianity's fear of female sexuality.

Crowley undoubtedly engaged in a great deal of animal sacrifice, and wrote about human sacrifice. This seems to be part of his addiction to giving offence – when he spoke of 'sacrificing babies', it's believed he was really boasting of the biblical sin of Onan, spilling his semen on the ground. As Crowley recognised, Sunday newspapers would always find it easier to print headlines of child murder than discuss masturbation.

Once again, contrary to popular opinion, animal sacrifice is frowned upon by the majority of Satanists (while human sacrifice is up to the conscience of the individual maniac). One of Crowley's better-known rituals, however, featured the crucifixion of a toad. As he performed this petty act of cruelty, the Great Beast addressed the hapless amphibian with the following words: 'Lo, Jesus of Nazareth, how thou art taken in my snare. All my life long thou hast plagued me and affronted me . . . all delights have been forbidden unto me . . . Now at last I have thee; the Slave-God is in the power of the Lord of Freedom . . .'

This strange little ritual typifies Crowley's attitude to Christianity. He clearly sees himself as its direct opponent, and his reference to the Christian God as a god of slaves is a Nietzschean concept much favoured by modern Satanists. While it seems most likely that 'the Lord of Freedom' was Horus, Crowley's 'Conquering Child', it's also resonant of 'Lord of Liberty' – the title given to the Satanic master of the medieval sabbat, who Eliphas Lévi identified with Crowley's namesake Baphomet.

Crowley revelled in the infamy of being 'the wickedest man in the world'. He yearned fiercely to be recognised as a modern messiah, and, if he could not be the reborn Christ, then he would be the Antichrist. The Great Beast constantly met public disapproval head on, deriving great satisfaction from his own shock tactics. Many rumours of his provocative behaviour survive, such as the story that Crowley liked to crap on carpets, insisting that his shit was sacred (it's not noted whether it was sacred enough for him to shit on his own doorstep).

In his book *Magick in Theory and Practice*, Crowley holds forth on the Prince of Darkness: 'The Devil does not exist. It is a false name invented by the Black Brothers to imply a Unity in their ignorant muddle of dispersions. A Devil who had unity would be a God.' (These 'Black Brothers' were accomplished magi, whose lack of spiritual development had nonetheless left them languishing in relative ignorance.)

However, criticisms of being muddled and lacking unity could easily be aimed at Crowley, who played many different roles and toyed with myriad belief systems. His modern apostles might say he was revealing the parallels that unite all valid mystical philosophies – more cynical observers might reply he was merely picking bits and pieces from various mythologies, stitching them together with seams of sub-biblical prophecy and obscure poetry.

In the gutter press that fed the popular imagination, Crowley's ability to alarm always qualified him as a Satanist. Better-informed detractors are still inclined to identify Aiwass – the entity Crowley saw as his patron and guide – with Satan, or His Egyptian predecessor, Set. Crowley himself wrote that Aiwass was the counterpart of the 'solar-phallic-hermetic Lucifer; the Devil, Satan . . . This serpent, Satan, is not the enemy of Man, but He who made Gods of our race, knowing Good and Evil; he bade "Know Thyself!" and taught Initiation.'

While Crowley described Aiwass as a tall, dark man, resembling medieval descriptions of the Devil who attended the Sabbat, it's worth noting this quote from his *Confessions*: 'I was not content to believe in a personal devil and serve him, in the ordinary sense of the word. I wanted to get hold of him personally and become his chief of staff.' In another passage, the Great Beast enthusiastically identifies with the title character from George Bernard Shaw's *The Devil's Disciple*.

Crowley's religion, Thelema, certainly has some of the darker, more brutal aspects of modern Satanism – particularly the elitist doctrine that some are born to serve, while others are destined to rule. But Thelema remains a religion – its adherents, most of whom blanch at the idea of their guru as a Satanist, are as locked into a Crowleyite personality cult as surely as fundamentalist Christians who worship a mythic Jesus, while Satanists, who embrace an 'anti-religion', are contemptuous of any herd mentality.

In the final analysis, Crowley was his own greatest work of art. He grasped life by the lapels, goosed the living daylights out of it and damned the consequences. His rebellion of both body and mind set him against the prevailing currents and placed him – in terms of influence at least – in the tradition of Western Satanism.

The underbelly of the early twentieth century yielded some far less ambiguous Satanists than Crowley. There were rumours of a new Hellfire Club in fashionable 1920s London, while William Seabrook, the American adventurer and writer, claimed to have attended several Black Masses during the 1920s and 1930s in London, Paris and New York.

Seabrook describes a ceremony supposed to return Lucifer, the 'light-bringer', to his rightful dominance over Creation: Latin Mass is said backwards, on an altar surmounted with the body of a naked virgin who has a chalice of red wine between her breasts. An acolyte, a whore dressed in red, is on hand to defile the heavenly host in her vagina. Most accounts of the Black Mass in this period dismiss the ceremony as a source of cheap thrills for wealthy tourists – which, given Satanism's pragmatic nature, also validates it as a magical ritual to attract financial reward.

This period also saw the publication of the study *Witchcraft and Black Magic* 1926 by the eccentric Reverend Montague Summers. The aggressively pious Summers – who had a medieval inquisitor's mind, trapped in a well-upholstered twentieth-century body – concluded his book with the biblical command, 'Thou shalt not suffer a witch to live.' However, Summers is a more interesting figure than this personal fanaticism suggests.

The good Reverend was interested in a number of other areas that seem suspicious for a man-of-the-cloth. An acknowledged expert on gothic fiction and Restoration drama (both considered morally suspect by the standards of the day), in private Summers' tastes ran to more overtly pornographic material. In his collection of essays, *The Books of the Beast*, Timothy D'Arch Smith notes that, after Summers died, among his possessions was found 'a treasured copy of *Fanny Hill* . . . and a portfolio of watercolours of guardsmen engaged in pursuits which only the confines of their sentry-boxes saved from the somatically impossible'. This valiant crusader against evil was an Anglican deacon, until investigations into a charge of pederasty obliged him to join his obvious spiritual home: the Roman Catholic Church.

Summers' homosexuality and hypocrisy are scarcely any great novelty amongst the clergy. However, D'Arch Smith claims that, on Boxing Day 1918, Summers conducted a Black Mass accompanied by two young men – the result of his sexual preoccupation with choirboys combining with a penchant for gothic melodrama. If the story rings true, then Montague Summers stands revealed not only as a twentieth-century inquisitor, but also as a latter-day Black Mass priest.

Sexuality, as repressed by the pleasure-hating Church, will naturally take on many pathological forms. In such an instance, Satanism can be used to liberate oneself from this trap – or, as in Summers' case, to wallow in it. Such a lust for uncorrupted innocence is a traditional priest's perversion. The Black Mass priests who have indulged this peculiarly Christian vice have traditionally turned to the powers of darkness as a temporary liberation – before returning to the arms of Mother Church, for absolution. Satanism preaches no such doctrine of forgiveness.

Charles Gray as Mocata in Hammer Films' 1968 adaptation of Dennis Wheatley's The Devil Rides Out, *one of many Crowley-inspired fictional villains.*

One similarly moralistic acquaintance of Summers, the inquisitor, was the novelist Dennis Wheatley – a man who, in his own way, contributed just as much to the twentieth-century notion of Satanism. Wheatley arranged to have dinner with both Summers and Aleister Crowley to research a book he was working on. Wheatley called Summers 'a very interesting man', though evidently found him a little unsettling in person. By way of contrast, he described Crowley as 'a fascinating conversationalist' with 'an intellect of the first order'. In 1935, the novel Wheatley had been researching appeared under the title *The Devil Rides Out*.

A prolific author, Wheatley specialised in action-adventure yarns of the John Buchan school, where pace and drama often substituted for atmosphere or character. It was a popular recipe, with his books selling nearly 30 million copies worldwide. Wheatley was a prolific writer, penning over 50 novels, of which only eight were black magic thrillers. Nevertheless, it's as an author of occult fiction that he's remembered. The public developed an appetite for

Dennis Wheatley's stories of Satanic cults and suburban Devil-worshippers – in satisfying that appetite, he helped create the popular image of Satanism.

Wheatley was a bluff gentleman of the old school – with a military background and stiff upper lip to match – who created the kind of Satanists that reflected his personal prejudices. They were sinister, swarthy foreigners, weak-willed, thrill-seeking young aristocrats and immoral sophisticates. However, Wheatley's heroes also showed hints of exotic darkness – particularly the vaguely Satanic good guy, the Duc De Richleau. Wheatley was very much a creature of his age, and his gradual decline in popularity, since his death in 1977, is due to the disappearance of the world he wrote about, with all its formal traditions and moral certainties.

It's telling that the source Wheatley relied on most for information on the dark arts was one Rollo Ahmed. According to Wheatley, Ahmed was half-Egyptian, half-West Indian, and had been brought up in the 'devil-ridden islands and the little-explored forests of Yucatan, Guiana and Brazil'. Such an exotic pedigree obviously gave Ahmed a good grounding in diabolism – it was a standard Christian assumption that primitive tribes worshipped devils.

Ahmed shared Wheatley's conviction that dabbling with magic was terribly dangerous, supposedly from personal experience: Wheatley claimed to have lost touch with him shortly after he 'slipped up in a ceremony and failed to master a demon, who had caused all his teeth to fall out'. In dim echoes of the Protestant Faustbooks 400 years before, the Catholic Wheatley prefaced his Satanic thrillers with dire warnings on the Devil and all His works – just thinking too long on Satan was dangerous enough, let alone engaging in a Black Mass. (As Ahmed was all too aware, the dangers were not merely spiritual but dental.)

Such warnings carried the implication that, while Wheatley was strong, virtuous and smart enough to survive the horrors and temptations of the Prince of Darkness, *you*, the humble reader, were obviously not. It added a delicious air of danger to the books, while feeding the author's authority (and ego). It did not hurt sales much either.

These warnings also reinforced the idea that Wheatley's stories were more than mere fictions, that the Satanic forces described in his novels were a real threat to the civilised world. In *They Used Dark Forces*, however, the hero tried to overthrow the Third Reich with black magic. Having served on Winston Churchill's Joint Planning Staff during the Second World War, Wheatley was at pains to insist that 'during the war Churchill had no truck with occultism of any kind' (to which Crowley would doubtless have taken exception, claiming to have suggested Churchill's 'V for Victory' sign).

However, Wheatley was not so sure about the opposition, dropping dark hints that the Germans had made recourse to black magic during World War Two. This was far from an isolated opinion, and, as the 1930s gave evil a new face for the twentieth century, some concluded that the power lurking behind its eyes was literally Satanic.

THE BLACK ORDER

Occultists at War

All good religions need some kind of Apocalypse. Thelema – the new religion of Aleister Crowley – was no exception. The Great Beast fully expected his new holy age, the Aeon of Horus, to be ushered in with an orgy of violence and bloodshed.

With the advent of the First World War, the prophecy seemed to have been satisfied. Over four long years, the optimism and complacency of nineteenth-century Europe drowned in the mud of the Western Front, along with hundreds of thousands of young soldiers.

However, Crowley seemed curiously indifferent to the whole affair. With typical arrogance, when the British Government refused his offer to produce war propaganda, the Luciferian man of letters travelled to the US to write anti-British propaganda. If he could not find recognition on the side of the angels, the Great Beast was always ready to side with the opposition. But Crowley later claimed he wrote deliberately absurd material to discredit the German cause. His article on the bombing of London by Zeppelin airships gives credence to this eccentric defence:

'For some reason or other in their last Zeppelin raid on London the Germans appear to have decided to make the damage as widespread as possible, instead of concentrating it in one quarter . . . A great deal of damage was done at Croydon, especially at its suburb Addiscombe, where my aunt lives. Unfortunately her house was not hit. Count Zeppelin is respectfully requested to try again. The exact address is Eton Lodge, Outram Road.'

If World War One had been too minor a cataclysm to introduce Crowley's Age of Horus, 1939 heralded a new orgy of human suffering. The Beast always maintained that the first nation to adopt his *Book of the Law* as a state religion would dominate the world. During the 1930s, however, as the Third Reich came to power, his ambivalence towards Germany – the country where his magical doctrines were taken most seriously – is perhaps understandable.

Some of his German followers saw in their new Führer a political equivalent to their prophet, the Great Beast (perhaps even his 'magical child') – a new world order was to be created by the pure will-power of these two extraordinary men. But in 1935 the Nazis banned the Ordo Templi Orientis and the Order of the Silver Star, throwing numerous occultists (including Karl Germer, one of Crowley's foremost disciples) into concentration camps. There may have been similarities between Crowley's Thelemic doctrines and emergent Nazi dogma (elitism, irrationalism, transcendence of morality), but the Great Beast could see on which side his future depended: Britain would 'knock Hitler for six!', he announced.

Whether or not the horrors of the Second World War signalled the advent of the Age of Horus, Adolf Hitler emerged from the blood and pain of that conflict as a secular Satan. Indeed, a minor literary industry has grown up around the idea of Hitler as a very literal Satanic figure. Above and beyond the almost universal consensus that he was profoundly evil, popular legend suggests that the Führer really did, in Dennis Wheatley's words, 'use dark forces'.

Nazi propaganda art from 1933 compares Faust's thirst for knowledge with Hitler and the Third Reich's quest for power.

The roots of this belief return us to the occult lodges of the late nineteenth century. In 1875, the writer and occultist Guido von List climbed a hill overlooking Vienna to conduct a strange ritual. Von List was dedicated to returning greater Germany to an older, purer faith – the worship of Wotan, and the other pagan gods of the Teutonic race. Upon the hill he commemorated the summer solstice by burying a number of empty wine bottles, carefully arranged into a sacred symbol: the swastika.

In 1908 von List founded the Armanen Initiates, the inner order of his modestly-titled Guido von List Society. His doctrines centred around ideas of racial purity – von List believed the Germanic peoples, the Armenen, had originally been a race of supermen, but mongrelisation had weakened the race until bashful old Guido was its last pure-blooded survivor. According to this racist mystic, 'the hydra-headed international Jewish conspiracy' was behind it all. To reverse matters, von List prescribed a study of ancient Teutonic religious runes and – more practically – laws to prevent further racial interbreeding. His eventual goal was a racial state ruled by 'a self-chosen Führer to whom [Germany] willingly submits'. Alongside the swastika, the emblems of this new state would include the sig rune: the symbol later used to form the insignia of the SS.

Guido von List was one of the leading Germanic mystics dedicated to 'völkisch' occultism. 'Völkisch' basically translates as 'folkloric', but this was also leavened with a hard-edged nationalism. Chief obsessions among the völkisch orders were the sacred nature of race (or 'blood'), an interest in the culture and beliefs of the Germanic peoples in the early Middle Ages, and a strong current of anti-Semitism.

Among the most important of the völkisch occultists – some of whom fancied themselves the priests of a revived Norse religion – was Dr Jörg Lanz von Liebenfels. In many ways a sorcerer in the classic mould, von Liebenfels adopted his aristocratic name to increase his mystique (his real name was Adolf Lanz), and began his career as a Catholic priest before being defrocked for 'harbouring carnal and worldly desires'. His response was to found an 'Order of New Templars' – quite what the original Templars had to do with racial purity isn't clear, but it did not stop von Liebenfels preaching a message of race war from his temple on the banks of the Danube.

In 1909, a young Austrian named Adolf Hitler secured an audience with von Liebenfels to secure some back issues of *Ostara*, the journal of the New Templars. In 1932, von Liebenfels would write to a fellow occultist that 'Hitler is one of our pupils . . . You will one day experience that he, and through him we, will one day be victorious, and develop a movement that will make the world tremble.'

The most direct link between the occult underground and the Third Reich is the Thule Society. Thule, according to northern European myth, was a version of Atlantis, an island that sank beneath the sea. Thule Society ideology decreed this legendary island to be the home of the Germanic supermen, who they hoped to contact using magical techniques. Most significantly, however, they also planned to further their cause with political methods. In 1919, the Thule Society formed a tiny political group called the German Workers Party in Munich – the seed from which Hitler's National Socialist Party grew.

In the 1920s Germany of the Weimar Republic, völkisch occult groups sensed that their time was coming. Losing the First World War left Germany politically chaotic, economically bankrupt and profoundly demoralised. Amongst those who could afford it, many turned to drink, drugs and sexual debauchery to forget their troubles. Weimar Berlin earnt a reputation for decadence exceeding that of 1890s Paris – though there was a cynical desperation among the German hedonists that never surfaced amongst their French counterparts.

For many ordinary citizens of 'Greater Germany' (which included Austria), however, their feelings of disillusionment hardened into suspicions of betrayal. One such was the young war hero Hitler – who was convinced Germany's forces were defeated by treachery at home, rendering the huge loss of life futile. Hitler, along with many others, was sure that the 'November criminals' (government signatories of a peace treaty in November 1918) were responsible for the fatherland's defeat and humiliation. And behind the November criminals were the treacherous Jews.

In this environment, völkisch occultists found an eager audience for their fables of an ancient, noble Aryan race. They not only offered up a scapegoat for their defeat, but also created the mythology of a sacred Germanic blood heritage from which a humbled people could rebuild their pride.

It's a long way from accepting that völkisch occultism helped create a spiritual environment friendly to Nazism to believing the Third Reich was a Satanic cult. The relationship between Nazism and völkism is similar to that between radical Afro-American political groups and black Islamic leaders who proclaim 'the white man' to be the Devil. Political leaders, as soon as they achieve any real power, are usually quick to distance themselves from such emotive spiritual propaganda.

But to understand Nazism, it must be seen as a profoundly revolutionary movement that extended far beyond mere politics. Total revolution also demanded a spiritual revolution. The Russian Revolution of 1917 had a similarly religious aspect. Communists were determined to uproot the Christian Church and replace it with religious loyalty to the State, and its socialist principles. Early Bolsheviks held wild revels, called 'African nights', where Christian festivals were parodied in atheistic rites such as 'Red Prayers' and 'Red Mass'. Obscene hymns were sung, and children were encouraged to spit upon and destroy puppets representing God, Jesus and other holy figures, in powerful echoes of the Black Mass celebrated by rebellious medieval peasants.

Hitler's doctrines were no less revolutionary. Nazism was designed to revolutionise every aspect of life – even the way people thought – and the old ways were denounced as 'Jewish', or 'liberal'. Hitler despised 'intellectuals', advocating intuition, or even irrationalism, over logical, rational thought. In many ways the Nazis turned back the clock two hundred years, to when science and sorcery were still reluctant bedfellows. In the field of military technology, innovation and instinct were promoted at the expense of methodology, liberating German scientists to create some of the most efficient weapons of war the world had seen. (Without the aid of the German scientists who enabled V-2 rockets to bomb London, the USA might ultimately have lost the space race.) But Nazi science was also prone to flights of fancy.

Left-right: Karl Maria Weisthor, Jorg Lanz von Liebenfels and Guido von List – the three völkisch magi at the nativity of Nazism. Portrait by Jason.

In April 1942 – when German resources were painfully short – an extravagantly-equipped scientific expedition was mounted to an island in the Baltic, to see if they could use high-tech instruments to spy across the globe at the British. This was the 'hollow earth theory': several influential Nazi scientists believed the earth was a hollow sphere, and that its inhabitants lived on the inside of it. Another Nazi scientist blended Germanic myth with astrophysics, concluding the entire cosmos was created by the conflict between fire and ice. The theory was sufficiently influential to halt production of the V-2 rocket for two months, for fear it might disturb the balance between these two primal elements. In many ways, the fruits of Nazi innovation were cancelled out by its eccentric irrationality.

The Nazi approach to war is best illustrated by Hitler's policy of 'Blitzkrieg', or lightning war, where decisive, rapid advances were the only priority. Blitzkrieg was formulated by Major General J. F. C. Fuller, one of only two Englishmen invited to Hitler's fiftieth birthday party – also one of the earliest converts to Crowley's Thelemic religion. It characterised Nazi methods in many other areas, where change was effected as rapidly as possible with little concern for coherence or consequence. That the Nazis also changed the face of German religion in a very short time is inarguable. Just what they changed it into isn't so clear.

The 'spiritual leader of National Socialism' was Alfred Rosenberg, an intimate of Hitler and high-ranking Nazi official. In 1930 he published his magnum opus, *The Myth of the Twentieth Century*, a rabidly anti-Semitic work which re-evaluated history as an epic process of racial conflict. It rapidly became a best-seller second only to *Mein Kampf*, taking its place alongside Hitler's book as a Nazi Bible.

Rosenberg – widely regarded as the most anti-clerical of the Nazi ideologues – included among his canon of Aryan saints the Protestant reformer Martin Luther. He also drew up plans for a National Reich Church, which was not going to destroy Christianity but 'supercede' it, and called his new faith 'positive Christianity'.

He concluded: 'On the day of its foundation, the Christian cross must be removed from all churches, cathedrals and chapels and it must be superseded by the only unconquerable symbol, the Swastika.' But what did the Swastika symbolise? Rosenberg wrote: 'Today a new faith awakens: the myth of the blood, the faith that by defending the blood we defend also the divine nature of man. The faith, embodied in scientific clarity, that the Nordic blood represents the mystery which has replaced and conquered the ancient sacraments.'

The historian Konrad Heiden begins his book *Der Führer: Hitler's Rise to Power* with a curious story concerning Rosenberg: 'One day in the summer of 1917 a student was reading in his room in Moscow. A stranger entered, laid a book on the table, and silently vanished. The cover of the book bore in Russian the words from the twenty-forth chapter of Matthew: "He is near, he is hard by the door."

'The student sensed the masterful irony of higher powers in this strange happening. They had sent him a silent message. He opened the book, and the voice of the demon spoke to him.

'It was a message concerning the Antichrist, who would come at the end of days. The Antichrist is no mythical being, no monkish medieval fantasy. It is the portrait of a type of man who comes to the fore when an epoch is dying.'

The book was *The Protocols of the Elders of Zion*, perhaps the most influential anti-Semitic document of all time, the student was Rosenberg, and the predicted Antichrist supposedly Hitler. However, this Satanic element reads as little more than gothic fantasy when considering how even the völkisch aspects of Rosenberg's new faith were later suppressed – at least when espoused by his rivals.

When Jörg Lanz von Liebenfels, the leader of the New Templars, boasted of his role as the spiritual godfather of Nazism, Hitler forbade him to publish any more material. Von Liebenfels got off lightly. The Nazis began suppressing occultists and secret societies in 1934, in a purge that reached its peak in 1937. Thousands of astrologers and mystics disappeared into the concentration camps, never to appear again. Völkisch occultists were not spared. Even the Thule Society – the magi at the nativity of Nazism – was devoured by its ravenous offspring.

In *Mein Kampf*, Hitler derides the 'wandering völkisch scholars' as 'the greatest imaginable cowards', having 'the feeling they are sent by dark forces who do not desire the rebirth of our people'. They were not – in that phrase so beloved of the Far Right – 'men of action', and were therefore useless as far as Hitler was concerned. The Nazis might have used some of their symbols to adorn the altars of their new faith, but that religion worshipped only the Nazi State and its embodiment: Adolf Hitler.

The Nazi State would not tolerate anything outside its control, or that it had not created itself. Its tenet of faith was the destiny of the Aryan race, as expressed by its prophet Hitler. If this policy of spiritual and intellectual monopoly sounds familiar, it's because it resembles the doctrines of one of the institutions the Nazis sought to replace: the Church.

The Nazi party created its own priesthood – the Black Order, better known as the Schutzstaffel, or SS. The SS began as Hitler's bodyguards, but, under Heinrich Himmler, manoeuvred and massacred their way to become the most powerful organisation in the Nazi establishment. Like 'the hounds of God' of the medieval Inquisition, the SS policed the souls of those under their ever-expanding jurisdiction. The faithful were monitored, the suspect – even the völkisch occultists who shared the Nazi vision of race – purged, the unholy exterminated.

As the Second World War progressed, Himmler's influence expanded until he became the second most powerful man in the Third Reich. A bundle of contradictions, Himmler was a quiet, gentle father capable of acts of staggering inhumanity, an industrious, realistic man and a fervent believer in numerous occult doctrines. He employed a personal astrologer, studied runic mysticism and believed himself the reincarnation of a ninth-century Saxon king named Heinrich the Fowler. Any occultist who wished to survive in Nazi Germany was well-advised to find a place under Himmler's wing.

Several such men did – most significantly Karl Weisthor. Weisthor was born Karl Maria Wiligut in Vienna, 1866, to a family with a long military tradition, and was decorated for his service during the First World War. Following the war he became involved in völkisch occultism, adopting doctrines which were extreme even by völkisch standards.

With the modesty characteristic of his ilk, Weisthor claimed to be descended from Aryan gods, the last living representative of the Irminist Church. The Irminists – who worshipped the true Christ, an Aryan called Krist – had been opposed throughout history by the false religion of the Catholic Church, their racial enemies the Jews, and Aryan heretics who worshipped the pagan god Wotan. Weisthor knew all of this because he possessed a clairvoyance that allowed him to recall the heroic lives of his ancestors, thousands of years ago. Not everyone was impressed by the evidence, however, and in 1924 he was committed to a lunatic asylum. Undeterred, when he was released he changed his name and headed to Munich. In 1933 he attracted the attention of Himmler, who installed the cranky medium in the Ahnenerbe department of the SS.

The Ahnenerbe were concerned with researching the history of the Aryan race, but also devoted time to more esoteric pursuits. These included some very odd projects indeed – such as working out if Oxford's church bells protected the town from German bombers, and whether Aryan bees produced superior honey. Even among such eccentric company, Weisthor was considered a nut – but he enjoyed Himmler's special favour and reached the rank of SS brigadier by 1936.

Under Weisthor's advice, a castle at Wewelsburg in north-west Germany was chosen as the spiritual headquarters of the Black Order. It became the Nazi equivalent of the Vatican, with great echoing chambers dedicated to the heroes of the Aryan race, and a central hall where Himmler and his twelve closest disciples would meet. Weisthor designed the SS 'Totenkopfring' – a sacred ring decorated with skulls and runes, personally bestowed upon SS members by Himmler and returned to Wewelsburg upon their deaths. He also conceived and presided over neo-pagan solstice ceremonies, and the weddings of SS officers to good Aryan girls.

The Black Order was not just a military organisation but a sect, a fraternity of warrior priests. Though it never claimed the heritage of the Knights Templar, the parallels between these two orders are striking. Both snowballed into vast international forces. Both maintained independent economic systems that allowed them to accumulate vast wealth. Both were composed of highly-disciplined warriors, fanatically dedicated to their creeds. Both were exempt from the laws that governed their contemporaries, answerable only to the head of their orders (Himmler or the Grand Master) and the representative of their sacred creed on earth (Hitler or the Pope). Both planned to establish their own independent states. And both were, at least ostensibly, Christian.

Weisthor's faith may have incorporated much bizarre Germanic paganism, but at the core he believed he was preaching Christianity. One of the oaths taken by SS candidates before full initiation ran, 'We believe in God, we believe in Germany which He created in His World and in the Führer, Adolf Hitler, whom He has sent us.' One of the titles Himmler had bestowed on him by his peers was 'the Black Jesuit', as he based the structure of the SS upon the fanatically-secretive Catholic Society of Jesuits.

Ignatius de Loyola, sixteenth-century founder of the Jesuits, is said to have boasted, 'Give me the child for seven years and I will show you the man.' In this sense Loyola is the patron saint of indoctrination, seeding received wisdoms and values that are virtually impossible to eradicate. Himmler, brought up in a devoutly-Catholic Bavarian household, never lost his belief in the importance of ritual and symbolism. When he used the term 'Satanic', or evoked the Devil, it was applied to the enemies of the Aryan race – never in connection with his own faith.

Hitler was also brought up a Roman Catholic, attending a Benedictine monastery school on the Austrian-Bavarian border. He played an active part in local religious pageantry and ceremony, and even dreamed of entering the priesthood at one point. Ultimately, Hitler's extermination of the Jews may have been colder, more calculatedly efficient than previous acts of genocide, but it was far from unprecedented. Murderous anti-Semitism had a long and shameful tradition in

The Wild Hunt *by Hitler's reputed favourite artist Franz Von Stuck. Note the resemblance to Wotan, the hunter, presiding over a pagan holocaust.*

Europe – a tradition that found its most powerful expression in the Catholic Church.

Persecution of the Jews was often inspired by accusations that they poisoned wells and drank the blood of children, or, more traditionally, that they had killed Jesus. They were commonly believed to be part of an international conspiracy – sometimes decreed to be Satanic – against all Christian values. The poisonous race-war fantasies of a few völkisch occultists were pretty trivial, therefore, compared to the Church-sanctioned tradition of anti-Semitic pogroms continued by Hitler.

In 1998 the Vatican would finally apologise for its anti-Semitic history, and for failing to oppose the Nazis. Pope Pius XII, it's claimed, would have been more forthright in his condemnation of Hitler if he wasn't so concerned about endangering Catholics. However, requests by Jewish leaders to view the Vatican's wartime records have been met with flat refusal.

The Catholic Church, concerned that the Third Reich was stealing souls that were rightfully theirs, had certainly preached against this new paganism. But the Church was more worried by the spread of atheistic communism, and Pius praised Hitler for his campaign against Stalin – 'the real enemy'. Bishop Berning of Osnabrück even preached obedience and loyalty to the State while visiting concentration camps in 1935.

The central ethos of the Church – obedience, ignorance, abstinence – found many echoes in Nazism. The totalitarian belief system that demanded the sacrifice of heretics. The sacred importance of blood. The joylessness of purely procreative sex – whether breeding babies for God, or 'for race and nation' – and fear of feminine sexuality. The potent iconography. While most Catholics would be horrified by these suggestions, they might like to ask themselves why the Catholic Church was so active in setting up 'rat-lines' – the escape routes that allowed Nazi war criminals to escape to South America at the end of the war.

Occultic suggestions that the Third Reich was, as one author puts it, a 'demonocracy' – with the Führer himself as a black magician, a 'psychic vampire', demonically possessed, or even as the Antichrist himself – are based on Hitler's skill at taking political and military gambles (precognition), his inner voices and violent rages (possession), and the way he simultaneously drew upon and released great emotion with his speeches (psychic vampirism).

All of these ideas have made for appealing books. They distance us from Hitler as a man, allowing the reader to regard the Third Reich as a manifestation of supernatural evil – despite the lack of any evidence at all. One suggestion in particular, that Hitler was a magician because he consulted an astrologer, really smacks of desperation. All of these theorists really have only one argument: Hitler was evil; Satan is Evil personified; therefore Hitler is Satan.

The Jews – lambasted in the New Testament as children of the Devil – have been the victims of violent persecution for millennia.

Otherwise level-headed historians have described Hitler as possessing almost supernatural powers – whereas the terms 'mesmeric' or 'hypnotic' best describe the psychological effect this frantic, grim little man had on the vast audiences at Nazi rallies. Political figures such as John F. Kennedy and Martin Luther King also based their careers on charismatic oratory, and few would suggest either man was possessed by demons.

Hitler's psychological demons may have been actually drug-driven: throughout his later career, the Führer was heavily dosed on a daily basis with methylamphetamine, a powerful form of speed. He also indulged in homeopathic remedies said to contain human shit, animal genitalia and a number of natural narcotics. More exotic theories suggest the Führer's relationship with his audience was sexual – with his climactic speeches as the equivalent to seduction, or rape. (Some claim Hitler reached orgasm at the climax of his speeches, and it's well established that the foundation of his popular support was female.)

However, after this attack of rampant rationalism, it's worth confessing that the Third Reich is of legitimate interest to occultists. Something about Hitler's meteoric rise – from penniless tramp to omnipotent dictator – and Germany's similarly rapid rise – from near-collapse to near-world domination – confounds rational explanation.

Occultism is, at one level, a language or terminology that describes extreme situations, individuals or events. The irrationalism at the heart of the Third Reich, its powerful use of myth and symbolism, the personal 'sex demon' with which the unprepossessing Hitler can be said to have seduced a nation – all reward examination from an occult perspective. Still, the philosophy of Hitler, and the psychological symbolism employed by the Nazis, are no more inherently Satanic than that of the Catholic Church.

Meanwhile, back in dear old Blighty, another group of occultists massed their self-professed powers in defiance of the Nazi threat. Military intelligence is said to have rejected agent Ian Fleming's idea that Aleister Crowley be used to interrogate Nazi Party deputy Rudolf Hess. Hess, who had been captured after flying to Scotland on a bizarre peace treaty mission, was believed to be obsessed with astrology and the peripheries of völkisch occultism. Fleming, the future James Bond author, knew the Great Beast's reputation from the Sunday tabloids, and thought he might be just the man to plumb the Nazi psyche. Churchill's backroom boys were not impressed. However, in the book *Witchcraft Today*, published in 1954, author Gerald Gardner relates the following eyewitness account of wartime sorcery in England:

'Witches cast spells to stop Hitler landing after France fell. They met, raised the great cone of power and directed the thought at Hitler's brain: "You cannot cross the sea. You cannot cross the sea. Not able to come. Not able to come." . . . I'm not saying that they stopped Hitler. All I say is that I saw a very interesting ceremony performed with the intention of putting a certain idea into his mind and this was repeated several times afterwards; and though all the invasion barges were ready, the fact that Hitler never even tried to come. The witches told me that their great-grandfathers had tried to project the same idea into Boney's [Napoleon's] mind.'

Though many worlds apart, both Nazism and New Age witchcraft cults have roots in early twentieth-century pagan revivalism.

Witchcraft Today was to have a profound impact on the occult world of the mid-twentieth century by exposing a faith which, according to Gardner, stretched back into the distant past. Gardner's revelations have remained controversial – doubts remain as to whether he may have invented the New Forest witch coven described in his book. Whatever the truth of the matter, converts were attracted to the modern witch-cult he named Wicca, with Gerald Gardner recognised as the head of this modern pagan creed.

Born in 1884, the irrepressible Gardner's childhood was spent travelling in exotic climes, tended by his nanny who applied regular physical discipline to the boy. From this classic upper-middle class British upbringing, the young Gardner developed a taste for flagellation and exotic erotica. One particular peculiarity was his tendency during rainstorms to strip naked and sit on his clothes until the rain passed.

After a long career as a civil servant in the British Empire's farthest-flung remnants, he returned to Britain. There, according to Gardner, in 1939 he discovered and was initiated into a Wiccan coven based in the New Forest. Their subsequent magical efforts against the Third Reich apparently terminated the lives of several members, and the rest weren't getting any younger. So, when the Witchcraft Act – which criminalised magic ritual – was repealed in 1951, Gardner resolved to give the ailing cult a new lease of life.

Wicca was a benign, life-affirming religion that combined worship of pagan nature gods with ritual magic. It was the Crowleyan elements, with which Gardner supplemented its whimsical framework, that raised many an eyebrow. Nudism, bondage, open-air sex and flagellation, all personal weaknesses of Gardner, became prominent Wiccan rites. These 'traditional' rituals were actually purchased from Aleister Crowley for the sum of £300, and many, not unnaturally, assumed the whole Wicca cult was simply a cover for the wily old goat to indulge his kinks.

However, völkisch occultism was not confined to Germany – an interest in folklore, and the lost gods of paganism, swept many European countries. In Britain, the early twentieth-century pagan revival focused largely on Greco-Roman gods, but aspects such as vegetarianism, nudism and traditional crafts had much in common with the völkisch movement.

The leading neo-pagans were interested in creating a youth movement – bizarrely, they infiltrated the fringes of the fledgling Boy Scout organisation. Unsurprisingly perhaps, Baden-Powell's reactionary little boy's club proved no place for their increasingly wacky doctrines. In 1919, the radical tendency split from the Scouts to form a völkisch-style youth movement called Kibbo Kift (an old rural English term for 'feat of strength'). As the new pagans grew in number, the less orthodox aspects of their creed began to surface.

In the mid-1920s, a series of schisms and scandals hit both Kibbo Kift and a similar pagan youth movement, the Order of Woodcraft Chivalry. Nudism was abandoned, the neo-pagan leaders ejected and the organisations steered back to the safe territory of Christianity. The real deathblow was their resemblance to the German völkisch youth movements that formed the basis of the Hitler Youth. When John Hargrave – a leading figure in the pagan movement – died, he left a sum of money to the London School of Economics on the condition they mounted an exhibition dedicated to the Kibbo Kift. The LSE, wary of the pagan-Nazi overtones of this otherwise blameless organisation, declined.

The remnants of these movements found refuge chiefly in the fledgling nudist movement, talking vaguely of 'sun worship' while letting it all hang out. Gardner discovered some of those remnants in the New Forest, re-inventing them as the basis for his 'witch-cult' of Wicca. Wicca, which claims to be an ancient pre-Christian cult, is in fact no older than the turn of the century.

Just as, in the 1920s, the German völkisch occultists found themselves in an environment friendly to their doctrines, so the British neo-pagans would have their day in the 1960s. They would play their own small part in a social revolution – an experiment of a very different kind to that of the authoritarian Third Reich.

SYMPATHY FOR THE DEVIL

Lucifer and the Countercultural Revolution

Post-war cultural rebellion first ignited in the bongo-playing, drug-loving, poetry-spouting 1950s world of the beatniks – but it exploded in a thousand colours with the advent of the hippie era. One of those colours was deepest black, and some of those questing for freedom and enlightenment looked toward the infernal.

The 1960s revolution, in many ways, seemed tailor-made for an Aleister Crowley revival. Thelemite maxims like 'Do what thou wilt', 'Every man and every woman is a star' and 'Love is the law' tripped easily from the lips of the 'flower children'. Crowley's insistence that sex and drugs were holy sacraments found eager acceptance. But exploration of the Great Beast's darker doctrines – of a world divided into masters and slaves, with good and evil sacrificed on the bloody altar of a new morality – would be the province of a far less gaudy crew than the hippies.

Spiritual renaissance was the aim of the hippie revolution – even more than changing the world, the hippies wanted to profoundly alter the way people looked at it. This was a revolution fought in the minds of a generation, running street-battles to re-order consciousness rather than national boundaries. If the engine of the flower children's rebellion was social and political, its fuel was spiritual. They saw the hypocrisy of a Christian establishment praying to a god of peace with blood-spattered hands, rebelling against a moral code more comfortable with fighting than fucking.

And if the hippie movement was mystical, its holiest rite was the love-in, its sacrament the LSD tab, and its high priests the young musicians who provided the soundtrack to the era. What made the movement so alarming to many was that it drew most of its converts from the respectable middle classes, the very bosom of polite society.

Marianne Faithfull – a former child of the upper-middle classes – was a long-time consort of English rock band the Rolling Stones, and an icon of 'swinging London'. In her autobiography, written much later, she displays little doubt as to the source of the era's dynamism. Speaking of her most famous lover, Mick Jagger, she says: 'He harnessed all of the negative forces into entities. Out of these destructive impulses, he created all the incredible personae of the late sixties: the Midnight Rambler, Lucifer, Jumpin' Jack Flash. They are all manifestations of malignant and chaotic forces, the ungovernable mob. The dark, violent, group mind of the crowd – chaos, Pan. That frenzied power caused many of the casualties of the sixties . . . '

Foremost among the musicians who pioneered the first colourful wave of psychedelia were the Beatles. Their high-profile transformation from chirpy, mop-headed scousers to long-haired peaceniks reflected the cultural tide of their generation. But not everybody greeted them with open arms and peace signs. American fundamentalist Christians spoke for many when they condemned the 'British invasion' – 190 years after losing the colonies, the limeys were counter-attacking with their pop groups – as morally and ideologically suspect.

Much of the concern was directed at the left-of-centre politics of the band's most talented member, John Lennon. In the USA, the FBI compiled a two-inch thick file on Lennon upon which FBI director J. Edgar Hoover scrawled, 'All extremists should be considered dangerous.'

However, it was fundamentalist Christians – with their endearing disrespect for facts or common sense – who discovered the occultic secret behind the Beatles' success. They maintained that the Lennon-McCartney sound was a magical beat stolen from the ancient Druids. According to them, in ancient times these pagan priests would beat out the demonic rhythm on drums made of human skin to summon evil spirits. In the hands of the Beatles, this Druid beat could be used to send the young people of America insane – or even worse, pinko. In one handy package they resurrected the spirit of McCarthyite commie-paranoia, introduced the brand new myth of teenagers hypnotised by pop music, and threw in a little racism for good measure.

This cover montage for the Beatles' Sgt. Pepper *album represents people admired by the band – including Aleister Crowley (back row, second from left).*

Back in the real world, Lennon upset the conservative establishment with his off-the-cuff 1966 remark that the Beatles were 'bigger than Jesus'. This minor blasphemy made their subsequent American tour into something of a nightmare. As Lennon later recalled, it was marked by Christian protests during which 'the Ku Klux Klan burnt Beatles records and I was held up as a Satanist or something'.

The next year, Christian suspicions of the Beatles were confirmed by detailed perusal of the cover of their catchy, innovative *Sgt. Pepper* album. The cover design is a collage of people admired by the Beatles, all standing behind the band: among them, in the top row, can be seen Aleister Crowley. As recently as 1994, a prominent Vatican official, Father Corrado Balduci, would reinforce the Christian view that the Beatles were 'the Devil's musicians'.

The Beatles' spiritual rebellion was actually no more than a dalliance with oriental mystics, the Maharishi and sundry other beardy-weirdies. But anyone who did not follow the authoritarian God of the fundamentalists was obviously Satan's stooge, spitting in Mom's apple pie. Sadly, it seems this madness finally caught up with Lennon. In 1980, he was shot dead outside his New York apartment by a dazed-looking young man named Mark Chapman. Chapman had been a big Beatles fan, but had become increasingly convinced that Lennon was evil. An interview with Chapman by a psychiatrist, published in *Rolling Stone* magazine, reported that the holy assassin could 'feel the presence of Satan's demons around him. "I can feel their thoughts. I can hear their thoughts. I can hear them talking, but not from the outside, from the inside."' The unfortunate Chapman had become a 'born-again' Christian, learning about the evils of Beatles music from his new faith.

The second wave of the British pop invasion came in the form of the Rolling Stones. The Stones were acutely aware of spending their early careers in the constant shadow of the Beatles – contriving to escape it, in part, by concentrating on shock tactics. Difficult as it may be to envisage today, in the 1960s the Stones were archetypal bad boys, symbols of aggressive rebellion who made the Beatles look like the cuddly boys-next-door they were.

Achingly raw, they carried off their sweaty ugliness with enough extrovert swagger to make it alluring. ('Would you let *your* daughter marry a Rolling Stone?' ran one horrified tabloid newspaper reaction.) The image the band cultivated owed its success to the confused messages they gave out: combining outrageous camp with macho posturing; toying with fashionable socialism while behaving like screaming snobs; posturing as streetwise cockney thugs while maintaining artistic pretensions. Next to the affable efficiency of the Beatles, the Stones were a maelstrom of creative chaos.

While the Beatles experimented with Indian spirituality, the Stones began charting darker, deeper waters. The slightly sinister, dangerous edge to their music became pronounced with the 1966 release of their beautifully morbid song, 'Paint It Black'. Songwriting partnership Mick Jagger and Keith Richards were becoming interested in the infernal works of authors such as Dante and the Marquis de Sade, and consulting the occultic manuals of nineteenth-century sorcerer Eliphas Lévi. Allen Ginsberg, poet of the psychedelic revolution, almost managed to convince Jagger to record a musical version of William Blake's *Songs of Innocence and Experience*.

The band's courtship of the infernal was consummated with the release of their 1967 album, *Their Satanic Majesties Request*. It was a deliberate exercise in provocation, with the band baiting their record company, Decca, as well as the public and the media. Decca put their foot down concerning a nude photo of lead singer Jagger on the inner sleeve, and vetoed the song title 'She Comes in Colours' (replacing it with the less innuendo-laden 'She's a Rainbow'). Even the original title, *Their Satanic Majesties Request and Require*, was considered somehow more blasphemous than its shortened version.

Upon release, the album was dismissed by many as an attempt to emulate the success of the Beatles' *Sgt. Pepper*. Certainly, the Beatles were more comfortable with psychedelia than their rivals, but *Satanic Majesties* was a far eerier record than *Sgt. Pepper*, its darker moments suggesting a sinister, melancholic emptiness. However, it was ill-conceived and over-ambitious.

Beggars' Banquet, which appeared a year later, was the album *Satanic Majesties* should have been. Where *Satanic Majesties* was confused, *Beggars' Banquet* had a definite infernal identity. Its charge of electrical energy expressed the angry streak of disgust and devilish mischief running beneath society's skin, a new mood that had nothing to do with the love revolution of the peaceniks. The most significant track on the album, 'Sympathy for the Devil', remains not only the Stones' finest moment but also a minor classic of Satanic art.

Originally entitled 'The Devil is My Name' (another title change was demanded by the increasingly-uncomfortable Decca), 'Sympathy for the Devil' is a monologue by Lucifer that reminisces about the evils of world history. The song is simultaneously sinister and seductive, as Lucifer – in the classic mode of the Romantics – comes across as a perfect gent. The lyrics twist across a background of primal drumming, interwoven with a samba-guitar sound Marianne Faithfull claims was suggested by a Santerian wedding she attended with Jagger. (Santeria is a Cuban occultic religion, similar to Haitian Voodoo, and the enraged celebrants chased Jagger and Faithfull away.) Inspiration for the lyrics came from Mikhail Bulgakov's black comic novel *The Master and Margarita*, in which a mischievous, philosophical Satan visits Russia to mock the artistic community and the Stalinist state in which they thrive.

Donald Cammell as Osiris in Anger's Lucifer Rising *(1972). Cammell who directed* Performance *(1970) was an occultist who was believed to be Aleister Crowley's 'magickal child'.*

Co-songwriter/guitarist Keith Richards said in an interview at the time, 'Before, when we were just innocent kids out for a good time, they were saying, "They're evil, they're evil." Oh, I'm evil, really? So that starts making you think about evil. What is evil? . . . I don't know how much people think of Mick as the Devil or as just a good rock performer or what? There are Black Magicians who think we are acting as unknown agents of Lucifer and others who think we are Lucifer. Everybody's Lucifer.'

One of the 'Black Magicians' Richards referred to was Kenneth Anger. Anger stood at the crossroads where many of the Satanic elements of the 1960s met. In his time, he has been a Californian pop guru, a Crowleyan sorcerer, a respected avant-garde film-maker, and a gay Hollywood gossip-hound – virtually a Renaissance magus.

Anger first drew mainstream attention to himself with his scandalous book, *Hollywood Babylon* (drawing the common comparison between the home of popular cinema and the city regarded in *The Bible* as the font of sin). Anger's book is a classic of unashamedly voyeuristic muck-raking, with the deliciously camp tone of a bitchy old queen swapping rumours at a trendy LA hair salon. Scraping away the veneer of glamour from the stars of the silver screen, Anger reveals enough drug abuse, sexual deviance and general depravity to make Aleister Crowley envious. Fittingly, perhaps, as the Great Beast is Anger's chief obsession.

It's easy to see how a Crowleyite might interpret the 'Age of Aquarius' (as astrologically-inclined hippies called their psychedelic revolution) as the Aeon of Horus predicted by Crowley. Two cataclysmic world wars had passed, and a lot of people were 'doing what they wilt'. The free love and wanton drug abuse so central to Crowley and his handful of followers were now common practice among many young people. Anger happily announced Crowley's dictum that 'the Key of joy is disobedience', and declared that not only was the Aeon of Horus upon us, but the Aeon of Lucifer.

Shortly before he became involved with the Rolling Stones, Anger helped found the Church of Satan. His blend of Crowleyism and Satanism entranced the band, though – in a familiar pattern – Anger was often keen to disassociate from Satanism, referring to his personal Prince of Darkness by the less inflammatory title of Lucifer. He later confessed, however, that his Lucifer had always been the 'cosmic villain', the Miltonic Satan.

In Anger, the Rolling Stones saw a short-cut to the spiritually-rebellious chic that was *de rigeur* in the late 1960s. 'Kenneth Anger told me I was his right hand man,' Keith Richards boasted to an interviewer. In the Stones, Anger saw attractively provocative heralds of his new aeon. Speaking of Richards, founder member Brian Jones and Anita Pallenberg (a member of the Stones' entourage who had been a lover of both Jones and Richards), Anger said, 'I believe that Anita is, for want of a better word, a witch . . . The occult unit within the Stones was Keith and Anita . . . and Brian. You see, Brian was a witch too, I'm convinced. He showed me his witch's tit. He had a supernumerary tit in a very sexy place, on his inner thigh. He said, "In another time, they would have burned me."'

The exact extent of Anger's influence on the Stones' music is difficult to quantify, but it's reasonable to assume the title *Their Satanic Majesties Request* was inspired by the demonic magus. The cover shows the band in the garb of colourful pantomime sorcerers. Examine it closely and you can see the planet Mars hanging high in the sky – according to Crowleyan doctrine, the god Mars is aligned with Horus.

Whatever effect Anger had on the band's professional lives, he touched them personally to varying degrees. 'Keith and Anita later got into this black magic stuff,' recalls Marianne Faithfull, 'but Mick never got into magic any more than he got into drugs. He's a dabbler.' 'We were all just a little afraid of Kenneth,' confessed Tony Sanchez, long-time associate of the band, in his book *Up and Down with the Rolling Stones*. 'Again and again, inexplicable things involving him would happen.'

Stories about the magus' association with the band include Anger seeming to appear and disappear in various places. He offered to perform a pagan wedding ritual for Richards and Pallenberg that involved a golden door. When they awoke the next day a heavy oaken door had been painted gold, with the paint already dry. The house was heavily secured, and nobody could explain this occultic interior decoration. Faithfull talked about falling off a mountain during the making of Anger's second version of *Lucifer Rising*, sustaining only a mild concussion. Anita Pallenberg was so spooked by all of this that she slept in a protective circle of candles with a string of garlic around her neck.

Some of Anger's most influential magic was performed through the media of film. In his *Magick Lantern* cycle of short films, Anger explores Crowleyan magic by casting the movies themselves as magic spells. The earliest films in the cycle, however, are expressions of his fixation with faded Hollywood stars and homosexual male icons.

In 1954 he made *The Inauguration of the Pleasure Dome*, a magical ceremony committed to celluloid. Anger explains: 'A convocation of magicians assume the identity of gods and goddesses in a Dionysian revel. Lord Shiva, the magician, awakes. The Scarlet Woman, whore of heaven, smokes a big fat joint; Astarte of the Moon brings the wings of snow; Pan bestows the grapes of Bacchus; Hecate offers the sacred mushroom, yage, wormwood brew. The vintage of Hecate is poured, Pan's cup is poisoned by Lord Shiva. The orgy ensues – a magickal masquerade at which Pan is the prize. Lady Kali blesses the rights of the children of light as Lord Shiva invokes the godhead with the formula "Force and Fire". Dedicated to the few; and to Aleister Crowley; and the crowned and conquering child.'

Anger's next overtly magical project, one decade later, was *Lucifer Rising*. His 'first religious film', a weird, mesmeric narrative combined with magical ritual, it also embodies his turbulent love/hate relationship with the1960s counterculture – both in the film itself, and the events surrounding its strange history. As Anger once observed, 'Making movies is casting spells.' As director and editor, the theory ran that the magus could fully control both the characters on screen and the entities they invoked. *Lucifer Rising* depicted the downfall of the oppressive Aeon of Osiris (or Christian era), and the movement into the Aeon of Horus (or Lucifer). 'My reason for filming has nothing to do with "cinema" at all,' explained Anger. 'It's a transparent excuse for capturing people . . . I consider myself working Evil in an evil medium.'

Lucifer Rising conjured more than its share of chaos. The original version was finished in 1967, but fate intervened. Anger – who picked his actors very carefully to match the particular deity they were to represent – wanted Mick Jagger to play Lucifer and Keith Richards as Beelzebub. The boys very politely refused. As a stop-gap Anger asked Jagger's brother Chris, but this new Lucifer proved impossible to work with. And so Anger finally selected a young hippie protégé of his named Bobby Beausoleil. (Jagger's girlfriend, Marianne Faithfull, would appear in the second version of *Lucifer Rising* as Lilith the Destroyer – though her decidedly unsteady walk and dazed expression made her look more like Lilith the Wasted.)

On 21 September 1967, Anger organised a celebratory event titled the Equinox of the Gods at the Straight Theatre in Haight-Ashbury, the epicentre of hippie culture in San Francisco. But Beausoleil proved a more capricious Lucifer than Anger anticipated – according to Anger, the pretty hippie he called 'Cupid' ripped off 1600 feet of footage from *Lucifer Rising* and some camera equipment before the performance. Anger was livid, smashing a rare magical cane that once belonged to Crowley. He then pronounced a curse upon Beausoleil, sealing it with an amulet he put around his neck. On one side was a picture of his erstwhile protégé, on the other a toad with the inscription 'Bobby Beausoleil – who was turned into a toad by Kenneth Anger.' Cupid never turned into a toad, but a cloud of uncommonly dark fortune did follow him as he headed south for Los Angeles.

Anger took the footage that remained of *Lucifer Rising* and fashioned it into *Invocation of My Demon Brother*. 'The shadowing forth of Lord Lucifer, as the Powers gather at a midnight mass' was Anger's description of this part-completed work. The wizard who performs the Satanic mass is played by Anger himself, draped in a swastika flag. He is intercut with other curious, foreboding images such as Hell's Angels and G.I.s landing in Vietnam. Also featured is Anger's friend Anton LaVey, High Priest of the recently-formed Church of Satan. The soundtrack music was played by Mick Jagger, consisting of odd, discordant drones on a decidedly flat-sounding Moog synthesiser.

In 1970 Anger remade his masterpiece, *Lucifer Rising* – though even now, he still tinkers with elements of the film to produce dozens of subtly different versions. Once again, Anger himself plays the Magus, invoking a new aeon through the door opened by the occult events of the 1960s: 'A film about the love generation – the birthday party of the Aquarian Age. Showing actual ceremonies to make Lucifer rise. Lucifer is the Light God, not the Devil – the Rebel Angel behind what's happening in the world today. His message is that the key of joy is disobedience. Isis (Nature) wakes. Osiris (Death) answers. Lilith (Destroyer) climbs to the place of Sacrifice. The Magus activates the circle and Lucifer – Bringer of Light – breaks through.'

Bad luck had begun calling upon the Rolling Stones, in the shape of a series of tragedies. The first was the death of the band's second guitarist, Brian Jones.

It was Jones who, in 1962, formed the band and named it after a Muddy Waters song. On 2 July 1969, in classic rock 'n' roll style, he drowned in his swimming pool on a cocktail of vodka and pills. In the seven intervening years, Jones had moved from the heart of the band to liability status because of his wild behaviour and appetite for chemicals. While Jagger increasingly took the limelight, shouldering the bad-boy image, in reality the lead singer was more cautiously conservative. It was Jones who left a string of illegitimate children, empty bottles and bruised knuckles in his wake. He tried to moderate his behaviour as, despite their carefully-cultivated wildness, the Stones became big business. But Brian Jones never quite got it together before death caught up with him.

Some, notably Genesis P-Orridge founder of magical movement Thee Temple Ov Psychick Youth, see Jones' death as symbolic. 'I see him as a shattered mirror of the sixties,' says Orridge. 'He encapsulates all the different threads, spoken and unspoken. The archetype angel destroyed.' Perhaps Jones, with all his fragile aggression, was closer to Anger's Lucifer than the low cunning of pretty boy Beausoleil, or the calculated camp of Jagger. Two days after Jones' death, the Stones turned their free concert in London's Hyde Park into a memorial for their ex-guitarist. Jagger read a poem by Shelley, then tried to release hundreds of white butterflies from boxes by the stage. They had been in the boxes too long and most of the delicate creatures were dead.

That summer, Woodstock free festival, in New York State, represented for many the hazy apex of the Love Generation. The spirit of love and rebellion had wafted across the western world like a mist of marijuana smoke, and myriad festivals, gatherings and love-ins had sprung up in its wake. The Stones, as ever, were desperate not to be outdone, planning their own free festival in the USA. They originally planned to hold it in Golden Gate Park, San Francisco, spiritual heartland of the hippie movement, but eventually had to move it to the nearby Altamont speedway track.

At the suggestion of scheduled support band the Grateful Dead, the Stones hired the Hell's Angels as security for their Altamont gig.

The Altamont festival, December 1969. Hell's Angels security guards 'keep the peace'. From the film Gimme Shelter.

The Angels were not only cheap (they charged 500 bucks' worth of beer, according to one account), but their brand of frightening freedom still had a devilish chic in the naïve 1960s.

The Hell's Angels Motorcycle Club was formed after the Second World War, by bike-loving ex-servicemen who found civilian life too bland to bear. The Hell's Angels moniker was taken from a notorious American Air Force squadron, but the Satanic implications of the name became increasingly appropriate. The Angels were hellraisers, prototypes for the whole biker culture – particularly the outlaws, or '1%ers' (the 'one percent of motorcyclists' labelled as 'hoodlums and troublemakers' by the American Motorcycle Association in 1967). Many 1%er gangs emulated the Angels' Satanic-sounding title, adopting infernal names like the Straight Satans, Satan's Slaves and the Pagans.

Some took their title at face value. One member of the powerful Canadian gang Satan's Angels said in a 1970s interview, 'There are definite spirits and we identify with that particular one that has been called Satan. It's an upsidedown world. Our virtues are other's vices. You could say we were Satanists.' In his book on the Hell's Angels which did so much to establish their legend, 'gonzoid' journalist Hunter S. Thompson identifies the club's ethos with the famous Milton quote, 'Better to rule in Hell, than serve in Heaven.'

Freewheelin' Frank Reynolds was a secretary of the San Francisco chapter of the Angels during the1960s. In his autobiography he says, 'Dig my definition of God Almighty is of a back-knifing second-rate cherub. And Satan is cursed because he was knifed in the back while laying it down the way it was and still lays it down one hell of a lot clearer beyond any doubt when weighing the facts. Any fact of God against the facts of Lucifer, who will someday regain his rightful place. A few pages from John Milton's *Paradise Lost* have put me exactly on the positive track that I am following. I am a child of his. I am a Hell's Angel. Along with all the other brothers in the Hell's Angels I no longer have to stammer and stutter: I will be able to lay down the trips of the righteousness of Lucifer.'

Hell's Angels, and other outlaw gangs, are symbols of the more destructive, volatile aspects of the Satanic canon. Their readiness to fight, their revelling in intimidation and fear, their rapacious passion for pleasures of the flesh in their basest forms, all these characteristics made them into icons of wilful alienation and violent self-indulgence. When the outlaw bikers collided with hippie culture, many of the flower children naively believed these rough outcasts would become police and protectors for their psychedelic revolution. But the appetite of the 1%ers for the love generation's drugs and free love wasn't matched by any shared ideals. They clashed most notably over the Vietnam War, which the Hell's Angels supported just as enthusiastically as the hippies opposed it.

Mick Jagger takes the stage at the ill-fated Altamont festival.

When Jagger finally came onstage at Altamont on 6 December 1969, things were beginning to get ugly. Marty Balin of support act Jefferson Airplane had been hit in the face with a pool cue by a Hell's Angel. He had tried to intervene when he saw the Angels beat up a black kid in front of him. Paul Kantner, band founder, began to shout at the Angels until his microphone was snatched from him in the brawl that immersed the front of the stage. (Kantner would enter into correspondence during the next decade with the Temple of Set's Michael Aquino on their mutual interest in space travel.)

Jagger took the stage clad in his psychedelic sorcerer's robes. Dancing under the red lights, surrounded by the dark wall of threatening, black-clad Angels, the vocalist could have been Anger's Lucifer served by a surly army of warlike demons. Two songs into the set, things just kept getting uglier. Naked hippies cast themselves at the stage as offerings for their rock gods, and the Angels cast them back into the audience after beating them bloody. The third song began, 'Sympathy for the Devil', and all Hell broke loose.

In the audience, a black youth named Meredith Hunter pulled a gun. According to some he was aiming it at Jagger, others claimed he was defending himself against the Angels. Whichever is true, it was scant moments before a pack of black-leather Angels fell upon him and, in a flurry of kicks and knife blows, Hunter was killed. The Stones could see that the Angels were brutalising the audience rather than controlling them – but Jagger was out of his depth, bleating weakly for everybody to 'cool it'. As the killing of Meredith Hunter played itself out to the strains of 'Sympathy for the Devil', the song had to be stopped briefly as Jagger quipped, with unintended understatement, that 'something very funny always happens when we start that number'. As the tide of panic and fury rose, the death count escalated to three with 100 injured.

Following Altamont, the shaken Stones turned their back on the whole Satanic scene. Jagger wore a large wooden crucifix for some time after. The revolutionary stance and allusions to street violence were quietly dropped in favour of the stately image of rock 'n' roll aristocrats. The Rolling Stones abandoned any pretensions to occultic chic or streetwise cool, letting themselves into the world of polite high society through the back door.

Kenneth Anger conducts a Black Mass in his film Invocation of my Demon Brother *(1968).*

For some, it was just one more death knell for the Love Generation. For others, it had a greater significance – it was a crack in the door through which demons from Kenneth Anger's Aeon of Lucifer could pass. A letter to *Rolling Stone* summed up the feelings of many who had seen Jagger's star 'As lightning fall from Heaven':

'To those who know, it's been obvious that the Stones, or at least some of them, have been involved in the practice of magick ever since the *Satanic Majesties Request* album. But there at least the colour was more white than black. Since then the hue has gone steadily darker and darker. At Altamont He appeared in his full majesty with his full consort of demons, the Hell's Angels. It was just a few days before the Winter Solstice when the forces of darkness are at their most powerful. The moon was in Scorpio, which is the time of the month when the Universal vibration is at its most unstable. It was held in a place dedicated to destruction through motion. Then Mick comes on only after it is dark enough for the red lights to work their magick. I don't know if they were truly aware of what they were doing or not. I feel they are sadder and wiser from the experience. But an agonising price was paid for the lesson. And we were all guilty because we have eaten of the cake the Stones baked.'

The Stones' flirtation with Anger was also over. Marianne Faithfull describes him as 'entertaining and appropriately creepy, but when his protestations went unanswered and he took to hurling copies of William Blake through the windows of Cheyne Walk, Mick took all our magic books and made a great pyre of them in the fireplace'.

Looking Back With Anger

An appreciation of the art of Crowley by a modern magus.

I met Kenneth Anger at an exhibition of art by Aleister Crowley in London during April 1998. He was friendly and open, if easily distracted, and was careful to be courteous to anyone who approached him. He seemed almost bashful when someone mentioned the 'Lucifer' tattoo on his chest and, dressed in a large, colourful sweater, it was difficult to think of him as the same man who played the role of evil magus in so many 1960s myths.

How do you see Lucifer?

Lucifer is the god of light. 'Lucem Fero' – I bring the light. So, in my take on it and Crowley's 'Hymn to Lucifer' also, Lucifer is the muse of the artist. He brings us colour, light, form and all of those things, as the god of the lower world. To me Lucifer is of great importance.

To what extent are your films magical in nature?

Invocation of My Demon Brother is the fragments of what remains of my first version of *Lucifer Rising* that was stolen from me by Bobby Beausoleil and his cohorts. It is necessarily a fragment and I put it together just to show I can make a film using fragments.

The ritual that's shown, where I dress as a magus and perform a circular dance, is the ceremony of the Autumnal Equinox. We performed the actual ritual in the Straight Theatre in the Haight-Ashbury district of San Francisco.

What's the ritual's purpose?

I'm supposed to call or invoke the forces of the new aeon.

Are these forces in any sense 'evil'?

I don't consider them evil. This was right in the middle of the Vietnam War, and while I have flashes of helicopters and things like that, we're banishing the forces of war.

You also use images like swastikas and Hell's Angels ...

Well, the swastika is a solar symbol, so that's why that's there. I'm also playing with darkness and light and there's a deliberate ambiguity. After all, Anton [LaVey] himself with his horns appears, with the Hell's Angels superimposed. It's the most Satanic film I've made, at least superficially.

How were you involved with the Rolling Stones?

I was a friend of theirs and I still am. A lot of the legends were just ridiculous things that somehow got pinned on me without verification (laughs). Like Keith Richards and Anita Pallenberg claimed I could walk through locked doors. They were getting married and I said I would paint their front door on Cheyne Walk with gold leaf that requires a special technique that I know. I made them a lovely gold door, which may still be there though probably not. They had forgotten they left the door unlocked for me so I got in with paints and so forth. I turned up inside their house, but there was nothing mysterious about me somehow breaking in or anything. It was because, frankly, they took so many drugs they tended to forget things. It was a heavily-drugged period.

It's often been suggested you were the influence that led to their brief infernal period.

The only thing I got out of it or put into it of a specific nature is they called their album *Their Satanic Majesties Request*. Then the song 'Sympathy for the Devil' mentions Lucifer by name. That's when Mick had agreed to play Lucifer. I asked him to play it in my film and he said 'Yes.' Then he changed his mind, not wanting to be too identified that way. Instead of playing in my film [the second version of *Lucifer Rising*] he went off and married Bianca. They invited me to the marriage, and I was rather pissed-off with him at the time. He'd started sporting this rather pretentious, large gold cross studded with diamonds. At any rate, I said, 'Thanks, but I'll wait for the divorce.' I had to wait five years.

Is there a connection between your passion for Crowley and golden-age Hollywood scandal? You use the 'every man and woman is a star' Crowley dictum and the quote where he, somewhat hypocritically, dismisses the movie crowd ...

As 'cocaine-crazed sexual lunatics'! You've got to understand Crowley – he's finding that amusing. He's dismissing it but he's also finding it a hoot. He's not being moralistic in any conventional sense. I daresay the side of Hollywood he saw was just people partying and taking coke at parties which he would consider wrong inasmuch as something like cocaine should be used in a sacramental way, not just to have fun. When he calls them cocaine-crazed that's what he's talking about.

How did you discover Crowley?

I feel quite fortunate in meeting up with his ideas through some people who had known him such as Jane Wolfe. When I met her she was an old lady living in retirement in Hollywood. She'd been an actress who'd played with Mary Pickford, then she went to live in his abbey, and knew Crowley quite well. She lent me some of his books. I met Marjorie Parsons, the widow of Jack Parsons, who was Crowley's magickal son. She played in a film of mine [*The Inauguration of the Pleasure Dome*] as the Scarlet Woman in 1953.

At that time you could go into used bookshops and find Crowley's books in the original editions. I kept doing that, not only in Los Angeles and New York, but when I got to London I completed my ten-volume collection of *The Equinox*. I ended up with quite a good library of Crowley material and read them all. The one thing I regret as a film-maker was that I was never able to find the backing to do a feature-length commercial film on Crowley, which I'd love to do. You could make a very entertaining film on him. Various people have threatened over the years to make a film based on Crowley. The worst idea I heard was that Ken Russell was toying with it. Of course he would just make a grotesque farce. I'm sure this film will never be made by him.

Various other people have made little noises, but nothing ever seems to happen. But his life is so complex that it almost defies being made into a film. If I did it, I would just do the episode at Cefalu, which just covers three years, but I've never found the backing I'd need, even though I've written up a proposal and have peddled it around a bit. Then of course, who'd play Crowley? . . . If you found an important actor who agreed to take the part, then it's 'bankable'. So, perhaps someone like Anthony Hopkins, or Gielgud though he's too old now. You'd need a top actor. You'd find someone who looks like Crowley looked at one time in his life – like Telly Savalas, with a bald head – but it would have to be an Englishman.

The one time Crowley's life was put on film in a sense was when a silent film was made of *The Magician* based on the story by Somerset Maugham. It was made by Rex Ingram and filmed in France in the late 1920s. Crowley wanted to play the part but it was played by Paul Wegener, a German actor that played the title character in *The Golem*. He was a tall, very imposing figure – taller and more giant-like than Crowley himself – with great, slashing, Slavic cheekbones and very deep-set eyes. The fact that he did not speak English did not matter in a silent film.

Do you believe in Crowley's vision of the world going through a trinity of 'Aeons'?

I think it makes as much sense as anything else. I'm quite prepared to accept that Christianity has had its day, in over 2,000 years, and is now in its twilight. In other words all religions go through this kind of cycle, and Crowley said it would be replaced by the Aeon of Horus who is 'the Crowned and Conquering Child'. It will be a much more joyful, life-affirming time.

But Crowley also suggests it will be a violent and turbulent time . . .

Horus is a war god, so it has that possibility, but this is fighting against ideas rather than physical warfare. As far

as physical war goes, well, Crowley was in London during the Blitz and he said it was exciting but a sheer waste.

Do you think Crowley's influence will continue to grow?

This is only the second exhibition of his artwork – the first was in 1931 in Berlin. I'm sure he'd find some significance in the fact that his influence is manifested by having his art publicly displayed. He thought that every time he published a book it was a manifestation. He is not only growing in stature – the stature was always there it just had to be found. His followers now number in the thousands. They're rather low key – they're not like the Scientologists that make a lot of

noise, or other groups that come and go like the transcendental meditators or whatever.

The interesting thing about his followers is in the quality of the people. These are people who are in their own right scholars, philosophers, artists, scientists – high-IQ people. They're not just a bunch of hanger-on hippies who want an excuse to have an orgy. Crowley had no objections to orgies in certain circumstances, but the whole point was not to make an excuse for that kind of indulgence. There's a serious end to it, and the expression of sexuality should be very carefully considered. Even what he called self-expression, or masturbation, shouldn't be indulged in just for relief or fun. It should be thought of as a giving-over to the god Pan.

That's one of the less palatable aspects of his creed, isn't it – turning pleasure into duty?

Enjoyment is a very flexible word. If it's just 'getting off' with someone else – Crowley said there should be a deeper side to it. In fact he had a similar philosophy to D. H. Lawrence – they were parallel thinkers in the new paganism. Between Lawrence, Nietzsche and Crowley they were seeing a post-Christian world.

THE DEFLOWERING OF AN AGE

Manson, the Process Church and Satanic Cults of the 1960s

hen Bobby Beausoleil hit LA, he quickly fell in with a band of hippies under the loose leadership of a short, bearded ex-con and would-be folk-rock singer. The group was later to become known as 'the Family', and their leader was one Charlie Manson.

Manson the myth has now almost totally swallowed Manson the man. Part of the myth depicts him as a Devil figure, a Satanist with very real supernatural powers. In reality, Manson fulfils very few of the roles in which modern legend has cast him – but this hasn't stopped the media and counter-cultural phenomenon we know as Charles Manson.

Manson often talks from his prison cell about mirrors, about reflecting those that purport to be examining him. This, as is common with his observations, hangs somewhere between the astute and the insane. Certainly, the significance of the Manson massacres lies not in events or actualities, but in how Charlie has become a symbol for so many different people: whether of a re-crucified messiah or a psychedelic monster. Most significant of all, perhaps, is how society seemed to need him to reinvent himself to fill these roles.

Bobby Beausoleil fitted into Manson's little group very well. The majority of them were young girls, who took to Cupid's pretty face straight away. Charlie's charisma and streetwise articulacy – mixed with the underground chic of being an ex-con in those revolutionary days – also proved a powerful aphrodisiac. With so many young hippie girls at his beck and call, Manson proved a popular character on the Californian scene, and an unlikely guru. The early life of the Family seems idyllic, in a squalid kind of a way – a carefree, nomadic existence, living from day to day on a diet of scavenged vegetables, playing idle games on LSD.

But the games did not last forever. Manson's very real resentment for 'the System' – which had mistreated him throughout his life – combined with drug-induced paranoia and the naïveté of his young companions to produce a volatile brew. The hippie scene attracted violent lowlife scenting easy meat, or a sympathetic audience for their own violent agenda. By 1969, frustration turned many of the love generation onto hate in the form of militant radical groups, like the Black Panthers, or hippie terrorists, like the Weathermen. Manson's education in the slammer had made him an accomplished survivor, and he prepared his flock for war within the darkening counterculture.

It's impossible to say exactly when the vortex of fear first caught hold of the Family. The group was growing in size and required greater funds to keep it together, only available through petty theft and drug dealing. The drug market wasn't becoming any more civilised, minds were becoming more and more acid-addled, and crises inevitably arose. Crises like an argument with black drug dealer Bernard Crowe, which led to Manson shooting him with a .22 pistol. Crowe survived, but Charlie's paranoia persuaded him he'd slain a member of the feared Black Panthers organisation.

This fed a growing siege mentality in the hellishly-hot desert locale of Death Valley, where the Manson Family had now retreated. Their leader felt increasingly trapped, between the forces of law and order and the threat of the black militants who had set LA ablaze in 1965. He turned their borrowed ranch home into a ramshackle guerrilla base, stockpiling salvaged dune buggies and weapons. Charlie was now keener than ever to court the friendship of outlaw bikers on the violent edge of the Californian scene. With the lure of his willing entourage of hippie nymphettes – providing blow-jobs on demand – and a plentiful flow of recreational chemicals, the ranch attracted hard-core cycle gangs like the Straight Satans, the Gypsy Jokers and Satan's Slaves.

The group's determination to maintain good relations with the bikers led them further into the exciting world of violence. Some bikers claimed that mescaline sold to them at the ranch had been phoney, demanding a refund. They did not return the suspect merchandise, so Charlie was dubious – but he did not want to upset them, taking Beausoleil and two of the girls with him to demand a refund from the

Cover design for the Video Werewolf documentary Charles Manson – Superstar. *The inspiringly-disturbed artist Joe Coleman illustrates the many faces of the 1960s' antisocial icon.*

supplier, Gary Hinman. Left to his own devices, Bobby's 'persuasion' got out of hand, killing Hinman with multiple stab wounds. Beausoleil used his victim's blood to daub the slogan 'POLITICAL PIGGIE' on a wall, which he hoped would implicate the Black Panthers – it may have been inspired by the song 'Piggies' from the Beatles' *White Album*, an acid-era favourite of the Family – then split. No criminal mastermind, Beausoleil was picked up a few days later, driving Hinman's car, which still contained the murder weapon.

In less than a month's time, on 8 August 1969, Manson's 'children' were involved in crimes which shocked the world and turned Charlie into a secular Devil for a whole generation. In opulent Beverly Hills, small-time drug dealer and film industry wanna-be Voytek Frykowski was sleeping off a night's partying. He awoke, on his friend's couch, to find a handgun barrel inches from his face. 'What do you want?' he breathed at the bearded intruder. 'I am the Devil and I have come to do the Devil's work,' responded the young hippie, then shot him. The intruder was Charles 'Tex' Watson, accompanied by Linda 'the Witch' Kasabian, Susan 'Sexy Sadie' Atkins and Patricia 'Katie' Krenwinkle, all members of the Family.

By the time they left, the crew, who dubbed themselves 'Creepy Crawlers', had taken six lives. Abigail Folger, coffee heiress, was stabbed 28 times; Jay Sebring, society hairdresser, was stabbed seven times and shot; actress Sharon Tate – wife of film director Roman Polanski, heavily pregnant with their unborn son – was stabbed fifteen times (Polanski, in England at the time, had recently directed *Rosemary's Baby* – a paranoid melodrama about urban Satanism, which employed Church of Satan leader Anton LaVey as technical adviser); Frykowski suffered 51 stab wounds and twelve blows to the head in addition to a gunshot wound. One further victim was shot dead in the driveway – Steven Parent, a young man who had been visiting the houseboy and had the misfortune to encounter the murderous hippies on his way home. Before leaving, the Creepy Crawlers daubed the legends 'WAR', 'PIGS' and 'HEALTER SKELTER' (sic) on the walls in their victims' blood. (The latter slogan definitely inspired by 'Helter Skelter' from *The White Album*.)

Charlie Manson in chains. Despite the reversed swastika cut into his forehead, 'one of the most evil, satanic men who ever walked the face of the earth' appears to be just one more little career criminal.

The following night, the Creepy Crawlers went on another mission. This time police found a middle-aged couple, Rosemary and Leno LeBianca, slaughtered beneath the familiar, crimson-dripping graffiti. Grotesquely carved into Leno's chest was the word 'WAR', with a knife and fork remaining stuck in his stomach. ('That's one man who won't be sending his son to war,' Sadie Atkins would later remark – drawing an insane parallel between Vietnam war-protest and the drug-crazed crime for which she expressed no motive.) Incredibly, they stopped afterwards for a snack amongst the blood and carnage, helping themselves to melon and chocolate milk.

Panic rippled across the West Coast, as the massacres seized the world's imagination. Not only were the killings unusually bizarre, but the pregnant, stunningly-beautiful Sharon Tate was the most poignant victim imaginable. Someone had ripped a Hollywood starlet and three other bright young things from the heart of the American dream, slaughtering them like livestock.

It was by pure chance that the Los Angeles Police found their butchers – a communal rabble of vegetarians living constantly in the shadow of the law. After a mass arrest for auto-theft, Sadie boasted in gaol of her part in the massacre. (Sadie – whose nickname came from another *White Album* song – may have been sexy, but she wasn't so bright.) Arrests followed, and the stage was set for a dramatic trial. The State of California not only had Manson, the Establishment finally had something concrete to pin on the hippie movement. The charge was that the counterculture wasn't just weird – it was *evil*.

The trial was a farce, part-circus, part-morality play. President Nixon publicly declared Manson guilty in print before the jurors' butts left the bench. Charlie and friends were also tried, and convicted, of the murder of one 'Shorty' Shea, a ranch-hand, in the absence of any evidence. (The eventual discovery of Shea's skeletal remains would corroborate the conviction.) The fact that Manson wasn't present at the Tate slayings – though he tied the LaBiancas up at gunpoint, promising not to harm them before sending his 'children' in – was regarded by the prosecution as a minor detail in convicting, according to prosecutor Vincent Bugliosi, 'one of the most evil, Satanic men who ever walked the face of the earth'.

The little misfit was convicted as the dominant ringleader of the group, paraded as an example before being sentenced to death. The sentence was later commuted to life imprisonment, with Manson cast back into the cold arms of the prison system that spawned him. In perhaps the most telling irregularity of his trial, Charlie was only allowed to state his final testimony once the jurors had been cleared from the court. In an echo of the witchcraft trials of five hundred years before, prosecutor Bugliosi believed Manson's 'hypnotic powers' might sway the jury to find him innocent.

In his statement Manson observed, 'These children that come at you with knives, they are your children, you taught them. I did not teach them, I just tried to help them stand up.' Bullshit? Offbeat insight? Buck-passing? Or was Charlie dropping the mirror for one moment, offering a brief glimpse behind his many masks?

Perhaps it doesn't matter, as mainstream society was too busy making up its own mythology. Charlie Manson became one of the twentieth-century faces of Evil, to hang alongside Adolf Hitler. Indeed, Charlie himself had some interesting things to say about the Führer: he insisted Hitler was the Second Coming of Christ, mocking the world for failing to recognise him and crucifying their messiah all over again. Some see this as simply a cracked manifestation of Manson's racist world-view. However, while Manson predicted a race war, unlike the Nazis he envisaged the blacks winning. In his warped philosophy of traditional redneck-jailbird values and mystical egomania, he believed the blacks to be too physically powerful for the Establishment to withstand, but cerebrally far inferior to a natural-born white leader – like himself.

Like Hitler in the 1940s, society wanted to blame Manson for the orgy of barbarism that briefly gripped California in 1969. But was Hitler, too, just helping his 'children' to 'stand up'? Like Manson, Hitler toyed with the role of messiah, and many commentators find it hard to concede his evident charisma without resorting to quasi-mystical ideas like 'hypnotic power'. Both men are commonly regarded as mass murderers – though their unprecedented notoriety is due not to crimes they themselves committed, but to atrocities committed by their disciples. Manson even compared his position to that of the US President, sending young Americans to Vietnam.

Orthodox Christian opinion insists that men like Hitler and Manson provide parables on the perils of following false messiahs, instead of the 'authentic' Jesus Christ. However, while there will always be charismatic, mystic malcontents like Manson and Hitler – or, indeed, Jesus – the responsibility for their supposed crimes lies with those who line up behind them. Without a reservoir of eager, empty-eyed disciples, even such charismatic men are relatively harmless. Maybe we just nail up the wrong guys . . .

The legend that grew up in the decades following the trial is more significant than the events of 8-9 August 1969, tragic as they were. In a world with no shortage of mayhem and pain, a car thief and small-time pimp like Charlie, with possibly only one squalid murder to his name (that of Shorty Shea), remains trapped like a hunted coyote in the torchlight of popular legend. The power of the Manson myth is demonstrated by the wide spectrum of attitudes reflected in his mirror. He has become, as one acidic commentator put it, 'the Elvis of alienation'.

Manson is seen as the ugly result of 1960s libertarianism – the Cain who slew the Abel of the love generation. Vincent Bugliosi – whose best-selling book *Helter Skelter* presents the standard Establishment viewpoint on the Manson murders – directly linked Charlie with the psychedelic revolution, making a connection between the massacres and the Family's shared passion for the Beatles. His theory centred on *The White Album* – particularly the song 'Helter Skelter' – acting as a psychological trigger for Manson's supposed idea to cause violent conflict between his enemies in the Black Panthers and the white Establishment.

On the other side of the fence, the radical fringes of the counterculture declared the drug-happy demagogue a martyr. Hippie terrorists the Weathermen told the flower children to 'dig it' (the savage murder of Leno LaBianca) and declared 1969 'the Year of the Fork'. The revolutionary Left revelled in the fear the massacre generated among their foes in 'straight' society, with *Tuesday's Child* magazine declaring Manson their Man of the Year. Over the ensuing years, some members of the radical Right hailed the hate-filled hippie as a 'man of action', reinventing him as a martyr to the cause of racial conflict. Charlie helped fuel this view by scrawling swastikas on his forehead (though, as some apologists are quick to point out, the swastika is an ancient religious symbol as well as a Nazi insignia).

In reality, as Manson has often observed, he was born in 1934 and was a child of the 1940s, sharing few of the hippie generation's values or aspirations. 'I got some friends that killed some people,' is his own estimation of his crimes. Beyond that, the motives and aims (if any) behind the murders are obscured by the veil of incessant drug abuse that fell over everything in the Manson Family's world.

One theory is that the girls inspired the killings in imitation of Gary Hinman's murder as committed by their beloved Bobby Beausoleil (rather than, as Bugliosi insists, to hang the blame on the Black Panthers and start a race war.) Their acid-addled logic may have reasoned that, if another high-profile murder were perpetrated in the same fashion, the courts would release Bobby from gaol as the killer appeared to still be at large. An opposing theory is that Tex Watson instigated the murders, after being ripped-off in a drug deal by Voytek Frykowski. (Supermarket owner Leno LaBianca, it's claimed, had mob connections, and his wife, it's also improbably asserted, was a big-time acid dealer.)

For our purposes, it's the occult aspects of the Manson phenomenon that warrants more investigation. The routine assumption is that Charlie was a Satanist – the girls liked to refer to themselves as witches, and designed a 'Devil's Witches' waistcoat to wear in their desert retreat. Manson's buddy, Dennis Wilson of the Beach Boys (the group recorded one of Charlie's songs, 'Cease to Exist', as 'Never Learn Not to Love' on their *20/20* album) said in an interview that he had a friend who was 'a little like the Devil' and 'likes to be called the Wizard'.

Certainly, Manson has said 'Satan to me would be God', and 'You could say I'm kinda like Satan.' But he's also keen on comparing himself to Jesus Christ, as well as a host of other historical figures including Eleanor Roosevelt. While obviously articulate and bright, Charlie is rarely consistent and sometimes thoroughly incoherent.

Many Christians remain convinced this is the result of being in thrall to Satan – rather than too much acid, and an appallingly abusive upbringing. Tex Watson and Sadie Atkins have both rallied behind the fundamentalist Christian banner, being 'born again' in gaol. Tex blames his bloodletting on demonic possession and is now a pastor, giving taped sermons in prison. Sadie, in her book *Child of Satan, Child of God*, even goes so far as to implicate Anton LaVey, head of the Church of Satan, as instrumental in her descent into evil. Cynics may agree with musician Phillip Kaufman, who served time with Charlie, when he suggested of Atkins and her compadres: 'Now she says she's sorry, she's found Jesus. Shit, they've all found Jesus – that's the best way to get out of jail.'

Charlie drops a few infernal hints in the book *Manson in His Own Words*, dictated to ex-con-turned-writer Nuel Emmons. He implies some kind of turning point for the Family at a place called the 'Spiral Staircase', in Topanga Canyon near LA. It was owned by 'a trippy broad, about 45 years old' who was 'pumped up about devil worship and other satanic activities'. Manson describes it as a place where 'freaks' could hang out and do as they wish, while 'straights' could shed their respectability and morals. 'To those who live within society's moral code,' he observes, 'the house might have resembled a movie scene of a massive party at a dope fiend's pad: music playing, often blaring, sometimes soft and sensual; strobe lights blinking, or hardly any light at all; guys and girls everywhere, seated on couches, chairs and pillows, on the floors and on the beds; marijuana joints being passed around; tables showing long lines of coke; pills and capsules of all colours, each providing a different high; long-haired bearded guys in weird clothes with exaggerated lengths of gold and beaded chains; scantily clad girls, obviously drugged, willing to have sex.'

Manson – if this can be assumed to be his authentic voice – adds that the Spiral Staircase was also a magnet for 'heavier shit – like chains, whips, blood-drinking, animal death and even human sacrifice. It was a hard-core multiple-devil worshipping bunch of people who passed through the doors of the Spiral Staircase.' Heavy shit indeed. 'In looking back, I think I can honestly say our philosophy – fun and games, love and sex, peaceful friendship for everyone – began changing into the madness which finally engulfed us in that house.'

Charlie Manson, King of the Scapegoats, seems to be getting in on the act and looking for someone else to blame. However, some have challenged the veracity of *Manson in His Own Words* – not least Charlie, who denounces the title's claim as 'bullshit' – and alert Mansonites will note the complete absence of his distinct, rambling, acid-anecdotal style. At the end of the day, as so often in the reflecting-mirror world of Manson, your belief as to what motivated the crimes probably says more about you than it does about Charlie.

There are, of course, numerous occult theories as to what happened. Legend has it that the curse Kenneth Anger placed upon his fleeing Lucifer, Bobby Beausoleil, caused Bobby's car to break down near the Family's hang-out. It's said Charlie Manson buried the stolen footage of *Lucifer Rising* in the desert, demanding a ransom of $10,000 from Anger for its return. (Anger and Beausoleil have since made up. Bobby recorded a musical soundtrack for the second version of the film, credited to 'Bobby Beausoleil and the Freedom Orchestra, Tracy Prison'.) Black Pope Anton LaVey also claimed that his response to the hippie invasion of San Francisco was a curse on the whole movement. The net result was, allegedly, the massacres that helped bring the innocence of the 1960s to an end.

Those who believe in links between Manson and the forces of darkness usually tie him in with the notorious Process Church of the Final Judgement. The Process has become legendary, both in the annals of hippie history and Satanic lore. Of all the psychedelic Satanist cults rumoured to exist during that era, only the Process Church was of significant size, made any impact outside the occult community, or left behind any notable literature.

Chief among the conspiracy theorists who weave Manson and the Process into a web of wickedness are Maury Terry, in his book *The Ultimate Evil*, and Ed Sanders, in his Manson study *The Family*. Terry is a sensationalist reporter with a nose for a good scare story, while Sanders is an ex-hippie mourning the death of 1960s innocence. Both would have you believe that, if you get hit by a car, then it's most likely driven by a member of the Manson Family and its license plates are a coded version of the name 'Robert de Grimston'.

De Grimston, an Englishman, founded the Process Church of the Final Judgement in 1965, with his new bride Mary Anne. They met while attending Church of Scientology seminars in London, and, while both proved promising students, they began to adopt increasingly personal interpretations of Scientology techniques. (This is one of de Grimston's few real connections with Charlie Manson, who made his own study of Scientologist-psychology while in prison on car-theft charges.) After one year, the couple broke away to found their own church. The Process gradually evolved, from a secular group based on unorthodox psychoanalysis to a religious cult assimilating psychiatric techniques into its mode of worship. This

Robert de Grimston, who, as leader of the Process Church of the Final Judgement, cultivated a deliberately Christ-like image. Portrait by Tim.

transition was achieved by the close bonding that developed from communal living – combined with shared traumatic experiences, both accidental and contrived.

As with the Manson Family, the closer their group became, the more alienated they were from mainstream society. The cult's pivotal experience was a disastrous trip to a place they named 'Xtul', in Mexico, during 1966 – when it was hit by a hurricane, the Process regarded the ordeal as a 'test' where 'we met God face-to-face'. At this point the Process briefly became an evangelical religious movement, travelling the world in search of converts. They began by defining themselves as unorthodox Christians, but by 1968 had given Satan a prominent place in their mythology.

The doctrines of the Process centred around the idea that if Jesus advocated loving your enemy, then God should love Satan and vice versa. Jesus was the intermediary whereby these two opposites would finally be reconciled during the apocalyptic 'Final Judgement'. (Later, a fourth deity, Lucifer, would be added to their doctrine.) God, or Jehovah, represented a stern authoritarian force, harsh and judgmental. Satan was the epitome of chaos, a god of destruction, death and violence. Lucifer embodied pleasure and indulgence, advocating drink, drugs and casual sex. Christ was the lord of understanding who taught compassion. Or, as expressed by Process doctrine: 'Jehovah is strength. Lucifer is light. Satan is separation. Christ is unification.'

Each member was instructed to follow the god who best suited them, exploring their own worlds through the universal truths expressed by their personal deity. Most Processeans were aligned somewhere between two gods. Robert was a Luciferian-Christian (basically just an old hippie), while the more dominant Mary Anne was Jehovan-Satanic. Opposing the Process were their equivalents of evil, the Grey Forces – representing mundane conformity, embodied in the arch-square 'John Grey', who, with his 'hypocrisy, mediocrity, blasphemy', was the antithesis of everything the Process strove for.

The group survived on funds supplied by new members (like many religions, the Process was keen on wealthy young converts) and by the extensive begging – or 'donating' – required of the lower ranks. In traditional cult fashion, familiar to Moonie and Catholic alike, much cash went to provide luxuries for the leadership, who became increasingly distant from the rank and file. Basic income came from selling the infamous Process magazines, strange seminars in 'developing telepathy' and

Artwork from a Process Church magazine, reconciling God and Satan.

associated psychic phenomena, and running Process-owned coffee-houses, such as Satan's Cavern in London. Decorated in the Process's inimitable style – Satanic red, with pictures inspired by the Book of Revelations – and featuring the cult's own weird form of folk music for entertainment, these offshoots of the 1960s counterculture attracted many converts.

The Processeans cut striking figures in their black robes, goat's head medallions and crucifixes. Early on, the de Grimstons bought German shepherd dogs: when emulated by the rest of the group this added to their distinct visual image, as well as providing protection from potential enemies. When not 'donating' funds, much of the lower ranks' time was spent attending rituals or mastering meditational or psychotherapy techniques. Discipline was strict and – despite the cult's Luciferian doctrines – hedonistic pleasures like sex, drugs or alcohol were rigidly rationed, to prevent distraction from the path. As with most religions, such restrictions did not apply to the upper ranks, who lived in comfort while wrestling with their various cosmic conundrums.

The Manson massacres had proven an image disaster for the whole hippie movement. Things were especially bad for the Process – if hippies were now treated with suspicion, then *Satanic* hippies sounded every alarm bell in polite society. Vincent Bugliosi – keen to prove Manson was not only a Nazi-hippie-Beatles fan, but also a Devil-worshipper – made a few limp attempts to connect him with the Process. Asked during the trial whether he knew Robert de Grimston, Manson, in a typically surreal moment, replied that he *was* de Grimston (alongside Jesus, Satan, Hitler, et al). De Grimston did not improve matters with the lurid 1971 *Death* issue of the Process magazine, cashing in on Manson-mania with a brief article by the incarcerated Charlie. Manson's take on death was that it was 'peace from this world's madness and paradise in my own self'. (This from a man who'd soon be relieved to escape the gas chamber, and go back into the arms of 'my mother, the jailhouse'.)

In an interview many years after the crimes, Bobby Beausoleil said of those commentators who gave the Manson murders a Satanic slant: 'Everything gets lost in blood and guts, devil worship, all that stuff that never went on. This satanic crap and brainwave master never went on. These things were taken out of light-hearted conversations.' More succinctly, Manson has described the theory of his supposed connection with the Process as 'horse-shit'.

Things became even more extreme when disillusioned hippie Ed Sanders targeted the Process in his Manson book *The Family*. They were the 'sleazo input which warped the mind of Charles Manson' or, even more colourfully, 'hooded snuffoids'. The Process successfully sued Sanders in the US, and the offending passages were removed. As far as their reputation was concerned, however, the damage had already been done. The novelty of their sinister black robes and Satanic emblems had worn off. Donations were drying up, and some members of the public were becoming downright abusive.

To try to compensate for their image problem, the Process uniform was changed – first to an ugly grey affair, then a more fetching blue ensemble. Process buildings were redecorated in jolly pastel colours. The psychotherapy business was becoming crowded, so they converted to the faith-healing trade. But nothing could shrug off the apocalyptic image they themselves had generated, notably in the *War*, *Death*, *Fear* and *Sex* issues of the Process magazine. The following is typical of the words placed in the mouth of Lord Satan by the Process: 'Release the fiend that lies dormant within you, for he is strong and ruthless, and his power is far beyond the bounds of human frailty. Come forth in your savage might, rampant with the lust of battle, tense and quivering with the urge to strike, to smash, to split asunder all that seek to detain you.'

The fact that the Process never endorsed or indulged in real violence did not help – few could be blamed for taking the cult's bloodthirsty literature at face value. It was their image problem which, combined with personal problems between the de Grimstons (Luciferian Bob wanted to invite another girl into their bed, but Jehovan Mary Anne wouldn't let him) caused the Process to split in 1974. With the Process already active in the USA, Mary Anne transformed her faction into the Foundation Church of the Millennium (now the Foundation Faith of God), which was specifically Jehovan and dropped all Satanic doctrines. De Grimston tried to keep the original Process alive, but it collapsed a year later amidst in-fighting, bruised egos and apathy. The cult's founder went to ground: when last heard of, Robert de Grimston was believed to be working for the US telephone company. Several self-styled Processean organisations exist today, but the most extreme is of the heretical 'hookers for Jesus' variety, of little interest from a Satanic perspective.

But this wasn't enough for the conspiracy theorists, who leapt upon rumours of occult activity on the Californian coast. One told of a cult near Santa Cruz, an offshoot of the Process called the Four Pi Movement, formed in 1968. They supposedly sacrificed animals and drank their blood in beach-side barbecues, where ritual glue-sniffing and fire-dancing turned the attendees into 'slaves of Satan'. More elaborate variations suggested the Four Pi performed human sacrifice on an ornate altar decorated with dragons. The bizarre ritual dagger used for these purposes had six blades, like a Satanic Swiss army knife: most were used to puncture the stomach before the last skewered the heart, which the cultists then ate. The victim was then disposed of in a portable crematorium – an improbable device that's become a standard prop in Satanic ritual-slaying myths.

Other related rumours concern an arm of the Four Pi Movement said to be more interested in kinky sex than violence – supposedly titled 'the Grand Chingon' after its leader, a wealthy, middle-aged LA businessman. The Order of Kirke (or Circe) cult's indulgence in animal sacrifice, particularly that of dogs, led some to suspect they were a branch of the German shepherd-owning Process (in fact, the Processeans loved their animals and were rabidly opposed to vivisection). Others pointed out that Mary Anne de Grimston sometimes called herself Circe, after the sorceress of Ancient Greek myth who transformed her enemies into swine. Despite all of the urban myths linking the Process to Satanic murder, however, hard evidence remains conspicuous by its absence.

From the notorious Fear *issue of the Process magazine.*

Aside from the Process Church, other Satanic cults undoubtedly existed in the psychedelic melting pot of the 1960s.

In the USA, Ohio barber Herb Sloane claimed to have been running a rather quaint Satanic lodge – known as the Our Lady of Endor Coven, or Ophite Cultus Satanus – since 1948. 'Satanism,' the cult explained in its literature, 'is the position opposed to the worship of the force that brought the force into existence as mind and matter out of the realm of pure spirit.' They credited Cain, *The Bible*'s first murderer, as the celebrant of the first Satanic Mass and declared that Satanism 'has no conception of sin, but rather puts ignorance (the lack of Gnosis) in the place of sin'. This revival of ancient Luciferian

Gnosticism had a certain profundity – but it wasn't nearly salacious enough for the conspiracy theorists.

Don Blythe, who ran the Satan's A Go Go disco on Hollywood Boulevard, had a much better grasp of the appeal of flesh and blood. Blythe also worked at an LA pathology lab, which helped furnish props for his Brotherhood of the Ram cult. At their meetings the cult would recite Baudelaire, Ron would give everyone a glimpse of his favourite pickled body parts, then one of the more decorative members of the congregation would flash her breasts. It may not have been the most spectacular show in town, but it sure beat Sunday service at the local Methodist Chapel.

In the Hollywood Hills, a wealthy housewife who believed herself the reincarnation of an Egyptian Princess named Leda Amun Ra carried out drug-enhanced rituals dressed in suitably theatrical garb. The costume did not stay on for long, the 'Princess' presenting herself naked on an altar where a swan was encouraged to 'mount' her. The grand finale involved 'capturing' the soul of a young man, who was symbolically crucified, then transferring it into the body of the swan. The unfortunate bird, by then thoroughly disorientated, was sacrificed in a special temple in the Princess's garden.

Back in Britain, the Wiccan movement went from strength to strength despite the death of its leader, Gerald Gardner, in 1964. In the experimental climate of the 1960s, the 'witchcraft revival' found a stream of willing converts. Under Gardner, Wicca had been a curious country club for kinky middle-class professionals. His successor as 'King of the Witches', Alex Sanders – a short, balding occultist with hauntingly piercing eyes – took full advantage of its potential as a mass movement for trendy youngsters. (This difference of style was significant enough for two camps to emerge, describing themselves as either 'Gardnerian' or 'Alexandrian'.)

Sanders had a flair for publicity, and he thrust witchcraft – formerly a mysterious, secretive pursuit – into the limelight. Tabloid editors were always eager for an excuse to feature photos of young people in the nude, and Sanders presented them with opportunities aplenty. His attractive blonde wife, Maxine, proved a big asset – as she once observed, she had 'the most photographed bum in Britain'. The King and Queen of the Witches appeared on TV programmes, recorded a record album, and even turned their rituals into a touring roadshow.

Sanders was astute enough to flirt with the glamour of the dark side. He affected a Satanic appearance – complete with dark glasses long before they became common fashion accessories – and bowed before a goat-headed high priest at his professionally-photographed rituals. He also revealed he had engaged in rituals that were 'pretty lurid and orgiastic, and pretty close to Satanism though I left any serious black magic out of it'.

Although Sanders died in 1988, such ambivalence towards Satanism remains characteristic of Wicca to this day. Any so-called 'white witch' interviewed in the media clearly enjoys suggestions of wickedness, but, at the same time, wants to point at 'others' as the source of any dark or sinister workings. Wicca allows them to court a little sinful chic, whilst adopting an offended tone if anyone accuses them of affiliation with the unholy. Today, Wicca is a loose amalgam of anodyne New Age spirituality, woolly liberal politics and twee occultic posturing. As eco-feminist, English Heritage pagans, they need those accusations of Satanism now more than ever.

Despite Alex Sanders' mealy mouth, there were some British occultists in the 1960s who made no bones about associating with the infernal. One such was a dark-haired Scot named Charles Matthew Pace. Born in 1920, Pace was a mysterious figure boasting the title 'the Jackal of Egypt', whose favourite gimmick was to draw a piece of red hot metal from a fire and lick it. One story about him tells of an acolyte turning up at a Black Mass wearing the same red robe – with a ram design on the chest – as Pace. Pace warned him to change. When he refused the robe supposedly caught fire, enveloping the rival in flames. But even Pace was never as black as the media liked to paint him: in a 1969 newspaper exposé, he confessed to attending Black Masses across the whole of Europe. When confronted by a priest in Rome about to sacrifice a child, however, Pace claimed he drew the line, drew his ceremonial sword and fought the bounder off.

The same exposé uncovered a Black Mass priest, an Irish clergyman named Father Basil Prendergast, who taught part-time at a convent in Sussex. Somehow, Prendergast lacked the dark gravitas of a Guiborg, or even a Montague Summers, seeming simply desperate to get his hands on a naked virgin. He told the female reporter, posing as a potential candidate for the post, that 'I can only say the idea [for the Black Mass] must have come from our father below. I'm not terribly interested in the history. I just like to do it.' Sadly, Basil lost his teaching post – and probably never got his naked virgin, either.

There were undoubtedly many more strange cults and unorthodox messiahs in the spiritual chaos that was the late 1960s. Most authorities agree the highest concentration was in the USA, its heart of darkness being the 'Golden State' of California. Satan, as lord of rebellion and indulgence, would undoubtedly have felt at home there (though He'd have found all the prattle about peace and love offensive).

One resident, quoted in Peter Haining's *Anatomy of Witchcraft*, put it like this: 'If you sense evil here, you are right, and I'll tell you what it is: too many people turned on to acid. If

Hippie-hating Satanist Anton LaVey (far left) confronts Bobby Beausoleil (far right) in the original version of Lucifer Rising. *The film's missing footage is believed buried in the desert by the Manson Family.*

you make a habit of tripping – well, acid is so metaphysical – you are going to be forced into making a choice, between opting for good, staying on a goodness or Christian trip, and tripping with the Lord Satan. That's the whole heavy thing about too many people turned on to acid: to most of them the Devil just looks groovier.'

There was one Californian who wasn't tripping out, but certainly thought the Devil was 'groovy'. In 1966 he established the basis of modern Satanism. His name was Anton LaVey.

Love, Freedom and Predators

Anton LaVey on the Summer of Love.

I spoke to Anton LaVey in March 1993 at the Black House, his home in San Francisco, and at a couple of his favourite restaurants. Interviews were conducted over two evenings in the company of LaVey's personal assistant and consort, Blanche Barton, and they both proved courteous and charming. LaVey's home was every bit as atmospheric and magical as it was reputed to be, though the abiding image that stayed with me was of his eyes, uncommonly penetrating and deep. Because of LaVey's importance to modern Satanism and the breadth of the topics we covered, the interviews are spread throughout this book.

Why did you react against hippie liberalism so violently?
I found the hippie movement distasteful on a personal level. Suddenly the ingestion of lysergic acid made every man a king. It made nincompoops self-assured – created a culture of people who, no matter what they knew or had done, considered themselves your equal. And my beloved San Francisco became engulfed by the movement.

Why then stay in San Francisco?
San Francisco has always been the centre of everything new. It attracted people like Ambrose Bierce [author of *The Devil's Dictionary*], Jack London and Dashiell Hammett who I think of as compatriots. Why abdicate from a place you love? We survived and flourished at the centre of it. I had a personal feeling of animosity towards the hippies that came partially from having to deal with them, my inferiors, who considered themselves everybody's equal: remember, one of the Satanic sins is pretentiousness. Their whole movement was supposed to be about love and freedom, but they attracted hordes of predators into Haight-Ashbury. Their pretentiousness brought them over-inflated egos, while, aesthetically, the movement made everything fall apart at the seams. I've always been enamoured of *film noir* imagery, so these new styles offended me aesthetically – it bothered me that they might take a beautiful purple velvet jacket, fit for a king, and then wear it with a pair of ragged sandals.

How did you become involved with Kenneth Anger?
I've known him now for 40 years or more. He's kind of been in and out of the picture ever since I was a kid,

we've always kept in touch. *Hollywood Babylon* was transcribed in the seat you're now sitting in.

Is he a Satanist or a Crowleyite?
He was definitely more of a Satanist. He spent a Hell of a lot of time with the Church of Satan – he was always hanging around.

What's Anger like?
Kenneth is a very sweet guy – he tries very hard to be angry but he can never keep it up. If you can believe it, he was also very innocent, very fey, trusting and outgoing.

Could you talk the about the films he made?
Lucifer Rising still contains the last remnants of the filming Kenneth did just after his split with Mick Jagger. *Invocation of My Demon Brother* was shot in a mansion here in San Francisco that used to be the Russian Embassy. Kenneth trusted the hippies and funded them to work on his films and they ripped him off. As ever: 'No good deed goes unpunished.' He vowed vengeance on the hippies after that. *Invocation* was designed as a way of capturing a psychological interpretation of a summoning or working. It was shot over a very brief period of time. Kenneth Anger really is an enchanted fellow – you give Kenneth an inch and he'll run off with a mile. He has this contagious enthusiasm – he's irrepressible.

How about Bobby Beausoleil?
Bobby was a sweet, mild-mannered guy that Kenneth took a liking to. Kenneth would often come back after walking in Golden Gate Park late at night, with a new protégé in tow that he thought represented some god or other. In Anger's mind, Beausoleil epitomised Lucifer. He funded Bobby, bought him a car with a gypsy caravan with a throne for Bobby to sit in, so Bobby could ride in high style. Unfortunately Kenneth couldn't drive, so Bobby usually had to sit in the front and take the wheel. Bobby was a nice kid, I don't know where he went wrong.

How about the rest of the Manson crew?
My open seminars facilitated the meeting of Bobby and Susan Atkins. Unfortunately my 'ex' absconded with my file of Manson papers so I can't give you as many details as I'd like. I employed Susan in my Topless Witches Revue – she would come out of a coffin dressed as a vampire. She was stoned most of the time and would do anything to get out of rehearsals. One time she claimed to have a temperature of 108. Susan was certainly a little flaky, but not possessed.

THE FOUNDATION OF THE INFERNAL EMPIRE

Anton LaVey and the Church of Satan

n the fateful night of 8 August 1969, a black-clad group gathered in a candle-lit chamber to launch this venomous curse upon the hippie movement: 'Beware, you psychedelic vermin! Your smug pomposity with its thin disguise of tolerance will serve you no longer! We know your mark and recognise it well. We walk the night as the villains no longer! Our steeds await and their eyes are ablaze with the fires of Hell!'

The ceremony, entitled 'The Rising Forth', was led by Anton LaVey, High Priest of the Church of Satan. LaVey claimed this magical working was the trigger that set the Manson massacres in motion, a ceremonial knife in the belly of the love generation.

In a perverse way, LaVey's Satanic group was the progeny of the 1960s revolution. In a fit of oedipal fury, the Church of Satan was butchering the father it loathed, the hippie movement, before turning to fuck its mother, the conservative establishment. LaVey was building a temple for true individualists who did not want to shelter beneath the hippies' thin veneer of non-conformity: a heretic creed that sneered at half-baked Eastern mysticism and naïve philosophies of universal love, recognising in the hippie ethos another Utopian movement – like Christianity – fatally flawed by its refusal to recognise the bestial nature of the human animal.

The group's San Francisco headquarters – which became known as the Black House – was to be a fortress against the ragtag, tie-dyed, egalitarian army who shouted, as one, that they were all individuals. LaVey extolled the true individualism he valued among the non-conformists who had always existed on the fringes of Western culture, placing them in a tradition he labelled 'Satanic'. But, for all that, it's unlikely he could have established his new church were it not for the spiritual and social turmoil of the 1960s.

The Church of Satan – unquestionably the most significant movement in modern Satanism – is a bizarre beast, sustained by a web of conflicting values and concepts. It is an anti-spiritual religion; a totalitarian doctrine of freedom; a cynical romanticism; a profoundly honest scam; a love of life, garbed in the symbols of death and fear.

To understand the Church of Satan, we must examine the formative years of its creator – a creature of the 1940's. Anton Szandor LaVey was born in 1930, a bright, unusual boy always destined to be an outsider, describing his peers as 'Barbary apes'. Nevertheless, young

'Tony' LaVey found a role among the local kids, as Blanche Barton relates in *The Secret Life of a Satanist*:

'Neighbourhood boys always chose Tony as a leader in their play, perching on his doorstep until he organised a club or game or something for them to do. But LaVey would get disgusted when other boys broke character, could not seem to concentrate on a game as seriously as he could, or were too heavy-handed, smashing his toys and going home.'

Anton Szandor LaVey.

It's a revealing little anecdote. LaVey's life seemed dedicated, even at such an early age, to organising a role-playing 'club' – only to be disgusted when the vast majority did not have the wit or temperament to appreciate it.

At age seventeen, this theatrical young cynic is said to have gotten into some sort of unspecified trouble, and, in the traditional fashion, run off to join the circus. There he found employment for his nascent musical skills as a keyboard player and discovered other talents, taking on the role of lion-tamer. Living on an unsteady wage, he also took work as a 'carny' in the carnivals and funfairs dotted along the West Coast. LaVey fell in love with this twilit underbelly of America, planting the seed for much of his future Satanic philosophy.

LaVey's road to Damascus – where he first 'saw the dark' – occurred on his twin stint playing bump-and-grind tunes for the burlesque shows and hammering out hymns for the travelling preachers who used carnivals to pitch their spiritual wares: 'On Saturday night I would see men lusting after half-naked girls dancing at the carnival, and on Sunday morning, when I was playing the organ for tent-show evangelists at the other end of the carnival lot, I would see these same men sitting in the pews with their wives and children, asking God to forgive them and purge them of carnal desires. And the next Saturday night they'd be back at the carnival or some other place of indulgence. I knew then that the Christian Church thrives on hypocrisy, and that man's carnal nature will out!'

The impact of the carnival on the young LaVey was as great as the epiphany that revealed the power of lust and desire. He'd recognised the language of the evangelical preacher and the occult magi, and it was the language of the carnival barker: 'Roll up! Roll up! The greatest show on earth! See the water turned into wine! Eternal salvation, once in a lifetime chance!'

LaVey began to perceive himself as a Satanic carny-hustler in the big funfair of life. All the glitz and magic was false, tawdry even, but if the punters wanted to believe it enough, then they'd swallow anything. The world was a freak show and everybody – whether they liked it or not – was drawn to the most colourful, shocking or sexually-provocative exhibits.

LaVey's grounding in showmanship, the references to deceit and delusion that recur in his work, have been used by detractors to dismiss him as a charlatan. But the same aspect that made people suspicious of him is the most novel characteristic of his creed. LaVey created the first truly twentieth-century occultic doctrine, the first *American* occult doctrine. Unlike his sorcerous predecessors LaVey was no deviant academic or renegade priest, swathing esoteric ideas in cryptic mumbo-jumbo. His Satanism was firmly based on the dingy fringes of 1940s America: shrines to the weaknesses of the flesh like pool halls, waterfront bars and strip clubs, where man could be found in his carnal element.

LaVey developed his world philosophy in an environment where a man lived on his wits. In the deceptive world of the carnival, the smart roustabout quickly became a master of street-level human psychology, learning how to prey upon his fellow man in a fashion that would not only go unpunished, but that he would be thanked for. According to LaVey, low magic is the application of such behavioural psychology. In a world of delusion and artifice, only the showman is honest.

Accepting that society is largely built on bullshit also allows someone to perceive it in himself. LaVey's writings owe much of their charm to his sense of humour and eye for the ridiculous. Just when it feels like his hatred, fury and bombast is becoming too much to swallow, LaVey defuses it with a wry aside or cheesy pun. When other occultists and religious leaders reach for the wand or the whip, LaVey produces the whoopee cushion. To those whom magic must be reverently mordant, this marks his work down as a flippant scam. But LaVey – in the tradition of the Hellfire Clubs and medieval Sabbat – believed blasphemy should be fun; devils and demons should not be stern masters or slaves, but welcome house-guests.

Marriage, and the threat of being drafted into the army, convinced the young LaVey to aim for a 'proper job'. In 1949, he enrolled as a criminology student at San Francisco City College. This led to employment by San Francisco Police Department as a photographer, shooting crime scenes. His assignments put him on a day-to-day acquaintance with the atrocities his fellow citizens perpetrated upon each other. They also put a cruel edge on LaVey's cynicism, convincing him not only of the non-existence of God, but also that the hand that shaped the world was of a profoundly brutal disposition. This was the seed for the 'Lex Talionis', or 'Lex Satanicus', the harsh social code that later became integral to Church of Satan doctrine.

SFPD, noting his penchant for the bizarre, drafted the photographer into answering '800 Calls': weird complaints concerning the paranormal or unexplained. This period as a municipal exorcist taught LaVey about people's responses to the supernatural: if offered a rational explanation, complainants seemed oddly disappointed; even the simplest folk secretly craved what they feared, valuing any element of melodrama in their lives. LaVey soon formulated the idea that showmanship and self-delusion were not antithetical to magic, as many (like Aleister Crowley) would maintain. One of the factors that would distinguish LaVey's Satanism was that the self-delusion was conscious – Satan was, after all, the Prince of Lies. When deliberate pretence provided pleasure, or achieved tangible results, then it was not only rational to indulge in it, but also, paradoxically, rather honest.

The late 1950s and early 1960s saw LaVey become a minor celebrity, occupying column inches in the San Francisco press as an eccentric local character. His distinctively flamboyant style, half Gypsy rogue, half medieval magus, and reputation as a psychic investigator – combined with the black panther he walked through the streets as a pet – made him stand out, even in the extrovert city by the bay. As this reputation turned LaVey into a beacon for the maverick fringes of respectable society, he began holding cocktail evenings at his home – an informal arrangement which gradually gelled into a 'Magic Circle'.

LaVey began delivering a series of seminars and lectures on the occult and the macabre. The popularity of these sessions owed much to his flair for the dramatic: one of the more striking examples was a lecture on cannibalism, reputedly illustrated by a human leg (obtained by a doctor who was a regular at these soirees) cooked in triple sec brandy by LaVey's new consort, Diane, and sampled by bolder members of the audience.

The core of LaVey's Magic Circle were an interestingly diverse bunch. Policemen, lawyers and doctors mingled with European aristocrats and property magnates. LaVey began to discern a common thread of 'productive alienation' among people who, like him, were regarded with suspicion because of their curious tastes and individuality, but who were more creative and *alive* than the masses who sneered at them. These 'productive misfits' were the lost tribe he would try to bond together under the banner of Satanism. Prominent among members of LaVey's Magic Circle was Kenneth Anger, who became a close friend, and the horror and science fiction authors identified with the pulp magazine *Weird Tales*.

Weird Tales – which published pulp-horror between 1923 and 1954 – was dismissed as trash by the 'literati' during its lifetime, but is now considered to be the birthplace of modern horror fiction. Its macabre short stories were notably more literate than those of its rivals, not least the work of the magazine's leading light – an eccentric Rhode Islander named H. P.

Eccentric horror author H. P. Lovecraft, with his 'dark gods' threatening to break through the bounds of reality. Portrait by Tim.

Lovecraft. Lovecraft is now legendary for his creation of a gaggle of alien gods, whose fictional histories weave together to form the 'Cthulhu Mythos'. These unspeakably horrific entities lurk in a dimension just outside our own, waiting to drag the earth back into the mire of chaos and insanity that exists beyond our thin tissue of reality.

Lovecraft died relatively young, in 1937, but the most distinguished of those who continued his tradition were drawn to LaVey's Magic Circle. They made a weighty contribution to the tone and development of his proto-religion – LaVey had been a long-time fan of *Weird Tales*, and would later go so far as to create rituals based on the Cthulhu Mythos. While most occultists based their beliefs on ancient legend and folklore, LaVey's use of Lovecraft demonstrated his belief that popular, well-crafted fictions were the myths of the age. The modern man takes his gods and heroes from best-sellers, TV and the cinema screen. The devils of modern mythology are invoked via the magic of mass media.

In 1966, all the elements were in place for the birth of LaVey's new creed. The Magic Circle was reaching conclusions which, if codified, seemed to present the basis for a whole philosophy. LaVey's ambitions now lay beyond magical parlour games. 'The amount of energy needed to levitate a teacup,' he later observed in *The Satanic Bible*, 'would be of sufficient force to place an idea in a group of people's heads halfway across the earth, in turn, motivating them in accordance with your will.' He planned to found a sacred institution dedicated to such esoteric ideas, and to the pleasures of mind and body – a Church of Satan.

LaVey blamed the Christian Church for most of what he despised in the world around him. The stupidity, self-destructiveness and mindless conformity of the herd were fostered by a belief that they weren't responsible for their own actions – there was a grand authority figure in charge, who would both baby and scold them, called 'God'. Strong people were discouraged from standing up for themselves; the foolish and mediocre were rewarded for not rocking the boat. LaVey's Church of Satan, rather than simply being a shadow-faith to off-load repressed desires and guilt, would actively invert and attack Christianity.

At its centre lay Nine Satanic Statements: '1. Satan represents indulgence instead of abstinence. 2. Satan represents vital existence instead of spiritual pipe dreams. 3. Satan represents undefiled wisdom, instead of hypocritical self-deceit. 4. Satan represents kindness to those who deserve it instead of love wasted on ingrates. 5. Satan represents vengeance instead of turning the other cheek. 6. Satan represents responsibility to the responsible instead of concern for psychic vampires. 7. Satan represents man as just another animal – sometimes better, more often worse than those who walk on all fours – who, because of his "divine spiritual and intellectual development" has become the most vicious animal of all. 8. Satan represents all of the so-called sins, as they all lead to physical, mental, or emotional gratification. 9. Satan has been the best friend the Church has ever had, as he has kept it in business all these years.'

On Walpurgisnacht (the night when, according to central European tradition, Evil holds sway over the world), 30 April 1966, LaVey shaved his head and declared himself High Priest of the Church of Satan. From original members of the Magic Circle he derived the Council of Nine, the new church's governing body, and threw open the door to new recruits. Weekly Satanic rituals followed at the 'Black House', almost all featuring a naked girl who served as the Satanic altar – blowing the cobwebs of Christian guilt and repression from the minds of the participants, and, of course, encouraging attendance. LaVey presided over these rites in voluminous black robes, clerical collar and horned skullcap, lending him the appearance of a vaudevillian villain.

By this time, San Francisco was fast becoming the Mecca of the hippie revolution. Its tide swept away much of the romantically-seedy underbelly of 1940s/50s America – as epitomised in *film noir* – that LaVey regarded as his spiritual heartland, replacing it with communes and crash pads. The hippies preached universal equality and that everyone should love each other. LaVey thundered that most human beings were worthless and should be punished for their inadequacies. The new liberals believed mankind's basic goodness would hold sway after everyone had been sexually liberated, freed of all their hang-ups. The Church of Satan countered that most people were a herd of undeclared masochists, and that genuine individuals should foster their fetishes as badges of individuality.

In its second year, the Church of Satan – and LaVey's sinister showmanship – drew the attention of the international media. During 1967, three major events established LaVey's project as a functioning religion. On 1 February, the Black Pope (as the press had titled him) conducted the Satanic wedding of radical journalist John Raymond and New York socialite Judith Case. On 23 May LaVey performed a Satanic baptism for his daughter, Zeena. In December, naval officer and Church of Satan member Edward Olsen was killed in an accident and, according to the wishes of his mother, was buried with full military and Satanic honours. This last ritual had the entertaining result of Satanism's inclusion in *The Chaplains' Handbook for the Armed Services*, the manual issued to military pastors as a guide for ministering to servicemen. All three ceremonies were masterminded as media events, with the presence of LaVey's pet lion, Togare, the buxom naked altar-girl and bombastic black pageantry all proving irresistible lures to the press.

LaVey's carnal religion started to attract some of the Hollywood set, taking the Church of Satan even further overground. The best-known converts were Sammy Davis, Junior and Jayne Mansfield. Davis, a black-Jewish song-and-dance man, was drawn in after playing Mephistopheles in the comedy film *Poor Devil*. As a member of Hollywood's notoriously rakish 'Rat Pack', alongside Frank Sinatra and Dean Martin, Davis was drawn to the novelty and controversy of Satanism – his unusual ethnic background making him something of a misfit in an all-white Hollywood.

Jayne Mansfield, a buxom B-movie Monroe (the self-mythologising LaVey also spoke of a sexual fling with unknown showgirl Marilyn back in the late 1940s), found LaVey's religion not only tolerated her outrageous sexuality, but applauded it. Doctrines declaring that fleshly desires were sacred seemed tailor-made for this busty, blonde sex-bomb. That same year, Jayne died in a tragic car crash with her lawyer and lover Sam Brody. Brody had disliked his beloved's new guru from the start, and the friction led to LaVey placing a ritual curse on his rival. The Black Pope warned the pugnacious lawyer – known to be a dangerous driver – that he would suffer a series of automobile accidents. It was no great surprise when a car crash ensued – but it made world headlines for taking the life of Jayne Mansfield, as well as the top of her cranium. LaVey grimly stated that on the night preceding the crash, as he cut out a newspaper clipping of Jayne, he accidentally snipped off the top of the blonde beauty's head.

Anton LaVey with a portrait of his one-time acolyte, Hollywood sex bomb Jayne Mansfield.

LaVey's flirtations with the press continued, in the shape of deliberately sleazy, showmanish publicity stunts like the Topless Witches Revue. But it was the 1969 publication of *The Satanic Bible* that made his doctrines widely available. This mass-market paperback, commissioned by a bold editor at Avon Books, collected the most important of the Church of Satan's initial manuscripts. It was a success, causing a ripple of delighted outrage and selling, to date, nearly a million copies worldwide. For every card-carrying member of LaVey's Satanic church, there were now thousands whose lives had been touched by the philosophy recorded in his black book.

The Satanic Bible was written as a deliberate affront – not just to Christianity and liberalism, but also to wilfully-obscure practitioners of the occult. As LaVey puts it in his introduction, 'occult bookshelves abound with the brittle relics of frightened minds and sterile bodies, metaphysical journals of self-deceit, and constipated rule-books of Eastern mysticism'. LaVey's tome laid down his Satanic philosophy in a startlingly-straightforward, common-sense fashion that could be grasped by anybody willing to lay down a couple of bucks. Much closer to a philosophy of pragmatism than any religious dogma, *The Satanic Bible* now reads like an early self-improvement manual.

Indeed, the most common response to LaVey's ideas was to ask why they went under the heading of 'Satanism'. Wouldn't it be easier to further his cause using a more innocuous title? LaVey responded by reasoning, 'It is most stimulating under that name, and self-discipline and motivation are easier under stimulating conditions. It means "the opposition" and epitomises all symbols of non-conformity. It represents the strongest ability to turn a liability into an advantage – to turn alienation into exclusivity.' To LaVey's thinking, modern rationalists who denied the power of ritual were just as deluded as the priests who maintained this same power was the product of imaginary deities.

The only dangerous aspect of *The Satanic Bible*, as acknowledged by its creator, is that while many are attracted by its doctrines of freedom, most people are too caught up in Christian conditioning to understand the rigid self-discipline and insight LaVeyan Satanism also demands. At this level, the book can be a blueprint for smug sociopathy, a spiritual refuge for the aggressive inadequate. To LaVey, however, unfortunate side effects such as violence and human suffering were a price worth paying. Everybody had to be made accountable for their own actions, and there would be casualties in the transition to this new philosophical state. Of course, LaVey's perception of most people as masochists and frustrated victims made the prospect of such casualties a lot more palatable.

The second book from this darkly fertile mind was *The Compleat Witch*, probably the only Satanic tract to get a good review from *Cosmopolitan*. Published in 1970, it was another provocation – a deliberate slap in the face for the feminist movement LaVey regarded as yet another drab trend, neutralising colour and passion while reversing natural instinct. As a militant proponent of the *vive la difference*-school of gender politics, LaVey, the self-professed misogynist, had no problem admitting to the power wielded over him by women.

At face value a self-empowerment manual for women, urging them to manipulate with their natural charms, *The Compleat Witch* is both revolutionary and reactionary – 'nine parts social responsibility to one part outrage,' as LaVey was fond of saying. 'Any bitter and disgruntled female can rally against men, burning up her creative and manipulative energies in the process,' he expounded. 'She will find the energies she expends in her quixotic cause would be put to more rewarding use, were she to profit from her womanliness by manipulating the men she holds in contempt, while enjoying the ones she finds stimulating. It's pretty hard to lose, using such tactics.'

But *The Compleat Witch* is more than a man-trapping manual, offering a treatise on the LaVeyan psychology implicit in all his work. This is most strikingly illustrated by the 'LaVey Personality Synthesiser', a clock-diagram suggesting how various personality types relate to different physical characteristics. LaVey also darkly suggested that a basic framework for eugenic breeding was hidden within the book. When it was re-printed two decades later as *The*

Satanic Witch, LaVey's strident daughter, Zeena, provided an introduction in which she claimed the book contained 'the lost science of preserving the able-bodied and able-minded while controlling the surplus population of the weak and incompetent'. Roll over Chuck Darwin, and tell Fred Nietzsche the news.

The Compleat Witch also clarifies the two main strands of LaVeyan dogma. The first relates to man as an animal, and attempts to set up a framework whereby the LaVeyan Satanist can understand human interaction in this light. Natural tendencies should not be suppressed or fought, but heeded, even revelled in. Ultimately, LaVey hoped to wear away the bogus veneer of 'civilisation' imposed by Christianity, in order to allow society to be governed by more primal laws. (This is an echo of the 'natural philosophy' of two centuries earlier – the idea that the only true god is callous nature, and the only true sin to deny instinct or appetite.)

Contrary to the impression given by this comic strip about the Church of Satan, LaVey condemned animal sacrifice and preached sexual freedom, not compulsion.

The other major aspect is the personality cult of Anton LaVey. As the Church of Satan preaches a religion of ego-worship, it's no surprise that its High Priest wasn't backward in coming forward. Many things defined by LaVey as 'Satanic' simply appealed to his personal tastes. Thus the popular music of the 1930s and 40s was Satanic; in *The Compleat Witch*, women were directed to LaVey's personal fetishes as the key to sexual attraction. LaVey advocated treasuring all personal tastes and proclivities as sacred badges of individuality. Ironically, this was a difficult message for many putative Satanists to grasp and led to them imitating LaVey's peccadilloes in order to become 'Satanic'.

The third of LaVey's unholy trinity was *The Satanic Rituals*, a DIY-guide to performing Satanic ceremonies. LaVey offers interpretations of some of the most historically notorious rituals – including the Black Mass as performed by Madame Monvoisin, and a Templar ritual – though he also prescribes a summoning for H. P. Lovecraft's fictional god Cthulhu. Each individual rite is described as a 'psychodrama' – interactive theatre, designed to entertain while unleashing desired emotions or states of mind in the participant.

The Satanic Rituals appeared in 1972, which was, ironically, two years after weekly ceremonies at the Black House ceased. LaVey had begun to farm out the Church of Satan's ritual duties to other branches, or 'grottoes', across the USA and Canada – such as the Babylon Grotto in Detroit, the Stygian Grotto in Dayton and the Lilith Grotto in New York. It was time, said LaVey, to 'stop performing Satanism and start practising it'.

A Church of Fantasy and Fetish

Anton LaVey on the foundation of the Church of Satan.

Contrary to the impression some have given (including, on occasion, LaVey himself), the founder of the Church of Satan was happy to debate the basics of his philosophy. He was frank, non-defensive, entertaining and surprisingly warm – if inclined to self-satisfaction. But then, this seems particularly fitting for the founder of a creed dedicated to ego-gratification . . .

The Temple of Set has alleged the Church of Satan is bankrupt and has ceased trading, and that you wrote little of its doctrinal material. What's the story behind that?
Michael Aquino used the Church of Satan mailing list to start his Temple. He's spread a lot of rumours about how he was my second-in-command and has set himself up as my 'Boswell', so to speak – in fact, he was only briefly in the Church of Satan. The bankruptcy rumour followed an alimony suit that was used as an opportunity by a feminist Catholic judge to pillory Anton LaVey. The Church of Satan was never bankrupt. My ex-wife also claimed she co-authored much of *The Satanic Bible*. She did type up the manuscript, which led to these claims, but my authorship is beyond dispute.

Do you have any regrets about how The Satanic Bible *came out – would you write it any differently today?*
If you'd have asked me that two or three years ago, I'd have told you it had too many exclamation marks – it was too loud. Since then, I've changed my mind. *The Satanic Bible* won't strain people's intellects too far and will get them thinking and doubting. You see, I get a lot of feedback from farm-boys who've never read anything apart from my book and the Christian Bible. I think *The Satanic Bible* is now timelier than ever.

Is Satanism just about blasphemy?
A lot of would-be Satanists are just interested in blasphemy. In effect they're just heretical Christians – which is what Satanists are often dismissed as by Wiccans. As an aside on Wicca, after the war I became involved with an English Satanist named Charles Pace. Everybody warned against him, because he dabbled in 'dark forces'. I have in writing a letter from him explaining how he suggested to Gerald Gardner the name 'Wicca'. In jest, he told Gardner it was an ancient

term for pagans. In fact it really meant those that had converted to Christianity! But the true Satanist need not believe in God. Peter Meyer defined Satanism as 'rational self-interest'. We occupy a grey area between religion and psychiatry.

What do you mean by this 'grey area'?
Back then, psychiatry had no room for the encouragement of fantasy or personal fetish. If anything, it was about negating or subverting them. That's where I found my grey area – keeping and treasuring your fetishes, dreams and fantasies, rather than subverting or expelling them.

The keyboard-playing, cinematic villain Dr Anton Phibes – seen with the android lover who reminds him of his late wife – was inspired by Dr Anton LaVey.

Does this fit in with your passion for 'artificial human companions'?
After all, what is 'natural'? Artifice can be very exhilarating, conscious self-deception. We already have 'artificial human companions', like the images on TV screens for example. People accept Johnny Carson into their living rooms every night. Soap operas provide 'surrogate lives' for many people, and these surrogate lives have become a very important consumer product. The artificial human companion I talk about comes

somewhere between that surrogate life and the inflatable doll many people first think of when I mention 'artificial human companions'. Rubber dolls are unsatisfying and surrogate lives are over-controlled. My vision of this companion is not relegated purely to the realms of robotics. It's about creating an artificial companion more stimulating than the people around you. This is a terrifying concept to many people because it shows how humans are far more expendable than they'd like to be. Artificial human companions enable politically-correct slavery. Most people aren't very exciting – Satanists have to be very special people, and, like outmoded classics, they can't be replaced.

There seems to me to be two distinct sides to the Church of Satan: what you call 'Lex Talionis' and the cult of Anton LaVey. How would you react to that?
The concepts of Satanism are there whether I approve of them or not. I may be an ideologue, codifying these laws, but they exist independently of me. There are those – I call them the stuffing in the mattress – who can't differentiate, for whom the Church of Satan is synonymous with Anton LaVey, but that's their problem. If it wasn't me expressing these laws, then somebody else, probably less qualified, would.

There are a number of Satanists who identify their ideas with Nazism and the Far Right. What's your opinion on that?
The link is often an aesthetic one. For example, there was this girl I saw not long ago wearing a long coat. The coat was unmistakably a Nazi artefact, while she was Jewish. Psychologically the two are irreconcilable, but on an aesthetic level they were understandable. The aesthetic appeal lies in the dramatic fashion of the Nazi militaria. The Nazis understood the meaning of visuals and sounds, and how to use them – take their use of a lot of black leather in their uniforms and 'oompah' music in their marches, for example. There were some pretty smart guys involved with the Nazi movement – they knew how basic material could reach the soul. Their aesthetics appealed to the religiosity in people. My own prejudices are not ethnic but ethical – somebody's race or background really has nothing to do with it. Under Hitler many prominent Jews were 'Aryanised'. This has all been documented, but it's been quietly swept under the carpet. There was a Zionist-Nazi pact establishing Madagascar as the Jewish homeland. Goebbels even struck a medal to commemorate the deal.

How much of the appeal of the occult, and Satanism in particular, derives from its secret, hidden nature?
There's a big link with 'the law of the forbidden': a concept pioneered by the photographer William Mortensen concerning the primal appeal of sex, sentiment and wonder. These are the basic human interests from which our compulsions and fetishes are derived. Like at the fairground where people will pay to go into the freak tent to avert their eyes.

How do you rate Aleister Crowley as an occultist?
I have one basic objection to Crowley. He knew what he was doing, had a sense of humour, wrote some very beautiful poetry, and knew his audience. But as a lucid, instructive guru, he's not nearly as good as Austin Osman Spare. The writings of H. P. Lovecraft are far more Satanic than those of most occultists.

How much is magic integral to Satanism?
Magic is only a physical or psychological effect that has yet to be explained, which means for many it is uncomfortable to entertain now. All good occultists must be sceptical – believe nothing in preference to believing everything. All proto-sciences could be defined as magic. You can see the ritual chamber as a kind of intellectual decompression chamber to prepare your mind for other atmospheres. People who limit themselves to the occult curricula and profess to be wizards are laughable – magic is an interdisciplinary pursuit. You must consider all of the options – investigate like a cop. To perform a summoning, for example, would involve finding the right environment, appropriate retrieval cues, the right atmospheric conditions. The effects of magic are demonstrable. A lot of simple magic is just to do with self-confidence, how much your antennae are up, how open you are to the world around you. Rituals and magical words are not necessary, merely tools or exercises to help train your mind. Scientists are now coming to the conclusion that there's a lot more interconnectedness between man and his environment than they originally supposed, which is a basic occultic concept.

How active is the Church of Satan in the UK?
We have a number of low-profile members in the UK in very responsible positions. We have many members operating quietly, leading ordinary lives, practising Church of Satan doctrines *sub rosa*.

Isn't overt drama part of Satanism though?
Drama and melodrama are very meaningful. Bombast has its place in Satanism – in some ways, Satanism takes up where Catholicism leaves off. Some, however, prefer carefully-adjusted drama in the privacy of their own homes.

You've mentioned the writings of H. P. Lovecraft. How influential has he been to your life and philosophy?
Lovecraft was the first writer I discovered who really scared me. Lovecraft was pretty heady stuff back then, and has proved a hard act to follow since. He become one of the protagonists in my life. Many members of Lovecraft's *Weird Tales* circle became friends

or attended my seminars or meets. I saw Clark Ashton Smith on a regular basis, he was very outspoken, not at all politically correct. Then there was Fritz Leiber and Robert Bloch [author of *Psycho*], and August Derleth, of course, who became Lovecraft's champion after he died. He was involved with my magical meetings in the early days, back in '65-'66; August held forth at one of our seminars on the history of *Weird Tales*.

What other Satanic groups do you come across these days and what do you think of them – are any of them dangerous?
There's a character called Joe Penner running something called the Synagogue of Satan. He claims to have been at it since the fifties and wants to inherit the mantle of the Process. Another guy named Mordecai Levi claims that Satan is directing his holy cause. These people are jokes. There's always some hard-core nut claiming to be part of some ancient cabal. They're just dillies. The only really dangerous characters are the ones who think they're generational Satanists and their grandfather told them with his dying breath what to do, or whatever. The Satanic scene is really too nebulous to pin down. The loquacious ones are like the drunk at the end of the bar who'll try and pin you down so he can fill you full of crap – we get stacks of that type of material every week. There are a lot of armies of one out there, a lot of coffee-bar revolutionaries. New information technology has bred a lot of desktop Satanists and bulletin boards mean that cyberspace seems to be just full of Satanists. The Christian heretics rarely get much further than designing letterheads.

But many Satanists are quietly applying Church of Satan philosophy to their lives in their own fashion in a very real way. The best thing we could ask for from those people is a passing nod of respect. We're not joiners. We don't expect fanatical devotion. We're not cudgel-pummelling evangelists. I do my own thing and I don't give a shit if people want to go along with me or not. I've no problems with a guilty conscience – this isn't some kind of scam. Left to my own devices this is what I'd be doing on my own anyway. In the very beginning it was a largely solitary pursuit.

It's like a story I was told about a new doctor who comes to work at a sanatorium. He comes across this

guy in his ward, naked except for a bowler hat. 'It's a lovely day,' the doctor says. 'Why don't you go outside and exercise?' 'Oh, I'd rather just sit here,' says the inmate. 'Well, why are you naked?' asks the doctor. 'Nobody ever comes to see me anyway, so why bother

The Black Pope, with a medieval mace from his extensive collection of weaponry.

dressing?' the inmate replies. 'Then why the hat?' asks the doctor. 'Well, you never know, someone could come along.' That's why I keep doing what I do – because somebody might come along.

A WITNESS AT THE BIRTH

Kenneth Anger on the early days of the Church of Satan

Anton LaVey died six months before my April 1998 meeting with Anger, who expressed evident regret, surprised that Anton had gone first. Despite LaVey's assertion to the contrary, Anger was adamant about his devotion to Aleister Crowley and eager to avoid the 'Satanist' label. However, he was a prominent celebrant in the Church of Satan's high-profile rituals of the mid-late 1960s. Anger's assertion that LaVey avoided Crowley's work because it was too complex, is another take on LaVey's own view that Crowley's writings are pointlessly flawed by deliberate obscurity.

How did you become involved with the Church of Satan?

I first met Anton when I moved to San Francisco in the early sixties. He was living there in the Black House – this was before the foundation of the Church of Satan. Anton thought it would be an amusing idea to gather a group of people around him and call it the Church of Satan. It was something that was kind of a lark but at the same time wholly serious. That was typical of Anton – he had this wonderful background in show business, having worked as a lion tamer and all sorts of wonderful things. He played the calliope in the circus as well as the organ in cocktail bars. He had all those talents, so it was pretty exciting to be around at the foundation and beginning of it all.

He held his Satanic Mass in the Black House.

There were always various beautiful women around – Anton tended to like rather buxom blondes, and he had one of his own at the time known as Diane, who was his high priestess. Much later, twenty years later, they had a falling-out which was very unfortunate. But I saw them when they were very much in love, and truly collaborating. He'd dictate and she'd write it out, or she'd get the thing printed up – they were working together. I met his daughter Karla, and babysat for Zeena, his daughter by Diane, when she came along. I knew him for almost 40 years previous to his death last year.

Will Anton LaVey ever be taken as seriously as Crowley by the occult community?

Time will tell. LaVeyan Satanism is an amusing, if somewhat superficial, take on the concept of self-indulgence. The basis of his philosophy, that you should be good to yourself, has certain similarities with that of Ayn Rand that she called 'objectivism'. It was a kind of pure selfishness. Ayn Rand had a deadly lack of a sense of humour, whereas Anton had a tremendous sense of humour.

Crowley would have been too much hard work for Anton. Anton may have been a little jealous of Crowley, he may even have been a lot jealous. But Crowley said, 'Don't follow me – find your own way', and that's what Anton did. There are aspects of Crowley that require a great deal of self-discipline. Anton's take on Satanism was to make it accessible for everyone – it's not a difficult, esoteric philosophy. He made it accessible by doing things like offering correspondence courses on how to become a witch, which seem jokey but were a lot of fun.

PART II

SATANISM IN 20TH CENTURY CULTURE

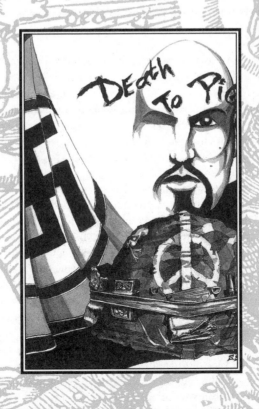

IMAGES IN THE
DARKNESS

Satanism in the Cinema

n the modern world, the spirit of the age often looms down upon us in strange, distorted forms from the cinema screen. Major production companies spend millions of dollars trying to trap the latest cultural trends on celluloid, while audiences make surprise blockbusters from movies which – accidentally or otherwise – tap into the anxieties and enthusiasms of the day. In the late 1960s and 1970s, the films which came to be regarded as the three 'Satanic blockbusters' – *Rosemary's Baby* (1968), *The Exorcist* (1973) and *The Omen* (1976) – all took the box-office by storm, transforming themselves into cultural phenomena which attracted public interest far beyond that of most 'mere' films.

Cinema has been the most potent legend factory of the twentieth century. Despite constant predictions that TV would devour the silver screen, the spectacle and ceremony of the cinema helped retain its status as the most sacred of modern temples. Film presents a super-real version of the world – louder, larger, essentially more mythic. More people take cues on how to live, love, fight – even on how to die – from the silver screen than from the pulpit or the gospels. Pagan worship is alive and well and being practised at you local multiplex, with Hollywood stars as the gods of our age. And, just as cinema has given us new gods, so it has supplied us with a new hierarchy of devils.

The relationship between Satan and the silver screen is a notable one. In the medium's earliest days, the Church aimed venomous sermons at the fledgling film industry – just as it had already lambasted music, theatre and dancing. In the early 1920s, resolutions condemning movies as 'evil' were overwhelmingly approved by the Baptist, Episcopalian, Methodist and Presbyterian churches. Preachers objected to every aspect of the early cinema – from its dramatic depictions of immorality, to the potential for personal sin in darkened auditoriums.

Canon William Chase, an ardent anti-film lobbyist, testified to the House Committee on Education that cinema was a 'threat to world civilisation', while the Reverend Wilbur Crafts was of the opinion that 'movies are schools of vice and crime . . . offering trips to hell for [a] nickel'. But while some religious conservatives campaigned for nothing less than the eradication of cinema, the Catholic Church had a far larger impact by advocating rigid regulation and censorship. One of the restrictions implemented at their behest was a ban on mockery of the clergy – as the Quigley Code, devised by influential lay Catholic Martin Quigley, explained: 'The reason why ministers of religion may not be comic characters or villains is simply because the attitude taken toward them may easily become the attitude taken toward religion in general.'

The father of fantastic cinema was a Frenchman named Georges Méliès, who made delightful short films crawling with demons and devils. Méliès was himself a Faustian figure, a stage conjurer and photographic illusionist who appeared out of the rump of the French Decadent era. Summoning devils on film, he defended this new sorcery in time-honoured fashion as 'white magic'.

In *The Laboratory of Mephistopheles* (1897), Méliès made Satan's head detach itself and float around the room – to the enchantment and horror of audiences in darkened 'picture palaces', resembling nothing so much as séance chambers. The success of this modern incarnation of the Faust legend (by then around 400 years old) led the pioneering film-maker to make *Faust and Marguerite* and *The Damnation of Faust* in the following year, while in 1899 he made two more Satanic shorts, *The Devil in the Convent* and *The Dance of Fire*. Significantly, Méliès – the mischievous Pandora who first opened cinema's box of delights – often took the role of a sorcerer, or even the Devil Himself, in his numerous bewitching little productions.

Hollywood's dream factory wasn't even at the planning stage by the turn of the century, but the pioneer of US cinema, Edwin Porter (partner of the man who virtually invented the movies, Thomas Edison), produced his own version of *Faust and Marguerite* in 1900. The most striking cinematic fantasies came from Germany at this point – stark, angular exercises in shadow and nightmare. *The Student of Prague* was an updated version of the well-worn *Faust* tale, based on an Edgar Allan Poe story, which transformed the lead from an ambitious academic to a devil-may-care student and Mephistopheles into a rakish devil called Scapinelli. The story was retold onscreen in 1913, 1926 and 1936. The 1926 version was by the master of German Expressionist cinema, F. W. Murnau – the last film he made before leaving his artistic roots for Hollywood, where he met with a tragically early death. As a minor masterpiece, it was a suitably grandiose climax to a career which produced *Nosferatu* (1922), the first great gothic vampire film.

One Satanic oddity that begs mention is the 1922 Scandinavian film *Häxan* (usually retitled *Witchcraft Through the Ages*). A truly extraordinary work, *Häxan* is a blend of historical lecture, melodrama and staged documentary stuffed to capacity with arresting images. Charting the history of the witch-cult and Devil-worship in the most phantasmagorical style, it employs the type of demonic imagery created by Church-sponsored artists like Hieronymus Bosch to condemn the excesses of the Church-directed Inquisition. *Häxan* is truly unique, and remains one of this writer's favourite films. (The director, Benjamin Christensen, went on to direct *Seven Footprints to Satan* for Hollywood in 1929 – a fine film sadly flawed by his decision to depart from the source novel, making the movie's Satanic cult into a hoax at the dénouement.)

In the USA, the dream factory was beginning to shift into full production. In 1915 audiences got to meet *The Devil's Darling* and, two years later, *The Devil's Assistant*. The trickster devil of New English folklore was the order of the day in early American films, most memorably rendered in the 1923 film *Puritan Passions,* where the Devil animates a scarecrow as a cruel gag. D. W. Griffith, the director who pioneered the American film epic with *The Birth of a Nation* (1915), revived Milton's tragic, anti-heroic Devil for his 1925 film *The Sorrows of Satan*. The prologue, depicting the war of angels in Heaven, demonstrates the talent for spectacle that Griffith was justly famous for.

The Magician (1926) is semi-legendary. Now sadly lost, it was an adaptation of a Somerset Maugham novel inspired by the exploits of Aleister Crowley, starring Paul Wegener – star of silent German horror movies – as the Great Beast. The film flopped commercially, amid charges of tastelessness which make its latter-day elusiveness all the more intriguing.

The 1930s are often referred to as the golden age of horror movies. However, the only significant Satanic effort of this era was Universal Pictures' *The Black Cat* (1934), purportedly based on an Edgar Allan Poe story to which it bears no resemblance. Featuring the two giants of black and white horror, Boris Karloff and Bela Lugosi, it tells the unusually grim tale of a bereaved man driven to take revenge on the cultured but immoral Satanist who murdered his wife (and preserved her corpse as a necrophiliac artefact after death). Notable for the hauntingly original art-deco atmospherics of director Edgar G. Ulmer (particularly in the Black Mass scene), this is the only horror movie in which Lugosi got to play the hero – albeit a hero driven to become a sadistic maniac.

Horror legend Boris Karloff as Satanist Hjalmer Poelzig in the 1934 classic The Black Cat.

In 1943, *The Seventh Victim* was produced by Val Lewton, creator of many urbanly stylish 1940s horror films. Predating the mass hysteria about Satanism by more than a quarter of a century, this moodily paranoiac feature tells of a Devil-worshipping conspiracy at large in Greenwich Village. Regarded by many as a minor classic, this exemplary exercise in quiet, psychological horror is, in many ways, too quiet – the Satanists are not really threatening for any other reason but for the fact that they *are* Satanists.

Lewton's sometime collaborator, French director Jacques Tourneur, created an altogether more satisfying Satanic chiller in 1957 entitled *Night of the Demon* (US: *Curse of the Demon*). Based upon the classic M. R. James short story 'Casting the Runes', it pits a sceptical academic against a Crowleyan Satanist in a war of science versus superstition. In a clever and genuinely unsettling plot twist, the scientist prevails – but only by resorting to his opponent's tactics, summoning a Lovecraftian demon from the netherworld.

Many of the more saturnine character actors of the day had a crack at portraying the ultimate Machiavellian smoothie in mainstream Hollywood movies. Walter Huston made a creditable Devil in the moral fable *All That Money Can Buy* (1941), Claude Rains attempted the role in the offbeat fantasy-thriller *Angel on My Shoulder* (1946), and even Ray Milland, usually a romantic lead, picked up the pitchfork for *Alias Nick Beal* (1949). Vincent Price, the most suavely Satanic actor of the silver screen, played Satan Himself in *The Story of Mankind* (1957). Sadly, it wasn't one of his finer moments, and is often included in lists of the worst films of all time.

From the late 1950s through to the early 1970s, Hammer Studios in England became a byword for colourfully-lurid gothic horror. However, Satan rarely reared his head – though, interestingly, when Hammer planned a film about the horrors of the Spanish Inquisition, the Catholic Church, not keen to have its dirty laundry aired, blocked the film by threatening to picket theatres. (Sets and costumes were used instead for *The Curse of the Werewolf*, in 1961.)

In 1968, Hammer got around to adapting Dennis Wheatley's Satanic thriller *The Devil Rides Out*. Set in fashionable 1920s England, it features the cultured Duc de Richleau, a swashbuckling good-guy occultist, against the fiendishly-decadent Satanist Mocata. Like the book it's fast-paced and atmospheric, if also starchy and pompous. Christopher Lee, normally typecast as a villain, got to play the good guy in another Satanic casting inversion. (Hammer followed it eight years later with *To the Devil - a Daughter*, based on another Wheatley novel, but, though much tawdrier, it lacked the zest and polish of its predecessor.)

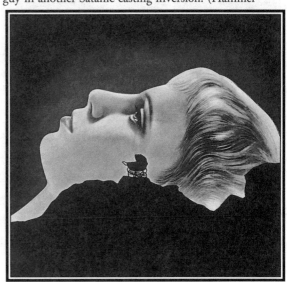

1968 was a good year for Devil movies. *Rosemary's Baby*, the finest Satanic film ever made, also appeared that year.

It was the first Hollywood film of director Roman Polanski, a master at conveying mundane madness and paranoia, starting the vogue for Satanic panic pictures. The acting is excellent, the tone a seamless blend of the ordinary and nightmarishly surreal. Innocent, likeable young Rosemary (played by Mia Farrow) realises her dream to have a baby while her husband achieves sudden success in his acting career – all due to a cult of eccentrically-quaint Satanists, who acclaim her baby as their Antichrist.

'Pray for Rosemary's Baby*' was the ad campaign slogan for Roman Polanski's classic of urban paranoia and domestic diabolism.*

As horror author Stephen King observed of the success of its source novel: '*Rosemary's Baby* was written and published at the time the God-is-dead tempest was whirling around in the teapot of the 1960s.' Very near the top of that particular 'teapot' was Anton LaVey, who was connected with the film in a number of ways. An adviser on occult ritual during shooting, LaVey appears in a drugged dream sequence on a boat, his sinister eyes representing those of the Devil as He ravishes Rosemary. His diabolic image was also used to promote the film, with personal appearances at screenings along with posters and badges proclaiming, 'Pray for the soul of Anton LaVey.' More darkly, it wasn't only such carnivalesque showmanship – stock-in-trade of the film's producer, William Castle – that made *Rosemary's Baby* such a rare treat for fans of demonic conspiracy and occult synchronicity.

Polanski's beautiful actress wife, Sharon Tate (who had recently appeared in *Eye of the Devil* [1966], for whom the adviser was Wiccan shyster Alex Sanders), would be murdered the year after the film's release by the supposedly Satanic 'Manson Family'. One of her killers was

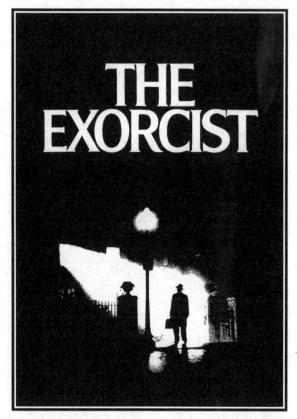

Susan Atkins, who played a vampire in LaVey's Topless Witches Revue. The tombstone that served as a coffee table in LaVey's front room originally belonged to one Lucas Machado – very close to the name 'Adrian Marcato', the founder of the cult in *Rosemary's Baby*. The film was also shot in the supposedly haunted Dakota Apartments, later to be the venue for John Lennon's murder by Mark Chapman.

While *Rosemary's Baby* was the better movie, it was *The Exorcist* (1973) which had the greater impact. William Peter Blatty's novel, a celebration of Catholic guilt, was turned into a viscerally-aggressive film by director William Friedkin. It tells the tale of a twelve-year-old girl, played by Linda Blair, who becomes possessed by a demon that inspires her to numerous unsettling performances, most notably masturbating with a crucifix. Two priests try to rescue her from its evil clutches, the film climaxing as a supernatural showdown between good and evil. Unbelievably, this morbid fantasy was described at the time of release by its director as a 'docu-drama'.

The influence of the Jesuit-schooled Blatty ensures that, at one level, the film is all about the crisis of faith within the younger priest. Despite this minor ambiguity, however, the viewer is constantly encouraged to cheer for the Catholic God and hope the priest regains his faith in time to save the poor little girl. This, for many, is the film's strength. It reminds an increasingly atheistic society of what it's turned its back on, and encourages – even amongst Protestant, Jewish, agnostic or atheist viewers – some good, old-fashioned Catholic guilt to atone for godless lives.

One clergyman, the Reverend Thomas Bermingham, observed, 'The second time I saw the film was in Rome, with all these bishops and a cardinal or two. They were enraptured by it, and they would be very critical of anything they did not believe in.' Blatty goes further, explaining, 'The Pope did make a statement shortly after the release of *The Exorcist* reaffirming the Church's position on the existence of Satan as a supreme and intelligent force of evil. I'm sure that had something to do with *The Exorcist*.'

However, most churches retained their traditional censorious position, picketing screenings and denouncing the film in pulpit and press. Mary Whitehouse, Britain's patron saint of censorship, much later managed to get a screening dropped from BBC TV's Halloween schedules. Ironically, none of these pious protesters ever seemed to perceive the pro-Christian ethos of the film.

Such hysteria reached its apotheosis with the British Board of Film Classification's refusal to allow the film to be released on video. BBFC director James Ferman claimed to have received letters from numerous poor, deranged little dears telling of how they came to believe themselves demonically possessed after a viewing of *The Exorcist*. (Commonsense did not prevail until 1999, when Ferman's departure allowed for the film's release on tape.) Only the Tunisian censorship board showed any sense of proportion, banning *The Exorcist* as Christian propaganda.

Temperatures had been pre-emptively raised by scare stories and rumours linked with the film: deaths, illnesses, accidents on set. Friedkin claimed strange double exposures on the print and distortions on the soundtrack had mysteriously appeared. Such visual and auditory effects should have been no surprise: the director had employed a double, Eileen Dietz, to cover for Linda Blair during the more controversial scenes. Dietz was also made up as a cadaverous demon for some unused sequences, and at least two subliminal shots of this creature – affectionately known as Captain Howdy – appear momentarily in the film.

The soundtrack also incorporated many weird noises, such as an angry bee trapped in a jar, pigs headed for an abattoir, and even the recording of an 'authentic' exorcism by the Vatican. Friedkin secured the services of award-winning actress Mercedes McCambridge to supply the voice of the demon. 'She said, "I haven't had a drink for twenty-five years,"' recollects Friedkin, '"but if you let me drink whiskey and if I start smoking, then you will find weird things happening with my voice."

'Then she said, "Why don't you tie me to the chair, and why don't you put me through some kind of physical torture as well?" Which we did.' Moving from method acting toward a makeshift occultic ritual, McCambridge unleashed the demon within herself.

Fuelled by the likes of evangelical preacher Billy Graham, the legend that *The Exorcist* possessed some kind of supernatural power gained impetus as 'experts' identified many other subliminal sounds and images on the print. When many of these rumoured 'subliminals' proved elusive upon re-examination, rumours began that the original print had been withdrawn, replaced by an expurgated cut to protect filmgoers from the movie's insidious effects.

Despite the high bullshit quotient surrounding *The Exorcist*, the film was powerful enough to create a panic among the cinema-going public. Breakdowns, hysterical 'possessions', even suicides were claimed as a result – but the overall silliness of the phenomenon is best illustrated by the punter who tried to sue an exhibitor on account of losing his jacket and trousers, purportedly due to the film's supernatural effects.

The Exorcist became the most successful horror film of all time, starting a vogue among evangelical priests and their flocks for staging demonic possessions and exorcisms. The film's power is partly due to a powerful hybrid of Catholic and atheistic guilt, which had also buoyed the box-office takings for *Rosemary's Baby* – but it also fed upon a growing fear of corruption of children then erupting in post-1960s, post-liberationist America. It was this same parental fear that was to be so astutely manipulated by fundamentalist Christians during the Satanic child abuse scare of the 1980s.

The Exorcist was followed, in 1976, by another successful Satanic-scare production: *The Omen*. The film resulted from a discussion between producer Harvey Bernhard and a born-again Christian friend, when Bernhard recognised fundamentalist prophecies for what they are: paranoid horror fantasies.

In *The Omen* the Antichrist (a mere walk-on part in *The Bible*) appears in the form of Damien, a little boy unknowingly adopted by the US ambassador to Britain, who believes him to be his natural son. The little fallen angel causes mayhem, suicide and gory accidents wherever he goes, clearing his way to the corridors of power. The film captured (and popularised) the fundamentalist fear of a Satanic conspiracy with some skill, but it's Harvey Stephens as the sinister child Damien and the excellent music by Jerry Goldsmith (an Oscar-winning blueprint for Satanic soundtracks ever since) which still shine.

The Omen wasn't the only horror film to use Christian dogma as a plot device. With two

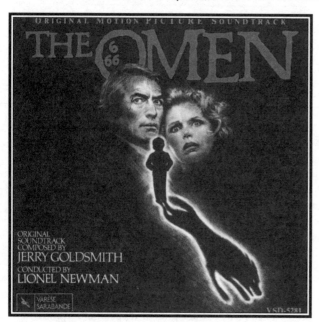

millennia of experience in terrifying their congregations, the Church proved a fertile source for movie directors looking for lurid scare stories. One obvious example is the evangelical Christian idea that rock music is a trap laid by the Devil to ensnare young souls. The 1986 film *Trick or Treat* employed the myth of 'back-masking': records played backwards as a hot-line to 'the Guy Downstairs'. With mischievous irony, the film's fundamentalist preacher was played by Ozzy Osbourne (a vocalist frequently targeted by Christian attacks on 'Satanic rock'), with the forces of evil manifested in a camply demonic heavy metal star.

The Gate (1987) employed the same wacky back-masking plot device. This time some bored kids use a heavy metal album to summon a huge Lovecraftian demon through the floor of their house, before anti-climatically despatching it with a skyrocket. *Black Roses* (1988) could have been adapted from one of the delightfully deranged Christian comic-books issued as tracts by evangelical publishers. A small town is thrown into disarray when the heavy metal band of the title descends upon it, dividing parents about whether they are harmless fun or literal hellraisers. Of course, as fundamentalist Christians have always warned, the rockers are servants of Satan trying to turn America's kids into degenerate zombies, and a risible showdown occurs between the wholesome hero and the powers of darkness.

The 1970s established Satanic cultists as stock movie monsters alongside vampires, werewolves and homicidal maniacs, and the past couple of decades have seen hordes of infernal chillers crowding the low-budget video shelves. Sequels to *Rosemary's Baby*, *The Exorcist* and *The Omen* jostle for space alongside their unofficial siblings like *The Mephisto Waltz* (1971) and *Satan's Cheerleaders* (1977). Anton LaVey was employed to teach Mexican peasants authentic Satanic chants for *The Devil's Rain*, an under-rated 1975 occult thriller featuring

Devil-worshipping redneck cultists. Even here though, the moral agenda is very orthodox and the good guys prevail.

Almost without exception, horror movies accept the Christian moral view – if the forces of darkness triumph, it's as a warning not a celebration. So many of these films – like *Black Roses* – come close to depicting what evangelists are preaching from their pulpits, or TV shows, that it seems strange for fundamentalist Christians to attack them as sinful or dangerous. It could be, however, that rendering the myths and fantasies of the Christian faith on film makes them look even more transparently ridiculous. Whether it's the feeding of the 5,000 or Satanic 'back-masking', there's something irresistibly comedic about many of Christianity's most fondly-held beliefs.

But it also seems the attitudes of those early twentieth-century preachers prevail: the cinema is the Devil's lantern. Movie-makers are in the business of temptation, using the traditional armoury of the Prince of Tempters – the pleasures and perils of the flesh. Sin sells,

in a way that the bland platitudes of Christian morality never will, while cinematic sin remains in the memory long after the credits have rolled . . .

As for what truly defines 'Satanic cinema', Satanists themselves don't always go for horror movies. Satanic cinema is a surprisingly broad church – it includes films that celebrate alienation, like *noir* thrillers or spaghetti westerns; horror or science fiction movies that punish or parody conformist stupidity, such as *The Texas Chainsaw Massacre* (1974), or *The Stepford Wives* (1975 – adapted from the novel by *Rosemary's Baby* author Ira Levin);

White Angel – Black Angel – *the Mexican title of Witchcraft '70, a 1969 documentary featuring salacious occult rites, including rare early footage of Anton LaVey's Church of Satan.*

movies with a magical sense of showmanship, like the horror movies of gimmick-king William Castle; or comedies that satirise religious morality, like *Monty Python's Life of Brian* (1979), or – a personal favourite – *Bedazzled* (1967), with the incomparable Peter Cook as the Devil.

Meanwhile, Satan continues to manifest Himself on the big screen, with many big stars unable to resist taking a crack at the role. Robert De Niro made a memorably enigmatic Louis Cyphere (say the name quickly) in the steamily-sinister *noir*-thriller *Angel Heart* (1987). In the same year, Jack Nicholson played the irresistible 'horny li'l devil' Darryl Van Horn in *The Witches of Eastwick*. Most recently, Al Pacino tried (unconvincingly) to make the role his own in a fable of demonic litigation entitled *Devil's Advocate* (1997). Cinema remains irredeemably Satanic because, just like De Niro, Nicholson and Pacino, all good Satanists know that the villain always gets the best lines.

SULPHUR AND CELLULOID

Anton LaVey on Satanic Cinema. LaVey always had a fascination for cinema, a compliment the movie industry occasionally repaid. He shared his typically idiosyncratic views on Satanic cinema with the author.

Were you happy with Rosemary's Baby*?*

It was the best ad for Satanism ever screened. The film-makers wanted to portray a woman whose maternal instinct overrode everything else. They played advance screenings for various religious groups and, like good Christians, they all applauded when Rosemary was going to kill her baby and hissed when she didn't. For the first time, *Rosemary's Baby* presented Satanists as sophisticated, reasonable people, instead of stoned freak-outs. Though I suppose you could say the Val Lewton film, *The Seventh Victim*, did the same decades before. I will always champion *Rosemary's Baby*'s producer William Castle, who also directed some wonderful films. Everything he did was right on target.

How about The Exorcist*?*

LaVey with the beloved auto (license no. 'SZANDOR') upon which the 'monster' in the 1977 occult thriller The Car *was based.*

I thought it was crap. William Peter Blatty, who wrote the book, is a rabid Catholic – I was banned from the set. I agree with Stephen King's assessment of *The Exorcist* in his book *Danse Macabre* – I think we're lucky we don't see much of Blatty anymore.

*How do you think the three landmark films – *Rosemary's Baby, The Exorcist *and* The Omen *– compare in their impact on Satanism?*

Rosemary's Baby generated an interesting blend of fear and attraction towards Satanism. It did for Satanism what *Birth of a Nation* did for the Ku Klux Klan; our membership soared after its release. You could say that it was 'an inside job'. *The Exorcist* sent everyone flooding back to the Church – it was designed or contrived to push people back towards Christianity. Of course, box office-wise it did great. Bill Friedkin, the director, has always said when asked that he knew me and had no problems with that. I have tried to read the novel but I really couldn't get through it. I was consulted on *The Omen*, but not really involved.

The first of these films, *Rosemary's Baby*, established Satanism as acceptable and modern. *The Exorcist* scared the shit out of people and sent them scampering back to the Church. It created a whole new market for instant exorcisms. Just like we have the current vogue for 'Satanic abuse survivors' now, then there was a rash of possessions and exorcisms. It was an exhibitionists' field day – they got to say all those naughty words they're not supposed to. *The Omen* established the idea of the Antichrist, of Satanists born-to-the-blood as it were.

Some people went so far as to change their names after that film – we started getting enquiry after enquiry at the Church of Satan from 'Damiens'. Michael Aquino became fixated with that film – he had '666' tattooed on his scalp. They wanted to film the second *Omen* film here in this house. They were so keen that they said they were happy to use a cardboard cut-out to film with if we objected to the young man playing Damien! A lot of producers have wanted to film here over the years.

Why are there so many Satanic movies?

Satanism sells. I've worked on a lot of films that have been swept under the carpet over the years, though. *Simon, King of the Witches* (1971) was a film which was magically very sound. *The Car* (1977) captured the metaphysics of fear. Many of the films I like are not horror, but *film noir* – about weak, flawed, inhibited heroes – films with a sympathy for the poor guy thrust into a role of incongruity. That incongruity doesn't exist anymore. We seem to have lost all the pure characters because we've lost all the contrasts. The lighting has changed, if you like. Satanists are trying to recreate those contrasts.

A Nativity
in Black

Satanic Psychedelia and the Devil's Music

usic has always played an important role in cultural outlook and identity. Hymns, marching songs, lullabies – there are a thousand different aspects of life which are ordered or inspired by a musical beat. Music helps to define your cultural tribe.

The Satanic underground was celebrated – and eventually propelled into the mainstream – by musicians at the tail-end of the psychedelic era. While the Beatles and the Rolling Stones were the public faces of 1960s youth culture, other voices of that same social and spiritual revolution sang dark hymns of rebellion.

Several weeks before the disastrous Altamont festival heralded the end of the Stones' brief flirtation with the Prince of Darkness, a more overtly Satanic gathering was planned. Billed as a 'Satanist's Woodstock', the Black Arts Festival was to be held in Olympia Stadium, Detroit, on Halloween 1969.

The event was to be blessed by Anton LaVey (rather incongruously, since he later claimed to have cursed the entire hippie movement that previous August – though his animosity toward that counterculture never became fully apparent until the 1980s), while Timothy Leary, the LSD guru – who coined the notorious 'tune in, turn on, drop out' adage – was also to deliver an address. The symbolic bridge between these two opposite worlds of love and darkness was the headlining band, Coven. Outrage at such a blatantly Satanic event was strong, however, and pressure from a coalition of Detroit churches forced promoters to cancel the event.

Some think that, had the Black Arts Festival gone ahead, Coven might have achieved the popular success that ultimately eluded them. The band's first album went under the uncompromising title *Witchcraft Destroys Minds and Reaps Souls,* boasting a gatefold sleeve featuring the band engaged in a Black Mass – complete with attractive blonde singer Jinx Dawson serving as a naked altar.

The album features a recording of this Black Mass at the tail end of side two: 'To the best of our knowledge, this is the first Black Mass to be recorded in written words or in audio,' explain the sleeve notes. (Anton LaVey recorded his own Black Mass shortly afterwards.) 'It is as authentic as hundreds of hours of research in every known source can make it. We do not recommend its use by anyone who has not thoroughly studied Black Magic and is aware of the risks and dangers involved.' The rite bears the hallmark of serious study, with notably authentic elements from medieval Gnostic and witchcraft lore. The overall effect, however is curiously naive, with the high priest's command to 'kiss the goat' sounding more Monty Python than Aleister Crowley.

The music that precedes the Black Mass is standard – if well-executed – 1960s folk rock. It's something of a jolt to realise that, behind the gentle acoustic guitars, the lyrics are exclusively about Devil-worship and black magic, while the alluring Miss Dawson's vocals give the effect of a demonically-possessed Joni Mitchell. Ultimately, *Witchcraft Destroys Minds and Reaps Souls* is an interesting musical exploration of the witchcraft tradition which suffused rural America ever since the Pilgrim Fathers landed in New England over three centuries ago. The infamous Salem witch-trials – which took place in Massachusetts during 1692 – had been one of the last major incidents of state extermination by religious fanatics from the 'old world', making the term 'witch-hunt' synonymous with the persecution of a minority. As such, it elicited the sympathy of twentieth-century hippies like Coven toward their satanic predecessors. (In sacrificing the lives of twenty suspected 'witches' to the fantasies of hysterical children, it also

Psychedelic Satanists Coven – with singer Jinx Dawson, top right – and their second album, Blood on the Snow.

predated the 'Satanic panic' of the 1980s-90s.)

Coven's second album *Blood on the Snow* followed but, despite its demonic sleeve, the Satanic elements were far more restrained. By the third album, imaginatively titled *Coven*, the sinister elements had all but disappeared, replaced by standard hippie material. Robbed of the distinctive image of their early days, Coven faded away.

On the other side of the Atlantic, British hippies were also dabbling with the dark side. Rock band Lucifer, formed in 1971, were a curious collection of characters whose sardonically-devilish promotional photos portrayed a Mansonesque image. They advertised their material via mail order in *Oz*, the legendary hippie magazine, in order 'to make evil music and sell it direct, without the usual crap and con'. Whether He liked it or not (and He probably did not), the Devil was enlisted to fight the capitalist-pig system.

Lucifer issued two albums, *Big Gun* and *Exit*, and a single, entitled 'Fuck You', which was seized by the police. 'Lucifer is English,' proclaimed the band, 'but we have this cave in Arizona where we record a lot of our stuff.' Unfortunately, it sounds that way – while there may have been some Satanic ideas beneath the thumping garage-rock, they rarely come through the primitive production.

Another band called Lucifer appeared in the US at around the same time. Formed by one Mort Garson, the American Lucifer released an album entitled *Black Mass* with a selection of occult-inspired electronics. Typical of early 1970s experimental music, it has dated badly. Lucifer, like their British namesakes, folded and disappeared.

Most outré of the Satanic psychedelicists, Roky Erickson had been the leader of the mid-1960s Texan garage band the Thirteenth Floor Elevators until a bust for marijuana possession. Facing a long prison sentence under the Lone Star State's sanctimonious laws, he committed himself to a psychiatric institution instead. This was a bad mistake. Three years later, in the early 1970s, the hallucinogen-loving Erickson came out of the nuthouse considerably crazier than he went in.

An obscure cult figure who became known for lyrical tributes to his favourite 1950s horror movies, in the hospital he had formed a close relationship with his own personal Satan. 'Ah'm not afraid of the Devil, the Devil is mah friend. He chose me to do his biddin',' drawled the deranged but loveable Erickson. 'Those doctors and nurses . . . They could not mess with the Devil's chosen one.' To cement this unholy pact, Erickson later vocalised his personal infernal visions in wildly sincere songs like 'I Think of Demons' and 'Don't Shake Me Lucifer'.

By far the most interesting of the Satanic-psychedelic bands were Black Widow. Their 1970 debut album, *Sacrifice*, was the result of guitarist Jim Gannon's research into the Black Arts, with occultic lyrics accompanying a blend of traditional folk music and progressive rock. The almost-ubiquitous Alex Sanders warned the band they had done their homework too well, and would attract dark forces. He was right for once, though only inasmuch as Gannon's lyrics boast a fair degree of authenticity, and some songs – like the catchy 'Come to the Sabbat' – are highly evocative of the medieval-European Satanic tradition. Other moments – like the horrible saxophone solo Satan uses to tempt some poor innocent on 'Seduction' – are diabolical in a different sense.

The band enhanced their image with an elaborately Satanic stage show, professionally choreographed by a Leicester theatre company, complete with sacrificial daggers and a naked girl to adorn the altar (at one point this was Alex Sanders' wife, Maxine). They reaped the reward for their oddly entertaining work, with *Sacrifice* reaching the Top 40 in the UK album charts. However, their second album, *Black Widow*, lacked both the Satanic themes and the power of its predecessor. The official explanation for this was that, true to Sanders' warning, weird things had started to happen – most alarmingly, near-fatal car crashes. (Satan seems particularly keen on causing road accidents, however much more impressive lightning bolts or stampeding elephants might seem.)

What's more likely is that, like many rock bands that use powerful Satanic imagery, Black Widow may have begun to believe that same imagery was holding back their career. As many have learnt to their cost, however, it's more often the other way around – few dabbling rock stars regain the early excitement once they stop playing the Devil's music. Suffice to say, Jim Gannon, the major creative force behind the band, can't have been unduly worried by the curse, as he tried to mount a stage musical version of the Black

Widow show on Broadway. Sadly, it never came off, and Black Widow – devoid of Devil-worship – dwindled into obscurity.

Further Satanic musical oddities came in the form of the bizarre Greek progressive rock band, Aphrodite's Child. In 1972 they released *666 – The Apocalypse of St John*, a curiously ambitious concept album based around the biblical Book of Revelations, which makes the end of the world sound like a surprisingly jolly affair. Members included electronic keyboard maestro Vangelis and kaftan-clad, blimp-falsetto Demis Roussos, no less.

Monument were more orthodoxly sinister. The sleeve notes for their 1970 debut album, *The First Monument*, declare that, 'Monument aren't the first rock group to profess an interest in witchcraft and the occult but in their case it is no mere gimmic [sic]. Vocalist and keyboard man Steven Lowe was a founder member of a thriving witches coven in Essex and the group's other three members all share his dedication to the occult . . . Haunting, eerie, mystical even at times a little frightening to those outside the shadowy half-world of the occult but compelling and demanding our attention . . . '

Monument's competent but unremarkable progressive rock did have a mildly macabre edge – while their sorcerous image helped gain their album an underground reputation as 'bad juju'. Even so, it did not compel or demand enough attention to stop Monument disappearing in a puff of smoke.

One band whose 'dedication to the occult' was always a little suspect (indeed, almost certainly a 'mere gimmic') were Black Sabbath. They have endured, however, considerably better than their contemporaries.

Founded in 1967 as Polka Tulk, then renamed Earth, the band comprised four down-to-earth, working-class lads from Birmingham. That they were the vehicle through which the infernal became a mainstay of rock music was far more by accident than design.

The origin of the name Black Sabbath, as with all the band's occultic connections, bears their trademark of good-natured confusion. Depending on which story you hear, the name may have been derived from the band's early song of the same name – an ominously-downbeat slice of original heavy metal, inspired by a Dennis Wheatley novel that bass player 'Geezer' Butler was reading. (Other anecdotes suggest both the song title and the band's name were inspired by the Italian horror movie *Black Sabbath*.)

'I'd been raised a Catholic so I really believed in the Devil,' Butler has retrospectively admitted. 'There was a weekly magazine called *Man, Myth and Magic* that I started reading which was all about Satan and stuff. That and books by Aleister Crowley and Dennis Wheatley, especially *The Devil Rides Out* which was meant to be a cautionary tale but which reads like a handbook on how to be a Satanist.

'I'd moved into this flat which I'd painted black with inverted crosses everywhere. Ozzy [Osbourne, amiably-demented vocalist] gave me this sixteenth-century book about magic that he'd stolen from somewhere. I put it in the airing cupboard because I wasn't sure about it. Later that night I woke up and saw this black shadow at the end of the bed. It was a horrible presence that frightened the life out of me! I ran to the airing cupboard to throw the book out, but the book had disappeared. After that I gave up all that stuff. It scared me shitless.'

More prosaic accounts of Black Sabbath's flirtation with occult imagery claim they were impressed by the interest Black Widow had enjoyed in their Satanic stage show. The truth is probably a combination of all these stories. Whatever, it's fair to say that intense interest in their demonic aspects surprised Black Sabbath as much as anyone else. Their eponymous 1969 debut album was recorded in two days for £600, treated with contempt and indifference by the press, and rapidly became a commercial success.

The *Christian Science Monitor*, of all publications, noted approvingly that the band did not 'condone or promote the less seemly aspects of . . . an interest in occult matters'. They were right. The song 'Black Sabbath' describes the narrator's state of terror at witnessing a Black Mass. Their attitude to Satan was chiefly the traditional one of fear and loathing, their lyrics even sometimes entreating listeners to turn to God as the only source of love. But the audiences weren't listening – they wanted a Satanic band, and that's what Black Sabbath ostensibly became. (Rumour has it that their management had the large cross that decorated the inside of their first album inverted without the band's knowledge or approval.)

Years later, in the liner notes to the band's retrospective *Reunion* album, Phil Alexander, editor of UK rock magazine *Kerrang!*, would note: 'Unbeknown to the band Black Sabbath was launched in the US with a party in San Francisco with the head of the Church of Satan, Anton LaVey, presiding over proceedings. For Sabbath it almost scuppered their US touring plans, the launch coming in the wake of the murder of Sharon Tate by followers of Charles Manson. All of a sudden Sabbath were Satan's Right Hand Men.'

Black Sabbath's lyrics presented a worldview that rejected both the dictatorial hypocrisy of the Church and the destructive Powers of Darkness. It was a philosophy most clearly expressed in 'Under the Sun', from *Black Sabbath Volume 4*, condemning Satanists and Christian preachers alike. Still, Satan appears in Black Sabbath's songs as a constant source of fascination and fear, an entity who brings

Tony Iommi, founder member of Black Sabbath, with trademark inverted crosses. The cover of their album Sabbath Bloody Sabbath *illustrates the demonic imagery that permeated the band's songs.*

colour into a drab existence but can also represent the overwhelming evil of the world.

In the classic 'War Pigs', Satanic witches are equated with the evil of politicians and generals who callously kill millions in their power games. (According to guitarist Tony Iommi, the title was derived from 'Walpurgis', the night when evil traditionally rules the world.) But the most fascinating manifestation of Satan in a Black Sabbath song is also the rarest: when they briefly allow the Prince of Darkness to speak for Himself. In the strange and haunting 'N.I.B.', Lucifer, the creator, sings a plaintive love song to His greatest creation and fellow sufferer, mankind. (The song 'Lord of this World' also recognises Satan as god of the earth.) 'N.I.B.'s title is the source of some confusion: according to drummer Bill Ward it was simply his nickname, derived from when the band were stoned and thought he resembled a pen nib(!). Typically, the fans perceived a more Satanic significance – to them, 'N.I.B.' stood for 'Nativity in Black'.

Inevitably, the band were quizzed on such apparent occultic beliefs during interviews. 'We're into God,' Iommi unhelpfully explained, to which Ward added, 'But sometimes I feel Satan is God.' Perhaps they were expressing the beliefs of the early Satanic Gnostic groups, fifteen hundred years before. Or maybe they were making it all up as they went along . . .

While Black Sabbath's material was never as 'authentic' or well-researched as that of Black Widow, Coven or any other occultic act of the era, they would have a dark influence on popular music for decades to come, while their Satanic contemporaries folded. The overall mood of their music and lyrics captured the spirit of the age: the hangover after the heady party that was the hippie era, a bitter realisation that the optimism of the 1960s had been mere naivety. Several such albums appeared in 1970, the year following the Manson massacres, all giving impetus to the general feeling that the hippie experiment had failed. (Aphrodite's Child even included a song about Altamont on their apocalyptic 666 album.)

Other bands may have had far greater knowledge of the occult, but none of them sounded as grim or foreboding as Black Sabbath. Before it attracted the label 'heavy metal', some described the music as 'downer rock' – reflecting both the music's mood and the depressant drugs used to compliment it.

As Osbourne observed, 'The world's a right fucking shambles. Anyway, everybody has sung about all the good things already.' This spirit of the Summer of Love turning to winter haunts much of the band's early work, dealing with drug addiction, depression and alienation. The doom-laden Black Sabbath sound is heavy with grim, grinding guitar riffs, while Osbourne's vocals sound simultaneously menacing and verging on a tearful nervous breakdown.

Neither Black Sabbath nor Ozzy Osbourne would ever fully recapture their early dark magic. Osbourne was constantly gnawed by his own personal demon, alcohol, which provided him with an archetypal wild-man persona but drove him into psychiatric care. The Satanic elements of the songs diminished, as Ozzy's relationship with the other band members – and reality itself – became increasingly distant. He would be replaced by Ronnie James Dio – a vocalist with a well-publicised interest in medievalism and the occult – but, like the many singers who followed him, Dio could not recapture the raw frustration and pain of early Sabbath. In latter years, even with the reformation of the original quartet, Black Sabbath sounded like they were trying to ape a style that they had, in their younger days, invented.

While Black Sabbath were the hands that truly fashioned heavy metal, the most overtly infernal form of popular music, the other great influence – to their own chagrin – were Led Zeppelin. Zeppelin emerged in 1968 from London's lively rhythm and blues scene, the baby of hotshot guitarist Jimmy Page. The band took off incredibly quickly, becoming a huge commercial success on both sides of the Atlantic. Their primal emotional intensity, phallic guitar worship, uninhibited sexuality and – in their quieter moments – passion for Tolkienesque fantasy made them the rock phenomenon of their era. None of this qualifies them as a Satanic influence on modern youth, and it's doubtful that Led Zeppelin's music has spread anything but idle pleasure. But the persistent rumours linking the band to the occult were by no means unfounded.

Like Black Sabbath, and any other guitar-dominated rock band, Led Zeppelin had their roots in traditional black blues music – though Page's outfit, much closer in its sympathies to the blues than to heavy metal, was far more preoccupied with the tradition. The original bluesmen – who followed nomadic existences across the USA in the early twentieth century – existed outside of polite society, becoming legendary for their drinking, drug-taking and womanising. Needless to say, this was frowned upon by the Church, then a very powerful force in black culture, and their maudlin blues became the antithesis of witlessly-exuberant gospel songs.

Hints of anti- and pre-Christian religion pepper the blues, with references to voodoo-style magical charms such as 'black cat bones' and 'mojos'. The Devil also makes His presence felt, either as a symbol of the inevitable fate awaiting the debauched bluesman, or as the hard-living musician's comrade and inspiration. The delta blues – the school that had the greatest influence on the rock-guitar style – became known as 'the Devil's music'.

Delta bluesmen included Peetie Wheatstraw, who liked to be known as 'the Devil's Son-in-Law and High Sheriff of Hell', and Robert Johnson. Johnson, the acoustic-playing grandfather of rock guitar, best illustrates the enduring legend of the bluesman who sold his soul to acquire musical talent. (As testified by Satanic rock star Glenn Danzig during my interview with him: 'A lot of the old blues songs are very heavily rooted in occultism. There's Robert Johnson, all the voodoo and juju stuff – "Got my Mojo Working", "Black Cat Bone".') Johnson's

Ad for Jimmy Page's unused soundtrack for Lucifer Rising. *Promoted as a Led Zeppelin spin-off, disagreement with the film's director reputedly led to the throwing of a 'Kenneth Anger curse'.*

pact with Satan was said to be struck at the 'Crossroads' – one of his best-known songs, and a traditionally magical location in many cultures – and thereafter he always claimed to live, as another of his song titles puts it, with a 'Hellhound on My Trail'.

Led Zeppelin, and Jimmy Page in particular, were heavily influenced by Johnson, lifting parts of his songs for their own compositions. As with Johnson, so the popular rumour went, Led Zeppelin had made their pact with the Devil, asking the Prince of Darkness to tune their instruments in return for their souls. Only Satanic aid, reasoned the myth, could explain the enormous success the band enjoyed so rapidly, or the sexual power these modern pied pipers had over young girls. These same legends had been linked with musicians from Robert Johnson to Elvis Presley and beyond, but with Led Zeppelin the Satanic-pact myth has proved especially enduring.

The reason for this is almost certainly Jimmy Page's early fascination with the occult, particularly Aleister Crowley. Page's commercial success allowed him to indulge his passion for the maverick occultist, obtaining a huge collection of Crowley books (the second largest in the world), opening an occult bookshop in London specialising in Crowleyana, and, as the final indulgence, Crowley's old house. Reputedly built on the site where a church had burnt down with its congregation trapped inside (and supposedly haunted by a disembodied head), Boleskine House sits on the edge of legend-wreathed Loch Ness in Scotland.

'I think Crowley is completely relevant today,' Page once affirmed in an interview. On a more sinister note, he observed that, 'You can't ignore evil if you study the supernatural as I do. I have many books on the subject and I've also attended a number of seances. I want to go on studying it.' It was also suggested that Page had used Charles Pace, one of the most notorious latter-day black magicians, as a consultant when redecorating Boleskine.

The spirit of Crowley subtly permeated Page's work. On the first pressing of Led Zeppelin's third album, the most famous of Crowley's doctrines, 'Do what thou wilt', is inscribed upon the record. In the band's film, *The Song Remains the Same*, there is an odd sequence filmed at Boleskine featuring a hermit (the same figure as in the Crowley-designed Tarot card deck) waving a sword. In one very brief shot, Page can also be seen examining a 'stele', or stone tablet, in front of an ornate portrait of Crowley. The 'ZOSO' symbol that became the band's trademark was also partly derived from the work of another influential British occultist, Austin Osman Spare – a contemporary of Crowley, and occultic artist, best known for his 'automatic drawing', which he claimed worked as a conduit for supernatural forces. On more than one occasion, Page hinted that much of Led Zeppelin's material (particularly their meditative anthem 'Stairway to Heaven') had been conceived in a similar fashion. Kenneth Anger, dedicated disciple of Crowley, was also a close acquaintance of Page for a time. Anger asked Page to record a soundtrack for his magic ritual film *Lucifer Rising*, but was bitterly disappointed with the results, saying, 'I had asked him for intimacy and strength, rhythms and counter-rhythms. But he gave me a short fragment of chanting voices and sounds that I thought were quite sombre and morbid.'

In October of 1976, the two fell out in grand style. Page threw Anger out of the basement of his London house, where he had granted the American magus use of a film-editing suite. Anger responded with a press conference. Asked if he felt vindictive towards Page, Anger responded, 'You bet I do. I'm not a Christian turn the other cheek kind. In fact, I'm ready to throw a Kenneth Anger curse.'

Asked about the incident in an interview the following year, Page observed, 'The whole thing about "Anger's Curse", they were just these silly little letters. God, it was all so pathetic . . . I had a lot of respect for him. As an occultist he was definitely in the vanguard.' Despite Page's scepticism, many fans and commentators linked the personal tragedies that were to strike the band with some kind of hex. On 26 July 1977, vocalist Robert Plant's young son Karac died of a respiratory infection. Three years later, on 25 September 1980, the band's drummer, John Bonham, died after a drinking binge. Enough was enough. On 4 December 1980, it was announced that Led Zeppelin were no more.

The band's demise only served to fuel rumours. The more lurid stories held that all of Led Zeppelin, with the exception of Bonham, had signed pacts with the Devil for earthly pleasure, supposedly explaining the drummer's untimely death. One fanzine reported that black smoke had been seen billowing from Page's house on the day following Bonham's death, and that the guitarist was overheard uttering strange curses in unknown tongues. Even the mainstream press got in on the act, with the London *Evening News* quoting an anonymous source: 'It sounds crazy, but Robert Plant and everyone around the band is convinced that Jimmy's dabbling in black magic is responsible in some way for Bonzo's death and for all these other tragedies.'

What are we to make of the 'Led Zeppelin curse'? Yet another version of the Faust myth, a warning to all who would overreach themselves? Another example of how some people would rather attribute success to supernatural forces than personal charisma or sexual magnetism? Or are those same qualities an authentic aspect of the occult, the most volatile results of which occur from the combination of occultic techniques with an art-form?

By the late 1970s, it may all have seemed immaterial. Fickle pundits and trend-setters derided the likes of Led Zeppelin and Black Sabbath, focusing their attention on the punk explosion. And punk rock, engaged in a mutually-satisfying, sado-masochistic relationship with the media, considered itself far too streetwise to be associated with anything as arcane as the Devil. But heavy metal – the generic term that denoted bludgeoning, riff-heavy rock music – had been blissfully unfashionable ever since the first appearance of Black Sabbath, yet remained perennially popular. Many young people still needed to hear guitar music that conjured the Devil, and Satanic rock would show a tenacity that surprised all but its most fervent disciples.

IN ANCIENT DAYS

An evening with Kip Trevor, former vocalist of Black Widow.

I drank with Kip Trevor in late 1993, at a couple of the London pubs that were Black Widow's stomping ground back in the late 1960s and early 1970s. Friendly and open, he's now a successful music publisher, but enjoyed resurrecting the Satanic concept album *Sacrifice* from the memory vaults.

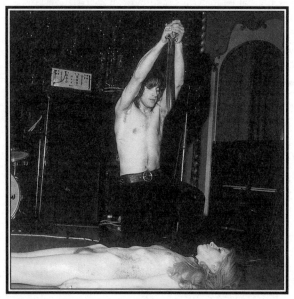

Kip Trevor and friend in Black Widow's notorious Sacrifice *stageshow.*

I've heard it said that Black Sabbath borrowed much of their Satanic imagery and mystique from Black Widow – to what extent do you feel that's true?
The publicity we got in the early seventies, they benefited from – in interviews, I've heard Ozzy admit as much. He's said, 'There was a lot of black magic going on back then,' and then mentioned Black Widow. We got coverage in papers like *The Sun, The News of the World* – all kinds of wild and wonderful publicity. A lot of it was with Alex Sanders – remember him? We stumbled across and became involved with him. We were so fucking naive.

If anything, your material seemed better researched than Sanders'...
It was heavily researched. It started out when we were

having a bit of an argument with our management company, Worldwide Management Artists. They eventually ended up managing Black Sabbath as well. We were having a little trouble deciding which direction to go in. We'd been playing American-style soul music, as we had quite a lot of brass in the band at the time. In amongst it all, Jim Gannon, our guitarist, came up with the idea of doing this occult thing and began writing a few bits and ideas. Since Widow he's become a teacher of transcendental meditation.

At this time we were working as musicians in the Phoenix Theatre in Leicester. Out of this came this occult thing which Jim had written. The research he'd done was very authentic. I remember going with him to the Victoria and Albert Museum, where he made an appointment to see this ancient magic book. They arranged for us to look through this book while a security guard watched over us.

I was totally amazed by the research that he did, from which eventually he came up with this very plausible story which was the basis of the Black Widow show. It was all to do with this Lady Astoroth, who was goddess of love, lust and the sexual organs and a whole list of other things to do with temptation and sex – which I guess all rock music is based on anyway. In this story this guy looks back in time and realises that he's existed before in another incarnation.

A rock opera of sorts?
Yes. I'd love to do it again and I've spoken to Jim a couple of times and we've toyed with the idea. I don't think we'd do it ourselves – they all do that, the old-fart rock artists, and I think that can be embarrassing and undignified. I'd love to find another theatre group, some young blood, and reform Black Widow with new musicians. Do the show how we originally envisaged it. It was a very credible, very well-staged show – beautifully lit – the whole thing was well structured. It would have been wonderful to continue things through the theatre group rather than bringing it out into the rock world.

But our management saw it and were totally blown away. Then gradually, they changed the show around to what they thought it should be. They commercialised it and introduced more nudity. The first thing that went was the girl we'd been rehearsing with, who was a very beautiful, sixteen-year-old art student. She was a fantastic performer, if a bit spunky. When the management came and started telling her what to do, she told them to 'Fuck off!' We did some publicity shots with Maxine Sanders, though she was nowhere near as attractive as the original.

Could you explain a little more about the story behind the show?

There's a guy who's lost his wife as a result of an accident to do with some kind of occultic ceremony. Something goes wrong, and she's killed. He comes back through the centuries, is reborn, and remembers this in a dream. In this dream he realises his wife can be returned to him, if he can perform another ceremony, like the one which had gone wrong. This time he would turn the tables on the Lady Astoroth, draw her, overpower her, and sacrifice her, then she would be banished and his wife would come back. So the first song, 'In Ancient Days', tells the story of this guy travelling through the centuries. Then there's the conjuration in which we bring in the Lady Astoroth and the girl appears. We'd have a lot of fun with that, as she would appear from all sorts of odd places, depending on where we were playing. We toured with it all over Europe for around eighteen months.

When Black Widow broke up, Jim and myself went off to try and revive the idea of the occultic stageshow. We spent a lot of time, money and effort on this new black magic concept, but it did not work out. Black Widow's first album was quite an achievement, but it would have been lovely to have developed it. The problem was that band politics got in the way – some of them wanted to be a 'normal' band and thought the whole black magic thing wasn't them. They thought it was overshadowing their playing.

The traditional story about why the band dropped the Satanic material was that Alex Sanders warned you that your material was too accurate, and that you began having bizarre accidents. Is that true?

That's a load of bullshit really. Alex Sanders and his wife were clever businesspeople who took the whole thing on beautifully. They latched onto what we were doing because it was very authentic. We were too naive to appreciate it at the time, but Jim and I were roped right into it. We stayed in his flat once, and it was an awful experience. It's laughable now, and I'm a bit embarrassed to tell you about it, but we were taken right in by it. Now it's so absolutely, totally clear that it was a big bloody con. Sanders was in it for making a bit of money and cleverly latched onto us, and we were more authentic than we realised at the time. We lectured colleges on it.

To what extent did the show transcend theatre and enter your personal beliefs?

The show was written with Jim's research, using proper conjuration ceremonies. The whole thing was done as authentically as we could possibly do it. We drew the magic circles, used all the props – fire, earth, air and water. We did it exactly as you were supposed to do it. Doing that has an effect, even if it's only psychological, because you know you're doing it in the correct fashion. You're stepping over the line. Combined with the power of the music and the power of the audience's involvement, weird things would happen.

DARK REFORMATION

The Temple of Set and Satanism in the 1970s

nton LaVey always claimed the numerous schisms and splinter groups that split the Church of Satan in the 1970s were part of a grand plan – to sort the wheat from the chaff, and achieve the stratification so central to his philosophy.

The ideas LaVey had promoted with his special brand of dark pageantry were not simply attracting the bright, alienated elite he had hoped for. A whole carnival of freaks was parading itself through the doors of the Black House: sexual inadequates ogling the naked altar; social misfits looking for an identity; intellectual poseurs trying to make themselves seem interesting. The success of the Church of Satan – founded as a refuge from the masochistic herd of conformists and compulsive 'joiners' – had left it in danger of becoming a magnet to such parasites.

Underlying this, LaVey was disenchanted with being the ringmaster of a media circus. He began to fade from the public gaze, making the transition from colourful carny to legendary recluse. The theatrical embellishments of his creed became the domain of others. From hereon, LaVey would judge his flock more harshly, measuring individual Satanists by how well they applied the pragmatic elements of his philosophy out in the real world.

This abandonment of the Church of Satan's religious trappings, in favour of a quieter, more sombre approach, caused significant disquiet in the ranks. Some saw this as an adroit move that stopped the Church becoming an over-familiar caricature of itself, a public joke. Others, however, saw it as symptomatic of LaVey's inability to carry his ideas through, believing that if he had stuck to his guns the Church of Satan would have entered the twenty-first (Christian) century as a force to be reckoned with.

Though many have assumed the Church of Satan made Anton LaVey a wealthy man, he resisted all temptation to turn it into a classic 'cult', sapping its members' minds and wallets. Despite the integral elements of pragmatism – and LaVey certainly saw nothing wrong with turning a buck – the creed was still dedicated to individuality. The Black Pope may have preached amorality, but encouraging sheep into his private fold just in order to fleece them would have been *im*moral.

Other Satanic movements had already erupted in emulation as early as 1970, such as the Cincinnati-based Cathedral of the Fallen Angel. Founder of the Cathedral James Guthrie distinguished his sect by abandoning the sexual emphasis of many of LaVey's teachings, replacing it instead with animal sacrifice. LaVey had described this practice as an 'inhibitive and asinine absurdity' in *The Satanic Bible*, condemning those who would sooner chop the head off a goat or chicken in an attempt to harness its death agony than have the 'blasphemous bravery to masturbate in full view of the Jehovah whom they claim to deny!' The Cathedral of the Fallen Angel was short-lived, merging with Don Blythe's lurid Brotherhood of the Ram in Los Angeles within a couple of years.

In 1970, the Black Pope began cutting apron strings. The Black House in San Francisco ceased to function as a public temple, becoming the Church of Satan's administrative headquarters. Charters were granted for independent 'grottoes' in over a dozen major American cities, as well as a couple in Canada. The membership was encouraged to refer to the Black Pope only for general direction and the settlement of internal disputes.

However, petty squabbles over titles, ranks and privileges did not bode well as to how this supposed fraternity of individualists would survive without their charismatic leader. The Church of Satanic Brotherhood attracted disaffected young recruits from the Church of Satan, and established 'templums' in St Petersburg, Louisville, Indianapolis and New York City. Despite supposedly rejecting LaVey's influence, much of their literature 'borrowed' from *The Satanic Bible* and his other works.

The Church of Satanic Brotherhood maintained a loose affiliation with Wayne West, another Church of Satan reject. West, British by birth, was an orthodox priest until defrocked by the Catholic Church – to compound the humiliation, he was then defrocked as a priest of the Babylon Grotto in Detroit. West responded by founding the Universal Church of Man, which he described as 'Satanism without Satan'. Sounding absurdly like the Church of God Without Jesus Christ in the Southern gothic movie *Wise Blood* (a 'Satanic cinema' favourite of LaVey), the Universal Church of Man lasted a couple of years before fading into obscurity.

The first issue of glossy 1970s occult magazine Witch, *featuring Alex Sanders as the cover star. Inside its salacious pages, Sanders exclusively predicts that Prince Charles will marry an American woman.*

While West wanted to remove Satan from the equation, more serious discontent came from Satanists whose concerns were completely the opposite. LaVey was making it increasingly clear that he did not believe in Satan as a literal entity – He was a name for the dark, brutal aspects of man and nature, as well as a symbol for the potency of man's untrammelled will. The Church of Satan was not a religion, and did not worship deities. For many, however, this was not enough. They wanted a *real* Devil to worship – belonging to a dark, mysterious coven, in the traditional gothic style, seemed much more appealing than being part of some cultural and social elite.

Though LaVey described the defectors as 'dependent parasitic groupies', his time and resources were increasingly wasted on the Church of Satan's dissenters. Fortunately, in 1969 the Church had attracted a bright, energetic recruit named Michael Aquino with a real flair for administration, and an interest in questions of rank and hierarchy. However, Aquino was not content with merely being Satan's secretary.

As a high-ranking officer in US military intelligence, with service in Vietnam and a doctorate in political science to his name, Aquino was the kind of deviant-Establishment figure that LaVey's organisation needed. But, in 1975, Aquino led a walk-out of disaffected Church of Satan members (the exact number is heavily disputed) to start his own Satanic order. The schism was precipitated by an explicit LaVey proclamation that priesthoods in the Church of Satan were available to those who demonstrated their success in the wider world – such demonstrations to include gifts of cash or valuable objects.

Just like the Pope in the sixteenth century, the Black Pope faced the challenge of attempted reform. As Protestant reformer Martin Luther had begun his protest as a criticism of the Papacy's sale of indulgences (spiritual 'get out of gaol free' cards, allowing sinners to pay their way out of damnation) so Michael Aquino, his Satanic equivalent, was upset that the Black Pope was running the Church of Satan as a business.

In both cases, the schisms reflected much deeper concerns. Luther's suspicion that the Catholic Church was being run for earthly profits led to accusations that the Pope was not a true believer in God.

Michael Aquino of the Temple of Set, and his wife Lilith.

Aquino's anxieties grew from a concern that LaVey no longer actually believed in Satan (nor – as LaVey would be the first to confirm – did he ever believe).

To make matters worse, LaVey had ordained his chauffeur as a priest of the Church of Satan – a man Aquino considered unsuitable for such a lofty position. Aquino argued that LaVey had cheapened his faith with an increasingly materialistic approach, never grasping that, as a Satanist, one should never be seeking the moral high ground.

From LaVey's point-of-view, the idea that he was sullying his 'faith' was risible – he preached doubt. As he observed of the original great reformer, in an essay on the benefits of meditating on the toilet: 'Martin Luther dreamed up Protestantism while sitting on the toilet at Wittenburg monastery, and we all know what a big movement that became.'

Just as there are parallels with the Protestant Reformation, so there are echoes of the schism between Aleister Crowley and the Order of the Golden Dawn in 1900. While Anton

LaVey was no more a counterpart of S. L. Mathers than Michael Aquino was another Crowley, it was to Crowley that Aquino turned for inspiration in founding a new magical fraternity.

On 21 June 1975, Aquino invoked the Prince of Darkness – to him, and his fellow heretics, a very real entity. The result was *The Book of Coming Forth by Night*, a work of automatic writing mystically dictated – according to Aquino – by an ancient Egyptian god, in true Crowleyan fashion: 'Reconsecrate my Temple and my Order in the true name of Set. No longer will I accept the bastard title of a Hebrew fiend.'

Set, the Egyptian god of evil, was an older deity than Satan. Indeed, Aquino – who maintains that this makes Set a more important figure – also claims the name Satan derives from Set. According to Aquino, on that summer night Set passed the 'Mandate' of the Prince of Darkness's emissary on earth from LaVey to himself. Aquino was the second Great Beast (as predicted in Crowley's writings), heralding the Age of Set. The Black Pope responded by lampooning Aquino's new order, the Temple of Set, as 'Laurel and Hardy's *Sons of the Desert*'.

The Temple of Set undoubtedly filled an important ritualistic need for some people, and – as LaVey was tiring of the media spotlight – the stocky, vampiric figure of Aquino became the new media persona of Satanism, expertly taking on the Satanic villain role on TV and in the tabloid press. While LaVey was codifying twentieth-century Satanism in a manner far removed from traditional sorcery, Aquino founded a fraternity in the classic mould of the late nineteenth-century magical orders.

The Temple did parallel the Church of Satan's grottoes with its own 'pylons', and created a number of colourfully-titled 'orders': loose groupings of people with a shared interest in various esoteric subjects. Instead of Nietzschean philosophy and *noir*-based cynicism, however, the Setians' interests were characterised by obsessively-footnoted, quasi-academic essays on space travel and psychokinesis.

This should have made for an amicable divorce, with neither side needing anything more to do with the other. But Aquino placed the Church of Satan at the heart of the Temple of Set's heritage. It was vital for him to demonstrate Anton LaVey was a once-great magus who once truly believed in Satan but had fallen from grace (or should that be 'risen from vice'?), a twisted, deluded shadow of his former self. In fact, Aquino nursed an obsession with his erstwhile mentor for a very long time – even shadowing LaVey's divorce proceedings to prove the Church of Satan was 'bankrupt' (though it's not clear how one 'bankrupts' a philosophy).

Nevertheless, the High Priest of the Temple of Set is a vigorously prolific writer (Arthur Lyons, author of *Satan Wants You*, unkindly accuses him of having 'computer diarrhoea'), who explains his aims thus: 'The Temple of Set is determined to preserve the principles of individualism, but to add to it the evolutionary 'higher self' aspirations of Aleister Crowley's pre-O.T.O. philosophy of Thelema. Glorification of the ego is not enough; it is the complete psyche – the entire self or soul – which must be recognised, appreciated and actualized. The process by which this exaltation of the psyche is sought is called by the name Xeper [a term borrowed from Ancient Egyptian hieroglyphics that the Temple of Set define as 'becoming' or 'being'].' As a psyche-worshipping (as opposed to nature-worshipping) religion, the Temple are dedicated to the 'sense of self-consciousness that places humanity apart from and above all other known forms of life'.

While Michael Aquino was trying to present an image of the Church of Satan in terminal decline, it was actually expanding in a number of areas. One of the least expected came in an attempt to establish a beachhead in Europe, via a charismatic young man named Martin Lamers.

Lamers was an energetic Dutch actor and entrepreneur, whose early career saw him found a theatre in Amsterdam and bring the popular nude musical *Oh Calcutta!* to Holland. In 1971, the 24-year-old Lamers discovered *The Satanic Bible*, which so impressed him that he vowed to meet its author. By the time Lamers left his first conference with the Black Pope, he was clutching a charter empowering him to form the Church of Satan's first European grotto under his new title of Magister Lamers.

The Magistralis Grotto began operations in 1975, from a grand old abandoned Protestant church in the town of Etershiem. The following year, they relocated to the bright lights of Amsterdam – the capital not only of Holland, but of Dutch tolerance, with particularly liberal sex and drug laws.

Lamers bought two buildings in Amsterdam's notorious red light district: one to act as headquarters for the 'Kerk van Satan', while the other, backing onto it, was named Walburga Abbey. At Walburga Abbey, the public were charged an admission fee of ten guilders by 'students in theology'. Visitors were required to hire a glass from 'the ecclesiastical bureau of religious goods' at 25 guilders an hour, after which the drinks were free.

Drinks coaster from the Kerk van Satan's notorious Walburga Abbey.

The highlights of the Abbey were the monastic sisters who wore nuns' habits and no underwear. 'Congregations' watched the young women perform carnal ministrations ('symbolic union with Shaitan', after one of the ancient Hebrew names for the Devil) on the altar in return for religious 'donations'. These most often took the form of banknotes folded over their noses, which were then removed by the monastic sisters and clasped inside their vaginas. The Magistralis Grotto had around 50 dedicated members at its height who met for sabbats every eight days, while larger festivals attracted hundreds of Satanists from all over Europe.

However, Lamers was to find the authorities less than sympathetic to this novel evangelism. Though ostensibly tolerant, Dutch Calvinism can also reflect the dour moralism one expects of the Protestant tradition. However, in Holland's liberal climate it proved difficult to close down the Kerk van Satan on the basis of their sexualised heresies alone.

The authorities began their witch-hunt against the Magistralis Grotto not long after its foundation, persisting for most of a decade. An irate Lamers complained bitterly about police harassment, taking his complaint to the law courts in 1984. His lawyer asserted that, 'The police raids disturb rituals and are completely unacceptable.' The monastic sisters were not prostitutes, he explained, but spiritual students in a Satanic seminary, their grotto a site of sacred rituals.

'Like the cigar show and banana show?' asked the judge. 'Yes,' argued the lawyer, maintaining that female adherents peeling bananas or smoking cigars with their pussies was an inherently spiritual practice. It was typically flamboyant of Lamers to challenge Judeo-Christian conventions about sex and spirituality with banana-peeling showgirl-nuns – as if he was reviving the four-thousand-year-old sacred bordellos of Babylon and Sumeria, rather than running a vice racket.

Eventually, as with Al Capone, the authorities nailed the Dutch Satanist with tax laws. Lamers maintained the Kerk van Satan was a religion and, as such, should be tax exempt, including the earnings from Walburga Abbey. The authorities were not convinced – and neither, interestingly enough, was Anton LaVey. LaVey never claimed tax exemption for the Church of Satan, believing that all churches should be taxed out of existence – including, eventually, his own. (The Temple of Set, by way of contrast, has been exempt from taxation since its foundation, Aquino making much play of the official recognition of the Temple as a religion.)

After LaVey's eldest daughter, Karla, paid a visit to the Dutch grotto, her father considered revoking their charter over the taxation matter. The fact that he never did proved immaterial, as Lamers lost his tax evasion case in 1987, when the Kerk van Satan was legally declared a sex club instead of a religious institution. Lamers was ordered to pay back taxes to the substantial sum of ten million guilders, and sentenced to a year in prison for tax fraud. After his release, Lamers turned his back on high-profile devilment, moving into the international communications business. Shadows of his past continued to haunt him, however, scuppering a lucrative deal with the Antillian government in 1988.

Chequered past notwithstanding, Lamers now runs a successful telecommunications company in Monaco. When recently tracked by a Dutch reporter, he cagily dismissed his youthful Satanism as 'one big joke that somehow got out hand. There are still people who think I was serious. That I really represented Satan. But it was the time of kicking against the authorities, against religion.' Despite this, Lamers is still insistent that the Kerk van Satan was more of a serious cultural experiment than a mere whorehouse: as the former Magister explains, 'Lust is a big part of Satanism.'

Europe's new demonic manifestations were not limited to satellites of the Church of Satan. In Britain, Raymond Bogart claimed to have been following his own variety of Satanism since 1955, leading a number of covens on the bleak Lancashire moors. Bogart, who often went under the magical name of 'Ramon', has variously described himself as a psychiatrist, healer and ceiling plasterer. His religion has also gone under a variety of names: the New Order of Satanic Templars, the Northern Order of the Prince, and the Orthodox Temple of the Prince.

Bogart called his creed 'Benelism' ('Benel' being, according to Bogart, another name for Satan), which he defines as 'non-malefic Satanism'. 'We believe,' explained 'Ramon', 'that Satan, although thrown out of heaven, was reinstated as the son of God and is directly in contact with him. We are a bit evil now and again – if any of our coven members offends he is either reprimanded, given corporal punishment, or is expelled from his coven and cursed. But we only do this sort of thing for our members' own good. We really believe in love, the sanctity of woman as the child bearer and procreator of life, and in worshipping Satan our master. We don't go in for Black Masses or public intercourse or anything like that.'

All of which is faintly reminiscent of ancient Gnostic Satanism – though Bogart added Ashtaroth, Queen of Heaven, as a kind of mother goddess to create a 'triarchy' of deities and give affairs a faintly Wiccan slant. And alongside the usual occultic curricula (tarot cards, candle magic, exorcising poltergeists), Bogart's Benelists also engaged in witches' sabbats.

During that newly-liberated era, the 1970s, the dividing line between the sexual side of the occult underground and the kinkier fringes of the trendy 'swingers' scene was pretty hazy. The Benelists came in for unwanted tabloid attention, claiming their sabbats were nothing more than deviant sex orgies. It has to be said that some of Bogart's recruiting plugs – 'We are looking for just a few prospective members, couples and genuine females to become an integral part of our Temples.' – did sound suspiciously like contact ads.

In defence, Bogart felt moved to include the following disclaimer in Benelist literature: 'WE DO NOT indulge in human sacrifice or vampirism. We do not practise any perverse or anti-Christian rituals, nor do we curse people for not following our beliefs, There are NO orgies of Sex, Drink or Drugs, nor any devious or perverted practices.' (So where's the fun in all this, one might ask?)

The witch-hunters finally caught up with Bogart in 1988 on UK TV talk show *The Time . . . The Place*, where he was described by a journalist as being a Satanist with a conviction for child abuse. In his defence, Bogart wrote a letter stating, 'Nothing we do has the remotest connection with child sacrifices or sex orgies. About my past, I was falsely accused of illegal sex with a fifteen-year-old girl, and I have spent the last twenty or so years trying to erase this from my life.' But persistent press interest prevented him from erasing the incident, and Bogart went to ground. Little has been heard from the Benelists or their leader since 1990.

Raymond Bogart, founder of the Order of Satanic Templars, and friend.

In terms of the international occult scene, London-based Kenneth Grant has had a far greater impact. While Grant probably wouldn't describe himself as a Satanist, he is one of the most influential figures at the dark end of the magical spectrum often known as 'the left-hand path'. An occultic term which refers to black magic, it reflects how the inherent conformism of many societies labeled left-handed people as deviant outsiders (the word 'sinister' is derived from the Latin word for 'left'). The right-hand path – or 'white magic' – is regarded as reliable, masculine, obvious, while the left-hand path is subtle, unpredictable and feminine by nature.

Kenneth Grant first came to prominence in 1972 with *The Magical Revival*, a book that represented the first of his ongoing 'Typhonian' series. In total they form an epic exploration of the magical currents conventionally regarded as 'evil'. Partly traditional grimoire, partly disturbing self-psychoanalytic tract, partly surreal nightmare fiction – Grant's work has compelled and confounded a generation of occultists hoping to find dark secrets in his esoteric lore.

Grant is one of the most convincing of those occultists claiming to inherit the leadership of the Ordo Templi Orientis from Aleister Crowley. Grant studied under Crowley in the three years before his death in 1947, and documents suggest the Great Beast was grooming the young man as his successor. Grant's work examines lost gods, strange spiritual traditions and forbidden symbols, often leading him to some disreputable spiritual neighborhood where devils and demons might be expected to reside.

(Among the more improbable denizens Grant makes regular contact with are the vile gods of the Cthulhu Mythos – as invented by horror author H. P. Lovecraft and featured in the rites of the Church of Satan. The most popular actualised version of *The Necronomicon*, the fictional 'bible' of Lovecraft's Cthulhu cult, was published in the US in 1977 – known as the 'Simon edition', after the pseudonym of the occultist who edited it. For decades, the paperback edition has sat opposite *The Satanic Bible* on the makeshift altars of young would-be Satanists, or in the gesticulating hands of evangelical preachers who denounce such dangerous texts.)

Respected comic-book writer and occultist Alan Moore says of Kenneth Grant: 'It is hard to name another single living individual who has done more to shape contemporary Western thinking with regard to Magic. If we should

An idol of the Lovecraftian god Cthulhu.

dismiss him and his work, on what grounds should we do so? That he's dark? That he's mad as tits on a piranha? That he's weird? As if the world of the occult was the last place one should expect to find darkness, insanity or weirdness.' Moore also describes Grant, admiringly, as 'Magic's Mr Kurtz seeking his Heart of Darkness.'

Of course, there is more than one 'heart of darkness'. While Grant searched for his in esoteric works of the occult and the murky depths of his subconscious, others rifled through the garbage dump of recent history. Inevitably, some of these scavengers searching for an unholy grail came up with a crumpled old swastika. Correspondingly, some of the more flamboyant fascists of the day sniffed around the haunches of the occult scene, hoping for easy converts.

Some of the 1970s defectors from the Church of Satan tried to liven up their secondhand

LaVeyism with Nazi regalia. In Detroit, one John Amend renamed himself Seth-Typhon, began ritually strangling chickens, and founded the Shrine of the Little Mother. He maintained contact with another Church of Satan refugee named Michael Grumbowski, who took the title Seth-Klippoth in order to front his Order of the Black Ram. (Rather than any perverse Hebrew allusion, 'Seth' seems to be, in both cases, an alternative spelling of 'Set'.) Their chief connection was 'völkisch' racism, both groups fostering friendly relations with mystical neo-Nazi groups like New York's National Resistance Party and Canada's Odinist Movement. Gradually, the spiritual taboo of Satanism, with all its theatrical trappings, was moving toward the black-shirted political rituals of the Far Right.

THE SINFUL SISTERS OF WALBURGA ABBEY

Reminiscences of Sister N'aama of the Kerk van Satan.

I spoke to Sister N'aama – as she was known in the Kerk van Satan – in early 1999. She had been a priestess with the Amsterdam Grotto for some years, cleansing celebrants before rituals. Loquacious and passionate, she came from a Russian-Jewish background, encountering Jewish mysticism early on in her upbringing in the form of *The Kabbalah*, more important in her household than *The Torah*. This blend of Jewish childhood and Satanic adulthood gave her an intriguing perspective.

How did you first become involved with the Church of Satan?
By accident. I was a student and I went to Holland to finish studying psychology. I'd started the course in Tel Aviv but didn't finish it because I got married and because of the war in '73. So I came to Holland to finish the course. Then I decided to study law, but I was about 33 when I started and I didn't get any money from the government. Then I read an advert in the newspaper about live sex conversations. My voice is very good and I am a strong personality, so I went along. I had no idea at the time that it had anything to do with the Church of Satan.

I met Magister Martin Lamers, who was the head of the Satanic church. He welcomed me to his company and said it would be good if I wanted to work for them. He really helped me through my period of study because I had to live, I had to pay my rent, I had to eat. He said I had a very sexy voice, and I was one of the first ladies who did live sex conversations, and he paid me very well. I was able to pay my costs and the university.

There was a party in December and they invited me to go. I was invited by some of the girls who worked with me as telephone operators, and also worked in the Church of Satan, though I had no idea as they never

spoke about it. I went to the party, and met many people I knew, including Martin Lamers. They told me they were involved in the Church of Satan and they asked me what I thought of that. I liked these people – they'd been so nice and kind to me over the years, so how could I hate them? If you have a lot of magic in you, you can be a Satanist and have no idea. They said, 'You're honest, you're a good person, we'd very much like you to come to our church.' I was very frightened, but it was okay, they were very supportive, and I saw these people every day in the office. They invited me to a service, I went, and I'm not sorry to this day that I did.

Was there much involvement between the Amsterdam grotto and Church of Satan headquarters in San Francisco?
Yes. Everything went through the Magister Martin Lamers, he was the high priest, and he spent a year in San Francisco under Anton LaVey's wing. We were involved with several other Satanic churches, but we always had problems with them. They were always coming to Amsterdam and they always caused trouble. We were the only aboveground Satanic church in Europe, the others were working underground. They were very weird people and I didn't like them. They

An infernal rite at the Kerk van Satan, presided over by Magister Martin Lamers.

always came with offerings of animal blood and we never sacrificed animals. We loved animals. On 30 April we celebrated the Satanic New Year [Walpurgisnacht]. It's also the Queen's birthday, so Amsterdam is upside down then. We partied all day and people from all over Europe would come to our Satanic church.

People from Germany, Belgium, France came and they wanted to bring sacrifices. We made our own blood from ketchup, syrup or whatever. Sometimes we worked with blood, but in a magical way. So if a girl was having a period she might keep the blood, freeze it and use it for a sacrifice in her house. But in the church we never used human blood or animal blood. These people came from outside, once or twice, and committed animal sacrifices and it got us a bad name. Everybody from our side was very upset. I hated it. Our Magister Martin Lamers hated it, but they wouldn't listen, and said they couldn't have a Satanic New Year without blood sacrifice. That's why, in the last years of the Church of Satan, only our Magister was allowed to conduct the ceremonies.

What was the connection between the Church of Satan and Walburga Abbey?

There were girls, some were witches, some priestesses, some nymphs, who worked there. The Abbey was very closely connected to the Church of Satan. For us the Abbey was another temple. It was a place where we conducted ceremonies, Satanic witches' ceremonies. The men were not allowed to fuck the women – the women were doing sexual magic on the men. Sexual magic is one of the highest spiritual ideals for the Satanist.

Was Walburga Abbey a business?

All they had to pay for was whatever they wanted from a big menu. The drinks are free, you can come in off the street and have a beer, pay five guilders entry, and you've found a very special place. This was no average whorehouse or strip club. They did shows. They could get banana shows for instance, where they put a banana in their pussy and the man was allowed to eat it. Or they did tricks with dildos. We had a five-guilder note, the man would put it on his face and lean back over the bar, then the girl would pick it up using the lips of her pussy. Then the taxman came and said, 'This is a whorehouse.' We said, 'No, it's part of the Church of Satan.' Then they said, 'You owe us money', and they started to try and calculate it. But we had no profits because we were not running it for a profit.

And this brought about the collapse of the Amsterdam Church of Satan?

Yes. In the last Satanic New Year we had a huge party and it was really great. I was there at the private party in the evening on the table. We had dinner on me! We had men dressed as equerries, in those beautiful clothes and wigs, walking around. They put me on the table naked, they put all sorts of salads all over my body, and they ate off me with a spoon. It was absolutely fantastic. For me it was the biggest compliment you could think of.

Later on we went onto the roof where we had a big party for all of the members of the Church of Satan. Then there was an attempted murder on our Magister. It was a woman who tried to seduce him. I found her rather strange because she wasn't a member and wasn't known from the Abbey. But she wanted to seduce our high priest. That night she tried to cut his balls off. He had to go to hospital and have surgery. It was very dramatic.

Why did she attack him?

She said her sister had become pregnant from one of our people and became involved in black magic and the Church of Satan. It absolutely wasn't true. She said, 'Because of Martin Lamers, my sister became a prostitute and a junkie.' But I'd never seen her sister and I'd been there for years. This woman was fantasising. Maybe she just wanted to become involved. You've no idea how many people tried to get involved in the Church of Satan but we wouldn't let them in. We'd talk to them, tell them to read books. We'd never seen this woman before. She was mad, she really wanted to kill Martin.

Then the taxmen came and we started really getting into trouble. Then Martin called us and said, 'We have no choice – we're going to have to close down.' Then he had to run away as they tried to arrest him, he left Holland during the night and went to France or Switzerland. They arrested his lawyer, Louis Velleman, who had become known as 'the Devil's advocate' because he worked for us. The taxmen were very cruel to all of our members. They went through all of our papers and destroyed a lot of them. Louis Velleman was in gaol, they broke into our offices as if we were the Mafia or something.

The press wanted to see us destroyed, the Christians were taking over again, it was very sad. Then the Queen said to Martin Lamers, 'Okay, you can come back to Holland if you throw in the towel and give up the Satanic cause.' So he did, and they put him in gaol anyway and he joined Louis. One weekend Louis Velleman was allowed to go home for the weekend, and he never went back, so now he lives on the underground.

Do you look back on the Church of Satan with affection?

Yes. Very much. I had two 'comings-out'. I had the coming-out as gay. Bette Midler came to Amsterdam and seeing her performing suddenly made me feel free to be gay. Many years later I met her in my synagogue on a high holiday and I said, 'I'm so grateful for what you've done for me.' Then I had the coming-out to be myself. Becoming free from a lot of pain that I'd been carrying because of all these fucking wars, and all this chasing after my people. I thought, 'Now you can never chase me again. You'll never get me. You can say what you want about Judaism – I'm so strong I can handle it.' The Church of Satan gave me power, power to come out and become myself.

Not Just Some Hebrew Fiend

**An afternoon with David Austen,
High Priest of the UK Temple of Set.**

When I visited David Austen in 1993, he was living in a flat in south London with his boyfriend and cats. Portly and congenial, with a soft West Country accent, he's a million miles away from most people's image of a Satanist. Involved with the UK occult scene for many years, Austen has a reputation for spreading gossip (particularly via the press), earning him a number of enemies. However, his usual defence, that he simply believes in speaking openly, was confirmed by the following interview.

Why did you join the Temple of Set?

For many years I'd been interested in the aspect of Set as a being or entity. Before I joined the Temple I had my own magical group with a couple of other people. We looked at the Prince of Darkness as something that occurs in every society or religious faction – there's always an opposite to the deity who they say is 'Good'. We came to the conclusion that we would refer to this entity as 'the Dark Lord', and he would be anthropoid but faceless. Looking at the concept as a diamond, Satan or Lucifer were just other facets of that diamond, purely ways of achieving workings which encompassed the whole.

So, if you were particularly drawn to the gothic Satanist current, fine, use rituals based around that. In our Temple of Darkness you could equally have Satanists, Setians, or followers of other paths, the principle being that the whole thing is a psychodrama anyway. Magic is basically the Western version of yoga. Everything that happens in magic happens first in your head.

Why do people join the Temple of Set?

They've read the introductory literature, they're seeking a philosophy, and they agree with ours. We then say, 'Show us what you've got.' They can write a magical CV of their own know-how, or they can meet a member of the priesthood who can then sponsor their application. That way you can find out what you've got, so you don't discover six or seven months in that your new initiate is sacrificing bugerigars or whatever. They then find they make a circle of friends. In the British scene we operate around pubs – not like the Salvation Army, I hasten to add, we sit in the pub and have a magical discussion.

The most important thing in the Temple for the first degrees is communication: we operate electronic mail networks and use a bulletin board service.

What does Set represent?

Basically the individual's psychic or mental energy – what they would call in Ancient Egypt the 'neter'. The 'me' that is talking to you is doing so through a series of meat cantilever systems and so forth. When that perishes or passes, instead of going into the cosmic whole – becoming one with the goddess or whatever – by sheer force of will the existence of that magician's mind can be sustained. This is the whole idea of the Temple of Set, and we use the word 'xeper', meaning 'to become', to define this. Set, whom we define as the Prince of Darkness, is a force about which you could say, 'As we are now, he once was.' When you die your force can survive.

David Austen, Setian Magister, and ritual accessories.

Where does the Temple stand politically?

We don't tie anybody to any particular political belief system. It is liberal in as far as it encourages individual input, and everybody's participation is important. We do have a system whereby we are a legal body, therefore we have to keep one foot in the material world, as it were – being registered as a legal church we have bylaws within which we operate. We have all races in the Temple. We have a couple of black people, I saw someone with the name Patel, which suggests a certain ethnic origin. Even in a sexual sense we operate across the board. These things just don't come into it in the Temple workings.

We don't rule out anything as long as it's legal. For instance, you could have a sexual working with two males – but they would have to be over the age of consent. Both parties must also be consenting, which is the Temple rule as well as the law of the land. We've got a couple of members of the British National Party at the moment in Britain. We have a couple of members of the Socialist Workers Party as well. It doesn't make any difference – they interact and discuss and politics doesn't come into it.

You have been accused of feeding 'witch hunts' led by the gutter press – how do you react to that?

They give me more credit than I'm due. The 'gutter press', as it's called, keeps people on their toes, thus I have respect for it because, while it's all hype, they do reveal some of the bad eggs in society. There was a leak in the Temple of Set which could only have occurred at priesthood level, and the gutter press were coming up with material that was directly from the membership roster. At the time all this was happening I was only a second-degree adept and wouldn't have had access to this material.

Set, ancient Egyptian god of evil. Portrait by Tim.

We had one woman coming over from the *Sunday Sport*, which I'd never read in my life. It was around '87-'88. She sat with our books and photocopied all the material – I prefer to give the press the benefit of the doubt and give them the facts. They came up with this cock and bull story about human sacrifice and cursing kids. She actually came back with a photographer and wanted me to pose naked in the East London Cemetery. I am not the world's most body beautiful, it was on a November night, it was nine below zero, and I had no intention of doing so. But the Temple's taken the pragmatic view that we're here, we exist, and people are interested in us.

What about the reports that you witnessed a human sacrifice?

Many years ago I was involved with a Wiccan group in Exeter, in the late sixties. I don't have any real recollection of what happened, and a lot of the report comes from words put in my mouth in a 1982 story. I was naive and thought reporters were nice people, and it was put to me: 'Could you have seen a human sacrifice?' I said, 'I couldn't really tell you. I was so zonked out of my box on the herbal potions that they could have been doing anything.' There you go – I'd given them *carte blanche* to say what they wanted. There was a guy on the phone the other day trying to get me to say that the Temple believes in human sacrifice. He's writing for a gutter tabloid where the readership are not going to accept the Hindu principle that you can sacrifice a leaf and a glass of water.

In some ways I think I was just too trusting – there never was any case of big bucks. I work it on balance these days, and try to be more selective. I've done two or three appearances on Sky TV because they tell you where they're coming from. The bulk of the hostility directed towards me is jealousy – the fact is that the Temple is very successful.

Is the Temple of Set a moral organisation?

We expect our people to abide by the laws of the country. The morals are down to the individual. There are guidelines set down in the Temple's bylaws – obviously you don't go around chopping up people or indulging in cannibalism. There is no basis for blood sacrifice at the end of the day. You start chopping up animals and you're out the door.

The overall colour of the Temple is rather dark though, isn't it?

I think we do tend to go in for the sinister and unusual. The theatrical side of it is obviously important. Dr Aquino, when he did a lot of TV, did appear rather theatrical, which may have sent out the wrong vibes. When I appear on TV I wear a clerical dog-collar and a blue shirt, which is a theatrical point. You then become the centre of attention and draw the camera, at which point you can deliver your message. Much of this sinister imagery is still a hangover from the Church of Satan. There is a certain tendency towards gothic theatrics. We say we're Satanists, but we're actually using a name far older than Satan. In *The Book of Coming Forth by Night*, Set says He doesn't want to be known by the name of a Hebrew fiend. But if we say we're Satanists it makes people sit up and say, 'Oh, my God!' It gives you a starting point for a conversation, or they run away.

What's the most impressive thing you've seen through your involvement with magic?

It's very much a personal experience. I recognised three Setians to the priesthood last year and that was a fantastic experience. You could really feel the ritual chamber fill up with a presence. I summoned Set and the visual effects were great. As I perform the priesthood ritual, I reach this one point where I ask the initiates if they accept this doom – becoming a member of the priesthood. As I pointed my finger at each one the incense flared and my amethyst ring glowed. It was a perfect, flawless ritual. That was fantastic, but it would mean nothing if you weren't there.

Magic is a mind-enhancing thing that serves the same purpose as these different yoga systems. It's our Western yoga system that has been suppressed by the Church. The philosophy of Satanism I follow is a modern invention, relevant to the modern age. We look at it from a fairly scientific, balanced point of view. It's a good working philosophy.

RAISING HELL

f fundamentalist Christians were unhappy with the birth of cinema in the early twentieth century, they were positively livid with post-1960s trends in popular music. When the dust had settled, they and their reactionary allies prepared to fight back, to reclaim the Western World – particularly the USA – for the Church. It was a crusade that gathered steam throughout the 1970s, reaching a climax in the following decade.

Grassroots churches and Christian broadcasting empires marshalled their armies of ignorance. While the various Christian coalitions failed in their efforts to get an evangelical preacher elected to the White House, the most powerful post on earth, they found an ally when Ronald Reagan became president in 1980. Evangelical Christianity was ready for a showdown with its ideological adversaries: humanism, liberalism, New Age mysticism and, of course, Satanism. And the world of rock music would provide one of the main battlegrounds.

As early as 1956, a Pentecostal preacher in Nottingham, England, addressed the rock 'n' roll 'problem' from his pulpit: 'The effect of rock and roll is to turn young people into devil worshippers; to stimulate self-expression through sex, to impair nervous stability and destroy the sanctity of marriage.'

Early criticisms of rock music attacked the form in terms that would be dismissed today as hysterically racist. In 1956 the *Daily Mail*, Britain's favourite reactionary rag, declared that rock 'n' roll had 'something of the African tom tom and voodoo dance', adding the following day that it 'is despicable. It is tribal. And it is from America. It follows rag-time, blues, dixie jazz, hot cha cha and boogie woogie, which surely originated in the jungle. We sometimes wonder whether it is the negro's revenge.'

Over the ensuing decades, things seemed to get considerably worse. Elvis Presley, once a prime target for moral condemnation, was described by evangelical author Jeff Godwin as 'like a shy, stuttering kid next to the rampaging, satanic, sex-stuffed rock rapists around today'. This shift – from a blanket condemnation of all rock 'n' roll as evil to a dewy-eyed nostalgia for the innocence of the 1950s – was a general trend as the anti-rock movement picked up speed.

Thirty years on, however, a psychologist from Ontario called Dr Walter Wright was still warning of those tribal rhythms: 'Rock has an incessant throbbing beat, the same beat that people in primitive cultures use in their demonic rites and dances. If the beat is monotonous enough it can induce a state of hypnosis.'

The fundamentalists and their crackpot allies attributed powers to rock music that were inherently supernatural, sorcery wrapped in a thin veil of pseudoscientific gibberish. As with Charles Manson, the appeal of rock stars was described in terms of the paranormal and hypnosis instead of sexual magnetism. During the 1980s, the supposedly chief paranormal aspect of rock music would be coined 'back-masking' – of which more later.

Rock 'n' roll was by now the most high-profile entertainment form in the Western world. In many cases, it not only depicted but celebrated sin, sex and drugs, challenging the Christian ethos of obedience, ignorance and abstinence. As such, it could be portrayed as a threat to the sanctity of the family, summoning up the irrational forces that emerge whenever good Christians are persuaded their children are at risk. As Jeff Godwin put it, 'Rebellion is the devil's trademark . . . when destroying a family. Satan and his demons continually throw more rebellion, rebellion, rebellion onto the raging family fires and rock music is the gasoline that feeds the flames.'

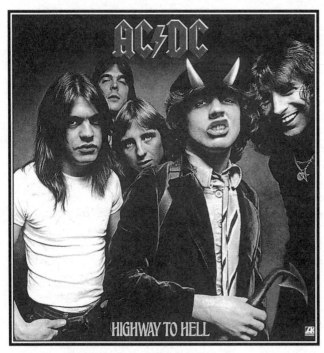

AC/DC, good-time bad boys 'on the highway to Hell'.

Inevitably, perhaps, heavy metal found itself at the forefront of the war between rock and the Church. Since its inception by British bands Black Sabbath and Led Zeppelin, heavy metal has always had a heady whiff of brimstone about it. As the new genre took off, and metal bands began filling sports stadiums with fans in the 1970s, the Devil increasingly symbolised their bombastic form of rebellion. The sign of the devil's horns – index and little fingers extended from a fist – replaced the peace sign as youth culture's salute. Here was an enemy the fundamentalist Christians could understand.

While heavy metal was born in Britain, it soon developed an international character. It's difficult to overstate the influence of the popular Australian band AC/DC on the growth of the genre – formed in 1973 by two Glaswegian immigrants, brothers Malcolm and Angus Young, they quickly perfected a distinctive style of rough, greasy, alcohol-fuelled rock 'n' roll. The comparative restraint of Black Sabbath and mystical hippie trappings of Led Zeppelin were out-shouted by AC/DC's saloon-bar humour and clap-clinic morality: the crude, hard-drinking, womanising ethos that became central to heavy metal's character.

It's difficult to believe AC/DC ever took anything seriously, living their lives with an overgrown-schoolboy smirk plastered across their faces. Still, the Devil was a regular in their bar-room world. In their contempt for traditional values and Christian morality, AC/DC not only expected damnation but welcomed it. 'Hell Ain't A Bad Place To Be!' shrieked one lyric, and the boys were willing to explore every pleasurable indulgence on the 'Highway to Hell', announcing on the song 'Hell's Bells' that, 'If you're into evil you're a friend of mine.' This was coarse, blue-collar Satanism of sorts – a light-hearted wink at the Patron Saint of Sinners, with a bottle of beer in one grubby hand and a cigarette hanging from the corner of their mouths.

While AC/DC created their working men's club version of infernal amorality, an American band took heavy metal deep into the realms of theatrical glamour. KISS was formed in 1972 with the intention of becoming a 'heavy metal Beatles'. Adopting heavy theatrical make-up, extravagant, explosive stageshows and lyrics that presented a comic-book version of the rock 'n' roll lifestyle, KISS made heavy metal into a merchandisable product.

To the cynical outsider, these fire-breathing, tongue-distending showmen looked like nothing more than pantomime demon kings. But to their adolescent target audience they were the essence of demonic defiance. As guitarist Gene Simmons once put it, 'We wanted to look like we crawled out from under a rock somewhere in hell. We wanted parents to look at us and instantly want to throw up.' Satanist Thomas Thorn, frontman of the Electric Hellfire Club, now cites KISS as chief inspiration for forming a band. 'KISS was rebellion incarnate,' says Thorn, 'and we identified with that in the same way we would later align ourselves with Lucifer and his rebellion against God.'

KISS lunch boxes, comics, socks, masks and even a cartoon show flooded the market, bringing the KISS carnival into the heart of high-school culture. In a 1977 Gallup poll, US fans voted KISS the most popular act in the country. Heavy metal had become the accepted popular culture for the adolescent youth of America. While always at pains to deny any links with Satanism, the youth appeal of KISS unquestionably rested on the marketing of their demonic

KISS – heavy metal's pantomime demon kings.

image, rather than their largely innocuous music. (Their 1990s song 'Unholy' – the promotional video for which features a choir of seemingly possessed kids – made that appeal fairly explicit, an attempt by the ageing Barnum and Baileys of rock to recapture past glories.)

Most parents regarded the likes of AC/DC and KISS as dumb, loud, tasteless – perhaps a little unhealthy, but not overtly dangerous. The fundamentalist Christians saw a darker threat. AC/DC, they said, stood for 'Away from Christ/the Devil Comes', while KISS were 'Kids in the Service of Satan'. Their outrage became incandescent by the mid-1980s, as KISS's popularity faded and a quartet of preening Hollywood 'glam rockers' named Mötley Crüe took centre-stage. As bible-basher Jeff Godwin explained, 'The Motleys wear tattered rags on and off stage. Their hair-dos look like the mangy pelts of rabid wolves. Their music is an unbridled, unbroken hymn to Lucifer and his legions.' (Godwin really should have been the band's press agent.)

Mötley Crüe attracted the ire of the righteous with their second album, *Shout at the Devil*, released in 1983. It was a deliberate, somewhat tacky attempt to create a little Satanic controversy, but it was a commercial breakthrough for the band.

Their attitude was typical of the less cerebral musicians who toy with the shock value of Satanism. 'We believe in the theory of Good and Evil,' opined bass player Nikki Sixx sagely in an interview, 'but, as for Satan and Black Magic and that kind of stuff, we really don't see any validity in it.' 'We're more into just raisin' hell and having a good time,' added vocalist Vince Neil, helpfully. 'Yeah,' summarised Sixx, 'drinking and fucking and doing drugs y'know.'

Still, such basic hedonism is many a good Christian's idea of how the Devil makes work for idle hands. To comat the supposedly 'Satanic' influence of hard-lining heavy metal bands, the 1980's saw the proliferation of de-programming centres. Run by fundamentalist Christians, these institutions endeavour to 'de-metal' and 'de-punk' troublesome teens, emptying their heads of the evil music and filling them with good Christian values. These Orwellian Sunday schools are populated by the children of desperate parents who feel their kids are beyond all control – but the treatment can also be recommended by secular law courts.

The most high-profile of the de-programming centres is the Freedom Village, founded and named – apparently without a trace or irony – by the Reverend Fletcher A. Brothers. 'Rock Music is one of the major factors in the downfall of today's youth! What's wrong with Rock Music? Everything!' announces Brothers, on the back jacket of his unintentionally hilarious *Rock Report*. 'Most of you kids are here because you couldn't keep things out of one of the holes in your head or holes in your body that were going to hurt you,' Brothers explains to a room full of new recruits. 'You live like the Devil because of the things that he put in your mind. The bottom line is he found a tremendous vehicle to get his ideas into one of the holes in your body – namely your ears – and that's through music.'

Each day starts at 6 a.m. for the 120 or so inmates of the Freedom Village, with prayer. During the year-long training course, girls must wear long skirts and take home-making classes while boys study carpentry and attend lessons on manliness. Outside media is carefully monitored – with no pop music and TV only on a Sunday – while the delivery of fundamentalist propaganda is both vehement and incessant.

Brothers has now established a Freedom Village in Canada and broadcasts his message across the USA via daily radio and TV shows. In theory, such 'de-programming' centres would never receive the blessing of the authorities in a nation where Church and State are separated by a Constitution such as that of the USA. In fact, fundamentalist Christian police officers – known in the field as 'cult cops' – produced ill-researched handbooks and delivered melodramatic seminars promoting various Satanic panics. The Union City Police Department, for example, produced a handbook entitled *Punk Rock and Heavy Metal: the Problem/One Solution* in 1985, while state probation officers in California founded the 'Back in Control' centre which advised police departments on the dangers of occultism in rock music.

The reason for all this was a covert alliance between evangelical Christianity and the American political establishment during the mid-1980s. In 1986, Fletcher Brothers took a busload of his charges to Washington, D.C. Sadly, it wasn't a jolly outing away from the Freedom Village, but a Senate hearing where the kids testified they had been 'abused by rock music'. These became known as the 'porn rock' hearings – although the term was beloved of Fundamentalists, the hearings were instigated by a secular organisation known as the Parents Music Resource Centre.

The PMRC centred around high-profile 'Washington wives' from across the political spectrum, notably Susan Baker, wife of Republican Treasury Secretary James Baker, and Tipper Gore, wife of Democratic Vice President-to-be Al Gore. The group portrayed themselves as concerned mothers who – First Amendment be damned – were determined to curtail the excesses of the recording industry. The PMRC were always at pains to distance themselves from their evangelical allies, but not everybody was convinced.

Anti-establishment musician Frank Zappa, testifying at the hearings, suggested the PMRC were merely fundamentalists in secular drag and asked if they considered themselves 'a cult'. Certainly the group enjoyed the unqualified support of Fletcher Brothers, and made frequent reference to material provided by evangelical Christian sources. Most tellingly, the PMRC marketed a 'Satanism Research Packet' containing 'clippings of crimes connected with Satanism and Heavy Metal music', largely derived from evangelical sources.

The PMRC initially lobbied for a system of labels alerting parents to the possible content of a record album. Those that featured profanity, homosexuality or suicide would receive an 'X' sticker, while those with occultic content would get an 'O'. 'Stickering' was finally adopted voluntarily by the music industry when they were threatened with a mandatory system in eighteen states, but a blanket 'Parental Advisory' sticker was adopted to cover the full multitude of sins.

Of course, such labels only served to increase the appeal of the product, with many teenagers refusing to buy recordings that hadn't earnt a Parental Advisory sticker. It even became a rebellious icon, with some teens wearing the label as a T-shirt design. The whole 'porn rock' affair ground to a halt once the PMRC seemed to feel their mission was accomplished, its members having more politically-advantageous crusades to fight. Christian fundamentalism was left out in the cold, while many young people felt more deeply cynical than ever about those who governed them.

The fundamentalists clearly needed a more powerful weapon against the Satanic rock conspiracy, and soon found one. It had its roots in 1983, when Texan evangelist Jacob Aranza published his book *Backward Masking Unmasked* – the earliest full 'exposé' of backward masking, or 'back-masking', on rock records.

The back-masking myth contends that messages recorded backwards and camouflaged with music can enter a person's mind without them knowing it, as a subliminal form of brainwashing. Like the hypnotic effects of the 'druid beat' they warned against two decades before, it had no basis in science whatsoever – the Christians were describing sorcery.

Some bands grabbed the opportunity, seeing it as a shorthand method of establishing Satanic credentials. Mötley Crüe got in early, embellishing the sleeve of their 1983 *Shout at the Devil* album with the legend, 'This record may contain backward masking.' With a degree of perceptiveness rare to them, few fundamentalists took this bait, searching instead for evidence of a secret 'back-masking conspiracy'.

Backward recording had been practised by studio engineers and producers since the 1960s, when many musicians were looking for ways to create weird sounds for experimental recordings. However, proponents of the myth were looking specifically for messages that supported their idea of music as a Satanic propaganda tool. It did not take long to find them. Alongside general messages of support for Satan, the 'experts' found more specific suggestions, such as smoking marijuana. In 1986, evangelist Jim Brown of Ohio led 75 young people in the mass burning of records containing the theme tune to *Mr Ed*, the popular TV comedy show about a talking horse. If the song 'A Horse is a Horse' was played backwards, Brown explained, the message 'Someone sung this song for Satan' could be clearly heard.

The most controversial back-masked messages were those advising heavy metal fans to commit suicide. Why 'Satanic' rock stars wanted their fans to kill themselves was never explained – but it

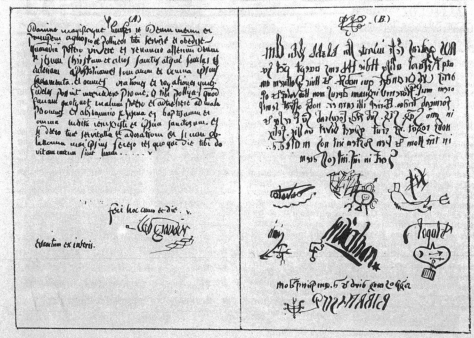

Satanic pact from the seventeenth century. This contract with the Devil is supposedly written backwards –
in the 1980s, demonic messages in reverse were believed to be recorded on vinyl, rather than parchment.

tapped into concerns about rising suicide rates among teenagers, giving a simple answer to a complex problem. It was also a godsend for Christian fundamentalists, who could attack rock music without appearing to attack freedom of speech. As there was no hope of the back-masking myth being accepted as fact in any scientific environment, its testing ground was to be the law courts.

Several attempts were made in the early 1980s to prosecute artists and record companies for causing harm with heavy metal records – all dismissed by sceptical judges before they reached court. But in 1985, two young men in Nevada made a suicide pact after a heavy marijuana, beer and heavy metal session, then shot themselves. One survived and – along with his devoutly Christian family – decided to pursue the band who recorded the album the pair had been repeatedly playing on the fateful night through the courts. The family's lawyers claimed the trigger for the suicide pact had been a subliminal message on the record urging the listener to 'Do it'. (Once again, why this should translate as an urging to 'off' oneself was never explained.) This pseudoscientific angle persuaded the judge there was a case to answer and, in 1990, the historic trial finally began.

The band in question was Judas Priest, an archetypal British heavy metal outfit who rose to international prominence in the late 1970s. Despite their blasphemous-sounding name the band made no use of demonic imagery, achieving their success with a studs-and-leather biker image, high-pitched guitars and even higher-pitched vocals. The judge blocked a number of attempts by the prosecution to introduce Satanic 'evidence' or 'experts'.

While psychologists for both sides conducted increasingly technical arguments, the trial teetered into the realms of farce. Judas Priest found some subliminals of their own, identifying phrases in their music like 'It's so fishy, perhaps I'll own it' to demonstrate how it was possible to 'discover' anything you wanted to in records played backwards. The judge ruled in favour of the band and their record label, CBS. The fundamentalists had lost the first round, but they were not ready to give up the fight – the next case would be against a rock performer whose Satanic credentials were, as far as they were concerned, impeccable.

Since leaving Black Sabbath, Ozzy Osbourne had pursued a successful solo career. Astute enough to see that much of Sabbath's appeal had derived from their Satanic flavour, Osbourne recorded albums with demonic titles like *Talk of the Devil* and *The Ultimate Sin*. Beneath the packaging, however, there was little Satanic substance in the music itself, 'Mr Crowley', the most satanic song on their album *The Blizzard of Oz,* is good fun – Crowley is invited to ride Ozzy's 'white horse', which is 'symbolic of course' of sex, or possibly drugs – but it displays a knowledge of its subject matter that's basic at best. Ironically, this album track is followed by 'No Bone Movies', with anti-porn lyrics which many Christian evangelists would enthusiastically support.

The now-portly Osbourne, ever the affable hellraiser, was less concerned with occultic devils than with his own personal demon: alcoholism. 'How can people accuse me of conjuring up the Devil?' he reflected. 'I have enough trouble conjuring myself out of bed in the morning.' But the Bible-bashers remained unconvinced, with one fundamentalist preacher estimating that 'a few thousand demons already live in his body'. In 1991, Osbourne's critics would see their quarry in court, faced with an accusation that back-masking on a song from *Blizzard of Oz* caused a young American fan to shoot himself in the head. The song in question had the sinister title of 'Suicide Solution' – despite his constant flirtations with devilish imagery, however, it was about the perils of the demon drink, to whom Osbourne had formerly given himself over too wholeheartedly.

Ex-Black Sabbath vocalist Ozzy Osbourne (left) plays a Christian preacher in the 1986 heavy metal horror-satire Trick or Treat.

As with the Judas Priest case, all efforts to have back-masking recognised as an authentic phenomenon failed. Several evangelical authors tried to sustain their attack by broadening their targets – Jacob Aranza dedicated two books to identifying back-masking in country and western; Rob Mackenzie may have attracted more sympathy when he conjectured whether the 'I' in Barry Manilow's 'I Write the Songs' was Satan Himself – but the whole back-masking hysteria smacked too obviously of desperation.

The back-masking myth has only ever prevailed in the most perverse manner. The 1990 UK Broadcasting Act incorporated clauses outlawing subliminal messages on radio and TV –

even though a subsequent 1992 report from the British Psychological Society concluded, 'even when backwards messages are present in a tape or record, LISTENERS ARE NOT AFFECTED BY THEM whether or not these messages are subliminal, because the meaning cannot be perceived by the listener'. (The emphasis is theirs.)

Indeed, if subliminal messages could be used to brainwash the recipient, the Church would have incorporated them into hymns centuries ago, while governments and advertising agencies would long ago have mastered the technique. (Though in fact, research by respected professional hypnotist Dick Sutphen has shown that evangelical preachers have been studying and using hypnotic techniques in their sermons for many years.) That fundamentalist Christians were prepared to make themselves look so foolish, by promoting such a dubious myth, speaks volumes about the climate of fear and ignorance they wished to nourish. In the words of British evangelist Robert Skynner, its success would have been the first step toward proving all rock music was 'a carefully masterminded plan instigated by Satan himself'.

In the meantime, however, another fundamentalist myth propagated in the 1980s was enjoying much greater success, and inflicting much greater damage. At the same time, unforseen by Christian activists, a new generation of rock musicians were emerging who would embrace, rather than protest at, accusations of Satanism.

BRANDY OF THE DAMNED

The Genesis of Black Metal

The popularity of heavy metal rock acts in the 1970s gradually started to work against them, as audiences associated them with big business rather than rebellion.

Punk rock took full advantage of this, presenting itself as distanced from the mainstream while keeping an eye on the masochistic liberals watching from the gallery. Punk proved to be little more than a series of pretentious tantrums – its failure and hypocrisy are apparent in its latter-day social acceptability, with punk retrospectives in art galleries, punk postcards for London tourists, and glib media pundits boasting of punk pasts as if they were Pulitzer prizes.

However, punk's increasing dominance of the youth-rebellion market made it almost impossible for heavy metal bands to get a record deal in the late 1970s and early 1980s. The scene would eventually strike back with what became known as the New Wave of British Heavy Metal. Every bit as gritty as – and infinitely less precious than – their punk rivals, these new acts also turned their back on the bland hard rock of the stadium bands. Unlike the punks, however, these greasy, byronic misfits were not interested in cider-fuelled anarcho-politics, but nurtured a passion for testosterone-soaked fantasy, dark melodrama and tawdry sex.

Heavy metal had, by this point, moved out of the Californian sunshine and cosmic otherworldliness of the late 1970s, back into the rainy alleyways and gloomy English pubs that were its birthplace. Satanism had also secured a prominent position in the iconography of the New Wave. For most bands, it was nothing more than an exciting image that sold records. But the Devil could be a risky card to play – as is His nature, for every potential fan He attracted, He also incited hostility. Iron Maiden's 1982 album *Number of the Beast*, which sported a leering Satan on the cover, proved to be their commercial breakthrough. The title track, like the eponymous 'Black Sabbath', describes stumbling across an horrific Satanic ritual. Despite bassist Steve Harris' limp insistence that '"Number of the Beast" is an anti-Satan song', the record not only took them to the top of the charts but also to the top of the hate list for Christian anti-rock campaigners.

The band were more than a little complicit in this, hyping the album with spooky stories about its cursed conception: mysterious power failures, radio interference and exploding amps apparently plagued the recording sessions; most sinister of all, the producer had a car crash at the time, his repair bill coming to £666.

More pertinently, as Anton LaVey once noted, you cannot employ Satanism without promoting it. True to this dogma, other young bands utilised Satan not as a throwaway reference but as the core of their identity. Their new sub-genre would become known as black metal, after a 1982 album title by the band Venom. In many ways black metal is the musical genre that never was – its style is basically the rawest, most malignant heavy metal, with a strong occult element in the lyrical content. The Satanic tag attracted a strange regiment of muscians who wished to test the musical and moral boundaries of what the rock business deemed acceptable.

Underrated occult-rock pioneers Witchfynde, recently reformed in the wake of the black metal renaissance.

Prominent among these bands was Witchfynde, founded in 1976. They never enjoyed much success, and were almost universally spurned by the music press, but some of their material retains a darkly naive charm – especially on their 1980 debut *Give 'Em Hell*. According to press releases of the time, 'It is no secret that guitarist Montalo does more than dabble in the occult and that both he and the band draw upon these sources for guidance.' The rock press cast scorn upon these claims, but there are moments on Witchfynde's early records when an ominous, almost baroque power oozes through their gruff cheesiness. In 1982, however, several band members disappeared – reputedly under sinister circumstances – and Witchfynde finally split, dejected by their lack of success, several years later.

Angelwitch, a south London-based band, enjoyed a much more agreeable relationship with the press than Witchfynde, and their first, eponymously-titled album, released in 1980, is regarded as a minor classic among black metal aficionados. Their style – pre-emptive of 'thrash metal' – possessed an inventiveness and intricacy that survives the limitations under which it was recorded. Though they disassociated themselves from the darker edges of the occult – notably in the song 'Hades Paradise', in which they accuse Satanists of being 'sick in the head' – there were suggestions that Angelwitch's occultic roots were darker than they would have their audience believe.

Other acts toyed with Satanic imagery, but once they attracted the 'black metal' tag tended to insist their Satanism was pure theatre. Typical of these were Satan, and the powerful if predictable Grim Reaper. More colourful were Cloven Hoof, who debuted in 1984 wearing garish face paint and leotards, after re-naming themselves 'Earth, Air, Fire and Water'. The idea of a comic-book demonic band had the potential to take up where KISS left off – but the theatrical budget was non-existent, and the band took the stage looking like psychedelic fairies.

Most unusual in their approach were Demon. Unlike their contemporaries, who boosted their Satanic imagery with aggressive guitars, Demon's keyboard-anchored sound emphasised more mystical, subtly sinister aspects. 'Shall I say that people have done your *Jesus Christ Superstar*, done your *Godspell*. It's always been our ambition to do something for the opposition,' explained vocalist Dave Hill. Like Black Sabbath, Demon hypocritically warned against the subject that clearly fascinated them. More importantly, their natural constituency, the progressive rock audience, had been dwindling steadily since the1970s, and those that were left were not interested in gothic or demonic themes.

The audience that eluded Demon flocked to a number of black metal acts who matched extreme Satanic lyrics with extreme, blistering tones. At the forefront were the Danish band Mercyful Fate, led by the unashamed Satanist King Diamond – who, taking the stage in black and white face paint, would influence the visual image of Satanic rock for decades to come.

Formed in 1981, the band debuted with the mini-album *A Corpse Without a Soul*. The cover boasted a scandalous sketch inspired by the song 'Nuns Have No Fun' – 'Upon a cross a nun will be hanged/She will be raped by an evil man/Knock spikes through her hands.' These gentle rhyming couplets were designed to generate controversy in the band's home country of Denmark, but only succeeded in denying them radio airplay. Elsewhere, the shock factor failed to draw the attention they were hoping for.

Mercyful Fate's image, like their sound, was dominated by King Diamond, his unmistakable vocals swinging wildly from a high-pitched shriek to a hoarse bellow – a directionless mess or a fresh breath of sepulchral air, depending on your taste. Lyrically, the band were held back by the fact that English was not their native tongue, a big drawback when tackling a subject as complex and prone to parody as Satanism.

Mercyful Fate's first full-length album, *Melissa*, came out in 1983, inspired by a skull owned by Diamond which he liked to believe once belonged to a witch. *Don't Break the Oath*, which followed the year after, contained a title track which was Diamond's most brazen dedication to Satan: 'By the symbol of the Creator, I swear/A faithful servant of his most puissant Archangel/The Prince Lucifer/Whom the Creator designated as his Regent/And Lord of this World. Amen.'

This album cover, for Witchfinder General's Death Penalty, *sold records but earned moral opprobrium from the press.*

King Diamond followed this same devotional approach to Satanism in interviews and everyday life. His inspiration was Anton LaVey, who Diamond visited in San Francisco (during this visit, the eccentric LaVey regaled his Danish guest with a keyboard rendition of 'Wonderful Copenhagen'). In return, King Diamond received an honourable mention in LaVey's 1990 biography, *The Secret Life of a Satanist*, as the only Satanic rocker then paying proper dues to the Prince of Darkness. He won the respect of figures in both the occult and rock worlds for his well-mannered sincerity and (strangely) humane philosophy – but the press regarded him as a laughable fake, while the anti-rock lobby perceived him as nothing less than a corrupter of morals.

It was a 1985 interview in Britain's high-profile heavy metal magazine *Kerrang!* that precipitated the break-up of Mercyful Fate. Rock journalist Dave Dickson purported to expose Diamond as a fake, but was only parading his own half-baked preoccupation with Aleister Crowley to pull some imagined occultic rank. This was the catalyst for all those who felt uncomfortable with Diamond's Satanism to let off steam at the unfortunate Dane. It was the last straw for Mercyful Fate: not only were the band not all Satanists, but some were avowed Christians, and there was mutiny in the ranks.

The shell of Mercyful Fate went off to form the uninspired Fate, while in Diamond's new band, the modestly-titled King Diamond, Satan was conspicuous by his absence. However, the

songs were atmospheric mini-horror movies, and the anti-Christian slant remained – most notably on their best release *The Eye*, which retold a historical tragedy surrounding the Catholic Inquisition – though records sold disappointingly. In 1993 Diamond reformed Mercyful Fate, but the wounds caused by his original dalliance with Old Nick obviously still smart, as this was Mercyful Fate *sans* Satan.

Danish Satanic rockers Mercyful Fate, with leader King Diamond (centre).

King Diamond was not alone at the forefront of black metal in advocating Satanism. British four-piece Venom were just as outrageous, musically uncompromising, and, if anything, more influential. While Diamond treated his subject matter with reverence and restraint (while his contemporaries might sing gleefully about fucking maggot-ridden corpses, Diamond would coyly 'make love to shame'), Venom were vulgar and base, with Satanism as a vehicle for their coarse obsessions.

The band was formed during 1980 in Newcastle, England by Abaddon, Cronos and Mantas: stage names culled from demons invoked in LaVey's *Satanic Bible*, as was the baphomet-pentagram that decorated their first album sleeve. However, little else about them suggested the Church of Satan's brand of predatory sophistication.

Venom's trump cards were frankness and rage, dosed with an admirable sense of (often unacknowledged) self-parody. All of these elements were scored deep into the grooves of their 1981 debut album *Welcome to Hell*, recorded in brief drunken bursts. It was a noise devoid of any social grace or artistic finesse, but its filthy, frantic immediacy attracted the attention of some of the rock press.

It was the band's Satanism, however, that convinced many young metal fans to buy the album. 'We're possessed by all that is evil. The death of your God we demand. We spit at the virgin you worship. And sit at Lord Satan's left hand,' ran the blurb on the back of the sleeve. At the same time, the rough and ready lyrics of songs like 'In League With Satan' suggested that if Venom conducted a Black Mass, crates of Newcastle Brown Ale would take the place of communion wine. The Devil-free tracks on the album also showcased the band's passion for the crude and the unacceptable, with numbers like the misogynistic, venereal disease-inspired 'Poison'.

Many have compared Venom's approach with that of punk rock, and there's some validity to this. Technically, Venom stank. They were fast, rude and keen to upset the apple-cart with a Molotov cocktail of confrontational attitude and unpredictability. But while punks nursed a disingenuous desire for media approval, Venom clearly did not give a shit, remaining both unacceptable and unfashionable throughout their career. The album *Black Metal* followed in 1982, defining the title of the new genre with more of the berserk energy that characterised their debut. The 1984 release *At War With Satan* was something of a departure – with one side of the album dedicated to a Satanic rock opera – but was still chaotic and crass by mainstream standards. Its gatefold

The Church of Satan's baphomet insignia – borrowed for numerous album covers, including Venom's debut Welcome to Hell.

sleeve took the band's Satanic imagery to new heights, resembling a black magic grimoire which opened to reveal a burning cross with 'Satan Laughs' inscribed over it. ('Damnation has sunk its talons deep into the womb of utopia, spilling forth great streams of Virginal Purity and Bliss . . .' ran the inner blurb.)

But the band continued to treat Satanism with loud irreverence. *Kerrang!'s* Dave Dickson attempted a similar hatchet job on Venom to the one he perpetrated on King Diamond, but the Crowley-bore was driven back by bombastic sarcasm. 'To put the record straight,' explained bassist/vocalist Cronos, 'the Devil was me Dad and I have got long pointed horns.' More pertinently, if just as boisterously, he added, 'The way Venom go about it – it's like what KISS lacked! You look at Simmons – and he was a demon! And there's fire and death . . . and he stands there going, "I was made for loving you baby!" And you say, what the fucking hell's this? You can't sing about sheep and lovely days and, oh, look at this lovely daisy with – AAARRGGGHH!!! – a thunderous bass line going on in the back and all these hellish drums.'

Venom were running on borrowed time from the start. The band's guerrilla warfare approach burnt a lot of bridges, while the constant friction between band members, which helped sustain their savage energy, inevitably began to grate. By the close of the 1980s Cronos left, precipitating Venom's collapse. He recorded a forgettable melodic rock album then, in an unusual career move, became an aerobics instructor. The Devil works in mysterious ways . . .

Venom reformed with a new vocalist and bassist, but the original fire – and most of the Satanic references – had gone. Nevertheless, they remain a seminal influence on the black metal scene, some feeling that their loud, orchestrated chaos has never been matched. Venom translated Satanic rebelliousness into a rage of drunken abuse and lechery which was not to everybody's taste, but made sense to many alienated young rock fans.

If anybody rivalled Venom for manic intensity in those early days, it was the Swedish band Bathory. Named after a homicidally sadistic seventeenth-century Transylvanian countess (Erzebet Bathory – 'Countess Dracula'), Bathory basically centred around one permanent member: vocalist Quorthon. Founded in 1983, Bathory were among the first to decorate their debut album with the now-obligatory goat's head. The music was a frantic assault of overheated aggression, topped with Quorthon's guttural bellows, winning no points for subtlety or elegance. More than either Mercyful Fate or Venom, Bathory – with their almost unintelligible vocals and atmospheric musical intros – pioneered the style that was to dominate the underground rock scene in the late 1980s: death metal.

Quorthon, of Swedish Satanic thrash metal pioneers Bathory.

Quorthon's Satanism had few, if any, historical sources, relying instead on the horror stories and late-night movies that inspired most youthful would-be Devil-worshippers. The lyrics suffered from the same translation problems that impaired King Diamond's work, as well as a degree of youthful naivety on Quorthon's part: 'The lies of Christ I lose/The ways of Hell I choose/I drink the floating blood/Defy the fury of God' ran 'In Conspiracy With Satan' – not without impact, but Lord Byron he ain't.

Three Satanic albums followed – *Raise the Dead, The Return* and *Under the Sign of the Black Mark* – each with increasingly polished execution. Then in 1988, Quorthon released *Blood, Fire, Death* based upon the Norse mythology of his native Scandinavia, followed by *Hammerheart* on the same theme – the most accessible of Quorthon's recordings. By this time, however, he was becoming lost in the genre he helped create and it became the Bathory project's swansong.

Norse paganism – the subject of Bathory's final recordings – is inherently linked in modern times with fascism, and Quorthon toyed with neo-Nazi imagery on these later albums. Simultaneously, the relationship between Norse mythology and Satanism was beginning to flower on the occult underground. The second wave of black metal would erupt in Quorthon's home territory of Scandinavia, taking the fascistic themes of 'völkisch occultism' to far greater extremes than Bathory ever did with their horror-movie melodramatics.

Don't Break the Oath

Words with King Diamond.

Affable, well-informed and well-mannered, King Diamond was a pleasure to interview when we spoke following the reformation of Mercyful Fate in 1993. The pioneer of Scandinavian black metal had none of the dour, hostile attitude that characterises his more recent contemporaries.

How did you first become drawn into Satanism?

It was through some experiences I had in my old apartment in Copenhagen. We were doing demo tapes for Mercyful Fate, which was when I had the first experience which I could not explain in any other way than that there are definitely powers around us. We were waiting to listen to the first demo – my brother, our drummer and myself, waiting for the other guys. We were sitting around a table and we'd bought a case of beer – we'd only opened one each, so we weren't drunk though. And we were wondering whether we should listen to the tape now or wait for the other guys. All of a sudden my brother's glass rose in the air, then slowly put itself back down on the table. I've used that in some lyrics: you'll find the experience with the glass in 'Welcome Princess of Hell'. I feel very comfortable when things like that happen around me, because I see the spirits as my protectors, almost as guardian angels, and I feel very comfortable knowing that they're still around me. In that song I say, 'I turn off the lights', and then you hear a choir responding, saying, 'We raise our glasses.' I took the experience as congratulations, saying, 'We're behind you.'

You were the first band to really advocate Satanism weren't you?

I guess so. If you look at Black Sabbath, they were interested in the occult but they were never Satanists. They were like standing on a hill looking over, while I was in the middle of it. Actually I didn't know anything about LaVey's church when things started happening. At that time I was reading a lot of books about the occult because I was fascinated by that first experience, and a lot of things followed that. But most of the books I read had the same view of Satanists – they slaughter babies, drink blood, whatever. I thought, 'God man, how sick.' But I had the openness that, when I came across LaVey's *Satanic Bible* I decided to read it and see what the Hell's really going on.

That was exactly what inspired the song 'Satan's Fall' – discovering LaVey's *Bible*. The interesting thing is that LaVey's book is not that occultic, it's mostly philosophy. In LaVey's Satanism he doesn't say you have to believe in this Devil with horns or whatever. When it comes to the spiritual side, there's just this huge void. LaVey realises, and I have the same feeling, that we're all born different with different needs and ways of thinking. No two people believe exactly the same way. When you realise that, you realise you should take whatever you want, whatever suits you best, whatever feels right for you to believe in. You can pick and choose

King Diamond, the first black metal star to be sanctioned by Anton LaVey, in distinctive demonic face-paint.

what you believe. One of the things I consider almost mandatory, though, is believing that there are powers around us.

Your early concerts were reputed to be Satanic rituals – is that true at all?

You could say any concert is a Satanic ritual because you are definitely letting so much energy loose. You could probably turn it into one of the most powerful Satanic rituals ever if you did it in the right way. With all of that energy, if it was directed in the right way, my God it could be powerful! But we never tried to do that – it would be taking advantage of people. We never tried to convert people, I never saw us as priests. I have my beliefs in spiritual things, but they are different from everyone else's. That's where the spiritual void in Satanism comes in again. Satanism is a lot to do with a life philosophy. There are also the steps of how to perform a ritual. But there too you have to be careful. Not just everybody can do it, you've got to have certain features and abilities so you can release the right energies at the right moment. If you can't do that nothing will come out of it. I've performed Satanic rituals at home, but never on stage.

You were harassed quite heavily by the rock press at one point, trying to prove you were a charlatan, weren't you?
There was one incident with an English journalist named Dave Dickson. He was so pathetic. It's pretty funny a guy coming up and telling me I'm not a Satanist, when I'm a member of the Church of Satan. He kept talking about a guy who claimed never to be a Satanist – Aleister Crowley – who was all he had on his mind. I said, 'Hey, I'm not interested in Aleister Crowley. I've heard of the guy, but I don't know much about him.' This Dickson guy kept going on – 'Aren't you afraid when you mingle with these powers?' I know what I'm doing. 'But you can't control it.' Did he know about what I'd done, or the results? No. But he kept saying, 'You can't do that, you have to follow Crowley, and it's still dangerous,' and so on. I said, 'Why do you keep talking about Crowley?'

Do you think you've turned a lot of kids on to Satanism?
That depends on what kind of Satanism you're talking about. There's a lot of people who'd like me to say, 'Well, maybe somebody got interested by listening to us and found a better way of living.' But the traditional way of looking at it is that you've turned some kids into killers. That has never happened because that's never what I've said. In fact it says in *The Satanic Bible*, and I agree with it 100 per cent on this point, that under no circumstances would a true Satanist sacrifice a child, or an animal for that matter. So, how could that be true? If kids are turning Satanism into something bad then they must have got it from somewhere else. Maybe the TV preachers in the US, or from the Church, which has always portrayed Satanism in this way. I have nothing against the Christian Church, I fully respect that people are different with different views, feelings and needs. If it feels right, do it. I judge people by their personality, not by their religious beliefs

Did you get a lot of flack in the early days because of your Satanic stance?
There was some. There was a priest in Denmark who really tried to finish our careers. Before the first mini-LP came out we had the chance of appearing on national TV in Denmark. That was a big break, because back then we were nothing. This guy heard of us and wrote to all of the national papers trying to stop us. I got really tired of listening to this guy. We did this mini-LP with this nun being burnt by this coven on the cover. That

cover was made purely to discredit that priest. I knew what he'd say when he saw it. He was all over the newspapers saying how dangerous we were to the kids. Then I got my turn because they wanted to hear my side of it. I said, 'Hey, get a grip, man. Try and look at reality. This is just a painting. You guys burnt people for real.'

Do you believe in Satan as an actual entity?
If you're thinking of this guy with horns and a tail who opposes some good force, then no. For me the word 'Satan' stands for the powers of the unknown, the powers of darkness, that are all around us which we can use for our or other people's benefit.

Why did the Satanic elements in your music start to take a back seat, particularly when you formed King Diamond?
That's not true. I know that's the way most people portray it, because they don't hear the word 'Satan' anymore. The lyrics are the same, apart from that we started doing concepts and stories. Writing about *Charon* the ferryman of the dead, we could have done that in the Mercyful Fate days too. He was in the Mercyful Fate song 'Satan's Fall'. The word 'Satan' got omitted because it became frustrating that so many people had that negative opinion of the word. No matter how many interviews I gave about it, it seemed as if it was too ingrained that the word meant 'Death' and nothing else.

It was a little tricky at first, because instead of using the one word which describes so many things for me – 'Satan' – I had to describe things more specifically. But it's worked, people have found out what I mean. I'm not saying that there are no rituals involved and that everything's fine. You hit back if someone hits you. It's the nature of the beast – the human animal. Of course, with these rituals you can harm people too. Not through sacrifice, but you can definitely throw these powers at people in a negative way.

Why does Satanism sell?
It's the twisted horror of it. Horror sells, death sells, anything nasty sells. You just have to turn on your TV and watch the news and there's more and more violence in your face. Why? Because people like to see it. They like to sit there and know it's not them – that they're better off. Sometimes it's healthy because these things happen, you can't avoid them. There's no way you can erase that part of life. I don't think we have more or less bad in the world since I've lived. It just moves around a bit. It's always going to be there, you might as well try and learn to live with it.

IN NOMINE SATANIS

An interview with Abaddon, founder member of
Venom

**Abaddon spends much of his time managing young
bands these days. He spoke to me in the spring of
1993 with the frank, friendly demeanour and
Geordie accent he still retains.**

How did Venom come together?
We began in '78-'79. We came together as a group of
friends who knew that there was something harder and
rawer out there, musically, image-wise and with
intensity. It didn't matter if nobody liked it. We were a
group of KISS, Motorhead and Judas Priest fans and we
always thought it was great to see Judas Priest but we
wished they had KISS's stageshow with the demon bass
player. We liked Motorhead's raw, don't-give-a-fuck
attitude, but they were always holding back because
they were a 'legit' band. We all loved the punk thing,
but if you strip the vocals and lyrics off punk it's all very
safe and wrapped up. Nothing was ever really let loose.
Black Sabbath used to sing about Satanism but they
always said, 'It's alright, God will come through in the
end.' Nobody was just saying 'Fuck off!' to everything.
You had to go to someone like Iggy Pop, but he still had
the melodic band.

So you were aiming at a nihilistic concept?
Absolutely. A concept of being massively disliked, but
never ignored.

How did Satanism creep into that?
It was part of that concept. We were never going to hide
our Satanism with backward masking or whatever. We
were always going to say, 'This is it, these are the images,
and if you want to buy it, you buy it – if you don't, leave
it. We're not trying to get into anybody's house to
preach Satanism.' We originally did a three-track demo,
and we sent it to Geoff Barton at *Sounds* magazine. We
got a gigantic two-page spread reviewing the material on
the demo: 'At War with Satan', 'Red Light Fever' and
'Raise the Dead'. It was very Hammer-horror Satanic
imagery. It was a good sample of what we planned to do
over the next five or ten years. The guy who owned the
studio we recorded at happened to own Neat Records.
Although he hated what we'd done, he said, 'I can see
you're going to be able to sell this.'

So we recorded an album for him – in about four
days it was recorded and mixed. Because of that we
managed to get quite a lot of violence into the grooves.
That was the album *Welcome to Hell*. Even by today's
standards, on 'best of death metal' charts it remains at
number one. It was released in 1981, and maybe it's a
little weak in places. Personally, I feel that stuff like

industrial music has left all of the death and thrash
metal behind now anyway. I don't feel that anyone in
Slayer or Metallica is going to touch what Ministry's
doing for intensity. That's what thrash metal was all
about. What Venom was all about was taking what
Judas Priest and Whitesnake were doing, and making it
totally unacceptable. Nothing like what we were doing
has happened until bands like Ministry and Murder Inc.
It's a completely new step.

You don't see death metal as one of these steps?
Not at all. I see death metal as slightly more hard than
us, slightly more intense, but it hasn't leapt anywhere.

*Cronos of Venom, with pet serpent. Rumour has it
the veteran black metal vocalist used to climb onto
the roof of his house and bark at the moon.*

Venom were a leap, that's why you're talking to me ten
years on with flagging album sales. It was a massive leap
into the unknown.

How did the 'black metal' tag come about?
People pigeonholed us, as they do every band. We
actually said in an interview, 'Fuck off, we're not heavy
metal. We're death metal, we're speed metal, we're thrash
metal, we're black metal.' We actually said that in anger,
but we created a whole range of new pigeonholes.
Because we called an album *Black Metal* you now get
people calling Black Sabbath black metal, and they were
happening long before we were in nappies.

Are there any Satanic bands you respect?
No. I've since come to realise that people who were

Satanists or really into the occult wouldn't use it as a tool for promoting music. It cheapens it. In the end it did with Venom. If Jimmy Page had gone out and said, 'Led Zeppelin are a Satanic band and I'm a Satanist' or whatever, it would have flattened Led Zeppelin. They would have become a joke band earlier. The Rolling Stones tried to do it, then got the fuck off it quickly.

Has your Satanic stance got you in any trouble?

Yes, then and just recently. Mainly with people's naive attacks on churches. They'd break into a church, desecrate it and then write 'Venom' on the walls. I don't know if they were fans of the music or fans of the fact that we were willing to stand up and take the rap for being Satanic. We accepted the blame. In the old days there were massacred animals in the church, blood smeared over icons, and doors hacked open. More recently, somebody in Scandinavia was arrested and taken to court wearing a Venom T-shirt. He might well say that our open-minded attitude and willingness to use the Satanic imagery inspired him. There's a guy on death row in the US who went out to murder someone, he couldn't do it, hit the guy but couldn't bring himself to kill him. He went home, put on a Venom album, and found the will to do it. He was asked if he blamed Venom and he said 'No.'

Has Anton LaVey been central to your interpretation of Satanism?

Very much so, yes. Very influential. There was a point when we received letters from his daughter in Holland in around 1983-4. The letters were very nicely written, but they basically said that we were a publicity stunt for the Church of Satan. That was the band's only limb of authenticity, somebody saying, 'Yes, what you're doing is right.' The studio we used to go to, there was a locked door, a long corridor, then some stairs and another locked door. At night-time the doors were all locked and alarmed. We went to the studio one morning and there was a letter there and it just said, 'Shemhamforash, Lord Satan approves.' We were recording at the time and we'd been the last ones in the studio the night before. It came as something of a shock, we thought someone from the Church of Satan must have been monitoring us. Since then, one of the guys who was a sound engineer has turned very strongly to Buddhism. I've always wondered if it could have been him and, as he was the engineer on the Venom stuff, whether there could have been some input from him musically onto the production.

Are you influenced by any other Satanists?

No. Personally I've always felt Crowley was too driven by narcotics, and you have to think with a clear head. I tend to drink a lot, and wake up thinking, 'Did I really do that?' I don't now subscribe to drugs very much. I got into cocaine in a big way then I stopped thinking about anything clearly. I wonder how the drugs affected Crowley. I've recently moved house to a village in Northumberland that's massively famous for its occult and Satanic connections. I find living there interesting, it's the kind of place where you have a hanging basket and there's this huge Satanic cross supporting it. All the windows are shuttered – people are very insular, very private, and I've learnt to honour that. It's drawn me away from using the occult in my music. People look at me in the street sideways – they all speak to each other, they speak to my wife, but they look at me askance. I won't apologise for having used the occult to fire my music, but I accept it looks cheap or even cheesy.

Do you believe in Satan as an entity?

No. It's a piece of me. Within me it's the positive – direct action, immediate decision, responsibility over my own actions, wisdom – which is why I don't automatically hate Christians. That's why I'd like to challenge Glen Benton of Deicide and say, 'You're full of bullshit, and I know you are. You can carry on doing what you do to small animals, but you won't do it to a bigger animal than you. And I'm a bigger animal than you.'

Do you think Satanism is dangerous?

Only because it has some radical fringes and it can be misinterpreted. You can take things literally, which is mistaken. I live in an old church, but not to desecrate it or fill it with inverted crosses or put a skull on the altar. I don't keep a lot of books on the occult in the house. I don't listen to black metal bands, and that includes Venom. Not because I don't like the music but because I don't like the way the lyrical content's gone. It's got to where people like King Diamond are saying, 'Come with me and worship.'

UNDER THE BLACK MARK

An interview with Quorthon of Bathory.

Quorthon has a reputation for being difficult to interview, but, in late 1993, I found him friendly and charming, with a well-developed sense of irony. Conducted over the telephone prior to the release of projects that looked set to close the book on his Satanic phase, the interview was, in one sense, a wake for Bathory.

How did the Satanism get into your music?
When we first started, we had no ambitions to make records or write songs – we just wanted to cover Motorhead songs, because that's what we'd grown up with. We'd just left school, so while the other bands sang about drinking beer, fucking women and riding motorcycles, we didn't know anything about any of that because we were too young. But we did have an innate interest in the dark side of life. It wasn't purely Satanic from the beginning, it just grew into that. It was a protest, revolt thing – we knew it would upset people one way or another. If you look at it today, it all seems so very innocent. The main inspiration came from a Swedish horror comic called *Shock*. It was just the blood and gore thing, with a tongue-in-cheek approach.

Do you think there's a particular link between Scandinavia and the Satanic metal scene?
Of course the second wave of black metal seems to have come from Norway and Sweden, but it would be very sad if people thought that was what Scandinavian rock was about. We have been Christian for only 900 years so it would be much more faithful for Scandinavian bands to deal with Norse topics. If they don't, and want to play Satanic stuff, okay, there's room for everybody. But I don't think there's a particular link with Scandinavia. Most Swedes are Christian for one hour on a Sunday morning at most. Though it's true that 70 years ago everyone had to go to church by law.

Is there anything about your early material which you regret?
You have to take the early material for what it was – horror lyrics written by a fourteen-year-old kid interested in the dark side of life. I didn't have much of an academic knowledge of Satanism, though that came later as I got deeper into it. I started reading into the Christian side of it too, which is when I decided it was all fake, so the Viking elements started coming into my work.

Horror-comic Satanic rocker Quorthon within the Devil's pentagram.

Why has Satanism had such a close relationship with rock?
Ever since Elvis shook his pelvis and John Lennon made his remark about Jesus, the conservative world has always been placing restraints on the younger generation. If you take something like Christianity and attack or mock it, then you have crossed certain forbidden lines, which is just what the Sex Pistols were doing with 'God Save the Queen'. It's rebellious. In our modern world, where we've begun space travel, we should really laugh at *The Bible*. But we don't because it remains such a very important stone in the building of modern society.

THE DEVIL HAS ALL THE BEST TUNES

Anton LaVey on music.

The affinity between art and Satanism is most apparent in the realm of music. LaVey, an accomplished keyboard player, put much emphasis on the magical potential of melody and rhythm. His own tastes ran to those tunes written during his 'Erotic Crystalisation Inertia' period (or ECI – the period in early life when an individual's tastes and aesthetic identity are formed and frozen in time) between the 1920s and 1940s: ditties like 'That Old Black Magic' or 'On the Level You're a Devil'. In the past LaVey had been dismissive of Satanic rock music, particularly heavy metal, once referring to it as 'the last big burp of Christianity'. Why did he dismiss it so out of hand and, in the 1990s, was he still of the same opinion?

Former professional musician Anton LaVey, with his snake Boaz.

What would you call Satanic music?

Music can be used as a litmus test of character. Musical taste can be telling as a psychological profile – you can tell a lot about a person by their choices of, and responses to, music. The Satanist is most likely to respond to evocative and descriptive music and be repelled by chaotic, disjointed or atonal music.

But isn't what you find atonal to do with what you've been brought up with?

Not really. It's to do with what are called 'ur songs'. These are atavistic, basic harmonies and intervals of sound which generate specific responses in the listener, and they transcend cultural boundaries. There are a

limited number of different ur songs – I've studied them and made a list and you can reduce that list to a handful of basic melodies which have been interpolated into diverse compositions. They give you that feeling – a shiver up your spine. There are different purposes to music and different ur songs generate different basic emotions – pathos or a marching tune, for example. These are not just my theories, they have been expressed by others – Lance Morrow in *Time* magazine, for example. Successful music feeds upon your emotional needs, while dissonant music feeds man's habitual masochism.

Who listens to this 'dissonant music' and what is it?

I can tell what I often call 'whipping music' when I hear it. It's the same kind of stuff used to urge galley slaves on. The element of habit in listening to this kind of thing is important. A lot of the people who listen to heavy metal have just become used to it. I've seen people of one or two generations removed respond to the same configurations of music in an identical manner. There are certain dynamics and harmonies you can play with – there's very much a science of music.

Do you think all rock music is 'whipping music'?

If I'd been born in 1970 I'd have a different ECI and I'd be moved or stimulated by different stuff. But I'd still discriminate – there are both ur songs and whipping music in rock music. Each generation has a different golden age. I believe our culture reached its creative apex in 1939. The world has become faster, but also more stagnant, musically since then. Rock music has been pretty generic since the fifties – the 'thought police' have been keeping everything pretty well suppressed. Take a band like Venom – how much resemblance do they bear to the Who? Are they generically the same? The creative process is too stifled, too repressed these days. Rock bands are being sold, as has Satanism, on brand names rather than content and rock, like Satanism, sells.

Do you believe subliminal messages on records work?

Subliminals make sense and visual subliminals certainly work. Audio subliminals can also work – you can train yourself to identify them. Pink Floyd use some wonderful subliminals where they interpolate a snatch of one song into another. I used a similar technique all the time when I was playing at rituals or working the bars and theatres.

Do you think music can induce violence or be dangerous?

To find out what will make someone aggressive, you

have to consider their proclivities. What's background music for someone can be very foot-tapping for another. Music can inspire people to murder or violence. But if someone contrives to play this overtly violence-inducing music, they'll find it works for them but not for others. For some people a lullaby can inspire them to shoot a mall full of people.

Which musical artists have you been involved with over the years?

I fully sanction King Diamond. The Dickies, the Sex Pistols, Sid Vicious – they were influenced by me. I actually like some punk and I've met some punks who are quite respectful of the Church of Satan and what we've achieved. Some artists would rather keep their affiliations with the Church of Satan quiet. We've had contact with a lot of people over the years. Alice Cooper was seeing a lot of my daughter Karla at one time. Dave Lee Roth recorded an album named *Yankee Rose*, which are the last words in *The Satanic Bible*. It's often difficult to say what is, or is not, Satanic music. I receive a lot of recordings from people that come preceded with a note saying, 'I know you won't like this but . . . ' But, to an extent, if they feel an affinity with me then there's probably some affinity in the music.

What do you feel about the Satanic bands who dismiss you as not extreme enough?

There is always a tendency in youth to defy your father, resist authority figures. They can't dislike me on any rational level – they don't know me. If they're at all intelligent – and remember, the first Satanic sin is stupidity – they'll realise that there's only so much I can say publicly. I will not be a martyr for them – be their Christ on a cross. I will not advance things in print which will make my position untenable – they can read the subtext in my work though. I started the Church of Satan in 1966, and they can only blaspheme the way they do right now because I opened the door back then.

How long would the Church of Satan have lasted if I hadn't appeased and outraged in just the right combination? It required a certain amount of discretion and diplomacy to balance the outrage.

How about the counterculture movements? You are accused by some of being over-authoritarian.

Counterculture is a very healthy thing. It aids stratification – counterculture can form society's cutting edge. It can help separate the wheat from the chaff. But counterculture for counterculture's sake is pointless.

How do you feel about Satanism's absorption into a medium like rock music?

Satanism as mass culture is great. If a car passes with a bunch of long-haired kids in it and they recognise me and make the sign of the horns at me, I'm very flattered. I consider it a compliment – these are, in a way, my children. There's a great advantage in mainstreaming and I'd be a hypocrite to dislike it. I'd rather see people dressed in black than in rags and I can't conceive of Satanic rock doing my cause any harm. It's like – do people who make movies promote Hollywood? Even those bands who just use the imagery and deny Satanism are promoting the concept. A lot of Satanic rock bands would rather just do their thing then stand back and watch everyone act shocked. I can't quarrel with that, but that's the sum total of a lot of them. They're just heretics – doing things because they're not supposed to. Whatever it is, they're against it – just biting the hand that feeds.

To those Satanic rockers who put me down, I'm expected to be 'understanding'. We, as Satanists, are on the move. Other Satanists might not be quite as 'understanding' as I am forever. Those using the trappings of Satanism for economic advantage should be careful not to slander their seminal roots in quite such a cavalier fashion. They may not care now, but they may very well have to care in the future.

SCAPEGOATS AND SINNERS

Satanic Crime, Conspiracy and the Ritual Abuse Myth

n 1980, a book was published with the innocuous title of *Michelle Remembers*. It was inspired by the therapy sessions administered to a troubled Canadian woman named Michelle Smith by her psychiatrist, Dr Lawrence Pazder. Smith had not enjoyed an easy life by any means, marred by three miscarriages, the early death of her mother and disappearance of her father, but Pazder's long course of therapy revealed the source of her mental problems was far more spectacular than these mundane tragedies. Using hypnosis, the Canadian psychiatrist 'discovered' his patient had been repressing memories of an horrific past in which she had been an unwilling member of a murderous Satanic cult since 1955.

The details of Smith's recollections would have convinced many mental-health professionals she was suffering from pathological delusions. Her 'memories' revealed a cult, led by the monstrous Malachi, who indulged in acts of unbelievable brutality in the name of the Devil, such as blood-drinking, sadistic orgies, animal sacrifice, murder and the ingestion of 'worm soup'. One might have thought that Michelle's later revelations – that she'd been visited by Satan Himself, a scaly character who spoke in bad rhyme, and rescued by the personal intervention of the Virgin Mary and Jesus Christ – would have given Pazder cause for scepticism.

However, the good doctor, a Roman Catholic, accepted Michelle's traumatic memories as gospel and published them in *Michelle Remembers*. The book reads like an X-rated Dennis Wheatley thriller, but many were convinced of its authenticity. Pazder and Smith – who divorced their respective partners and married – were invited to the Vatican, where Bishop Remi de Roo wrote a preface to the second edition of *Michelle Remembers*.

The bishop, however, was a little guarded in giving total credence to the book. Others were not so sceptical. Fundamentalist Protestant sects, more aggressive than the wily old Roman Church, seized upon the book as proof positive of their Satanic foe's existence. *Michelle Remembers* was to trigger an urban myth of epic proportions, inspiring a whole army of deluded crusaders to fight the good fight against a shadowy Satanic conspiracy.

The genuine innovation of the book was the introduction of child abuse as a central feature of Satanic conspiracies. The idea wasn't wholly new: sexual perversity had been a regular charge against medieval witches; in the fifteenth century, when wholesale sexual abuse, torture and murder of young children might have seemed enough to condemn Gilles de Rais as a monster, the courts added the charge of Satanic sorcery.

De Rais's crimes found an echo in twentieth-century Britain, where, between 1957 and 1971, the island of Jersey was terrorised by a sex criminal the media dubbed 'the Beast'. The perpetrator of the crimes was one Edward Paisnel, duly convicted of brutal sexual assaults on one woman and five children. The press hinted at black magic, a suggestion reinforced by the revelation that Paisnel (very dubiously) believed himself a descendant of Gilles de Rais.

When police searched Paisnel's house they discovered a secret room, holding an apparently sacrificial altar with a wooden dagger suspended above a glass bowl. Also within was the costume the Beast of Jersey had worn to perpetrate his crimes: a strange ensemble consisting of a fawn raincoat, home-made wig, sinister rubber mask and bracelets studded with nails. Clearly, Paisnel held occult beliefs, but whether these originated anywhere but in his own deluded imagination is impossible to know. (Paisnel died in the early 1990s, after being paroled from prison.) The Jersey High Court resisted all attempts to introduce the black magic angle to proceedings, dismissing it as a distraction from the real issue of whether Paisnel was guilty of sex crimes.

Others were not so pragmatic, not least the press. Occult 'experts' were encouraged to pontificate on the magical significance of every aspect of Paisnel's deviant behaviour – even down to his peculiar passion

The sinister costume worn by Edward Paisnel, the Beast of Jersey.

for painting things blue. Few listened to suggestions that Paisnel's confused fantasies implied the loathsome character might be mentally unfit to stand trial. Interestingly, despite his personal cocktail of misunderstood pop-occultism, Edward Paisnel was always adamant, both before and after the trial, that – like his idol, Gilles de Rais – he was most certainly *not* a Satanist.

The revival of Satanic conspiracy panics was mirrored, unsurprisingly, by the gathering impetus of the evangelical Christian movement.

During the mid-1970s, stories began circulating around America's mid-West about the carcasses of cows discovered drained of blood, with their eyes, lips and genitals removed. The mystery of where their blood had gone, and how and why these animals had been operated on with seemingly surgical precision, gave birth to the 'cattle mutilation myth'.

In reality, a thorough 300-page report in 1980 – compiled by ex-FBI agents, veterinarians and animal pathologists – determined that these 'inexplicable' mutilations were the natural results of dead animals being eaten by scavengers. But, as Anton LaVey could have told them, people don't like to have their fears deflated quite so quickly.

The cattle-mutilation myth has survived despite being comprehensively discredited – indeed, it has almost become a barometer of American paranoia. During the early1970s, cattle mutilation was regarded by the myth's believers as the result of sinister experiments by UFO occupants. By the early 1980s the perpetrators had changed to Satanic cultists, who travelled in special pickup trucks and vans containing surgical and blood-draining equipment. Why Satanists should want to sacrifice cows, and why they did not simply take the aftermath home for a barbecue, was never explained. Once the Satanic panic subsided, the rumours changed again: government agencies, conducting monstrous secret experiments, are now the favoured culprits in this bovine mystery.

Of course, Satanic cults have been accused of far worse than massacring farm animals. Whether Satanic conspiracy theories are started by Christian fundamentalists on a crusade, sensationalist hacks trying to turn a buck, or attention-seeking neurotics with genuine mental problems, it often pays to have real criminals (like Charlie Manson) at the forefront of the pitch. To their evident delight, some convicted killers have found themselves cast as members of all-powerful underground cults.

The poster child for the Satanic conspiracy myth might have been Stanley Dean Baker, who has been linked with more than his fair share of imaginary Satanic groups (including the Four Pi movement). This bearded hippie hitchhiker was arrested in California during July 1970, after a traffic violation. Confronted by the police, Baker made the immortal confession, 'I have a problem. I'm a cannibal.' In their search for proof the cops only had to go as far as Stanley's pocket, where he'd secreted a human finger to snack on. The fact that his other pocket contained a copy of *The Satanic Bible* ensured his place in folklore. Baker was convicted of the murder of the finger's unwilling donor, who he had stabbed – apparently inspired by a thunderstorm – then, as an afterthought, cut out and cannibalised his victim's heart, before taking a few fingers for later.

Baker made a dubious confession that he belonged to a blood-drinking cult in his home state of Wyoming, implicating himself in a series of other murders. Once in gaol he revelled in his reputation, preaching his Satanic 'beliefs' to alarmed fellow inmates. He also took to barking like a dog and howling at the moon (Baker was clearly not the most inconspicuous of Satanic conspirators). In 1976, Baker made an application to join the Church of Satan, but the kooky cannibal's request was turned down. Upon his release, however, Baker blamed his crimes upon mind-altering drugs, not the Devil.

Another Satanic conspiracy favourite is David Berkowitz. Between July 1976 and August 1977, this self-styled 'chubby Behemoth' stalked lovers' lanes in New York, shooting necking couples with a .44 pistol. Before his arrest, Berkowitz had killed six and wounded seven more innocent victims. He earned the nickname 'Son of Sam' from a series of letters left at crime scenes and sent to newspapers, in one of which he announced, 'I am a monster. I am the son of Sam.'

It turned out that 'Sam' was his next-door neighbour, whose dog barked all night and – according to Berkowitz – was possessed by demons who told him to kill. His spartan bedroom was daubed with messages reading: 'IN THIS HOLE LIVES THE WICKED KING', 'I TURN CHILDREN INTO KILLERS' and 'KILL FOR MY MASTER'. Sentenced to 365 years in prison, Berkowitz began spinning increasingly lurid fantasies of involvement in a Satanic cult, eagerly encouraged by conspiracy theorists.

Depending on the particular theory, he was a member of the Four Pi movement, or 'the Twenty Two Disciples of Hell', or a secret group called the Coven which Berkowitz described as containing 'a mixture of satanic practices which included the teachings of Aleister Crowley and Eliphaz Levi [sic]. It was (still is) totally blood orientated and I am certain you know just what I mean. The Coven's doctrines are a blend of Druidism, the teachings of the Secret Order of the Golden Dawn, Black Magick and a host of other unlawful and obnoxious practices.' All of which sounds like a mixture of half-digested occult gibberish (Druidism?) – but some were convinced and, on the back of his 'reformed Satanist' act, Berkowitz managed to secure a level of macabre celebrity coveted by many serial killers.

Henry Lee Lucas was another such notorious attention seeker. Since his capture in 1983, Lucas claimed to have killed – in the company of his companion and bisexual lover Ottis Toole – over 300 people. A simple-minded drifter with a distinctly feral approach to life, many came to believe Lucas was making multiple confessions in order to please his captors and earn prison privileges. His confessions had a habit of contradicting each other, or simply being chronologically impossible. Some less credulous lawmen and journalists concluded that Henry was guilty of only one murder: that of his mother, which he'd already served time for. In time, Lucas would recant all of his previous confessions.

At one point, however, Henry claimed he'd been a member of 'the Hands of Death' – a Satanic cult that indulged in mass murder, cannibalism, drug trafficking, the production of pornography and snuff videos. All of the wicked activities that Christian fundamentalists claimed Satanists got up to. He never explained why the Hands of Death would recruit a pair of half-witted, chronic substance abusers like himself and Ottis. For their part, the authorities continued to treat the case as one of recreational homicide.

Sure enough, fickle Henry changed his mind again, disowning the Hands of Death fantasy. Regardless of this, he was convicted on eleven counts of murder and sentenced to death. Retarded Ottis milked the myth right up until his death in prison from Aids in 1996, calling himself the 'Devil's child'. Letter-writing correspondents would receive primitive tracings of his own 'Hands of Death', or infantile drawings depicting the supposedly Satanic crimes he'd committed. Meanwhile, Henry became a born-again Christian and revived the whole Satanic fairy tale. Untroubled by the complete absence of evidence or logic to his tale, fundamentalists claimed Lucas had been beaten and drugged by police officers who wanted to suppress information about the cult.

If Lucas and Toole's claims to Satanic affiliation were extremely dubious, one serial killer was at least consistent in his dedication to the Prince of Darkness. His name was Richard Ramirez, though he became better known by the title of the 'Night Stalker'. Between June 1984 and August 1985, Ramirez terrorised Los Angeles with an opportunistic campaign of burglary and sadistic murder, mutilation and brutal sexual assault. His 'calling card' was a pentagram drawn on the wall, or, in one case, carved into the body of one of his victims. When he was apprehended, his charge sheet included fourteen counts of murder, 24 of sexual assault and one of attempted murder.

Ramirez was an enthusiastic drug abuser, ardent AC/DC fan and self-styled Satanist. He prepared himself for his grotesque crimes by listening to AC/DC's song 'Night Prowler' over and over again. Indeed, it appears that Ramirez's sketchy Satanic doctrine, such as it was, was derived from drug fantasies and AC/DC albums. (It was galling for him when the press somehow managed to get his title – 'Stalker' instead of 'Prowler' – wrong.)

Ramirez put on a good show in the courtroom: winking, blowing kisses at the cameras, flashing a pentagram drawn on the palm of his hand, holding fingers to the sides of his head as 'horns', muttering 'Evil, evil, evil . . .' Sentenced to death, he responded, 'Big deal, death comes with the territory . . . see you in Disneyland.'

Less extreme than Ramirez, there are dozens of cases where the discovery of *The Satanic Bible*, a Black Sabbath T-shirt, or a crudely-drawn Devil have led religiously-motivated police or sensation-hungry journalists to label the crimes 'Satanic'. Perhaps the classic case is that of Ricky Kasso, a high school drop-out from Long Island whose heavy involvement with drugs earned him the title of the 'Acid King'. In 1984 he stabbed another youth to death in woodland, insisting his victim pledge allegiance to the Devil as he attacked him. This melodramatic image led to the crime becoming forever associated with Kasso's demand: 'Say you love Satan.'

Ricky Kasso was only seventeen when he committed murder. He owned a copy of *The Satanic Bible*, but, if he'd read it, he clearly hadn't understood that LaVey's book is a manual for *productive* misfits and *creative* outsiders. Kasso's Satanism was merely a way of trying to earn status within his limited social circle. To describe his lifestyle – of compulsive substance abuse and petty crime – as self-destructive is a

Richard Ramirez, the sadistic 'Night Stalker', who told the court, 'I will be avenged . . . Lucifer lives within us all!' before being sentenced to death.

definite understatement. Indeed, he hanged himself in his cell before he could be tried.

Kasso had once been arrested for grave-robbing, but the young delinquent did not take his grisly trophies for some macabre rite – he sold the Indian bones to a local curio shop to raise drug money. Similarly, his stabbing victim was not killed in some intricate ceremony, but attacked in a drug-fuelled frenzy. (Kasso and his victim had been in a long-running feud over the theft of some PCP.) But 'black magic murder' makes good headlines in a way that one more squalidly-mundane story of drug-related killing does not.

Another story of a juvenile 'Satanic slayer' attracted even more attention than that of Ricky Kasso. In 1986, in Oklahoma City, teenager Sean Sellers shot his stepfather and mother with a .44 pistol, before ransacking the house in an attempt to make it look like the murderer had been an intruder. Despite his efforts, Sellers was soon apprehended. It soon emerged that he had killed before, shooting a store clerk in September 1985, and on 6 March 1986 he was charged with three counts of first-degree murder.

His defence mounted an insanity plea, and it soon became apparent to observers that Sellers was no average teen. He was in the habit of drinking vials of his own blood in the school cafeteria, painted one of his nails black, and conducted Satanic rituals in a deserted farmhouse. Shortly before he killed his parents, Sellers' school contacted his mother after he submitted an essay on Satanism that quoted heavily from *The Satanic Bible* and concluded, 'I can kill without remorse. I have seen and experienced horrors and joys indescribable on paper.' The court threw out his insanity plea, so the defence produced a police 'expert on Satanic murder' willing to testify that Sellers was not mad but 'possessed'. A bold legal foray into the unknown, or the last ploy of a desperate lawyer? The jury decided on the latter, convicting Sellers on all three counts and sentencing him to death.

Despite this, Sellers' case became a *cause célèbre*, with fundamentalist Christians holding him up as an example of the very real threat Satanism posed to American youth. The media gave him air time on high-profile shows like *Oprah* and the cover of *People* magazine. Sellers was 'born again', announcing how he'd always loved his parents till he'd been possessed by a demon. Poor little Sean really was the injured party. However, his 'not guilty by reason of Satanism' plea falls apart under scrutiny.

Sellers' 'coven' had only two members – Sellers and his one friend. Their first 'sacrifice' was not conducted according to any sacrificial rites, but motivated by the fact that the victim once refused to serve the two Satanists beer on account of their age. Previous to the murder of his mother and stepfather, there had been a great deal of tension in the family, not least because his mother refused to allow Sellers to see his girlfriend. Perhaps most tellingly, like Kasso, Sellers had been taking an awful lot of recreational drugs, leading to long periods without sleep and blackouts. Away from the glare of publicity and popular opinion, justice was finally done in 1987 when psychological tests determined Sellers was insane and his death sentence was quashed.

But the likes of Sellers and Berkowitz made good television. In 1985 the popular TV show *20/20* ran an episode entitled 'The Devil Worshippers', highlighting 'Perverse, hideous acts that defy belief. Suicides, murders and the ritualistic slaughter of children and animals.' The programme did indeed 'defy belief', but it also attracted record viewing figures – with Phil Donahue, Oprah Winfrey and Sally Jesse Raphael all following suit with shows dedicated to 'investigating' the Satanic menace. To an uncritical audience, these paranoid fantasies were 'real' because they had been on television, and a wave of rumours and panics followed the screening of each 'Satanic special'.

None of the talkshow hosts did as much to promote the Satanic conspiracy myth as Geraldo Rivera who, between 1987 and 1995, ran no less than four shows dedicated to Satanism. In the first of these, Geraldo claimed, 'Estimates are that there are over one million Satanists in this country . . . The majority of them are linked in a highly organised, very secretive network. From small towns to large cities, they have attracted police and FBI attention to their Satanic ritual child abuse, child pornography and grisly Satanic murders. The odds are that this is happening in your town.'

Rivera's description of police interest, unlike the rest of the scenario, was not wholly imaginary. Satanic 'experts' were now lecturing fellow law enforcement officers on the subject. These 'cult cops' may have been pious Christians with a bee in their collective bonnet about Satanism, but their presence on the programme earned the myth a vital sheen of respectability.

The dynamics of how the Satanic conspiracy myth became so widespread have been analysed by a number of eminent sociologists. The original theories were far-fetched in the extreme, often involving literal demons and conspiracies that stretched to the corridors of power.

Figures were produced from the air – such as 100,000 people sacrificed to the Devil every year in the USA alone – as hard fact. Many fundamentalist claims were unintentionally hilarious, their literature identifying the Smurfs and My Little Pony as demonic propaganda tools.

Once these myths were diluted for secular consumption, however, the source material remained much the same. TV programmes quoting fundamentalist sources were then quoted back by these same sources as further 'evidence' of the existence of the cults, generating a self-sustaining vicious circle of unsubstantiated rumour.

During the 1980s, evangelical Christians were particularly active in promoting their views through videos, information packs and presentations. It became a very lucrative trade when 'experts' in Satanism routinely charged hundreds (or even thousands) of dollars for their cocktail of paranoia and hearsay. Police departments were targeted as markets for these seminars, which proved popular among officers at grassroots level. Not only was a course on 'Satanic Crime' more exciting than the mundane alternative of, say, immigration law or traffic violation, but the attending officer could return to his station as a newly-appointed Satanic expert. After this preliminary training, he would find traces of Satanic crime everywhere: in heavy metal albums, porcelain animals, candles and 'drawings of any geometric shape'.

The influence of occult crime seminars on law enforcement led to numerous embarrassing incidents. In 1990, in a place close to Albuquerque, New Mexico, aerial photographs revealed the presence of a gigantic pattern set out next to the word 'TERF', made up of around 400 tyres. A senior Rio Rancho officer sent out to investigate concluded, 'The pattern is identical to a "seal" used in Egyptian mythology for some type of initiation. It is definitely a ceremonial site used by a cult. A form of church. And it's probably still in use.' An officer from Albuquerque Police Department was more specific: 'This is definitely witchcraft . . . And I'd stay away from there if there are any people around. They'll hurt you.' Another 'occult expert' observed that it was 'a very powerful and spiritual symbol'.

Once the story ran in the local paper, the mystery of the 'ceremonial site' was quickly resolved. 'Terf' was a team sport invented by a local man, and the tyres were used to lay out the field. Local officials, including the police department, had all fielded teams. The ex-mayor of Albuquerque, who once captained a terf team himself, observed that that the whole debacle was 'the best belly laugh' he'd enjoyed in years.

Of course, not all of the idiocy uttered by cult cops was so harmless. The Satanic conspiracy myth not only wasted vast amounts of resources that should have been expended on genuine crime, but ruined the lives of numerous individuals caught in the hysteria. And it very nearly opened a backdoor for radical Christians to re-introduce their totalitarian philosophy into secular law.

Among the public at large, the Satanic conspiracy myth gained credence via the 'no smoke without fire' thesis (though it's more accurate to say that where there's smoke, there's usually hot air). The myth dramatised crime in a way in which people could understand: the heroes and villains were clear-cut, murky moral questions cast aside in favour of a witch-hunt. As more than one commentator observed, World War Two had made it unacceptable to persecute Christianity's traditional scapegoats, the Jews, leaving imaginary Satanists (an archetype that could be projected onto all kinds of innocent people) to carry the sins of the world.

In 1983, three years after the publication of *Michelle Remembers*, a criminal case erupted in a comfortable Los Angeles suburb called Manhattan Beach. Centring on the popular McMartin Preschool day-care centre, it would become the most expensive trial in Californian criminal history up to that point. It began when some parents voiced suspicions that their children were sexually abused by staff at the centre. Seven staff members were arrested to face 208 different charges. Then things got weird.

The children began telling increasingly bizarre stories – stories curiously familiar to readers of *Michelle Remembers*. They had been forced to drink blood and eat shit, and had witnessed robed adults sacrificing animals and eating babies. To many, this seemed like a morbid, childish fantasy. But to others, it was verification of Michelle Smith's lurid description of child-molesting cults. The trial split the whole community, including those prosecuting the case. One prosecutor proudly announced the discovery of 'toy rabbit ears, a cape, and a candle' proved the existence of a Satanic cult. Another resigned in disgust at the shabby proceedings.

Meanwhile, things just got weirder. One child said he was kept in a cage with a live lion. Another identified film star Chuck Norris, and the lawyer questioning him, as being among his abusers. As the trial turned into a circus, it emerged that the mother who made the initial accusations had a history of mental problems. Five of the accused were released without charge because evidence against them was, according to the District Attorney, 'incredibly weak'. The case dragged on until January 1990, when the last defendant was released as the jury deadlocked on a verdict. That following July, a second trial produced the same result.

This inconclusive verdict is emblematic of the Satanic ritual abuse myth. On one side, those

Myths about demons stealing our children are nothing new, as illustrated by this late medieval woodcut.

who wanted to believe in it emphasised that the accused had never been fully exonerated. On the other, the sceptics pointed out that nothing had been proved – despite huge public expenditure – and wondered aloud whether the therapists who interviewed the children had helped inspire their macabre tales of cultists and demons.

Nevertheless, the myth continued to gather pace – with reports springing up all over the USA and, later, the UK, Holland and Australia. Dozens of cases either collapsed before they even got to court, or reached verdicts that were inconclusive at best. Each time the sceptics asked where the evidence was, credulous believers responded by asking how the children's accounts of their experiences could be so similar.

One answer is that dissemination of this new urban folklore had implanted aspects of the myth into children's minds. The other, more sinister, is that the evidence of the children was contaminated by their contact with adults. Overzealous foster parents, childcare specialists and therapists were prompting them to release 'suppressed memories'. Tellingly, the vast majority of accusations, ostensibly by the children, could be traced back to the same few adults.

In the same way that police departments had attended Christian-fundamentalist seminars on Satanism, so a worrying number of childcare organisations were relying upon information supplied by evangelists. Like the police, many childcare professionals refused to believe they were facing the depressingly mundane horror of everyday child abuse, rather than an international cult of metaphysical evil.

Child abuse appeared to have risen rapidly between the mid-1970s and 1980s. The National Resource Centre for Child Abuse in the US reported a seventeen-fold increase in reports between 1976 and 1985. However, research suggested it was not the actual incidence of child abuse that was increasing, so much as awareness and willingness to bring it to the attention of the authorities. It was a particularly nasty can of worms. Many simply did not want to believe that ordinary people – people like themselves – could be responsible for such awful cruelty to their own children. The Satanic ritual abuse myth offered a comforting alternative reality, in which child abuse was the work of strange, inhuman cultists.

Sceptics of the myth had long been dismissed as professional cynics, apologists for evil, or even agents of the Satanic conspiracy. Now they demanded their say. Since the mid-1980s Kenneth Lanning, head of the FBI's Behavioural Science Unit, had endeavoured to bring a little sanity to the ritual abuse debate, but remained a lone voice in the wilderness. It's difficult to say when the myth began to drown in its own drivel, but the publication of a British newspaper article was a significant turning point.

In August 1990, Rosie Waterhouse wrote an article for *The Independent* commenting on a recent case of 'Satanic ritual abuse' in Rochdale, northern England: 'There have been police investigations across the United States, in Canada, the Netherlands and now in Britain. They have produced no evidence. No bodies, no bones, no covens, no underground tunnels, no animal carcasses, no bloodstains. Nothing.'

This first high-profile British manifestation of the myth mirrored its American blueprint, the McMartin case, in many ways. In a series of dawn raids on 14 June 1990, seventeen children were taken from their parents by police and social workers. After weeks of questioning, the social workers announced that the children were victims of protracted sexual abuse by a secret Satanic cult. However, a later judicial inquiry ordered them returned to their parents and severely criticised the authorities' action, prompting the resignation of Rochdale's director of social services.

Independent journalist Brian Appleyard made the following observation: 'Within half an hour of arriving in the town I had been persuaded that these allegations could not be substantiated. The council assured me that there was further evidence, but there was nothing more than some ill-written reports by social workers. The whole affair was a depressing mess and one which was turned into a national scandal by the appallingly gullible and ill-judged use by the social workers of the single word "satanism".'

In her 1990 *Independent on Sunday* article, 'The Making of a Satanic Myth', Rosie Waterhouse dissected the genesis of the hysteria: 'The panic spread to Britain early in 1988 through several channels including the evangelical Christian movement, in books, testimonials of survivors and "Deliverance" ministries, and through "experts" from the US who spread the message here, in newspapers and on conference circuits.

'Once here, the stories have been spread by Christian organisations such as the Association of Christian Psychiatrists and the Social Workers of the Christian Fellowship, by churches, anti-occult campaigners and by born-again "survivors" of satanic abuse.'

Books began to appear which denounced the 'Satanic conspiracy' as an orchestrated delusion. *The Satanism Scare*, edited by sociology professors James Richardson, Joel Best and David Bromley, criminal justice analyst Robert D. Hicks' *In Pursuit of Satan* (both published in 1991) and sociology professor Jeffrey Victor's *Satanic Panic* (1993) all comprehensively debunked the myth with rational enquiry. Perhaps most devastating was the 1994 report by Professor Jean La Fontaine, commissioned by the British government, which stated that Satanic abuse in the UK was officially non-existent.

But outlandish stories continued to surface. In 1992, Nebraskan senator John DeCamp, himself a Republican, published a book claiming that the Republican party was infiltrated at the highest levels by a paedophile Satanic cult. DeCamp even claimed that George Bush had been at one of the cult's perverse parties, prior to his presidency, though he stopped short of actually implicating Bush. By now, however, less and less people were willing to take such stories seriously.

In 1995 even Geraldo Rivera – the talk show host who played no small part in popularising the Satanic abuse myth – turned his back on it. On the air, he made the following apology: 'I want to announce publicly that as a firm believer in the "Believe the Children" movement of the 1980s, that started with the McMartin trials . . . now I am convinced that I was terribly wrong . . . and many innocent people were convicted and went to prison as a result.'

Previously, when investigating claims of abuse, child welfare professionals had treated the testimony of children with caution, on the basis that some are inclined to lie or invent stories, considering it necessary to back up accusations of child abuse with corroborative evidence. This new 'Believe the Children' doctrine, bolstered by various Christian movements, held children's testimony to be sacrosanct, preaching that they would never lie about something as grave as sexual abuse. By inference, they suggested that prosecutions should be pursued even when no verifiable evidence supported a child's accusations.

It's easy to see why this theory has a special appeal to Christians: it confers a sheen of virtue upon the believer, who appears to be siding with a defenceless victim; it also chimes with the Christian myth of childhood innocence. Children, according to the Christian ethos, are like mankind before the fall from grace, prey to corruption by 'the world, the flesh and the devil'. Church of Satan leader Anton LaVey also held a special reverence for children, calling them 'natural magicians' – but this was because of their talent for fantasy and invention. The Satanist does not regard the child as an angelic innocent, but as a selfish, feral creature. This does not imply condemnation of any kind, but merely confirms the Satanic view of natural, unfettered human nature.

With a couple of notable exceptions, the Satanic ritual abuse myth left real Satanists untouched. The myth's proponents levelled their accusations at more vulnerable social outcasts, random victims or, interestingly enough, members of their own fundamentalist sects. Official Church of Satan policy, as far as there was one, was to treat the Satanic conspiracy myth with lofty disdain, and to dismiss the likes of 'Satanic slayers' Sellers and Ramirez as 'lone nuts'.

The relationship between Satanism and crime is an ambivalent one. Many young potential recruits are surprised (and perhaps disappointed) to discover that most established Satanic orders take a hard line on law and order. Many early members of the Church of Satan were lawyers and policemen – indeed, one story of the organisation's origin has it that the church's foundation was suggested to LaVey by a friend on the force.

On the other hand, LaVey talked with admiration about gangsters like Bugsy Siegel and Meyer Lansky, referring to them as seminal influences on his own philosophy. With typical perversity, the Black Pope also told a story of how, he once bumped into Ramirez, the Night Stalker, on the street. LaVey's recollection of the feral serial killer was that he was a polite young man, subsequently regretting not having stopped to speak with him.

LaVey's penchant for offending the self-righteous should not be overlooked, but the basic attitude toward crime is, as ever, one of cynicism. Human societies will eventually stratify the natural governors and the governed, the masters and the slaves. The rule of law is not sacred, but necessary in order to avoid disruptive, wasteful chaos. All sensible career criminals have, as their ultimate aim, the goal of becoming legitimate businessmen. The criminal is, like the occultist, just trying to take a shortcut, to avoid too much hard work in getting what he wants. Our ancestral leaders were the robber barons of yesteryear, the mobsters of today are just the government in waiting.

'Son of Sam' David Berkowitz. Portrait by Tim.

Ruminating on the Satanic conspiracy myth in Blanche Barton's 1990 history of the Church of Satan, LaVey observed, 'It all works eventually in our favour . . . All these *Pray TV* evangelists have had their last gasp. It's almost back to the old days when the words "evangelist" and "huckster" were synonymous. So who else do they turn to but the Devil? He's always been their real Saviour. They dress themselves up as "experts", start railing against the Devil, the Enemy trying to drag them down and how they need money, lots of money to fight the Devil. But people see through it. They're tired of the noise. We couldn't have planned it any better. When the Satanic hysteria gets to the point of absurdity, people start questioning the whole line of crap. It will eventually get so no one believes anything Christian ministers say anymore. When they hear about the Devil and how rotten he is, it just makes them curious about what the Satanic viewpoint might be.'

The following commentary is by Robert Ressler, former FBI agent, coiner of the term 'serial killer' and co-founder of the VICAP criminal profiling system – as interviewed by the author in 1997.

'*The Ultimate Evil*, a book by Maury Terry, created a great deal of the basis for the Satanic conspiracy theories. It had links between Berkowitz and Manson which were all nonsense. Terry actually booked Berkowitz into a three-part TV programme where he would finally reveal all about his crimes. You watch the three-part series and Berkowitz did not admit to anything. He did not bring in the Satanic or occult activities. It was a big put-on. When I interviewed him he said he was just looking for a justification for his behaviour. He did not really have any realistic motivation he could draw upon, apart from that he was a very lonely person who was sexually frustrated. The "Sam the dog story" just came out as a verbalisation of his motives, but he said none of it was true.

'Police were coming from all over the country, having big parties after the Henry Lee Lucas interviews, going down to local bars and dancing. It became a social event. They were taking Henry

[left] on trips too. They'd take him to California to look for where some of the bodies were buried. Instead of staying in a dingy Texas gaol cell with no air-conditioning, Lucas was staying in Holiday Inns and having steaks delivered to him. I think he's a serial liar, rather than a serial killer. He may have killed people because he was a drifter and a bum and led a lifestyle that was conducive to killing someone over a card game or something. He may have killed half-a-dozen people, which is all the more reason to keep him where he is. But from the standpoint of killing even dozens, I don't believe it.'

While Henry was imprisoned in Huntsville, Texas, the brain-damaged Ottis Toole, incarcerated in Florida State Prison, fantasised about a Satanic upbringing (as told to prison literature anthologist Sondra London): '. . . I used to go with my grandmother into graveyards . . . we used to dig up all kinds of bones . . . and she used to take the bones and do devil worship . . . take a chicken and wring the chicken's neck . . . she told me I belonged to the devil . . . I said, well maybe she's akin to the Hands of Death . . . but she was a real witch . . . she had skulls in her

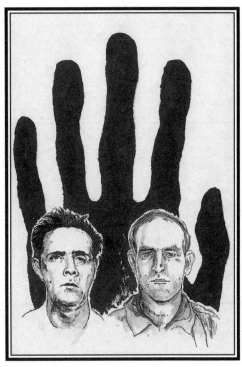

Henry Lee Lucas and Ottis Toole. Portrait by Tim.

house . . . she showed me how to take a drawer and turn it upside down and build an altar out of it . . .' As noted by Anton LaVey, the most dangerous self-styled Satanists are those who construct fantasies of 'generational Satanism'.

PART III

THE SATANIC
MILLENNIUM

THE APOCALYPSE GENERATION

Social Darwinism and Satanism in the 1980s

he defining episode of Satanism in the 1980s occurred at the Strand Theatre in San Francisco on 8 August, 1988. Dubbed the '8/8/88 Rally', it was a self-conscious cross between an occult ritual, performance art and fascistic political rally. Militaristic drums pumped over snatches of strange, quasi-classical music and nursery-rhyme melody in a dark hall bedecked with Teutonic runes and Satanic symbols. An audience clad in evening dress and black stared reverentially or whooped with joy when addressed from the podium by a quartet of grim-faced young orators in their twenties or early thirties. These individuals were the four most prominent figures at the axis between the unholy and the culturally taboo.

One of them, Nikolas Schreck, described the event as 'an evening of apocalyptic delights . . . very deliberately designed as a ceremony and a ritual to celebrate the death of the sixties for one thing. The Sharon Tate murder was a symbolic representation of the end of an entire way of thought, of compassion for the weak, peace for its own sake, pacifism that breeds stagnation. That entire way of thinking was destroyed on August 8th 1969 and that is why we chose this evening to perform a ritual of cleansing and of purification. It is also symbolic of the unholy alliance of various Satanic entities in the world – Radio Werewolf, Non, the Church of Satan, and the work that Adam Parfrey has been doing.'

Parfrey was the figure behind a new independent publishing company, Feral House, dedicated to 'thinking the unthinkable'. The other West Coast 'Satanic entities' were Schreck himself ('Alpha Male' of Radio Werewolf), Boyd Rice (the non-musician behind Non), and Zeena LaVey, daughter of the Church of Satan's Black Pope. (Anton LaVey himself was conspicuous by his absence – more of which later.)

The themes that dominated the 8/8/88 Rally ran throughout much of the Satanic current during the 1980s: fascination with Charles Manson, and a tendency to treat the convicted killer as a gifted philosopher or political messiah; representation of the 1960s as a nadir in Western culture, when the Christian ideals of egalitarianism and compassion briefly took hold; the merging of Satanism with a dour, often racialist version of Europe's pre-Christian, pagan past. All were bound together by a nihilistic belief that the world was in the throes of a bloody apocalypse, slowly purifying the overpopulated planet.

Within the Church of Satan, doctrines from the dark undercurrents of the movement had risen to the surface: social Darwinism, the idea that the brutal laws of natural selection applied not just to the natural world but to human society; the romantic, almost mystical elitism of nineteenth-century German philosopher Friedrich Nietzsche; the theories of nineteenth-century English economist Thomas Malthus, a Christian clergyman who saw the cure for problems of overpopulation in human 'culls', by war, disease and natural disaster.

Nikolas Schreck, then in his twenties, was not born with the name that embodies his sensibilities. It's reasonable to assume he chose his surname with care: 'Schreck' is German for dread; Max Schreck was a German horror movie star of the silent era, known for his portrayal of the repellent title character in the 1922 vampire classic *Nosferatu*; Julius Schreck was the original head of Hitler's SS, replaced by Himmler in 1929.

Nikolas Schreck was the self-styled leader of the Werewolf Order – named after the 'Werwolf Korps', a Nazi guerrilla force established in the dying months of the Third Reich to try to hamper the Allied advance. In 1988, the Werewolf Order affiliated itself with the Church of Satan – this was more than a symbolic union, as Schreck was personally involved with Zeena LaVey, who he appointed as the Order's Alpha Female.

The relationship between LaVeyan Satanism and fascism is a complicated one. In his only reference to Nazism in *The Satanic Bible*, LaVey says: 'From every set of principles (be it religious, political or philosophical), some good can be extracted. Amidst the madness of the Hitlerian concept, one point stands out as a shining example of this – "strength through joy!"'

This is certainly a pragmatic attitude to that traumatic episode of history, but not a ringing endorsement. In *The Satanic Rituals*, LaVey also includes a rite entitled 'Die elektrischen Vorspiele', credited to the Black Order – a term applied here to the völkisch occult groups of late nineteenth-century Germany. However, a far greater influence on this strange ceremony, invoking the demonic power of electricity, are the expressionistic German horror films of the silent era, such as *Nosferatu*.

Satanic Magister Boyd Rice, with Totenkopf (death's head) tattoo.

Indeed, LaVey made a poor candidate for an Aryan superman – not least because of his own mixed blood (partly Jewish), and affection for the 'degenerate' carnivals and sideshows of his seminal years. The early Church of Satan membership – prominent among whom were homosexual film-maker Kenneth Anger and black-Jewish entertainer Sammy Davis, Junior – would have been substantially depleted by a Nazi pogrom.

Despite this, LaVey's doctrines held much appeal for the revolutionary Right. Indeed, his church had attracted interest from a fascist group, the US National Resistance Party, as early as the 1970s. While unwilling to be seen publicly condemning an organisation as 'evil' (the role of villain being a particularly delicate balancing act), LaVey derided the organisation in private.

Nevertheless, during the 1980s the Church of Satan was widely regarded in the occult community as having slid from a position of aesthetic elitism into brutal authoritarianism.

Some, like writer Burton Wolfe – who did much to establish the LaVey legend in his 1974 biography *The Devil's Avenger* – left in disgust at the membership's perceived swing to the Right. Inevitably perhaps, many of the younger Satanists he objected to had placed the twentieth century's secular Satans, Hitler and Manson, on their altars alongside the mythic Devil.

'Fascist' – a word much used and often little understood – has become little more than the ultimate term of political abuse. In a time when 'democratic' has become a synonym for 'good' and 'undemocratic' for 'evil', the heretical position is to suggest that the 'will of the people' is far from perfect, and often (or usually) wrong. Many Satanists, recognising the power in invective, began to label their own pragmatic elitism as 'fascism' – but, for the most part, this fell short of neo-Nazism, with all of the racist doctrine and enthusiasm for genocide it implies.

Nikolas Schreck had no truck with any such ambiguity. According to its promotional propaganda, the Werewolf Order was formed 'after a private study of magical techniques that culminated in a pilgrimage in 1983 to various occult power points, including Heinrich Himmler's SS castle in Paderborn, Germany and the ruins of Karnak Temple in Luxor, Egypt'. Schreck cites as primary influences Guido von List, the Armanen Initiates, the Thule Society and other völkisch occult schools associated with the rise of Nazism.

Werewolf Order literature states, 'Nikolas Schreck teaches that the ancient mythological figures of the werewolf and vampire are actually archetypal role models for the next step in evolution: cruelties of the natural order and man's animal origins, and yet the master of a new science of pagan technology.' This concept – that the mythical creatures of the night were the most highly-evolved form of humanity – would be combined by Schreck with revived Germanic racial occultism, inside the broader church of Satanism.

His self-styled 'propaganda unit' was titled Radio Werewolf, after the propaganda stations set up by the Nazis at the end of the Second World War: 'Radio Werewolf stands as the standard-bearer of a new kind of youth . . . Orderly, disciplined, drug-free, proud and re-awakened to their pagan heritage; the cadres of the Werewolf Youth Party.' Contemporary youth culture was labelled 'a sewer of mind-numbing drugs, primitive African rhythms, the unbalanced encouragement of androgyny and homosexuality, the blurring and muddying of racial cultural boundaries'.

Performing midnight rituals to send signals to the sleeping masses in furtherance of their 'demonic revolution', the Werewolf Order were a gothic extreme of modern facism. 'The black-clad warrior priests and priestesses of the order form a lycanthropic legion who are shaking the axis of the world,' asserted their self-published propaganda. 'There are thirteen designated Power stations of the Werewolf movement situated in such cities as San Francisco, London, Berlin, Seattle, Vienna, Brussels, Colorado Springs, with headquarters in Los Angeles overseen by Nikolas Schreck.' Not one for half measures, Schreck declared his aim as 'world domination', remaining resolutely dour when the situation called for gales of egomaniacal laughter.

American recording artist and writer Boyd Rice, a former associate of Schreck, remains a high-ranking member of the Church of Satan. Together with Schreck he formed the Abraxas Foundation, a 'fascist think tank' – though Rice's relationship with fascism was always more ambivalent than that of his cohort. Abraxas – an ancient Gnostic deity embodying the marriage of opposites, particularly good and evil – is a very appropriate patron for Boyd Rice, a man whose preoccupations are divided between the saccharinely kitsch and venomously grim.

As a commanding presence on the fringes of the avant-garde, Rice is a cultural agent provocateur. One of the ways in which he first came to prominence was as a major contributor to the *Industrial Culture Handbook* and *Pranks* editions of the highly influential Re/Search books published during the 1980s. Relating a few of his favourite practical jokes in the latter, Rice describes presenting President Reagan's wife, Nancy, with a skinned sheep's head. I guess you had to be there . . .

Rice was also associate editor of ReSearch's *Incredibly Strange Films* book, which was instrumental in taking the fascination with low-budget cult movies mainstream. Surprisingly, perhaps, Rice doesn't champion existential horror or political propaganda films, but sings the praises of surreallistically – bad oddball efforts such as Ray Dennis Steckler's *The Incredibly Strange Creatures Who Stopped Living and Became Mixed-Up Zombies*.

However, rumours of Rice's political beliefs caused a permanent rift between him and the Re/Search team – rumours that were not unfounded. In an interview after the 8/8/88 Rally, Rice observed, 'what appeals to me about the SS and the Nazis is order. Bringing things back to order . . . This isn't official Church of Satan doctrine, but to me personally, Hitler was an occultist trying to bring about a pagan revival. It was completely against the Judeo-Christian ethic, and he was bringing that to an end and bringing something new forward. I feel that's what we're doing today.'

More recently, however,

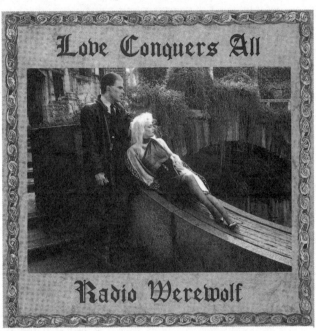

Church of Satan renegades Nikolas Schreck and Zeena LaVey pose for the sleeve of a Radio Werewolf album – appropriately titled Love Conquers All.

Rice has downplayed his involvement with the revolutionary Right, conceding his fascism while insisting it's of an aesthetic, not political, nature. 'I find the extremist stuff of whatever bent stimulating and interesting,' he explained in a 1994 interview. 'It provides more grist to the mill than normal mainstream opinion. I don't necessarily adhere to it as a political agenda. I sometimes err on the side of excess, because if it ends up being incorrect at least it's more interesting and colourful.'

Rice is almost as notorious for erring 'on the side of excess' with his passion for pop-culture kitsch like the Partridge Family and early Barbie dolls as he is for his flirtation with taboo politics. This same unlikely marriage characterises his musical career. Since the late 1970s, Rice has established himself – chiefly under the name 'Non' – as a seminal figure in the gratingly-atonal industrial music scene. At the same time, he expresses great admiration for the girl groups of the 1960s and other trashy 'bubblegum' pop music most people have long since discarded. This interest in the ephemeral culture of his formative years chimes with Anton LaVey's ideas about the power of lost popular classics.

Significantly, Boyd Rice and Nikolas Schreck were first brought together by their mutual pen-pal Charlie Manson – Shreck even referring to him as one of 'the more important thinkers of the twentieth century', despite his over-indulgence in the 'mind-numbing drugs' the Alpha Male so disdained. Manson enjoyed a quasi-messianic role among right-wing Satanists in the 1980s as 'the man who killed the sixties' (as one TV documentary later put it), largely because his curious psychobabble lent itself to any number of interpretations. Chiefly, though few liked to admit it, it was also because the infamy of his criminal convictions made Charlie such a potently anti-social icon. Manson received his new disciples on prison visits in the same way he'd learnt to deal with everybody – reflecting back at them their own desires and preconceptions.

Schreck was the chief editor of *The Manson File*, a 1988 compendium of Charlie's thoughts and 'philosophy' published to coincide with the 8/8/88 event. One of his co-editors was Adam Parfrey, who went on to found the publishing company Feral House. 'I want to get dangerous information out into the world,' explained Parfrey of his project. 'I think it's necessary for people to make up their own minds rather than some publishing house to decide what's right and wrong.'

One of the most epochal works of 'dangerous information' was compiled by Parfrey and published, in its original edition, by Amok Books in 1987. *Apocalypse Culture* was a landmark, a document that defined an ominous zeitgeist. Its contributors and 'thanks' lists read like a *Who's Who* of Western culture's darkest extremes. In the words of the cover blurb, its interviews, articles and rants offer 'a startling tour through the nether regions of today's psychotic brainscape'. Necrophiliacs rub shoulders with advocates of eugenics, racist conspiracy theorists struggle for space against champions of self-castration. The worlds of science, art and the occult collide in a bewildering pile-up that leaves few standing.

Apocalypse Culture distilled the pre-millennial angst and nihilism of people who grew up under the shadow of a mushroom cloud. The possibility of mass destruction, as imprinted on the subconscious of a generation, had produced a state of amorphous unease. In the hands of Parfrey and his friends, this took on a worryingly coherent form. According to them, the imminent apocalypse – which Parfrey described as a 'Malthusian mud flood'– was already underway. As Boyd Rice observed after the 8/8/88 event, 'The end of the world came ages ago, but it happened slowly over a period of time and nobody noticed it. It's an ongoing process. The world today is different than the world 30 years ago. It's decayed so much, and it's decaying more and more all the time. The entire world is rotten and corrupt and they're [the masses are] ordaining their own death. To us they're just dead people who refuse to lie down.'

While Schreck cultivated a menacing Aryan-ubermensch image, and the clean-cut Rice came across as a sinister parody of a wholesome all-American, Parfrey portrayed himself as a rakish, cigar-smoking *bon viveur*. 'I don't worship anything called Satan with the hooves and so on,' he explained of his attitude toward Satanism. 'It's more a philosophical thing. It's an understanding of power and how it operates in the world.'

Indeed, a disclaimer inside certain Feral House publications states that the company is not affiliated with the Church of Satan. These very same publications, however, include a new edition of Anton LaVey's *The Compleat Witch* (retitled *The Satanic Witch*), reinstating material originally censored from the Avon Books edition, *The Secret Life of a Satanist*, the authorised biography of LaVey by enthusiastic young disciple Blanche Barton, and two compendiums of

LaVey's essays, *The Devil's Notebook* and *Satan Speaks!* (the latter published posthumously as the Black Pope's final work).

Asked who early Feral House publications were aimed at, Parfrey observed that it was 'people who don't see anything out in the world right now, feel lost, feel unattached, feel swirling in a world of despair and boredom and seeing some glimmer of hope that there are at least some people like-minded'. If this makes 1980s Satanism sound like Generation X gone rogue, then it only reflects how LaVey had been consciously widening the gap between the Church of Satan and occultism, until Satanism became more of a cultural or social movement than a magical one.

Magical Satanic orders in the traditional mould were also prominent during the 1980s, many of them borrowing liberally from early Church of Satan material. Among these was the Church of Satanic Liberation, established in January 1986 after its founder, Paul Douglas Valentine, was inspired by reading *The Satanic Bible*.

With a background in Wicca, English teacher and romance novelist Valentine initially styled himself as a Satanic playboy. The Church of Satanic Liberation now claims branches in Antwerp, Calais, Edinburgh, Heidelberg and London, as well as their headquarters in New Haven, Connecticut, and Valentine pitches his Church as a less misanthropic, more accessible successor to the Church of Satan – though few, outside of his own organisation, take his claim to LaVey's legacy seriously.

The Temple of Set continued to flourish under Michael Aquino's leadership. His pre-occupation with his erstwhile mentor Anton LaVey also persisted, Aquino making much of the increasing fascist presence in the Church of Satan. When it was pointed out that Aquino himself had made a special study of the Third Reich, in his defence he explained he was simply interested in techniques used by the Nazi occultists, rather than their racial or political views. Nevertheless, in 1986 several disaffected members of his order defected to form a feminist version of the Temple of Set – the Temple of Nepthys – while citing Aquino's increasing interest in Nazi-inspired ritual as their main complaint.

Undeniably, in 1984 Aquino – like Nikolas Schreck – made a visit to the SS castle at Wewelsburg, conducting a rite in the notorious Hall of the Dead. 'The reality of this chamber rushed in on me,' he later wrote. 'This is no Hollywood set, no ordinary room painted and decorated to titillate the senses. 1235 inmates of the Niederhagen concentration camp died during the construction of Wewelsburg for the SS. If the Marble Hall and the Wallhalla were memorials to a certain unique quality in mankind, they also serve as grisly reminders of the penalty mankind pays for that quality.' Clearly, Aquino's 'pilgrimage' to Wewelsburg was not as enthusiastic an embrace of the Third Reich as Schreck's.

However, by 1987 the Temple of Set's Magister Templi had more to worry about than an accusation of fascist sympathies. In August of that year, his house in San Francisco was raided by police, military and FBI agents, who seized a substantial amount of Aquino's personal records and belongings, and noted, portentously, that his living room was painted black. The motive for the raid was the accusation that Aquino and his wife, Lilith, had engaged in the sexual abuse of children. It was a classic Satanic ritual abuse case, inasmuch as the only evidence was the vague testimony of children, reeking of cross-contamination and, ultimately, failing to stand up to the scrutiny of the court. The case rumbled on for two years before Aquino's pursuers reluctantly conceded they could not bring him to ground. Ironically, the only person to actually be prosecuted for the crimes was a Christian priest.

The least typical aspect of this case was the attempted prosecution of a known Satanist. In the vast majority of cases of alleged ritual abuse, the connections between the defendants and Satanism are tenuous to say the least. So why was Aquino targeted? He himself referred to the debacle as a 'modern witch hunt in the most classical sense', hinting darkly that somebody in high office was out to get him. Their motive was supposedly his position as a senior officer in US Army Intelligence, and one of the USA's leading experts in psychological warfare, which – though protected by constitutional rights of freedom of religion – seemed incompatible with his role as the head of a Satanic order to many of his superiors. Added to this was the fact that he'd visited Wewelsburg while on secondment to NATO in Europe, and that a dozen or so other high-ranking members of the Temple of Set were also in Army Intelligence.

The strange career of Michael Aquino is not the only instance where Satanism intersects with the murky world of governmental conspiracy. Victor Norris had founded the Anglican Satanic Church in the UK during the late 1970s, under the name Father Belphlegor. To assist him in producing literature for his organisation, Norris secured the services of a Blackburn-based occultist named Magda Graham who took the ritual name of Mother Lilith. (Lilith, a popular Satanic-*femme* pseudonym, is the archetypal illustration of Satan's longstanding penchant for powerful women. Created out of filth by Jehovah in the Old Testament's Book of Isaiah, she was the first wife of Adam. Cast out into the wilderness for not submitting to her husband, she hooked up with the Devil and they made lots of little demons together.) The organisation's magazine, *Dark Lily*, promoted the Anglican Satanic Church as a secret order of great wealth and power, with origins dating back to the turn of the century. Its content was also heavy with dark sexual overtones.

During the 1980s there was a split between Father Belphlegor and Mother Lilith, who found a new 'Satanic Master' in the form of a Scot named John Allan, and renamed her organisation the Order of the Dark Lily. *Dark Lily* magazine continued publication, though Graham – who seems to have become alarmed at Norris' involvement with a number of revolutionary right-wing groups – was now insistent that occultism and politics did not mix, going so far as to publish an article urging Satanists not to tar Jews with the same brush as Christians. Content was dominated by lessons from 'the Adept' – ordering his students to stand on their own two feet and think for themselves – while more private Dark Lily literature continued to carry a heavily sado-masochistic undercurrent.

During the early 1980s, Norris – in his role as a freelance undercover investigator, trading under the name Contingency Services – was, by his own admission, involved in 'dirty work' on behalf of the UK government. This chiefly involved infiltrating left-wing and anti-nuclear groups. In 1984 Hilda Murrell, an elderly but vigorous anti-nuclear protester who campaigned against the Falklands War, was found sexually assaulted and stabbed to death in a wood near her home in Shropshire. Several political figures soon challenged the official version of events, that the old lady had been the victim of a random burglar. Events took a strange turn when investigative journalists established that Norris had been employed to monitor the groups Murrell had belonged to.

Ex-MI5 undercover agent Gary Murray observed in *Enemies of the State*, his book on abuses by the British secret services during the 1980s: 'No one is saying that he [Norris] was one of those who broke into Miss Murrell's house and abducted her. But as [journalist] Paul Foot said, "It is just a chilling thought that such a person is used by the Home Office.

As the security services showed no hesitation about employing a known neo-Nazi and professed Satanist, it throws up the question of whether Norris' major role may have been to monitor dissident right-wing and occultic activity. Unfortunately, by this stage the truth will probably never be known.

Another British Satanist group with definite Far Right connections, the Order of the Nine Angles (ONA), first appeared in northern England in the late 1970s. By the late 1980s, the ONA had become vigorously involved in publishing extreme occultic-fascistic material – most notably with the 1988 introduction of the order's journal, *Fenrir*, named after the Norse myth of 'the wolf who swallowed the sun'.

The doctrines of the ONA call for entry into a new aeon of human development, via the overturning of current social dogma. More specifically, individual members are encouraged to evolve personally by overcoming various physical and psychological ordeals. The ONA defines itself as more 'sinister' than established Satanic movements – such as the Church of Satan and the Temple of Set – who are dismissed as not 'evil' enough. The group's efforts to establish its philosophical wickedness include, inevitably, flirtations with the Far Right, which the ONA acclaims as the most radical force on the current political scene. Conversely, most neo-Nazi Satanic orders claim they're merely using the occult world as a potential recruiting ground for their fascist groups. Nazis posing as Satanists, or Satanists posing as Nazis? In the cloak-and-dagger world of the occult-political axis, many of the adherents themselves are no longer sure which is which.

In the introduction to the ONA's version of the Black Mass, author Anton Long writes: 'One of the most shocking Satanic Masses used by Satanist groups today is based upon an evokation [sic] of Adolf Hitler – and not as something artificial, still less as a psychological "game", but rather as a genuine identification with the positive aspect of National-Socialist philosophy. (To most readers this, of course, will be blasphemy, outrageous – which is exactly the point.) As with the traditional Black Mass it is the stress placed upon the positive, vital qualities of opposition that is of paramount importance because these contradict in their very essence all that is assumed. Thus in the particular Satanic Mass, Adolf Hitler is not represented as he is portrayed by his opponents – or as he is today assumed – as some sort of "evil" monster but as exactly the opposite, as a kind of saviour.'

If this glib endorsement of Nazi iconography shocked the ONA's anti-fascist opponents, they were moved to even greater outrage by the group's open advocacy of human sacrifice in order to 'release energy' and 'draw down dark forces'. An article in *Fenrir* describes three forms of sacrifice: the first is of individuals who voluntarily offers themselves up; the third is the human carnage that ensues as the result of political or social upheaval, to be brought about by the actions of the Order. It is the second that gives most pause for thought – the secret murder of individuals considered to be opponents or impediments to the ONA's goals.

While the essay on human sacrifice is prefaced by a disclaimer that it is of 'historical interest only', the list of potential victims sounds alarmingly sincere: 'Candidates are zealous interfering Nazarenes [Christians], those attempting to disrupt in some way established satanist groups or Orders (e.g. journalists) and political/business individuals whose activities are detrimental to the satanist spirit.' Most occultists, however, are inclined to dismiss the ONA's more outrageous material as macho posturing, or a misguided effort to generate controversy.

While Satanism in the 1980s was dominated by its flirtation with fascism, the wider occult community remained predominantly liberal and politically left-of-centre. Perhaps the most important of the burgeoning movements during this period was chaos magic, a new occult school with strong ties to the post-punk counterculture. As a style of ritual magic preoccupied with 'anti-dogma', chaos magic blended the latest developments in 'chaos theory' science with ancient traditions of sorcery and shamanism. Dominant influences include the eleventh-century 'Old Man of the Mountains' – head of the heretical cult of Assassins, who declared, 'Nothing is True. Everything is permissible.' – and twentieth-century author and guru William S. Burroughs, who spoke of deconstructing reality using language and drugs.

Chaos magic first surfaced during the early 1970s in the form of a loose confederation known as the Illuminates of Thanateros, though it wasn't until the 1980s that it became a dominant thread in occultism. Advocates of this system (or 'absence of system', according to adherents) proclaim that the practitioner can invoke any tradition of gods, demons, angels or symbols – even those derived from fiction – as their personal meaning, rather than literal existence, is vital in achieving the individual's magical aims. This imaginative freedom has created more crossover between Satanism and chaos magic than any other area of the occult.

The fictional alien gods of the Cthulhu Mythos, as created by H. P. Lovecraft, are among the demonic entities found in chaos magic literature. In 1980, the Esoteric Order of Dagon was formed – heavily influenced by the writings of Kenneth Grant, the group drew parallels between Lovecraft's fictional demons and those Aleister Crowley claimed to have conjured. (Michael Aquino is a one-time member of the EOD.) Boasting a dozen 'lodges' situated in locations as diverse as Texas, Australia and England, the Order's literature explains that while members 'do not believe in the absolute existence of the deities which are portrayed in the Cthulhu Mythos, they find the iconography of Lovecraft's work to be a useful paradigm for gaining access to deeper, non-rational areas of the subconscious. The oneiric [dream] origin of Lovecraft's stories is of crucial importance here, in pointing the way of access to parts of the human mind which are identified with alien and (literally) nameless horrors in his fiction.'

Much of the group's works are relatively benign, dedicated to dream interpretation and ritual magic. However, beneath the surface the Esoteric Order of Dagon nurses a more ominous, apocalyptic ethos: 'From day to day the probability grows that the increasingly repressive social structure of Western Civilisation will crush and destroy all expression of True Will. When it collapses completely the EOD will welcome the return of the Elder Gods from beyond the Abyss and with Them breed a New Race. This is the Aeon of Cthulhu Rising.'

Perhaps the most influential new occult order of the 1980s was a countercultural chaos magic group known as Thee Temple Ov Psychic Youth (TOPY). Founded in 1981 by avant-garde musician and self-styled 'esoterrorist' Genesis P-Orridge, TOPY was as much an artistic movement in the tradition of the Dadaists or surrealists as it was a magical order. Broadly anarchic in perspective, TOPY occupied a grey area between art school experimentation, post-punk political activism and mind-altering magic ritual, its idiosyncratic spelling supposedly being one of its methods of breaking the chains of conventionality.

P-Orridge had been with the band Throbbing Gristle, a seminal act on the industrial music scene, and would front the experimental musical project Psychic TV during his years with TOPY. The use of musical beats to alter consciousness and the concert experience as ritual were primary concerns, and the group can take a large cut of the blame for popularising the acid-house scene in Europe. Similarly, spiritual extremes of pleasure and pain were prominent features of TOPY ritual, playing a prominent part in inspiring the fashion for 'body modification' and piercing.

In February 1992, officers from the Obscene Publications Squad raided a house in Brighton, on the English South Coast. The raid was inspired by a decidedly fuzzy video of a 'ritual' which informants alleged had taken place in the cellar of the house (though the house, in fact, had no cellar). It belonged to Genesis P-Orridge, who was in Thailand with his family at the time, aiding Tibetan refugees. The video in question depicted P-Orridge, and others broadly associated with TOPY, in a collage of intercut film sequences portraying a kind of performance-art Black Mass.

What it did not depict was what advocates of the Satanic ritual abuse myth claimed was occurring onscreen: child abuse, abortions and anal sex. The appearance by P-Orridge's heavily-pregnant wife, Paula, in this cheaply-filmed ritual, was somehow interpreted as a woman being forcibly made to abort. Christian activists proudly held up this muddy footage as the evidence that had been lacking for so long, and even presented a woman who claimed to have been abused at the group's Satanic revels. A documentary was made for UK TV's Channel 4 series *Dispatches* – entitled, appropriately enough, 'Beyond Belief' – featuring clips from the video and 'experts' who backed up the ritual abuse hypothesis.

However, the programme – which used as advisers Christian campaigners closely associated with the ritual abuse myth – met resistance from critics and viewers alike, some of whom were well aware that the 'evidence' of Satanic abuse was, in fact, a performance-art video, *Stations of the Cross*, made for TOPY by highly-respected avant-garde film-maker Derek Jarman in 1983. The programme's chief 'witness' was also exposed as an inmate of a psychiatric hospital, her interview taking place within its grounds, while pivotal experts complained about being quoted out of context and misrepresented. The whole farce turned out to be the Satanic abuse myth's last gasp, a last desperate stab at credibility before media and public credulousness were exhausted.

Self-styled 'esoterrorist' Genesis P-Orridge, founder of Thee Temple ov Psychic Youth.

None of which helped Genesis P-Orridge, who regarded the episode as an attempt by the Establishment to fire a shot across the bows of deviant culture. It became clear that if he returned to the UK he could expect, at the very least, to be held up to severe scrutiny by the authorities. As there was a distinct possibility they might insist on taking his (by all accounts happy and well-adjusted) children into 'care', P-Orridge flew to the USA for nearly a decade of self-imposed exile. In truth, many of his less supportive peers weren't sorry to see him go – even though he'd left TOPY, the cultural organisation he founded, in 1990. There was always an undercurrent of resentment between P-Orridge's immediate clique and several factions within TOPY, not least because outsiders regarded him as the group's leader while other members insisted there was no hierarchy within their anarchic order.

P-Orridge had a habit of taking everything into dark territory that made fainter-hearted TOPY members uncomfortable. He shared the by-now-common occultic obsession with Charles Manson, who he regarded as an icon of 'de-control'. (Perhaps ironically, charismatic little criminal Charlie was as much of a countercultural control freak as P-Orridge himself was perceived to be.) He also openly fraternised with Anton LaVey, and other members of the Church of Satan, who made his more liberal brethren nervous with their fascistic reputation. With a dark irony, those who dragged P-Orridge into the Satanic ritual abuse myth seemed blissfully unaware of his connections with the world's most notorious Satanist.

And what of Anton LaVey during the 1980s? The Black Pope's gradual retreat from the public gaze had progressed into reclusiveness. He had, he reasoned, laid down the framework of LaVeyan Satanism and earned the right to privacy. While he always maintained that the Satanic ritual abuse myth was too fatuous to represent any threat to genuine Satanists, it's also true that the cultural environment hadn't got any friendlier since the Church of Satan's foundation in 1966.

A pearl-handled pistol, and a big cat for a pet, had provided enough protection in the past. But, in an atmosphere where fundamentalist Christians were bombing abortion clinics, and paranoid communities were forming vigilante squads against outsiders who might be 'cultists', LaVey could be forgiven for being a little more circumspect. The Black House, once open house to those interested in LaVey's creed, was beginning to resemble a fortress, or perhaps an abbey . . .

The most significant policy statement from LaVey during the 1980s was his 'Pentagonal Revisionism' and corresponding 'Five Point Program': '1) Stratification' – LaVey's belief in meritocracy and hatred of egalitarianism was stronger than ever. '2) Strict taxation of all churches' – the issue over which he fell out with Martin Lamers of the Kerk van Satan. Christianity was a racket, but if it was an honest racket it would go bust overnight. '3) No tolerance for religious beliefs secularized and incorporated into law and order issues' – already enshrined in the US Constitution, though the antics of Christian fundamentalists during the 1980s made it worth restating. '4) Development and production of artificial human companions' – an increasing preoccupation of LaVey's, illustrating his wish to use androids for 'politically correct slavery' and also – in its freedom from reliance upon human beings for social stimulation – his belief in the disposability of most people. '5) The opportunity for anyone to live within a total environment of his or her choice, with mandatory adherence to the aesthetic and behavioural standards of same.'

'Total environments' had always interested LaVey – they were now beginning to obsess him, as Satanists followed suit by quoting more heavily from Walt Disney than Milton or Baudelaire. Boyd Rice, who once referred to LaVey as 'the Walt Disney of the dark side', shared the Black Pope's admiration for Disney himself and his creation, Disneyland – a haven of artificial fulfilment among 'animatronic' companions.

Just as the eighteenth-century Hellfire Clubs had created their 'Abbeys of Thelema' in deserted caves, and Crowley had established his in rural Sicily, so the Black Pope was creating his own private world in the cellar of the Black House. As is evident from his writings, the mass of humanity now not only disappointed LaVey, but distressed or disgusted him. His response was to insulate himself in a *film noir*-fantasy world of seedy gin joints and run-down hotel rooms from 40 years previously, occupied only by his mannequins, half-living creatures that seemed to move in the twilight.

But even a fantasist – or 'sorcerer', as the two are often interchangeable in the occult world – as imaginative as LaVey could not insulate himself from familial conflict. On 30 December 1990, his daughter Zeena made public a letter she had written to Michael Aquino, not only resigning her membership of the Church of Satan but dissociating herself from her father, its founder. To rub salt into the wound, Zeena, along with her paramour Nikolas Schreck, eventually threw her lot in with the Temple of Set – which had for so long shadowed and derided everything LaVey had done.

'I was born a Satanist,' wrote Zeena, 'my unfather was raised in the mundane world of humankind where he remains. He unwittingly served as the agent of the true daemonic energy needed to sire me as a genuine magical child. I have never seen any evidence that he honestly believes in the force whom he has exploited for so long as a "good gimmick". Nevertheless he did succeed in attracting the ideal sorceress needed for my conception. My mother, a natural magician as incarnation of Diana the Huntress, was the driving force of the most positive aspects of the Church of Satan.'

Anton LaVey relaxes in his famous Den of Iniquity.

The full story behind this very public and bitter schism is probably only known to those involved. LaVey had been through a bitter divorce from Zeena's mother and the court proceedings were dragging on. He was spending increasing amounts of time with his secretary and biographer, Blanche Barton, who would later bear him a child. Zeena criticised Barton's biography of LaVey, *The Secret Life of a Satanist*, deriding 'the sickeningly repetitive flattery she (he) extends to Zionism, Bolshevism, and the state of Israel while safely negating any Norse or Teutonic mythology'. The rift seemed to be both personal and ideological. Whatever the case, the 1990 split of the Werewolf Order from the Church of Satan took some of the more grimly fascistic elements of the movement back into the periphery.

Beyond Good and Evil

A beer with Boyd Rice.

I spoke to Boyd Rice, a tall, affable fellow, at a Non concert in spring 1999. Provocative and extreme in print and on record, it was difficult to reconcile his anti-social ideas with his agreeable personality. In common with most media villains, in person Boyd proved friendly, open and articulate. Why do so many notorious misanthropes seem so much more likeable and reasonable than their celebrated humanitarian equivalents?

Fascism's a word that's used a lot more than it's understood. What do you think it means?
I use the word in a modern, bastardised sense where it's just some kind of harsh doctrine or creed. Fascism is actually just the corporate state, it's about economics and that sort of thing, and that doesn't interest me at all. For years what I talked about publicly was a harsh, Satanic philosophy, and people would say, 'That sounds really fascistic', and I'd respond, 'No, no.' Then at one point I just thought, if fascism is just being anti-democratic and against the consensus-reality we live in, I might as well just say I'm a fascist.

What does Satanism mean to you?
For me, Satan is a path to God. I believe God is a balance of good and evil, a creative and destructive force that underlies everything in the universe. For me that power is God. It encompasses everything – good and evil, God and the Devil. I feel today that people are very one-sided and one-dimensional. The way back to a balance is Satan.

Has this balance ever existed?
Yes. For instance, the symbol I'm wearing comes from an old rune, which meant the balance between light and darkness, destruction and creation. It's the thirteenth rune in the oldest runic alphabet, right in the middle. This suggests to me that there was a time when people understood that the creative force and destructive force were just aspects of nature, and one was just as important as the other. But by the time the second runic alphabet appeared, it was gone. People once had sight of this concept, but have lost it.

I think early on, a lot of the people considered to be Satanists were just pagans who had a completely different approach to worship, which was misunderstood by orthodox Christians. A lot of the early pagans and Satanists were just people interested in hermeticism, alchemy, Zoroastrianism and dualism. In the early Black Masses, you wouldn't just eat a communion wafer, there was a white wafer and black

wafer, suggesting a balance between good and evil, that both were necessary for life to function.

You must be aware that the way you present your ideas – using fascist imagery, for example – will provoke and offend people . . .
I've always thought every single thing I do is the most reasonable thing in the world, and there are other people who don't. There are people coming to protest the show because I use banners with this runic symbol on it, and they think it looks fascistic. I just spoke to a woman from the Anti-Nazi League and she kept saying, 'You're using fascist imagery, you're using swastikas', and I kept trying to explain that I'm not. The symbol I use is an ancient symbol but certain people will think it's Nazi because it has the kind of look or aura to it.

Abraxas, a Gnostic demon representing reconciled opposites – beyond good and evil. Portrait by Tim.

I describe the 8/8/88 Rally as the defining moment in 1980s Satanism – would you agree?
Yes – I can see that. When I met Anton LaVey he was a recluse by his own choice. He'd put up with all these

people through the sixties and early seventies and he got to a point where he didn't want to deal with them anymore. He just wanted to live in his own world with things exactly as he wanted them. He'd become tired of the whole public Satanism thing. He met me and I introduced him to this whole circle of people, like Adam Parfrey, who'd grown up on his books and been totally inspired by him. During the seventies, we'd heard that the Church of Satan no longer existed and Anton LaVey didn't have anything to do with that sort of thing any more. Then, when we met him, he was just like one of us, a kindred spirit. I think he got really excited by the fact that there were people out in the world, on their own, who'd been influenced by him and were doing all this stuff. It got him into high gear again.

In the Church of Satan, Anton LaVey claimed to have discovered a lost tribe of productive misfits . . .
It's amazing how I will meet people who, down to the last detail, are into the same stuff. Like LaVey – I went for years not knowing anyone else who was into Tiny Tim – and Anton LaVey thought Tiny Tim was one of the greatest performers of all time. I would meet other people in the Church of Satan into Tiny Tim too. Not because LaVey was into it, and they checked out all his reference points, they were into it because it was great stuff they discovered on their own.

Many people see contradictions in the Church of Satan's stance. How can the same organisation ordain a decadent performer like Marc Almond and a radical right-winger like Nikolas Schreck?
LaVey understood that there wasn't one cookie-cutter for everybody. What makes one person happy might well make someone else miserable. In terms of sex, for example, some people are happy living a totally monastic lifestyle, others are happy being total libertines. Sexual freedom doesn't mean having as much sex as possible, it means having the kind of sex you want. What makes Nikolas Schreck happy might not be the kind of thing that makes Marc Almond happy.

But might not one of the things that could make Nikolas Schreck happy be making Marc Almond unhappy?
I think for Nikolas Schreck, just having his name mentioned will make him happy. Nikolas and Zeena are now with the Temple of Set preaching these things that sound like Christianity with a different god. They used to call the Temple of Set the Temple of Shit – they realised Aquino was just a laughing stock.

It seems to me that, during the 1980s, the entity the Church of Satan was invoking looked more and more like the Old Testament God . . .
I like the God of the Old Testament. We should get back to some of those old ideas like 'an eye for an eye, a

tooth for a tooth'. Some of that stuff sounds like it's straight out of the Church of Satan.

How do you see Satanism progressing?
I wrote a piece recently for *The Black Flame* and I ended it saying, 'Only time will tell whether Anton LaVey was the first modern Satanist or the last modern Satanist.' I'm not an organisation man, I'm not a joiner, so I have a real difficult time with some of these modern Satanists, people who can quote Anton LaVey front-to-back but can't really apply the ideas. There are so many people who can talk it, but can't really live it.

Can a society for non-joiners ever work?
I think when you take an idea, no matter how good it is, if you get a bunch of people involved, you degrade the idea. Anton LaVey was aware of that. There's this inner circle of people that were great, who didn't really need each other. I'd say, 'What if we get all these good people, and they come from wherever they live in the world, and all gather in one place. Imagine the power that could generate.' And he'd say, 'No. We're loners. People in other groups need to rub elbows, be with all the lemmings. Divided we stand, united we fall.'

Fear and Loathing in Los Angeles

Hobnobbing with Count and Countess von Dreck.

While in LA during the summer of 1993, I bumped into two affable ex-compatriots of Nikolas Schreck, the head of the Werewolf Order. Count and Countess von Dreck hosted an off-the-wall horror show on a local cable TV channel and oozed enough sleazy, cheesy gothic chic to match their monstrous hair-dos. Unable to track down Schreck himself, I asked the Count and Countess to reminisce about their times with the fledgling werewolf.

I've had trouble tracking down Nikolas Schreck, why's he so difficult to get a hold of?
The problem is that he's scared he's going to get murdered all the time so he stays very secretive. When we first met Nikolas we were extras during the punk era – there was a big punk scene in Hollywood and plenty of money to be made as extras. Nik was on set, he had two-tone hair at that time, and still had two ears, and he had these fishing boots on. We were in this terrible movie called *Fast Forward* and we all had to be real fools. Radio Werewolf was going strong then, but they

couldn't play as they were getting bomb threats all the time. This was because they were really pushing the Nazi thing. A lot of the lyrics had a lot to do with Nazism and he was seriously into it – a lot of the Nazi youth were beginning to gather around.

The Count and Countess von Dreck with the author.

The person who really put them out of commission was the music editor for *LA Weekly*, though he's dead now. He did a big article on them and basically ended up saying that Radio Werewolf will not survive. The band went down after that. Shortly after that Nikolas moved to San Francisco where he hooked up with Anton LaVey. They became friends and he got close to Zeena LaVey. In fact he tried to get us to join the Church of Satan, but we're not into that – we said, 'No thanks, we don't want to be little Devil worshippers.' He came back to LA with Zeena, who has a son, and they lived together in Hollywood for another year or so. It was while he was in San Francisco his ear got chopped off. He was driving in his car and some people kept smashing into him until his car wouldn't go any further. He rolled his window down and someone came up and cut his ear off. Then every time you'd see him, if you came up behind him he'd freak out, because he'd got really paranoid. Then they went to Vienna. He doesn't like his face photographed anymore, he's got really paranoid about it.

What caused the schism with LaVey?
This is just rumour and opinion, but it was partly Nikolas's overt Nazism. Also, Nikolas is a real power freak and he wanted what Anton had. He wanted to be Anton. He's still with Zeena though, and I think she's also rebelling against her father.

It must be damn difficult rebelling when your old man's a Satanist.
If you're a Satanist and a Nazi, isn't that more impressive?

CONSERVATIVE SATANISM

Paul Douglas Valentine on his
Worldwide Church of Satanic Liberation.

I spoke to Paul Valentine over the phone in 1994 from his new home in Texas, and he proved to be both articulate and charming, living up to his loquacious reputation. A polite man, with some forceful points of view, Valentine was clearly at home dealing with the press.

How large is your organisation?
We have exactly 2,342 members worldwide, most of whom are in Europe. About 600 of our members are in the States. We're not as controversial as people would want us to be. We're not militant: we don't go down the street dressed in black; we don't go up against Baptist ministers. I certainly did it when I started out, but it got tired and boring. No one took us seriously. They looked at this facade, and that was all they saw, and my message was more important than the facade. My philosophy is that every person has the right to achieve with every ounce of their being. I don't believe in putting limitations on anyone or anything. I'm anti-government intervention in people's lives. This may sound strange, but I'm a strict conservative when it comes to politics. I don't go as far as Aleister Crowley – every person is a god or a star, nonsense like that. You are either born with magical ability, or you're not. I believe in a separate entity, which I call Satan. It has absolutely nothing to do with the Judeo-Christian concept – my concept is a glorified nature god. I started out by being involved in various kinds of nature-orientated magic, which I still have a soft spot for. But I differ from Wiccans because I don't believe in the very Christian-type concepts of love thy neighbour, love thy enemy.

Why choose Satan as the name for the entity you believe in?

Quite honestly, it was for show. It's a very potent, shocking term – LaVey was right about that. But, as I got older, I realised Satan was the perfect term because He embodies ideas of freedom and individuality you don't find in other concepts of religion or God. Satan represents liberty in its utmost form. There's no guilt involved in being who you are, standing up for what you believe in, even if it is contradictory to social mores. I have many gay men in my organisation – that doesn't bother me in the least. Be what you want as long as it doesn't infringe upon the welfare of another person or animal.

Are you the liberal arm of Satanism?

I'm very conservative in many ways. I show no quarter to those who cannot follow basic rules and regulations. Child molesters should be shot, for example. There is no allowance for Nazis and neo-Nazis in my organisation, though – I have no use for that.

What is it you dislike about the Church of Satan?

I do the talk-show circuit and people within the occult world have said I'm crude and I have very little class because I speak my mind and use coarse terms. But those within the Church of Satan kiss Anton LaVey's ass. Nobody in my organisation kisses my butt, and if they do they're out. I don't want to be put on a pedestal because I'm only going to fall off. Everyone in the Church of Satan takes everything LaVey says as gospel. I don't think any of them have ever pulled him up and said, 'Some of this is idiotic.' In *The Satanic Witch* he has that nonsense about salad dressings, how some are more Satanic because they smell like a woman. If I ever went down on a woman and she smelled like Russian salad dressing, I'd run screaming.

I respect LaVey in many ways for what he's given the occult world. But these days it sounds like I'd rather be dead than be him, because I like to go out and meet people and interact with individuals. I have been shot at, and I've had one of my apartments fire-bombed. But if it got to the point where I had to walk about with armed guards and set up electric fences because of who I am and what I am, I'd stop. But I like getting up there and being confrontational. Most people are pretty pathetic with their beliefs. It's based on what their parents have told them, and what their grandparents told their parents, and so on. I like getting up there and saying, 'Look folks, question your beliefs.'

The Church of Satanic Liberation has a reputation as a Satanic swingers club – how did that come about?

When I first started out, I had a lot of people who came to me that were young and most of the people in my organisation are female – about 70 per cent. I was very quick to be seen on the street with these girls. I always said, 'If they're within the age of sexual consent, fine,

there's nothing wrong with that.' But that was stupid, because I was just looked at as someone who was a rush to be with because I was Paul Valentine – Satanist. I took advantage of the situation, and them. It should never have happened, and it made the Church of Satanic Liberation look like nothing more than a Satanic sex club.

You like to be confrontational.

I've done numerous talk shows with so-called Satanists, and I've said, 'Look, these people are fools, they're not real Satanists.' A lot of the heavy metal/death metal Satanists that have run the gamut of talk shows have said they won't appear with Paul Valentine. Many times I agree with the talk show hosts. I was on *Geraldo* and he wouldn't air the show. I found out it was because I wasn't anything he wanted, the show got out of hand, and he was offended by some of it. Also, most tellingly, I agreed with him on some very important points. They had these other guys on who publish this magazine called *Infernal Grotto*. They started saying this garbage to Geraldo: 'You're the reason we get so many problems with that two-hour special you ran.' I said, 'Shut up. We made our beds, we have to lie in them. That documentary was a good representation of what could be going on.' They were really offended by that – me turning against a 'fellow Satanist'. But you can't go blaming Geraldo Rivera for the public's reaction to Satanism.

Are you active magically?

Yes, but all of my magic deals solely with personal and private matters. I'm very selfish when it comes to my magic. I haven't done a destruction ritual in about eight years. I'm the type of person who'd sooner walk up and punch someone in the mouth – I'm six foot four, so that's not too hard – than to waste my time and effort. A magical working's just not worth it. Unless they'd hurt one of my family members and they were somewhere I couldn't get at them, such as in gaol, in which case you can bet your ass I'm going to do a working and it's going to work. I have a very high success rate.

THE SINISTER DIALECTIC

An afternoon with Christos Beest of the Order of the Nine Angles.

I met Mr Beest, at his request, on a glorious day in 1994, in the beautiful Shropshire hills on the Welsh border that he believes are the heart of his personal Satanic tradition. After a bracing walk to the crest of a bracken-topped hill (which did no favours to a person's hangover), we paused and talked. Beest was not at all how I'd imagined him. He was a serious, personable, well-spoken man in his mid-to-late twenties who seemed closer to a mature sociology student than the bloodthirsty fanatic I'd anticipated.

Tarot card no. 3 from the Order of the Nine Angles deck: the Mistress of Earth, the 'dark, menstruating woman' who embodies the left-hand path and feminine power.

What is the Order of the Nine Angles?

It's a tradition which goes back 7000 years – that's according to legend. It was born when there was a civilisation around here called Albion which had various rites associated with a dark goddess who we know as Baphomet. Baphomet's been handed down through the ages as a composite figure. The famous goat-headed symbol was actually a distortion, a lie which took away from the real power of the goddess, who was actually a dark, menstruating woman. It was very much a code of honour centred around war and the brutal realities of life, and actually the original paganism for thousands of years before Christianity arrived. It's basically an oral tradition I received from my predecessor, Anton Long. He received it from a Mistress of the Order and she had it passed on from someone before her.

How large is your order?

Very small, probably around ten people with a few hangers-on. We are small because it is a genuine magical way and it requires people to live a certain lifestyle. The archetypal ONA member is a lone sorcerer, somebody who defies their own limits, defies themselves. They find out their true potential, usually through ordeals. There's one ordeal, for example, which requires living alone for three months, completely alone, bereft of any possessions whatsoever. The actual aim is, on an individual level, finding your god within yourself. What it aims to produce is a unique individual who doesn't need anything. There's a lot of strands from a lot of esoteric groups, but the ONA is essentially a Western tradition.

Why is there such prominent mention of human sacrifice in your literature?

Because it's part of the tradition. There was an issue of *Fenrir*, our magazine, which centred around human sacrifice. A lot of things are not what they seem. All manuscripts that are written serve a certain purpose – they illustrate a certain point. A lot of people at the Temple of Set and the Church of Satan are trying to re-establish Satanism as a moral religion. Something which is sanitised, something which is misunderstood, and really quite nice. What the ONA is doing is countering that by saying, 'No, it isn't.' It's regaining the original darkness of what Satanism is, because if Satanism isn't evil, then what is?

Could this effect not be achieved without human sacrifice?

Maybe human sacrifice doesn't go on. That's part of the point. The manuscripts are illustrating an ethic.

So what you're saying is that the effect the manuscript has is more important than anything it actually says or advocates?

Yes. The manuscripts are collected to illustrate points. Here it says that people should stop allowing laws to treat them like children.

Have you been involved with human sacrifice in any form?

Obviously I can't tell you.

Is there an element of macho occultism in your order?

There's more women involved in the group than men, which is quite interesting. There is the man I inherited the tradition from, Anton Long, and he's fought in wars as a mercenary. That was a form of sacrifice. To outline the theory behind human sacrifice again: ultimately it could be anything, that's just the most extreme form. It also aids the sinister dialectic, it regains a certain darkness that has been taken away from Satanism. It gives back to an individual their own judgement over things. Saying that you can actually do this – you can go out and kill somebody if you feel it's important to do it – but you take the consequences for it. In other words, anybody who gets involved in 'the sinister' can do anything they want, or anything they judge useful. There's nothing in the Order which says you can't do this or you can't do that – that would be contradictory to what we're aiming for. All it's saying is – find yourself and use your own ethics and judgement. You could go ahead with a sacrifice, but you could get caught and spend the rest of your days in gaol – is it worth doing that?

What is the role played by 'aeonics' in your philosophy?

An understanding of how energies flow through civilisations. What moves people. What creates certain kinds of individual. All civilisations start off as a creative minority, a small group of people in a certain area who did certain things which drew the masses. People are putty, basically, and it's always going to be a small number of people who can effect changes; the artists or whatever, the people who dare to break out of the constraints of society.

What's the ONA's political position?

I regard the ONA as the only true anarchist group. A group which can use extreme right-wing politics and extreme left-wing politics. We're not seduced by either side, we don't regard them as 'true' in any sense, they're just a means to an end. So far it's been judged that it's the energies which imbue right-wing organisations that are useful and will flower, say within 100 years, and certain things will follow on. This is the essence of aeonics. It is a cold, rational, almost scientific judgement of certain means to achieve further ends. The archetypal ONA member considers any form to be a suitable means to an end. That's part of the point of the ordeal of spending three months alone. You actually go through a withdrawal where you're not swayed by anything, any abstract ideas, you are just yourself. An ONA member doesn't 'become' a Nazi or a communist, he just uses those movements. Obviously, in order to use them you have to enter into a role in a very demonic sense, you also have to know where it ends.

Why does so much ONA material seem to have such a negative, destructive approach? Could you not, for example, write something about the beauty of walking in these hills?

There are actually four novels, *The Deofel Quartet*, which deal exactly with that. It deals with love and life in a very real sense. It deals with all those feelings which would make an archetypal Satanist confused, because the archetypal image is of a dark master who could kill just at the drop of a hat. That image is very important because it allows people to play a role which people are swayed by. What some of the ONA manuscripts do is allow people to play that role. But it has to end at some point, and if it doesn't end they become possessed by that role, and their whole Satanic or magical quest is finished. They've lost insight. If they do derive insight from it, then they'll know there's something beyond that. It may be something that's the opposite, something quite beautiful perhaps, but they have to go through a role to find its true opposite in a real sense.

If you say that people can explore their limits by contemplating human sacrifice, could they not, by that philosophy, feel they ought to abuse a child?

No, not at all. The background of sacrifice is that it's about culling, accepting that there is certain dross in society. A right-wing concept perhaps, but that's just labelling it. It's something which is not right- or left-wing, it's a concept that goes back to the Vikings, or before that. The Vikings weren't right-wing. We're imposing modern political views on things to raise emotive responses. People have to see beyond that, to see the essence beyond the appearance, which is what a lot of the manuscripts are about. People are swayed by forms – what is racism but a word often used to make people feel guilty about feeling certain things?

Is it possible to be black, oriental or whatever and a member of the ONA?

There's a gentleman in Singapore who's working with us.

There's a suggestion that the ONA has something to do with neo-Nazi groups, is that true?

It's rather the other way around. Someone in the ONA felt that involvement in the British National Party would be useful to them. There is somebody who is involved in the ONA who is involved in right-wing politics, but he used it as a form to achieve something, then got out of it and went on to something else. We have something of a reputation for dressing in Nazi uniforms and invoking the spirit of Hitler. It stems from the deeds of the past which people haven't seen from a magical perspective. There's very little that's dangerous about becoming a radical anarchist or a communist. But there are people in Germany right now being executed for their involvement in right-wing organisations. There was a certain individual found dumped in Holland who was a leading light in the political Right of Germany. You mustn't confuse 'right-wing' with conservatism or anything like that. The political format that's gripped this society has nothing to do with right-wing politics and actually leans more towards the Left in essence. The Hard Right is a very dangerous thing to get involved with. Particularly for Satanists – the ONA has received threats from certain national socialist groups who don't like the idea of Satanism being linked with them. Unlike left-wing groups, when stirred right-wing activists will do things others wouldn't consider. That's why it's a good thing to get involved with, in one respect: because it offers genuine danger on all sorts of levels and offers a moral dilemma as well. The whole point of insight roles is that you undertake a role for around a year which is the complete opposite of your own personality.

Tarot card no. 5 from the Order of the Nine Angles deck: the Master, who embodies masculine power and organised religion. This monk has blinded the Christian worshipper with his rigid belief system.

What are you aiming for in the ONA?
The real secret of Satanism is that a Satanist restores balance within society, acting as a counterbalance. For example, if we were in a right-wing situation at this time, there would certainly be a communist Satanic organisation. This may all seem rather frivolous and aimless, but what Satanism represents is basically an energy for change. Evolution. An energy which provokes insight and adversity. Satan represents movement. Something which moves and that isn't tied down by moral abstracts or ideas.

Culling is portrayed in your literature as helping nature along, isn't it?
Yes, you could remove someone you feel is detrimental to your cause, but you could be wrong in that. It could turn out to be the opposite. War is the perfect example of culling in that it is removing a massive number of people, and when you do that you effect certain changes. What those changes will be, how you can control that, is all part of it. It's like moving pieces on a chessboard. People are removed who you judge to be detrimental to certain things. It could be a large number of people, it could be an individual. Not everyone will cull, not everybody should.

It's suggested in your literature that it's something which is expected of ONA members.
Would you kill if ordered to do so?

No.
Well then, we have already established an insight upon yourself, albeit in a split second. This is actually the secret of the manuscripts. They are designed to attract people who can think and judge for themselves. That includes when a Satanic master comes along and tells you to despatch someone – you are faced with a choice: if you do it you will please the master, but do you want a master like that? As the master, do you want somebody serving you who is weak, or do you want somebody who will turn round and refuse to obey? We're looking for the latter.

How would you like people to look on the ONA, do you want to scare people?
The work is very extreme, it has to be that way. The manuscripts are designed to produce certain changes in society, to create certain preconceptions and destroy others. We are very elitist, because very few people ever stay the course. It involves real hardship, a certain way of living which few people are willing to follow.

CHILDREN OF BLOOD, DEATH AND THE DEVIL

Satanic Thrash, Speed and Death Metal

ach generation needs a new soundtrack to define their coming of age. Most people are inclined to dismiss the popular art-forms of the previous generation as dull or staid, and those of the generation that follows their own as gaudy or excessive. Anton LaVey referred to this phenomenon as Erotic Crystallisation Inertia, or ECI. Rock music, in its worship of impetuous youth, is forever in search of the next wave of ECIs.

For the kids that first got into Bathory or Venom in the early 1980s it was an electric revelation, defining the newly unacceptable extreme of black metal. For those who'd been brought up on the previous generation of metal bands, like Black Sabbath or Judas Priest, this new variation sounded like an overheated mess. For young black metal fans throughout the decade, however, it was what they craved – the hardest, fastest, evillest music possible.

Some of the kids who formed their ECIs in the early 1980s did so to an accompaniment of the likes of Mercyful Fate and Witchfynde – bands who cemented the musical pact between Satanism and heavy metal. As the New Wave Of British Heavy Metal died off, the younger musicians it inspired began to generate a sound which was even more intense. The result exploded as thrash metal, a genre that took the rapid guitars of black metal bands like Venom and increased their musical complexity whilst supercharging them to ever-greater velocity. Speed was the order of the day, turning raw adrenaline into a sound that matched the frustration and energy of the young people who created it.

The recording commonly regarded as the first thrash metal album was *Kill 'Em All* by the American band Metallica. Released in 1983, it was an exuberant, frantic piece of work, dismissed by the old guard as immature, but embraced by a new generation of fans as the yardstick for speed and aggression. James Hetfield, the main force behind the band, had endured a strict Christian upbringing manifested in apocalyptic, biblically-inspired epic tracks like 'Four Horsemen'. Later, he wrote bitterly of religious hypocrisy in songs like 'The God That Failed'.

Despite their links with black metal and vaguely anti-Christian sentiment Metallica never dabbled in Satanism, concentrating instead on the corruption of political power, the futility of war, and their own earnest dedication to freedom and honesty. These themes were to become trademarks of the new thrash movement that followed in Metallica's smoking footsteps and dominated the metal scene in the mid-1980s. The music that sounded so extreme in 1983 is pretty tame today, now that the musical barbarians have left the temples of good taste in smouldering ruins.

Second only to Metallica as pioneers of thrash metal were Slayer, whose debut album *Show No Mercy* appeared in 1984. While Metallica replaced the theatrical aspects of heavy metal with a sweatily-honest approach, Slayer fully endorsed the potent armoury of symbols and imagery. Their stage appearance was an exercise in over-the-top aggression: huge inverted crosses, demonic black make-up and wristbands studded with nine-inch nails. Their sound echoed this, a musical beast driven by a thundering heartbeat which sounded fit to burst. The songs were howls of hate in the face of a grey world – fantasies of massacre in the name of Satan. Slayer were the bastard sons of Venom, the next step down the musical left-hand path, who made their predecessors sound like easy listening.

If there was a Satanic philosophy behind any of this, it did not show – Slayer were purely celebrating the catharsis of aggression, frustration and pain through music. Slayer's Satan was a god of apocalyptic destruction, a symbol of deep alienation and blind rage.

1985 saw the release of their second album, *Hell Awaits*, which demonstrated the band's growing popularity by selling over 100,000 copies, followed by the 1986 recording *Reign in Blood*. Typically, their popularity was often

Satanic Californian thrash-metal band Slayer in a bloodthirsty early promotional shot.

mirrored by negative press. Among the bloody rants featured on *Reign in Blood* was 'Angel of Death', a song about the notorious Nazi torturer and medical researcher Dr Josef Mengele. In the USA, their record label Def American bowed to pressure and refused to release the album because of its offensive lyrics (though it later received a UK release).

Since their earliest days Slayer had toyed with Nazi imagery, (at one point giving Iron Crosses away free with one of their releases,) but their interest in radical right-wing ideology was no greater than their appreciation of Satanic philosophy. The band had merely identified a couple of icons – the Devil and Hitler – who, for very different reasons, generated alarm and discomfort, nihilistically wallowing in the depths of taboo. The hideous images that decorated their album sleeves were unashamedly dark fantasies, their songs an attempt to translate the hellish paintings of Hieronymous Bosch to vinyl. As guitarist Kerry King explained in a 1985 interview: 'I'd rather sing about the Devil than God . . . I like to read up on it because it's something I want to know about . . . We don't sacrifice babies or burn churches or anything.'

Slayer began to leaven their death-fixated ballads with songs that carried ethical messages, however grim the context. ('Silent Scream', for example, is an anti-abortion song, ironically putting Slayer in the same camp as fundamentalist Christians.) Likewise, their overtly theatrical Satanic stage personae became a dim, embarrassing memory as the band's image came closer to the everyday street garb of a Californian heavy metal fan. In an interview to promote their 1990 *Seasons in the Abyss* album, Slayer confessed they weren't entirely in tune with the fans who took their Satanic tag at face value. 'If we told them that we weren't seriously into it they'd get offended,' pleaded bassist/vocalist Tom Araya. 'You sit there and try to be honest with them and say, "Hey, mellow out dude" and they don't understand. There is a handful who take this stuff seriously and you don't really know what to say to them.' Sharing the mild hypocrisy of many established metal bands, an older, more comfortable Slayer wanted

to portray their flirtation with the dark side as a warning against it.

Of the many tensions in the band, which perhaps helped Slayer attain their early level of fraught intensity, not least was the friction between King – source of most of the band's Satanic references – and front-man Araya – who, since the release of *Show No Mercy* in 1984, had converted to Christianity. Reflecting, in a 1998 interview, on the conflict between his beliefs and the blasphemies he sometimes found himself singing, Araya rationalised: 'I look at it like it's bringing happiness to people, so it's a sacrifice I'm willing to make.' Guitarist Jeff Hanneman more candidly observed: 'The major change in the lyrics is we got out of Satanism. We were never seriously in it. We like to

dabble. We got drunk and drew pentagrams on the floor and read *The Satanic Bible*. And when people thought we were crazy we got off on it.'

Slayer weren't the only thrash band to adopt Satanism as a badge. Sodom, a German band, combined Satanic imagery with lyrics about the horror of war – though their musical limitations and poor English took them closer to parody than potency, as exemplified by their stage names: Aggressor, Witchhunter and Angel Ripper (the latter replaced by the splendidly-titled Grave Violator). Even more flamboyant were the Swiss band Hellhammer, consisting of Savage Damage, Bloodhunter and Satanic Slaughter. Hellhammer went on to become avant-garde thrash act Celtic Frost, but, sadly, changed their memorable names (though Mr Slaughter did opt for Tom G. Warrior).

Other infernal thrash bands included the influential Exodus, Onslaught, who evolved from punk to thrash, and the Californian band Possessed, who suffered from the reputation of being a poor man's Slayer. Their first two albums, recorded in the mid-1980s, *Seven Churches* and (in a suitably hellish gatefold sleeve) *At the Gates*, were full of demonic aggression, machine-gun riffs and crude horror-story lyrics. Like Slayer, Possessed revelled in medieval visions of Hell and apocalyptic biblical themes, but, beneath it all, were just a bunch of West

Coast kids who liked beer, scary movies and making a lot of noise. Reformed in the mid-1990s due to the recent vogue for extreme Satanic rock, Possessed have been feted as one of the chief forerunners of the next wave of underground rock – death metal.

The roots of this furthest musical extreme sprang from the alienated kids who swapped demo tapes and photocopied fanzines. The more unacceptable a band was – whether in terms of musical aesthetic or 'bad taste' – the stronger its underground credentials. By the mid-1980s, thrash had become too safe a form to be embraced by the underground. Hard-core metal fans were looking for something even louder, less civilised, more demented.

The style that surfaced was a blur of bludgeoning guitars and manic piston-drums, rode by an indecipherable growl of inhuman vocals. To outsiders, it was a painful cacophony that sounded the same from one song to the next. But to its teenage adherents, death metal – which began in earnest in 1987, with the release of *Scream Bloody Gore* by the appropriately-named Death – was a rollercoaster ride of aimless fury that crushed all worldly cares in its wake.

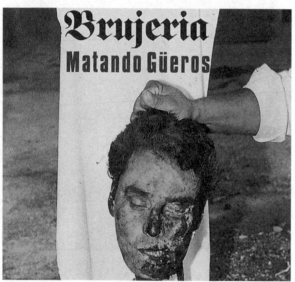

Brujeria ('black magic') are a spoof death metal band who claim to be Devil-worshipping Mexican bandits. This scene-of-crime photo supposedly represents the Matamoros case, where drug-dealing killers were dubiously assumed to be Satanists.

Completely confounding its critics, the fans' criterion for death-metal perfection was 'uncompromising brutality'.

Lyrical content seemed almost irrelevant, due to the growling generic vocal style that made the words inaudible. (Leading exponents Obituary reputedly did not even use lyrics, just bellowing nonsense into the microphone.) Still, the one distinct theme was – as Death's debut-album title suggests – gore and viscera. Death metal lyrics describe, in as much nauseating detail as possible, painfully messy deaths as epitomised in 'Multiple Stab Wounds' by Malevolent Creation, or 'Hammer Smashed Face' by Cannibal Corpse. Forever seeking new ways to express their visceral subject, death metal lyricists often sounded as if they'd swallowed a mortician's thesaurus. The genre's abstract approach – taking a hideous moment out of context, combining it with alien noises produced by out-of-tune guitars played at implausible speed – gave the material an almost surreal effect that also appealed to underground music fans outside the metal subculture.

Independent record companies, sensing another burgeoning trend, rushed to sign young death metal acts. American band Morbid Angel, with their classic album *Altars of Madness* in 1989, were the first to abandon the death metal fixation with gory mayhem to adopt an overtly Satanic stance. On *Altars of Madness* many of the songs have the feel of overheated black magical chants or prayers, caught in a storm of black hate and contempt for the world. The second album, *Blessed are the Sick*, released in 1991, continued in the same black vein. Notable among the medieval demons featured in the band's lyrics are references to unfamiliar names like Yogsothoth and Shub Niggurath – creatures from H. P. Lovecraft's Cthulhu Mythos. As the band progressed, it became apparent that much of their Satanic perspective was derived from Avon Books' dubiously-authentic *Necronomicon*, the bible of evil conceived in Lovecraft's fiction.

At the same time, a rival death metal act named Deicide stepped into the Satanic limelight. Deicide, formed in 1987 under the name Amon in Florida – which, for no obvious reason, became the spiritual home of death metal – created their name to describe the act of murdering faith, or God Himself. From the outset, Deicide's biggest asset was its bassist and frontman, Glen Benton. Benton infuriated press and public to the point where they could not help but react – sporting an inverted cross branded on his forehead (the rest of the band talked proudly of their own self-inflicted burns), his interviews rarely progressed beyond the vocalist

Glen Benton of Satanic death-metal band Deicide.

alternately baiting, and being baited by, the interviewer, followed by a tirade of bombastic threats and abuse.

One such interview, with *New Musical Express* in 1992, led to a typical bout of controversy. Benton was quoted as boasting that he shot and tortured small furry animals at his Florida home, bringing him to the attention of European animal rights groups. The tour to promote Deicide's second album, *Legion*, was beset by problems – not least death threats from militant animal lovers, resulting in a bomb scare in the UK and an explosion at a Scandinavian gig. Animal rights activists – who have conspicuously avoided obvious, low-publicity, high-risk targets such as halal or kosher butchers – got very excited about coverage in the music press for threatening the lives of young metal fans. For his part, Benton was happy to ignore the evidence and blame the whole episode on 'Christian bastards'.

Benton freely admits the inspiration for his Satanism comes mostly from his own dreams. This is hardly surprising. The 'trifixion' symbol that decorates the sleeve of *Legion* has no historical Satanic pedigree. Their lyrics are dominated by images of despair and suffering wrapped in fevered blasphemy, while genuine Satanists are opposed to misery or self-sacrifice, considering themselves above the uncontrolled aggression that typifies Benton's approach. It's true, however, that Deicide's bitter musical salvos and Benton's gruff howls combine to create a dementedly menacing – if one-dimensional – sound, and the vocalist's manic 'Heavy Metal Manson' persona is entertainingly well-executed.

On the first Deicide album, the song 'Dead by Dawn' is obviously inspired directly by the high-octane splatter-movie classic *The Evil Dead*. This suggests the band's Satanic creed originated in modern popular fictions – born out by their first demo recording, entitled 'Feasting the Beast'. There is no 'Feast of the Beast' in any historical Satanic tradition, but there is a very definite reference to this mythical event in *Michelle Remembers*, the book responsible for launching the

Satanic ritual abuse myth. Deicide, therefore, were either alluding to a secret practice which other, better-informed authorities on Satanism were ignorant of, or – more likely – they were taking their inspiration from the huge volume of anti-Satanist propaganda pumped out by fundamentalist Christians. Satanic rock bands, it seems, had learned to play the opposition at their own game.

Since the early 1980s, the USA had seen increasing evidence of minor juvenile crime influenced by Satanism – graffiti, vandalism in graveyards, impromptu animal sacrifice. In their spurious attempts to apply scientific methodology, evangelical theorists have styled the perpetrators as 'Dabblers' – foot-soldiers, or outer initiates, of the vague, all-powerful, Devil-worshipping conspiracy. 'Stoners', the more common term applied to these improvised Satanists, is, in youth parlance, just a loose term for an unmotivated kid who likes rock music and marijuana – more *Beavis and Butthead* than Richard Ramirez. However, to self-styled experts on Satanism, stoners are an amorphous cult dedicated to the service of Satan Himself.

Worryingly, such 'experts' have included a number of law-enforcement officials. The idea that somebody's musical preferences predispose them to crime puts us back on the road to the Freedom Village. As we have seen, back during the fevered climate of 'cult-busting' and Satanic paranoia in the 1980s, some police departments began to address the Punk Rock and Heavy Metal Problem (as a Union City Police Department workbook put it) as a cultural or religious challenge, as opposed to an issue of petty crime.

To put things into perspective, however: while vandalising cemeteries, persecuting small creatures and playing loud music late at night may be anti-social behaviour, compared to the war zones created by Uzi-toting crack gangs in the USA's inner cities, 'stoners' are a trivial problem, only worthy of special attention to someone with a fundamental religious agenda. One of the few studies on the teenage Satanic delinquency problem was conducted in Texas in 1991 by Kelly Richard Damphousse, his conclusions summarised in Professor Jeffrey Victor's book *Satanic Panic*: 'white, middle class, highly intelligent teenagers, who have a high need for control in their lives, are those who are most likely to justify their criminal activity in terms of a Satanist deviant ideology'. Furthermore, Victor observes, 'When the claims-makers focus our attention on so-called Satanic beliefs, symbols and rituals, they deflect our attention away from the real underlying problems of teenagers involved in pseudo-Satanism. It is much more useful to find out why so many emotionally disturbed and delinquent teenagers suffer from severe feelings of powerlessness and feelings of hostility. That should be the focus of our concern.'

But from where do these teenage pseudo-Satanists derive their 'deviant theologies'? Believers in the Satanic conspiracy myth point at LaVey's *Satanic Bible*, or imply they are commanded by some secret cabal. More sceptical observers glibly state that 'stoners' are merely aping things they've seen in horror movies or read in gory comics. Victor has a more intriguing suggestion, which strikes a parallel with death metal band Deicide's partial embracing of the Satanic myth: 'When so-called experts in teenage Satanism are brought into communities to lecture at schools and churches, one unintended effect is that they provoke curiosity about Satanism among hostile, marginalized adolescents. Ironically, these "experts" even provide youthful rebels with the Satanic symbolism, rituals, and beliefs, which they use to fabricate new ways to shock adult authorities.'

All of which brings to mind what the redoubtable Charlie Manson said in a letter to President Ronald Reagan in 1986: 'All the distorted thoughts and rules make problems worse . . . Cops teaching kids what not to do only shows them what they can do if they want to go against someone . . . Keep projecting what not to do and you make the thought in their brains of what can and will be done.'

DEAD BUT DREAMING

The beliefs of Glen Benton, frontman for the band Deicide.

Glen Benton is a provocative figure who deliberately baited the media throughout the early-mid 1990s. True to form, when we spoke just after the release of the *Legion* album in late 1992, he was by turn engaging and evasive. Benton speaks completely unrehearsed and spontaneously, in a low, abrasive voice, and he peppered our conversation with contradictions, rants and mind games.

Could you define your Satanism?
I would consider it a spiritual philosophy and a life philosophy. I like to tie them both in, because in one way I'm creating a blasphemy within my soul.

Is there any religious aspect to the performance of your music?
I'm not into flooding our stuff with things like that. I think it's been done and overdone. That's like looking for a commercial value on it, that's just Hollywood. I'm not into sampling or shit like that. What you're getting is the testimony of all I've seen – that's what you hear in my lyrics and that's what I'm all about. It's about my experiences, the things I think of, dreams that I have. You're hearing the life of torment that I go through because of what I believe in. Maybe I'm like a speaking tormented soul.

Not all of Satanism is about violence and death, so why do they dominate your lyrics so much?
I don't care what you've been told, there's death and violence in Satanism. They are what I consider to be the true demonic spiritual links.

Are dreams an important part of how you perceive life?
Dreams are existence. When you dream it is the closest to death you can get while alive. If you're dreaming and your mind is travelling that is very close to death.

Do you believe in an afterlife?
I believe in torment. I believe in a lot of pain at the end of my existence. A person can judge his life by his dreams and that's what I do. I have a lot of things that have come into my dreams, that I have reacted on, that have come true. I have made a lot of predictions based upon my dreams. Dreams forecast the future – you've just got to be intelligent enough to be able to decipher it.

Do you believe your Satanic faith can lead to special powers?
I believe there's a lot of power in the mind. I believe you can kill someone with a simple thought.

So not using a traditional curse?
A curse is an exhortation. You can call pitching hatred at somebody the same thing as cursing them. So creating imagery in your mind to cause death or other problems to somebody, that's the best way of accomplishing this curse.

Glen Benton, seen here with an inverted cross branded on his forehead, once claimed to want to die at 33 – giving him the same lifespan as Jesus.

Is it possible to do positive things in this way?
Of course.

This magic is achieved just by positive or negative thought, rather than any ritual involving candles or anything like that?
There needs to be more than just waking up one day and deciding you're going to pull your dreams apart or be able to use your mind. You have to do more than just wishing. I don't consider myself self-owning. I belong to something, and what I belong to is Satan.

Do you believe in Satan as a corporeal being?
I believe in Him as a spiritual being. I believe in Him as if I was in a dream state or dead. I believe in Him in the same way that death exists, in your soul and in your spirit. We could call it another dimension, we could call it raw energy, and just like anything else, there's a negative and a positive.

You believe in Satan, do you believe in . . .
Hollywood Satan? No I don't.

I was actually trying to ask . . .
Do I believe in 'harmonisers'? No.

Do you believe in . . .
Do I believe in pure raw evil? Yes I do.

What I wanted to ask was, do you believe in a kingdom of devils and demons who serve Satan?
There'll be a place for everyone when they're dead, good and evil. That's the day when peace will come to me and no longer will I have to live in a world full of Christians. I will be surrounded by my people.

Do you believe in God?
No, I acknowledge His existence, but I don't believe in this God. I hate this God.

Many Satanists in the past have questioned the use of rock music, for example Anton LaVey. How do you feel about that?
I don't do rock music. My message is what I am and what I believe in. If Anton cannot accept that I believe in the same thing he believes in, maybe in a different way, then he's the one that's being ignorant, not me. We're all on the same side, we shouldn't fight amongst ourselves. I have the same beliefs he does, he just lives by a philosophy that I find a little bit confusing. Well, it's not that confusing, it's quite simple. You just need to accept Satan. Satan is you. You are Satan. You are alive until you're dead. The thought of Satan is in your head every second of the day. You have no choice, it just becomes a part of you. There's no escape other than death.

Does everyone have this 'Satan' inside their head?
Humans have been greedy and evil from the start. It's just this book of lies has created this false standard for life. People have the thoughts they do, then think, 'I can't do that, that's evil.' If they were so holy they wouldn't even have those thoughts. Everybody has evil inside them, it's just that the normal average human is afraid of it. I have accepted it and I love it.

Are there any positive aspects to your work?
I collect souls. That's what I do. If I can collect one soul

to the side of Deicide then I've done something good, because maybe I've made that person aware of what Christianity's all about. If I can convert one person to accepting evil as a part of their life rather than denying it as Christians do, then this world, and that person, will be better off.

Do you believe in Satanic child abuse?
Let me put it this way: I have a son, his name is Damon, and in the state I live in there's a child protection agency called HRS. Some stupid, anonymous asshole phoned these people and told them my son was being Satanically abused, and they came to my house and found a very healthy little boy. Whoever phoned these people made this organisation look like a bunch of idiots. Because of legal repercussions, I wouldn't want to make a statement like that: but yes, it does happen. I don't have to ritually abuse my son to have my beliefs. But there are some freaks out there who think that the only way they can express themselves to the Lord is to do something like this.

Do you believe Satanic human sacrifice occurs?
Of course. A certain sect of people in a certain part of the country might believe that represents a sufficient offering, and if that's what they think then that's what they must do. If that's what brings them closer to it then that's what they must do.

Do you think then that it's justified?
It depends. I've already made my offering. My offering is myself. I walk around this world with the mark on my forehead. I don't regret it at all. In fact, I love speaking the truth. I love speaking from His lips to mine. I love letting the world know what's going on.

Are there any historical Satanists you identify with?
I am just a person who says what I have to say and I am one person in this world who says I'd rather go with evil. Going with evil has brought me more than goodness ever could. Once you get past that point there's nothing that can interfere with your life, other than things that are brought down because of your own stupidity and ignorance. I belong, and I enjoy where I belong, and my beliefs have done a lot for my personal insight. I consider the mark I have on my forehead to be the mark of the Beast and that's where I stand.

So is wisdom something that Satanism can offer?
Wisdom, self-satisfaction, security within your soul, a willingness to go on through life without fear of death.

What do you feel about the fundamentalists? Why have they been so active?

Because they're scared. They keep throwing people out of church and they don't have any money. If they don't have money they can't have a church. Their religion depends on a book, our religion depends on ourselves, not a building, not an establishment, not a book of lies, and not a dollar. That's what Christianity's all about. You can put Christianity out of business by breaking their pocketbooks, you can put them out of business by burning their church to the ground: there's a lot of ways of putting a church out of business. When churches start regulating the way people should live, that's when ordinary citizens go and burn churches down to the ground. That's how favoured Christianity is in this country. We're not going to be governed by religion. I'm tired of it and the mass population of the US are tired of it. Religion shouldn't have anything to do with the way a person lives.

Is there anything at all about* Christianity *or* The Bible *that you could admire?
Just the publisher.

MORE THAN ONE LEFT-HAND PATH

Satanism and Alternative Music

It's a constant source of frustration among many Satanists that, as far as many people are concerned, Satanic music begins and ends with black metal's blizzard of angry guitars. The marriage between Satanism and black metal is, they ambivalently suggest, made in Heaven. Metal is bombastic, theatrical, sinful, iconoclastic – all devilish traits, to be sure – but Satan should also be seductive, sophisticated and saturnine.

The relationship between music and the Devil is age-old. As with literature, theatre, and all popular art-forms, the Church has always regarded music with great suspicion – happy to patronise it when it could be utilised, quick to suppress it when not under ecclesiastical control. The Church even proscribed certain tones on the musical scale, referring to these unholy sounds as the Devil's Tritone. Modern US evangelical broadcaster and anti-Satanic campaigner Bob Larson continues this tradition – claiming that, while God invented music, the Old Testament's Book of Ezekiel implies Satan was the first musician.

On the other side of the fence, Blanche Barton, in her history of the Church of Satan, dedicates an appendix list to Satanic music – none of which is black metal, or even rock music. Ms Barton notes: 'Like scientists, or anyone else who has tried to move the human species forward, most classical composers were, in their time, denounced by the Church and the general public as being practising Satanists, heretics, possessed and, in certain cases, accused of having actual pacts with the Devil. They were blasted from every pulpit for being diabolical, leading our children into the Devil's hands, glorifying pre-Christian and anti-Christian themes, and inciting people to too much bestial, sexual and emotional fever.'

In the interests of redressing the balance against the neutering and sanitisation of classical music, Barton may have overstated her case. Just as William Blake suggested all true poetry was the Devil's work, she seems to be insisting all genuine creativity, including music, is the result of an implicit pact with the infernal. However, Christian dominance of Western culture for much of the past two millennia has ensured that religious themes dominate the classical canon. Despite this, blasts of infernal passion still break through.

The lives of many of the classical maestros were debauched enough to rival that of the most depraved rock star. The celebrated nineteenth-century violinist Niccolo Paganini was popularly supposed to have gained his virtuosity from the Devil – he even took to carrying around a signed letter from his mother to prove his mortal origins. However, the gaunt violinist relished his Satanic notoriety, pausing only from his histrionic performances to indulge in orgies of gambling and womanising. The Church was less than impressed and Paganini was denied a Christian burial for 70 years, while rumours maintained that ghostly violin playing accompanied the wandering of his restless soul.

Many composers have given the Devil his musical due, causing more than one churchman to wonder why the Devil should have all the best tunes. Satan supposedly manifested Himself to the eighteenth-century Italian composer Tartini in a dream, showing him a few infernal tricks with the violin. When Tartini awoke, he put what the Prince of Darkness had taught him into the composition of *The Devil's Trill*. However, it is Modest Mussorgsky's *A Night on Bald Mountain* which remains the archetypal Satanic classical composition. Initially created for a musical play called *The Witch*, it accompanies a scene entitled 'The Sacrifice to the Black Goat on the Bald Mountain' (as it would later accompany the macabre Satanic sequence in Walt Disney's classic feature-length cartoon *Fantasia*).

In a letter to a friend about the piece, Mussorgsky wrote: 'Witches used to assemble on that mountain, there to jabber and disport themselves pending Satan's arrival. When he appeared, they formed a circle around his throne and glorified him. When he felt sufficiently stimulated by the praise he gave the signal for the sabbath to begin . . . Well that's how I've done the thing!'

Originally Satan remained triumphant at the piece's climax, but this dark exuberance proved too much for Mussorgsky's more timorously unimaginative contemporaries, who dismissed it as 'hideous' and 'rubbish'. Later revised by the less passionate Nikolai Rimsky-Korsakov, the new arrangement (now sadly the standard one) ended with a tranquil coda – signifying a church-bell and sunlight – to banish the Prince of Darkness.

Other classical composers have represented Satanic rites in music, including Hector Berlioz, with his 'Dreams of a Witches' Sabbath' (from *Le Symphonie Fantastique*) and the opera *Faust*. (The enduring legend of Faust has inspired, according to one calculation, no less than 33 compositions.) Late nineteenth-/early twentieth-century composer Alexander Scriabin's work straddled the traditional and the progressive, moving from gentle romantic compositions to exercises in experimental atonality. The eccentric Scriabin was a fervent believer in occultic and mystical theory, using colours and scents to supplement his musical tones. (The arrangement of a Scriabin piece as the musical theme for the *Twilight Zone* TV show became a signature tune for weirdness in popular culture.) His infernal compositions include a *Black Mass* for piano and a *Satanic Sonata*, influencing the darkest of modern composers, George Crumb. Crumb – using such unusual effects as gongs lowered into cold water, and chants of mystical number sequences – also created several Satanic compositions, most notably the very strange *Black Angels*.

Arguably the most significant composition in terms of modern Satanic culture is Carl Orff's *Carmina Burana*. At the root of Jerry Goldsmith's excellent 'Ave Satani' refrain for his Oscar-winning soundtrack for *The Omen*, *Carmina Burana* is a celebration of barbaric power and brazen sensuality. While dull music critics have concentrated on his cosy relationship with the Third Reich and the völkisch elements in his work, there is an undeniable Satanic electricity to Orff's music. As his widow observed in a television interview: 'He had such a demonic force inside him that even I – his wife and friend – was frightened of him . . . He dreamt of witches. He'd wake up screaming and screaming . . . and said, "I have seen the Devil."'

It's a mistake to assume contemporary Satanic music has been wholly dominated by black metal. Just as the fringes of the psychedelic revolution were touched by darkness, most other modern musical movements have had their Satanic exponents. However, the punk explosion of the late seventies yielded comparatively little: Johnny Rotten may have drawled, 'I am an Anti-Christ!' in the Sex Pistols' anthemic 'Anarchy in the UK', but it was just as throwaway as the band's anarchic political stance.

It took the pioneers of the early gothic punk movement, Siouxsie and the Banshees, to distinguish themselves at the seminal punk festival at London's 100 Club in 1976 by reciting an interminable, inherently blasphemous rendition of 'The Lord's Prayer'. Formidable gothic icon Siouxsie would also introduce her band's cacophonous version of the Beatles' 'Helter Skelter' (so inextricably associated with the Manson murders) with a callous dedication to Roman Polanski, widower of the murdered Sharon Tate.

Still, there were very few direct manifestations of the infernal in the punk scene. It wasn't until 1981 that the American West Coast punk act 45 Grave released their debut, 'Black Cross', with a Satanic pentagram emblazoned on the cover – but even this outwardly Satanic band tinged their hymns to Hell with Hollywood irony. (The remnants of 45 Grave now record as Penis Flytrap, fronted by flamboyant *femme fatale* Dinah Cancer.)

Gothic rock, the morose, vampiric younger sister of brash, loutish punk, added the visual aesthetic of a Victorian funeral to the fetish-wear once common to the punk movement. Musically, it toned down the aggression to create mesmeric dirges with an evocatively morbid air. Within its world of incense smoke, cobwebs and shadows, one might expect to find many musical apostles of the Prince of Darkness – but Satan is largely conspicuous by His absence from the gothic scene.

One reason for this is that, by the 1980s, Satanism was seen as firmly the province of heavy metal; another is that the modern gothic counterculture is preoccupied with appearance rather than the Satanic aesthetic. *The Addams Family* TV show and horror author Anne Rice figure far larger in their world than the decadent poetry of Baudelaire, or the libertinism of eighteenth-century Hellfire Clubs.

Several gothic bands have had infernal connections, however. British goth-rockers the Fields of the Nephilim created a curious cocktail from strands of heretical Christian lore, the doctrines of Aleister Crowley and the creations of H. P. Lovecraft – largely at the behest of the band's vocalist Hank McCoy, who made little secret of his involvement in the darker regions of the occult. The band split in 1991, with McCoy going on to form a more aggressive and overtly occultic act called the Nefilim. Another British gothic act, Inkubus Sukubus (incubi and succubi are legendary sex vampires, sapping vital energies), explored the realms of medieval demonology and witchcraft in an unusual blend of goth-rock and traditional folk.

However, Inkubus Sukkubus are avowed Wiccans – while their musical approach is notably darker than any anodyne New Age drone, the band remain pagan rather than Satanic in their beliefs. Like many on the gothic scene, the closest they get to any malevolent aspect is an interest in vampires. This dominant strand in the gothic subculture – known as 'darkwave' – represents a growing number of bands who abandon guitar-based rock in favour of electronic or industrial sounds, marrying funereal elegance with cyberpunk chic. While acts like Project Pitchfork or Mephisto Waltz may sport infernal names, they almost always aspire to the part of putative vampires rather than Satanists.

The opera singer Diamanda Galas recorded an avant garde version of Baudelaire's Litanies of Satan.

Industrial music began as an artistic movement as much as a musical genre, its exponents exploring radical forms of expression divorced from traditional, organic creativity. The first breakthrough bands in the genre blended electronic technology with punk rock to create a danceable barrage of nihilism, such as Al Jourgensen's Ministry and Trent Reznor's Nine Inch Nails. The early 1990s saw these bands enjoying a rare combination of critical acclaim and commercial success with their grinding anti-songs of hate, disillusionment, cynicism and serial murder. Ministry's biggest hit was the darkly satirical 'Jesus Built My Hot Rod', while Jourgensen talked at one point about forming a country and western band called Buckskin Satan and the Six Six Six Shooters. Reznor went so far as to record Nine Inch Nails' *Downward Spiral* album, an atmospheric nightmare of substance abuse and self-destruction, in a studio built within the house in Cielo Drive, Hollywood, where Sharon Tate and her friends were murdered by the Manson family.

The origins of industrial music were in the occultic avant-garde. This incestuous community of artists at the cutting edge of experimentation – seldom danceable, occasionally unlistenable – often collaborated on each other's projects. Many, too, were directly affiliated with Satanic organisations. Genesis P-Orridge is often credited as the godfather of industrial music, on account of his band Throbbing Gristle – described by one critic as 'aggressively anti-melodic', their 1970s concerts were events, or ordeals, rather than shows.

In 1979, P-Orridge formed Psychic TV as a musical vehicle for his magical group Thee Temple Ov Psychic Youth (TOPY). Utilising insane collages of ballads, white noise and pop music, Psychic TV experimented as much with their audiences as their music in a project blending magical evocations and mind-altering mantras. P-Orridge's personal relationship with Anton LaVey also led to a collaboration on the Psychic TV single 'Joy', which features the Black Pope reciting 'The Lord's Prayer' backwards (a traditional feature of the Black Mass, according to some accounts). From 1988 onwards, Psychic TV became increasingly interested in the consciousness-altering potential of acid-house music, and were influential in introducing this vapidly repetitive brain-melt to the mainstream in Europe.

Another member of TOPY with connections to the Church of Satan, Swedish occultist Carl Abrahamsson fronted the experimental rock band White Stains (their name taken from a collection of erotic poems by Aleister Crowley). The project crossed a broad range of sounds, combining skeletal guitar with some imaginatively offbeat arrangements. Perhaps their most obviously Satanic release was the sinister, unsettling 1992 album *Misantropotantra*, though much of White Stains' material has a less overtly macabre, but equally profound Satanic slant with a distinctly LaVeyan edge. (They also recorded a cover version of Black Sabbath's Satanic classic 'N.I.B.' on the tribute album *The Legacy 1990 – The Sabbath Continues*.)

Coil also had their roots in TOPY, formed by ex-Throbbing Gristle member Peter 'Sleazy' Christopherson. Using a diverse selection of instruments, from the orthodox to the bizarre, they created what some critics called 'audio sculptures'. The most obviously Satanic of these 'sculptures' appear on the 1988 album *Unreleased Themes from Hellraiser*. Reflecting the interests of Coil member Stephen Thrower, who edited and published the cult horror-movie magazine *Eyeball*, the album consists of music commissioned – but never used – by horror author Clive Barker, for his classic film of sado-masochism and demonic temptation.

Current 93, formed by musical occultist David Tibet in 1983, represent a mystical journey expressed in music. Chilling ambient melodies combine with gothic chanting and traditional folk elements to create dark industrial soundscapes. To give some idea of the territory covered in this journey, guides include ghost story writer M. R. James, the Great Beast Crowley, Satanic surrealist de Lautreamont, and the children's character Noddy. Similar territory is occupied by Death in June, whose moody compositions – veering between surreal studies in alienation and folky evocations of Europe's pre-Christian past – and grim demeanour give the direct impression of fascist sympathies. Death in June are a more authentically dark example of 1980s 'totalitarian chic', epitomised by the seemingly tongue-in-cheek Yugoslavian group Laibach. Admired by some for their martial pastiches of pop classics, Laibach released a 1988 EP with no less than four cover versions treating the Rolling Stones' 'Sympathy for the Devil' in similar style.

The growing influence of traditional folk music on the occultic musical avant-garde led to the coining of the term 'Dark Ambient' – describing a genre moving away from the mechanical towards more organic, if equally disturbing regions. One of the more controversial exponents is the American Michael Moynihan – former collaborator with Sleep Chamber, whose 1988 album *Satanic Sanctum* combines trance-like, ritualistic ambience with a disturbing sado-masochistic thread.

More heathen than Satanic, Moynihan's current project, Blood Axis, is essentially a vehicle for heretical, extremist philosophy, blending classical influences, sampled dialogue and electronic music to evoke a pre-Christian world of strength, beauty and purity, kind of *Nietzsche: The Musical*. Moynihan's chief tactic is deliberate provocation of the liberal media, with such politically-incorrect features as a sampled speech by British fascist leader Oswald Moseley.

Satanist Nikolas Schreck, 'Alpha Male' of the Werewolf Order, is no stranger to controversy either. The essence of Radio Werewolf, the Order's 'sonic propaganda unit', was predictably incendiary. Sleeve notes for their 1989 album *The Fiery Summons* indicate the intended purpose of this 'sonic magic': 'The very act of hearing this music serves as an initiation into the lycanthropic mysteries. This particular exercise is intended to awaken dormant regions of the human mind, thus stimulating a process of resurgent atavism. This process has previously been understood as lycanthropy and indeed this is a ritual to unleash the beast in man.'

The concept of this musical equivalent of Anton LaVey's Werewolf Ritual is more intriguing than the results. Carnivalesque mood music, translations of Norse sagas and deadpan nihilistic rants are the order of the day, with a recitation from the correspondence of Victorian serial killer Jack the Ripper thrown in for good measure. At its best, Radio Werewolf was unsettlingly sinister – though the material's over-ambitiousness and deadly lack of humour was enough to make a werewolf howl.

The dour Herr Schreck's sense of humour finally surfaced on a 1996 release from his company, Wolfslair Inc. *Christopher Lee Sings Devils, Rogues and Other Villains* consists of the

saturnine English actor, best known for his villainous film roles, tackling a series of songs ranging from classical opera, to show tunes, and even cowboy ballads, quite competently. Schreck had long admired Lee (the actor seeming blissfully unaware that his record producer was a Satanist), and chose an enjoyably witty selection of songs to outline his own misanthropic philosophy, as in Steven Sondheim's 'Epiphany' from the musical *Sweeney Todd*:

'There's a hole in the world like a great black pit

And it's filled with people who are filled with shit . . .'

Boyd Rice, one of Schreck's former heretical brethren in the Church of Satan, first made his name as an experimental musician in the late 1970s under the name Non. Early releases included 7" singles with three or four different holes drilled so that they could be played off-centre, and an album called *Pagan Muzak* which – featuring a dozen locked grooves offering twelve looped tracks – could, theoretically, play for all infinity. Rice was a pioneer of the industrial genre, working in pure noise, sounds that stretched definitions of the word 'music' to breaking point and beyond.

On the sleeve notes to *Easy Listening for Iron Youth*, a Non 'greatest hits' compilation, Adam Parfrey, Feral House publisher and long-time comrade of Rice, says: 'The sounds that issue forth from the recordings of Boyd Rice (a.k.a. Non) have been known to cause anxiety attacks and even physical illness in the faint of heart and weak of mind. The bold and adventurous few, however, will find this music to be pure balm. This swirling vortex of sound is mood music, pure and simple; like some soundtrack to a frenzied blood-letting at the foot of the mongol steppes. There is no better tonic I know for today's true connoisseurs of that stimulating region that exists one step beyond good and evil.' The American music magazine *Trouser Press* was less enthusiastic, describing Non as 'structurally impressive but aggravating in the extreme'.

As with Boyd Rice's political and social pronouncements, his music can be wilfully hard to swallow – some go so far as to equate it all with his notorious pranks. Over the last dozen years, however, a number of his projects have taken him into musical regions generally considered unlistenable for altogether different reasons. The 1989 release, *Music, Martinis and Misanthropy* was inspired by the album *Music, Martinis and Memories* by Jackie Gleason, the 1960s king of suffocatingly-schmaltzy easy listening. Rice's take on this, as its title suggests, combines cheesy cocktail bar melodies with jarringly poisonous, social-Darwinist lyrics, extolling Hitler and Stalin as 'gardeners' necessary to prune humanity of its superfluous population.

Expressing similarly taboo sentiments, the 1994 release *Deep Inside a Cop's Mind* is credited to S.W.A.T., a sociopathic supergroup featuring several prominent Church of Satan members (including Rice and Anton LaVey, in spoken-word cameos), Adam Parfrey, Jim Goad – editor of the 'hatezine' *ANSWER Me!*, a journal of insightful provocation – and members of Poison Idea, a resolutely crude and nihilistic post-punk rock band. Sub-titled 'The soundtrack to the new police state', the album features a series of rock, country and movie soundtrack covers, altered to become perverse tributes to the forces of law and order.

While the liberal-minded may have been happy to believe *Deep Inside a Cop's Mind* was somehow ironic, the follow-up album *Hatesville*, by 'the Boyd Rice Experience', challenged even the most broadminded listener with its tirade of provocative bile, delivered over deceptively innocuous melodies. A celebration of hatred, featuring tracks like 'Race Riot' and 'Let's Hear it for Violence Towards Women', Hatesville stakes its claim as the furthest extreme on the lyrical scale of unacceptability.

Not all of Rice's projects play so rough. Spell was a collaboration with Rose McDowall of goth-pop band Strawberry Switchblade, featuring the pair's favourite, forgotten downbeat pop songs of the 1960s by the likes of Nancy Sinatra and Dolly Parton. Played totally straight (though Boyd's voice is pretty flat), they reflect Rice's sincere passion for the 'uncooler' end of the classic pop spectrum. 'It made you feel emotional,' he explained in a 1994 interview, 'and I think people find that threatening, to have some sappy, sugary pop song make them happy or sad. They want to be in control of their emotions. They don't want to submit to something which is just good fun.' Rice's passion for the tunes of his childhood echoes one of Anton LaVey's theories: of the magical power inherent in immersing oneself in the lost music of one's formative years. As an accomplished keyboard player, music played a far bigger part in LaVey's occult activities than the more traditional sorcerer's paraphernalia.

In an interview for the popular *Ben is Dead* 'zine, Rice explained: 'Anton's form of ritualizing nowadays is just playing his music and getting together with like-minded people and discussing things that are important to them. I have been over there when a definite mood has started to take place and he'll start playing certain frequencies on his synthesizer and the next day unbelievable things will happen. Incredible catastrophes relating to what we were talking about. One night he was playing this frequency that was a combination of black noise and white noise which he said is his ideal sound for releasing adrenal energy, and while he was doing this he was talking about when he was in the police department and there was a specific radio frequency or code that meant dead bodies on the highway. So the next day there was this bus driver that lost control of the bus, ploughed through a crowd of people, smashed through all these cars, and this one car that looks just like LaVey's car got hooked on the front of the bus and sort of led the bus around in this rampage of destruction. The car also had personalized license plates very similar to LaVey's. This stuff happens all the time.'

The Black Pope always championed the popular songs of the 1930s and 1940s as the most truly infernal ditties of the twentieth century. Tunes like Irving Berlin's 'Stay Down Where You Belong' were hailed by LaVey as being truly Satanic for their emotive, evocative qualities, as opposed to the rock music he once memorably dismissed as 'the last big burp of Christianity'. More than one black metal fan must have been nonplussed after buying LaVey's album *Satan Takes a Holiday* only to discover a medley of jaunty popular melodies from yesteryear. Similarly, both LaVey and Rice enhanced their affection for longhaired 1920s/30s revivalist Tiny Tim by a belief in his music's 'magical powers'. In replicating old tunes like 'Tiptoe Through the Tulips', his big hit, by listening to scratchy old 78rpm discs, he invoked the spirits of their era with his ghostly, unsteady falsetto.

Other musicians influenced by this aesthetic include Marc Almond, the decadent torch singer and long-time member of the Church of Satan. His varied career has embraced sleazy electronic dance with the chart-topping Soft Cell and camp cabaret material, but LaVey's influence is most clearly heard on the mini-album *Some Songs to Take to the Tomb Volume One*, featuring an eclectic selection of forgotten ballads ranging from the 1950s to the mid-1970s. Hip American lounge-kitsch

Rose McDowall and Boyd Rice, harnessing the occult power of resurrected 1960s bubblegum-pop in their project Spell.

band Combustible Edison have collaborated with Boyd Rice, giving a tip of the hat to the Prince of Darkness in an interview where founder member 'The Millionaire' claims easy listening 'has the reputation for being bland and toothless. Whereas I find it opens a window to a world of wickedness.'

Perhaps the most shamelessly Satanic modern band outside of black metal, however, have their roots in the Chicago industrial dance band My Life With the Thrill Kill Kult who, during the late 1980s, layered their electronic disco sounds with lurid blasphemy. (Their 1989 release *Kooler Than Jesus* featured such songs as 'The Devil Does Drugs'.) In the early 1990s band member Buck Ryder became disillusioned by the diminishing infernal content in the material. Changing his name to Thomas Thorn, he left to form the Electric Hellfire Club.

Influenced by the psychedelic Satanism of the1960s, filtered through a contemporary barrage of heavy metal guitars, electronic dance rhythms and sampled dialogue, the Electric Hellfire Club are a colourful, carnivalesque explosion of devilish kitsch and macabre mood. While the mainstream music media treat them with suspicion or indifference, these latter-day rakehells are attracting a growing following. Like the original Hellfire Clubs of the eighteenth century, their stateside spiritual descendants recognise that Satanism is not all blood and hellfire. True Satanism is chiefly about unashamed pleasure and laughter in the face of moral sanctimony – making the most of this earthly life instead of immersing oneself in gloom and nihilism. In a world where it's too easy to slip into a comfortable depression, and only idiots usually wear smiling faces, the Electric Hellfire Club's life-loving spirit is a lurid beacon of light.

Cover art by Timothy Patrick Butler for Alive With the Taste of Hell *by 'dark ambient' band Neither/Neitherworld – the project of Wendy Van Dusen, editor of Satanic 'zine* Primal Chaos, *whose Satanic folk-rock is heavily influenced by 1960s hate-messiah Charlie Manson.*

Is It Real?

Chewing the fat with BJW of GGFH.

Californian duo GGFH (Global Genocide Forget Heaven) were an intriguing presence on the industrial music scene in the early 1990s, painting pictures of pain, ignorance and perversity with a harsh electronic palette. Their debut album *Eclipse* concentrated on the media circus surrounding the Satanic conspiracy panic. I met BJW in 1993 while on the London leg of a European tour, tired and more than a little disillusioned. Though their live act utilised multiple TV screens showing talk-show hosts, convicted killers, horror-movie scenes and autopsy footage, all reflecting the earthly Hell we've created for ourselves, the venue refused to let them use any stage blood. Nevertheless, the deadpan Californian took time out for a drink and a few words before he went on stage.

Would you describe yourselves as a Satanic band?
No, we're not. When put out the *Eclipse* record we were interested in the way Satanism was being exploited at that time as a scapegoat for all the violent behaviour of a bunch of disturbed individuals. I'm talking about serial killers and the whole blame-everything-on-a-Satanic-cult thing. Sort of like a paranoia – 'It's there! It's in your town! They're killing and molesting your children! Even though you don't know who they are, they're there! Believe they're there!'

Are you parodying that paranoia or commenting on it?
We're saying that it's a bunch of shit and the real root of it all is people's personal paranoia and their inability to deal with their own repressed nature, society's repressed nature, and society's facade versus what's really underlying our modern culture.

You're obviously having fun with it as well though.
Absolutely. We find it very amusing that people can be so serious about something as silly as that. Taking it seriously to the point that, at the time we were recording *Eclipse*, every show was running Satanism specials. 'Satanism's Underground Exposed', *Geraldo*, *Oprah* – we used all that stuff because we thought it was awfully funny. These kids were committing suicide for Judas Priest, all that stuff, it was just so silly. It's all about finding a scapegoat. We thought that was funny because of the tradition of Satanism and the goat, and Pan the pagan symbol that became the scapegoat. Essentially blaming everything on the Devil.

You include some sampled dialogue from LaVey and Aquino in your music – how do they fit in?
Oh, we think that they might have some interesting ideas, but their organisations aren't something we'd be a part of because thinking for yourselves is not about being a part of a hierarchical religion, with all of its little levels. My personal theory is that Aquino is doing research for the military, and the Temple of Set is an experiment.

Ghost and Brian J. Walls of techno-terrorists G.G.F.H.

There was a government experiment where the military wanted to investigate parapsychology and mind control. They tried it in clinical conditions and it was a total failure. By recruiting people who are interested in it, under non-clinical conditions as it were, they're hoping to learn something. It's not for me. They all take it awfully seriously – I find it both a little amusing and a little scary.

Do you think there's a danger of the Satanic panic going so far that people will begin imitating the things they're being warned of?

I think it's already happened. I think it's mostly played-out though, you don't see it so often on TV in the States. Our music's now more about individual characters, which is how we originally started. We do songs about people who do sick, twisted things, who felt free to do what they felt like doing despite all of society's taboos. We got a lot of shit for it, and all the Satanism thing started, so during *Eclipse* we focused on that. Then we went back to what we'd done before, focussing on people like Ed Gein, Jeffrey Dahmer. Your normal guy next door who got up yesterday and blew his family away. Mundane, normal, ordinary, pathetic sadists and serial killers. What happened to them which hasn't happened to all of us who aren't likely to go out and kill someone for fear of gaol, living with the guilt or whatever? How come they're so out of touch with society and humanity? That's kind of an interesting thing. Could it be that TV is so fucked up? Could parents be so fucked up? We're just having a laugh while we ask these questions. We play with the media because the media pretends to have all the answers.

What do Satanists make of what you do?

They find it a little amusing and a little aggravating.

Are you an anti-Christian band?

Personally, I think Christianity has been responsible for many good things. Music for one (Western music as we know it has grown from the Church), cathedrals, a lot of works of art. Catholicism, despite all of its evils, is a lot better than fundamentalism. Fundamentalists just sit in their square rooms, they're just boring people with no passion. A lot of martyrs and saints were quite cool, trippy people. Whereas the Mormons never did a fucking thing for art, music or anything in particular. They should all be eliminated – not in a violent sense, I just mean we don't need that shit. Catholicism at this point may be dead, but for what it did for art and music it was overall a good thing, even if a lot of people got burnt.

On The Road From Inner Fear

A few words from Carl Abrahamsson of White Stains

I communicated with Carl Abrahamsson by phone and letter in 1994, just before he went on tour with his band. He was helpful and enthusiastic, with a genuine interest in advancing knowledge and promoting his vision of LaVeyan Satanism.

Are you a Satanist?

The role of Satanism in modern popular culture is an interesting one. Although hard to define, the true light of Satanism shines brightly amidst the pathological and criminal offshoots. I would regard myself as a LaVeyan Satanist because of its focus on creativity and stable, deserved progress. It's more of a philosophy than a school of magic, which is healthy in a world full of would-be gurus, full of shit and promises of dark and sinister energies for their dazed and confused nitwit-disciples.

Is White Stains a Satanic band?

We have never expressly claimed that White Stains is Satanic per se, and I don't think that will ever happen,

Crowley-inspired Swedish esotericists White Stains: Peter Bergstrandh and Carl Abrahamsson (right).

as I play with people who are not Satanists and don't wish to be associated with Satanic philosophy or magic. But personally I see the music we make, and all other projects I'm involved in, as a creative expression of myself, which in itself is of course Satanic.

How did you become involved with the Church of Satan?

The first White Stains 12" was 'Sweet Jayne', which is a love song to Jayne Mansfield and also about how she became involved with the Church of Satan. I sent a copy to Anton LaVey in early 1988 whereupon he made me a member. He is on our *Dreams Shall Flesh* CD performing a 'Satanic hambo'.

Is your work in any way evangelical?

I don't see myself as on some sort of mission to proclaim 'the word' to the populace. What's occult should remain occult. In the LaVeyan 'school' we don't look very highly upon people in general. But . . . on the other hand, I, and many like me, feel very uncomfortable when criminal acts are performed 'in the name of Satan' (this is usually an excuse to get a reduced sentence, disclaim mental liability, etc.) and don't like to see the philosophy dragged down by the disgusting and truly sick fundamentalists and others who don't want to see the individual strong, beautiful and happy. That's why I personally dislike a lot of the metal stuff, because of the nonsensical violent imagery and the actual criminal acts sometimes perpetrated by these so-called Satanists. So, I guess it will always be a balancing act of working quietly and countering, in an intelligent and educated fashion, the forces of stupidity who have, for some reason or other, chosen to associate themselves with the term 'Satanism'.

Burn Baby Burn

Discourse with Thomas Thorn of the Electric Hellfire Club.

I spoke with Thomas Thorn just previous to the release of the Electric Hellfire Club's first album in 1994. I'm no fan of dance-oriented music, but his passion for Satanism was obvious and I soon found Thorn's enthusiasm damnably contagious. Witty and amusing, he made a pleasant change from the solemnity that can dominate Satanic music.

What's the relationship between your band and the original Hellfire Clubs?
Going by what information we have, there's a lot of what they did that bears a relation to what we do. For example, we're not some horrible, infant-murdering sect so much as a social, political statement that blasphemes against the existing order. We also share the great emphasis on indulgence in whatever pleasures take your fancy.

How did the psychedelic elements make their way into your music?
It was definitely intentional. One of my interests is that era, the 1960s, when the Church of Satan was formed, and the whole element of psychedelic Satanism. Any books that catalogue Satanic crime always say that just outside the fringes of the Haight-Ashbury scene there were gangs of outlaw bikers, Satanists and all manner of ne'er-do-wells waiting to make a buck out of it all. I just find the

characters from that time fascinating and exciting.

What's your relationship with the Church of Satan?
We have connections with – and I appreciate – the Church of Satan, and I think a lot of LaVey's writings are brilliant. But, at the same time, I don't necessarily tow the party line because there are parts of it I disagree with. We run this no-man's-land between the organised Satanic churches and the teenage dabblers or self-styled Satanists. Somewhere between there is psychedelic Satanism – the kind of acid-tripping, Haight-Ashbury Devil-worshipper.

There's a large element of humour in your approach to Satanism isn't there?
I think that's very important. Once you lose your sense of humour about something, it becomes more laughable than if you're able to laugh at it yourself. The people who, to me, seem rather foolish in their Satanism are those who spout, 'I serve my dark lord Satan' or 'We do everything in homage to Him', and try to sound as evil as they possibly can. I think people find us a lot more frightening because, while we are serious, we're not this

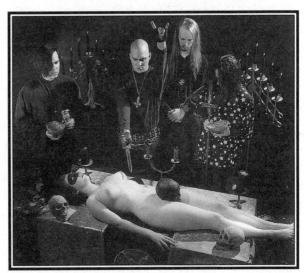

Thomas Thorn – centre, with sacrificial dagger – leads the Electric Hellfire Club in a Black Mass.

caricature of Satanism which has been invented by the Christian Church. We're not limited by that caricature and it's really important to me that we have fun with what we're doing.

My house is equally decorated with traditional carved devil masks and tacky plastic dolls of devils you might buy at Halloween. I think our music is honest because it's multi-dimensional. At moments we tow a very demonic hard-line on Satanism with songs like 'Fall From

Grace' – which are written in biblical metaphor, shaking a fist in God's face – then we turn around and write something campy or flippant like 'Psychedelic Sacrifice' or 'Black Bus', with clichéd lines like 'Satan is my main man.' That's a natural expression of being people with different moods and ways of looking at the world.

How do you see Satan?
Not to quote LaVey directly, but I don't see Satan as some anthropomorphic deity who's going to appear in my living room in a puff of smoke. Your god or gods are personified with your personal vision of them, and I'm content with a lot of the popular-culture images of Satan. To me Satan is a force rather than a being, and I think there are a lot of individual demonic entities within that force that can manifest themselves in different ways, in anything from someone you meet in the street to some little clown doll you purchase from the second-hand store.

What's your live show like?
It all depends on the song – the mood changes from song to song. We have a go-go dancer who comes out for some of the songs. In the more psychedelic numbers she might come out in spangly platform shoes and a pink fur jacket. In other moments she might appear as a classic gothic vamp. Likewise we change the lighting,

changing the mood with fog and so forth. We're taking the audience on a rollercoaster ride through an amusement park in Hell. There are parts which are 'the house of horrors', parts which are 'the funhouse'.

How does your music affect people?
At the best shows we get a lot of feedback, it becomes this electric exchange between us and the audience. There are a couple of responses we get. One is the 'Oh, you guys totally rock out and I had a great time and let loose', which is fine – we're definitely interested in providing pleasure for people. Then there are those who show a deeper interest in the subject matter and lyrical content and are inspired by what we do, and I enjoy that. There are some weird things that happen at our shows. We've played shows where people do some bizarre things and take on, for all practical purposes, the appearance of being possessed. We've done shows where people have started having sex in the audience, another time a guy started rolling around and burning himself with candles – the guy threw himself down on the stage, tore off his pants and was pouring hot candle-wax on his genitals. Granted, there are people who will do that anyway, but we have had more than our share of such occurrences at our shows. I wouldn't necessarily say we have conjured demons that have entered members of the audience, but I wouldn't deny the possibility either.

RAGNAROK AND ROLL

The Second Coming of Black Metal

lack metal, as a 1990s phenomenon, is a creature with an identity largely distinct from its parent heavy metal music. Growing like a poisonous fungus away from the light of mainstream media interest, it developed its own bizarre sounds, imagery and philosophies.

Fostered upon a diet of xeroxed fanzines with names like *Thanatography* (after Thanatos, Greek god of death), *Hammer of Damnation* and *Baphomet*, its white teenage male exponents were keen to make their mark with a genre too wilfully obnoxious for outsiders. Visually, bands tried to outdo each other with outrageously macabre or offensive imagery: fire-breathing; tattered black clothing or robes; blood-soaked or naked flesh; medieval weaponry; bullet belts and spiked leather; insane calligraphy – spattered with profane images – which rendered band names illegible or scarcely identifiable. The most striking black-metal 'fashion statement', however, was the sepulchral black-and-white make-up worn by many bands which became known as 'corpse paint' – a mutated offspring of the theatrical greasepaint worn by KISS in the 1970s, by way of King Diamond.

At the movements genesis, few band members had racked up enough years of experience to excel at their instruments in the traditional fashion – instead, they concentrated on producing unearthly, crazed, ugly sounds with guitars, drums, the human voice and keyboards. Specialist independent record labels, founded by fans or the bands themselves, sprang up as a truly international underground: Osmose Productions in France; Candlelight Records in the UK; Wild Rags in the USA; Black Power Records in Greece; Drowned Records in Spain. The list continues to proliferate to the present day, but the most influential of all was a small Scandinavian label called Deathlike Silence – of which, much more later.

One of the more arresting rock artists of the early 1990s bridged the gap between the musical extremes of black metal and rock 'n' roll's demonic roots in the blues. Far subtler than most black metal bands, Glenn Danzig still operated at the infernal end of the spectrum.

An anomaly who stubbornly refused to bow to the expectations of either purists or populists, Danzig began his career at the height of the punk revolution in 1977 as vocalist for New Jersey band the Misfits. No ordinary punk band, Danzig's classic rock 'n' roll delivery gave a quasi-1950s feel to their abrasive sound, while they spurned the usual punk look in favour of an all-year-round Halloween image. Sporting monstrous black quiffs they dubbed 'devil locks', the Misfits often took the stage in skeletal garb – indeed, Danzig's skull make-up was prescient of the 'corpse paint' popular among 1990s black metal bands.

The Misfits were one of the first punk bands whose songs possessed a strong gothic undercurrent. Many reflected their love of cheap schlock movies, such as 'Teenagers from Mars' and 'Return of the Fly', but others were genuinely disturbing explorations of hate and violence. Their second recording, *Bullet*, featured a song entitled 'Hollywood Babylon', inspired by magus and film-maker Kenneth Anger, while another track included an authentic Latin chant for effecting a werewolf transformation.

Black Aria, *Glenn Danzig's album of Satanic orchestral music.*

In what was to become a familiar pattern, Danzig tired of the more tongue-in-cheek aspects of the Misfits, forming Samhain (pronounced 'Sow-En' – the precursor to Halloween, a Celtic festival dedicated to fire and death) who released their first album, *Initium*, in 1984. This was a stark journey into primal evil, threatening rhythms and bleak guitars combining with Danzig's lupine vocals to create a musical beast that howled at the world. It was all too bleak for most audiences and, in 1987, the vocalist dissolved the band in order to enter his third incarnation – called simply Danzig.

Danzig was in many ways the singer's most innovative project, as well as the most overtly Satanic. Voodoo blues as deep and black as Mississippi mud met predatory heavy metal, with a vocal style redolent of early rock 'n' roll's late-fifties/early-sixties crooners. Typically, Glenn Danzig's insistence on treating his Satanic subject matter without a trace of irony did not endear him to the press. Short, powerfully built, with raven black hair and prominent side-burns, the music media dubbed him an 'Evil Elvis' or, more irreverently, 'Fonzig'. Some audiences were also perplexed: younger black metal fans wanted a less subtle Satanism, while rock fans who appreciated Danzig's musical approach found his lyrical preoccupation off-putting.

Nevertheless, the band attracted a dedicated fan base, appreciative of a familiarity with demonic subject matter that most shock-horror rockers could only envy. Nietzschean howls of defiance against the Creator, such as 'Godless', complemented more traditional takes on hellish suffering like 'Tired of Being Alive'. At his quietest, Danzig was at his most sinister – like the poet William Blake, Danzig identified love as 'a Devil's thing'. In 1994, the band received mainstream attention when MTV picked up on the video for the anthemic 'Mother'; in the same year, an uncompromising Glenn Danzig released a solo project entitled *Black Aria*: an album of quasi-classical music retelling the story of Satan's fall from grace.

In 1996, after four albums of powerfully-infernal rock music, Danzig took his eponymous band in a new direction. *BlackAcidDevil* was predominantly an industrial record, many fans mourning the passing of the classic Danzig sound and dismissing at as 'a poor man's Nine Inch

Nails'. In truth, when the industrial grind is layered with the dark velvet of Danzig's seductive tones – as on 'Come to Silver', an exploration of temptation – then the material becomes really interesting.

The indifferent sales and reviews that greeted *BlackAcidDevil* tested Danzig's already-strained relationship with the music business. He let the band slip back into the cult status he was perhaps happiest with, and began spending the money he'd made from his musical career on other projects – most notably a comic-book company named Verotik. As the company's name suggests, these comics are crammed with violence and erotica, combined with the fascination for all things infernal that has become Glenn Danzig's trademark. Scripting many of the comic-strips himself, Danzig introduced overtly devilish characters, like the vamp Satanika, to stake his claim as one of the main modern contributors to Satanic popular culture.

On the continent of Europe, particularly in the Norwegian capital, Oslo, things were being taken to a less subtle extreme. Deathlike Silence was an independent record label owned by a young man who re-named himself Euronymous – according to some folklore traditions, a cannibalistic demon with skin the bluish-black colour of a meatfly's carapace – who also ran a dank, dingy specialist record store named Helvete (meaning 'Hell') and founded a band called Mayhem.

Mayhem formed in 1984, just as the original black metal scene was peaking, debuting with a demo called *Pure Fucking Armageddon* and an album called *Deathcrush*. Interest in Satanic imagery, with its attendant gothic spikes-and-leather garb, was faltering among audiences at this time, but Mayhem clung onto its uncompromising style. They sounded like a rawer, more grinding version of Venom, screaming and thundering between militaristic marches and growling rage. As the tastes of young underground fans in the 1990s swung further towards diabolical excess, Euronymous' obsessive dedication made him a potent force on the newly-burgeoning black metal scene.

During the early 1990s, Euronymous' store became the focus for a small circle of like-minded Scandinavian metal fans who all started their own bands. This loose group

An early shot of Count Grishnackh in 'corpse-paint'.

named itself variously the Black Metal Circle, Satanic Terrorists or Black Metal Mafia, and was influenced by the supposedly Satanic doctrines of Euronymous – based around a vague reading of the biblical concept of war between Heaven and Hell. For Euronymous, siding with Satan meant endorsing everything that was considered evil, spiteful, hateful. Hate motivated his philosophy, coloured by the cold, depressive morbidity that characterises the negative edge of the Scandinavian psyche.

All of the releases on Deathlike Silence were stamped with the 'Anti-Mosh' symbol (moshing is a raucously combative form of dancing common to thrash and death metal fans). Around the symbol were stamped the messages 'No Mosh', 'No Core' (a reference to the hardcore punk revival), 'No Trends' and 'No Fun' – these sentiments taking against those metal audiences who were introducing splashes of gaudy mainstream colour, in the form of Bermuda shorts, baseball caps and skateboards.

In the centre of the 'No Moshing' symbol was a red line struck through those figures Euronymous professed to hate most: Scott Burns, the Florida-based record producer whose work had come to dominate the death metal scene, and, curiously, Anton LaVey. Euronymous divorced himself from all Satanic tradition, loathing LaVey because of the Church of Satan's philosophy of self-empowerment and individualism. Euronymous' simple faith expressed all that was negative: a cold core for a violent code of self-destructive nihilism.

Joining Mayhem in their isolated world of hate were several other extreme bands. Burzum – chiefly a vehicle for Count Grishnackh (given name Kristian Vikernes, though he legally changed his first name to Varg, Norwegian for 'wolf'), who'd lived in the damp, lightless cellar of the Helvete record shop for some time – were a prominent presence. Burzum were an odd blend of frustrated insanity and strange, sad, ambient mood music, pained pathos and gibbering fury – oddly effective, but distinctly disturbed.

Founder member Grishnackh took his name from one of the evil 'orc' characters in J. R. R. Tolkien's fantasy trilogy *The Lord of the Rings*, while Burzum meant 'darkness' in the orcish language conceived by Tolkien. Perverse as this seems, it should be remembered that *The Bible* is just a book of stories – in this light, perhaps using *The Lord of the Rings* as the basis for an (im)moral philosophical code is not wholly ludicrous. However, it does an infernal philosopher's credibility no favours to identify too closely with 'hobbits' (glorified goblins).

Grishnackh's personal mythology combined the darkness-versus-light motifs of 'mystic quest'/sword-and-sorcery sagas with the violent Viking tradition he believed true Northern Europeans belonged to. While this seems symptomatic of Scandinavia's peripheral removal from – and distorted imitation of – Western pop culture, it also has an authentic dark side. As is common among Norse pagan revivalists, the Black Metal Circle began to espouse race-based Nazi political views. (Though totalitarian-loving Euronymous also expressed admiration for communist despots and Cambodian genocidalist Pol Pot.)

Also pivotal in this new movement were the bands Emperor, Immortal, Enslaved and Arcturus. The last to join Euronymous's Norwegian cadre were Dark Throne, who'd already recorded one death metal album, *Soulside Journey*, in 1990. In the following year, they disowned their debut, donned corpse-paint and joined the 'Satanic Mafia' with their album *A Blaze in the Northern Sky*. If Euronymous exemplified the nihilistic hate at the heart of the Black Metal Circle, and Burzum represented its violent Norse/Nazi fantasies, then Dark Throne symbolised the Circle's isolation and sociopathic need for solitude. Taking their country's sombre, anti-social reputation to extremes, the band never met to record, spoke little, and spent increasing periods alone in the frost-bitten Norwegian wilderness.

In the spring of 1991, Mayhem's vocalist died: a Swede who, by way of black comedy, had re-named himself 'Dead'. Dead blew his head off with a shotgun, leaving a note to say he felt he was not of this world, but belonged instead to the cold solitude of the forest. He also apologised for the mess. As is common with obsessively inward-looking groups like the Black Metal Circle, a crisis of this type either causes the grouping to dissolve, or re-enforces their convictions. The latter instance applied, and the Circle hailed Dead as a hero.

Euronymous, who found the corpse, rushed out for a camera to take his final photograph of Dead before alerting the authorities – claiming a morsel of brain to make into soup and a fragment of skull to fashion into a necklace. At this point, the Black Metal Circle were no longer merely a group of disaffected teens and early-twentysomethings, but a subculture who believed themselves to be at the centre of significant, apocalyptic events.

Euronymous' demented, anti-social rants were making him a regular feature in the underground metal fanzines; despite the continued indifference of the global music media, black metal was rising from the grassroots across the world. The 'legend of Dead' contributed to a growing international interest in extreme, Scandinavian Satanic metal, with Deathlike Silence treating the grim event as a grotesque promotional gimmick.

For the first time, European countries bordering the Mediterranean also began throwing up a slew of black metal acts – most notably the Greek band Rotting Christ. In contrast to the cold hatred of the Northerners, the Southern European scene was inclined to a less self-destructive, more LaVeyan approach – though Anton LaVey would have regarded many of them as blasphemy-fixated novices, struggling to topple the repressive Christianity that dominates their cultures.

Black metal was emerging all over the developed world. Influential Finnish band Impaled Nazarene played what they described as 'Industrial Cyber Punk Sado Metal', composed of jagged sonic jigsaws of profanity, obscenity and sexual aggression. They were very much in tune with blasphemy-loving American band Profanatica, who took the stage naked and bathed themselves in a cocktail of bodily fluids. (The first Pofanatica release, 'Weeping in Heaven', was smeared with semen and blood by their frontman Paul Ledney. After Profanatica broke up, Ledney formed a new band called Havohej – Jehovah backwards.)

Post-Cold War Eastern Europe entered the black metal underground with a number of influential acts from Hungary and Czechoslovakia, including the classically-inclined Master's Hammer and the heavily LaVey-inspired Root. In Canada, a Satanic skinhead band named Blasphemy combined the music and imagery of black metal with a combative attitude and right-wing dogma. The scene continues to expand, with dozens of new bands releasing demo tapes for the attention of a shock-hungry young audience.

Back in Scandinavia, Swedish bands evidenced a very similar attitude to the icily-obnoxious Norwegians. One band, Abruptum, so impressed Euronymous that he recorded them on his Deathlike Silence label, in defiance of his own professed Norwegians-only racial policy. (In reality, Deathlike Silence also planned to release efforts by Italy's Monumentum and bizarre Japanese black metal exponents Sigh.) Abruptum's debut, *Obscuritatem Advoco Amplectere Me*, features the band's demented dwarf vocalist, It (too evil to possess a name, apparently), screaming as he mutilates himself in the studio. Once heard, never forgotten . . .

Despite this moment of cross-pollination, the insularity of the Black Metal Circle was growing to parodic levels. Members of its 'Inner Circle' had taken to declaring Norway as the Aryan homeland, while dismissing all others, including the Swedes, as racially inferior. Most of their venom was reserved for rival metal bands who responded in kind, instigating a curious war of insults, telephoned threats and general intimidation between the young musicians.

In 1992, the posturing of the weapon-wielding nihilists began to assume tangible expression. In June of that year the stave church of Fantoft, a small Norwegian town, was burnt to the ground. The destruction of stave churches – magnificent early-medieval wooden buildings – represented not just the defilement of a place of Christian worship, but irreparable damage to Norwegian historic monuments and national treasures. This was the first of many such arson attacks. In January 1993, Grishnackh gave an interview to a local paper as 'an anonymous source', boasting he knew the identity of the church arsonists. It led the police to his door, and he was arrested – along with a number of accomplices from the Black Metal Circle – and convicted on three counts of arson.

The Scandinavian tabloids had a field day with these obnoxious antics, and the Black Metal Circle revelled in their villainy. However, for all the derision, Euronymous and his peers had succeeded. They had taken their grey existence and filled it with black melodrama – dragged the world, for the briefest of moments, into their Hell of frustration and animosity. But this perverse victory would exact a price.

While everybody expected these anti-social kids to melt back into obscurity, later that year the Black Metal Circle exploded into the headlines with the violent death of Euronymous. He was discovered on the stairwell leading to his apartment on the morning of 10 August 1993, wearing only his underwear, having sustained 25 stab wounds to the face and chest. Rumours abounded concerning the perpetrators of this frenzied attack: fundamentalist Christians, a rival from the Swedish black metal scene, fanatical anti-Nazis were all suggested on the grapevine.

Several weeks later, Count Grishnackh was arrested and charged with the murder. His alibi for the evening, a twenty-year-old friend, cracked under police questioning and recanted his story.

The international nature of black metal in the 1990s is illustrated by the Brazilian band Mystifyer – seen here performing a mock crucifixion guaranteed to offend in their Catholic homeland.

Then another associate of Grishnackh's confessed he'd accompanied the Count to Euronymous' home, where he saw Grishnackh stab his erstwhile comrade. A detailed search of Euronymous' flat revealed extensive records of the Black Metal Circle's activities which, police maintained, demonstrated a merit system whereby status was determined by the number of evil acts perpetrated, like some troop of Satanic boy scouts.

A further fourteen arrests followed, for crimes ranging from arson to rape, suspects ranging from fourteen to 22 years of age. Faust, the drummer with Emperor, confessed to the murder of a homosexual who propositioned him in a park during August 1992. The following night, he went out and torched a church. Few were surprised at a further bizarre turn of events – it was alleged that, when placed under arrest, Grishnackh was in possession of 150 kilos of dynamite with which he hoped to blow up the church that housed the Norwegian crown jewels. The Black Metal Circle disappeared as quickly as it had risen, its founder dead, its most prominent members facing trial with little hope of acquittal. Their use of crime as part of a self-publicity campaign had definite limitations . . .

Grishnackh came to trial in May 1994. In a surprise move, he confessed to the events of that fateful August night: '[Oystein] Aarseth [Euronymous' real name] opened the door. He looked tired and just wore his underpants. I tried to give him the contract [for Grishnackh's new mini-album *Aske*] and suddenly we were arguing. Among other things, he accused me of talking meaningless shit. He started threatening to beat me up. I told him only weak men threaten. Strong men take action. He then kicked me in the chest. I was dumbfounded, and pushed him over. As Aarseth stood up, he began to run toward the kitchen. I am sure he was going for a knife. I therefore drew one of mine. I stabbed him, thereby preventing him from reaching the kitchen. He then started running around the living room, screaming at the top of his voice. He kept screaming for help. Then I got really mad. He ran out in the hallway, with me close behind. I kept stabbing to make him shut up. I stabbed because I was angry at him for screaming for help instead of putting up a fight.'

Grishnackh's defence counsel made an insanity plea on their client's behalf, but the prosecution's expert witnesses opined that, 'Vikernes [Grishnackh] is polite, well-mannered and correct in his behaviour. His intellect is well-developed. He has shown in court that he is definitely not schizophrenic. There are no grounds to conclude that he suffered from temporary insanity during the murder either.'

The Count was found guilty of the murder of Euronymous and three charges of arson. He was sentenced to 21 years in gaol, the maximum allowed under Norwegian law. The young man who drove Grishnackh to and from Euronymous' house on the night of the murder received an eight-year sentence as an accessory. Faust received fourteen years for the park murder, while two other members of Emperor – the band most active in the Black Metal Circle's brief, blasphemous rampage – were gaoled for the church arsons, armed assault, burglary and 'desecration of a sacred property'.

An early promotional collage by Black Metal Circle members Emperor, utilising Nazi iconography.

The crimes split opinion among Satanists as to their merits, or otherwise. At the libertarian end of the spectrum, the reaction was one of contempt – destroying beautiful old buildings like the Fantoft church was mindless vandalism, with no regard for aesthetics or history (all ancient churches being cultural museums), which could only strengthen the Christian case against Satanism. Oddly, this opinion was expressed by Euronymous himself, who declared that the church burnings were aimed at strengthening Christians while weakening his enemies in the organised Satanic churches.

The most interesting reaction came from right-wing Satanists. There had long been a degree of crossover between proselytisers of social-Darwinism and the fascist fringes of the pagan movement: indeed, some regarded Satanism as a stepping stone for Europeans, a rejection of Christianity before embracing the traditional pagan faith of their Aryan ancestors. In their acclaimed 1998 book on 'the bloody rise of the Satanic Metal underground', *Lords of Chaos*, Michael Moynihan and Norwegian journalist Didrik Soderlind identify the Black

Metal Circle's crimes as an example of 'resurgent atavism' – an expression beloved of right-wing mystics, denoting a return to primal nature. Just as Christian churches were often built upon sites sacred to pagan gods in order to exorcise them, so the authors interpret the church burnings as justified revenge for these ancient wrongs – evidence that the Aryan youth of Scandinavia were rising to cast off the twin bonds of Christianity and liberal democracy.

Count Grishnackh had had connections with the Far Right before his brief career in the Black Metal Circle. In gaol, with the luxury of time for reflection, he re-invented himself – returning to the name of Varg Vikernes and abandoning all pretensions to Satanism in favour of a blend of Teutonic mysticism, Norse mythology and fascist politics. He even proudly claimed to be related to Vidkun Quisling (the Norwegian politician notorious for selling-out his country to the Nazis in World War Two, his name now synonymous with 'traitor'), expressing a desire to revert to Quisling as his surname.

Ironically, the very liberal laws that Vikernes had mocked allowed him to continue recording as Burzum while in gaol. This new material reflected the re-invented Vikernes, consisting of weird, haunting hymns to the Norse gods of old. This electronic music, almost New Age in feel, reflects Vikernes' desire to divorce himself entirely from rock music, which he regards as tainted by its origins in black American blues. (This same attitude – a search for a purely European form – is reflected in the work of a lot of avant-garde, occultic musicians who experiment with traditional folk melodies.) Varg Vikernes, who took to the stage as a Satanic 'orc' – and was briefly, according to a lawyer at his trial, 'a troll' – has transformed himself into a Viking martyr . . .

The true motives behind the crimes only became clear as the media frenzy subsided. Dead's suicide had energised Euronymous into a pathological game of oneupmanship wherein he and Vikernes spurred each other on into greater outrages. Asked if the black metal culture contributed to his most serious crime, the murder of a stranger in the summer of 1992, Faust opined: 'Of course it might have influenced me a bit and made it easier. But all this really could happen to anyone if you get approached by a homosexual. Whether you are like me into this underground scene, or if you were working in a bank – you might react the same way.'

However, several insiders suggested Grishnackh wanted to 'better' this bloodthirsty crime, and some say he even boasted he'd leave a corpse with more than the 37 stab wounds Faust inflicted on his victim. The rock media also played its part, albeit unintentionally. The March 1993 issue of *Kerrang!* – the world's best-known heavy metal magazine – had featured them on the cover, a privilege usually only afforded to metal's most successful artists. It was heady stuff to the Black Metal Circle – a gaggle of adolescent nihilists who found themselves transformed into a 'cult' – and Euronymous' murder proved a fitting climax.

Inevitably, the death of one of its foremost exponents at the hands of another had a substantial impact on the black metal revival. The media, which had long treated the bands as a joke, became decidedly nervous. Young fans in Scandinavia, who could previously have expected their outlandish garb to elicit mockery, now found themselves subjected to outright hostility and police harassment. Musicians and record label staff disassociated themselves from black metal, or at least laid low for a while. Many anticipated a wave of copycat violence.

In *Lords of Chaos*, Michael Moynihan makes a strong case for some kind of mythic aspect to the murder of Euronymous, but it's difficult to go along with his suggestion of black metal as an embryonic revolutionary movement. However, while it's true that the killing of Aarseth was motivated by such mundane concerns as money and peer-group status, there are a number of similar cases that received plenty of press on account of the 'Satanic' angle.

In April 1993, three German teenagers murdered an unpopular fifteen-year-old classmate. They belonged to a band, Absurd, who had never recorded but boasted Satanic affectations. Their chief motive appears to have been silencing the boy, who threatened to reveal one of them was having an affair with a married woman, and the evidence suggests they only meant to frighten their victim before the violent momentum led them to kill him. In France, on Christmas Eve 1996, a disturbed young black metal fan announced he was possessed by demons before stabbing a priest to death. In 1997, in a crime reminiscent of the murder committed by Faust of Emperor, a homosexual Algerian was killed when shot in the neck with a stun-gun in a park in Gothenburg, Sweden. Two young musicians were convicted of the crime, both members of the black metal band Dissection.

While these murders – which occurred alongside a spate of grave desecration and arson attacks – are disturbing, compared to the weekly death toll among hip-hop fans in the USA's inner cities, this 'wave' of violence qualifies as barely a ripple. Maybe they are all the more shocking because those involved are largely white, bright and middle-class. Given that they flag their rejection of mainstream values with the most anti-social icons they can find, perhaps it's remarkable their Satanic posturing doesn't lurch into literalism more often.

Recent black metal scares are not confined to the West. One example from the Middle East is particularly revealing. In Egypt – the meeting point between the Islamic and Western worlds, source of some interesting violent tensions – during January 1997, around 100 youths, chiefly from affluent families in Cairo and Alexandria, were arrested and charged with 'Satan worship'. Their homes were ransacked and 'evidence' – such as heavy metal CDs, T-shirts, key rings with little plastic skeletons, and a Chicago Bulls basketball cap with a horned logo – was seized. A local paper quoted the brother of

Johnny Hedlund of Norse metal band Unleashed gives a pagan salute with Satanic musician and writer Michael Moynihan (right).

one of the accused, who observed, 'All the proof they have they took from the kids' homes. They took some CDs, a T-shirt and a sketch of Bob Marley.'

It was rumoured that teenagers held 'Satanic parties' in a Second World War cemetery outside the capital. One of the accused observed, 'I don't have anything to do with Satanism. I joined because their parties were exciting. I used to go to feel up the girls when they were dancing.' Another, less reluctant recruit to the forces of darkness, said, 'We want to be different, to be unconventional. Satan encourages instant enjoyment and permits what religion forbids.' The Minister of the Interior, Hassan Al-Alfi, was not impressed, stating, 'I call on Egyptian TV to adopt a project to reform these deviant thoughts through religious programmes.' More radical Muslims demanded the death penalty for those proven to be apostates. Significantly, many in the media identified Israel as the source of this Satanic threat, fingering the McDonald's hamburger bar in Heliopolis as their high temple.

In Russia, during early 1997, an anti-personnel mine was defused in beautiful Elokhovsk Cathedral, just as Christmas service was about to be addressed on the iniquities of local youth. The following day, a tabloid newspaper identified those responsible as 'the Black Metal Brotherhood . . . the most powerful grouping of Satanists in Russia today. At present the Russian branch of the Brotherhood contains nearly 200 members.' A spate of arson attacks, vandalism and explosions was directed at Russian churches and synagogues, the Russian Orthodox Church responding with a statement that, 'There is no justification for those who stir up hostility, commit acts of blasphemy, vandalism, violence and even murder. The destructive work of the nationalistically-inclined and other political extremists, devil-worshippers and pseudo-religious opportunists and criminals exploiting the national and even religious factor for their own ends must be halted.'

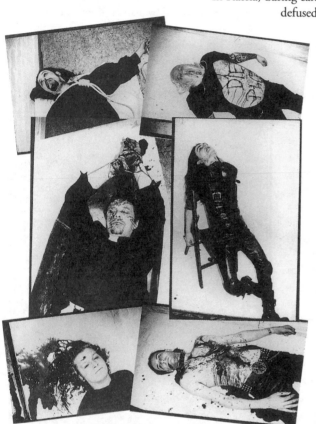

Characteristically-tasteful promotional shots for British black metal act Cradle of Filth.

To many heavy metal kids – who had endured years of repressive atheistic communism only to witness the Orthodox Church getting back into bed with an incompetent, corrupt government – there might have seemed every justification. One Russian black metal fan, quoted in extreme music magazine *Terrorizer*, observed soberly, 'A lot of people in the police are looking for an excuse. The Mafia are running rampant, and tackling that problem would mean denting their pockets. So they have to look for someone else. And when they start arresting people just for wearing Burzum shirts, they know there is going to be a response . . . they would like nothing better than to start a war with us.'

Back in the West, the prospect of 'war' between the black metal underground and mainstream society became an increasingly distant prospect. When the feared tide of violence failed to break, business as normal resumed. In 1999 Dimmu Borgir, leading lights of the black metal revival, were nominated for a Grammy award in their native Norway – whereas only a few years before no black metal fan would even have been allowed at the awards ceremony. (The award actually went to another Norwegian black metal band.)

Dimmu Borgir – whose name refers to a traditional Norwegian entrance to Hell – have alienated some purists because their sound has a level of melody and polish some consider anathema to their underground status. However, it's this very blend of metallic aggression and quasi-orchestral atmospherics that has seen the band chalk up impressive sales. Black metal is in danger of becoming big business.

With two of their number released from gaol, Emperor are back in the game. Displaying little remorse for past indiscretions, they do at least concede their crimes may have been a little foolish. Musically, they've learned to structure their dark hymns with melody lines that have won healthy international album sales and even a cover feature from *Kerrang!* – the magazine they once declared unofficial war on.

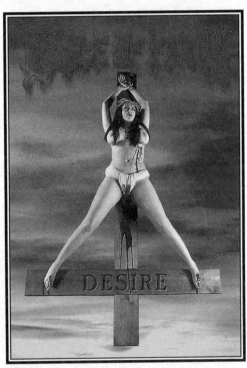

Other bands still play with the raw 'Norwegian sound' of the early 1990s – notably Mayhem, still regarded as the most unremittingly 'evil' black metal band, who endure despite their melodramatically-fluctuating line-up. Just as Euronymous once traded on the death of band-mate Dead, so Mayhem enjoy 'legendary' status thanks to the death of Euronymous.

Ironically, though the criminal antics of the Black Metal Circle attracted the international attention that led to the genre's global renaissance, most current black metal bands distance themselves from the excesses of the early 1990s – while conceding that they lent the genre a pathological allure. There's an ambivalence at work that is almost classically Satanic. Cradle of Filth, the British act currently riding high on the black metal revival, are disdained by many 'traditionalists' as overly commercial while enjoying album sales many less flamboyant acts would sell their

Cradle of Filth's blend of erotic, blasphemous and bloody imagery has helped establish them at the forefront of the black metal movement.

souls for. Since their foundation in 1991, the band have become something of an institution – their singer, Dani, writes a regular column for *Metal Hammer* magazine, and they even took part in a BBC TV documentary wherein they helped dispel the fears of a fan's dear old mother about her son's Satanic tastes.

Cradle of Filth have popularised a style that blends the velvets of gothicism with the razorblades of black metal, combining corpse-paint and profanity with a Hammer-horror aesthetic and funereal dignity. Some critics, however, have challenged the poetic aspirations of the band's most controversial output to date: their 'Jesus is a Cunt' T-shirt, which led to a number of young fans being arrested on charges of public indecency.

The sheer number and diversity of bands involved in the black metal scene today is breathtaking: 'black metal' is defined not so much by a musical style as by a lyrical fixation with the Satanic (though not necessarily Satanism itself), evoking dark passions and gothic moods. Within these boundaries, black metal is arguably the most vital and creative force in contemporary music.

Black metal musicians plunder almost every aspect of the Western musical canon, from folk and techno to orchestral and jazz influences. (There is even a Japanese band, Sigh, who are heavily influenced by traditional Oriental music.) They are also becoming increasingly literate and well-informed. Whereas, three decades before, Black Sabbath were inspired by a Dennis Wheatley novel, the new generation of demonic rockers are exploring writers like Dante and Milton, with the Norwegian act Ulver releasing an album based upon William Blake's *Marriage of Heaven and Hell*.

Blasphemer, guitarist with the current line-up of Mayhem, flanked by a butcher's parade of severed cow's heads.

The seemingly limitless present-day ambitions of black metal are evident in the mission statement of blackmetal.com, an American on-line store influential in fostering the genre stateside: 'Black Metal is the state-of-the-art pinnacle in extreme music and the most alternative, most underground form of demi-monde culture this side of Hades! BLACK METAL, blackmetal, 'BM', 'Norwegian', 'Northern', 'true', 'elite', 'modern black', 'dark-metal', 'Greek', 'blackened death', 'gothic-metal', 'Pagan metal', 'vampyric', 'death-industrial', 'black-noise', 'dark-ambient/black-ambient', etc. – these are the nomenclature that sets our music apart from the mediocrity of conventional culture and brings us all together in the most cutting-edge community! . . . Hail Satan!'

A TWIST OF CAIN

Words with Glenn Danzig.

I met Glenn Danzig in 1992, while he was touring Europe. He's a Satanic artist in the most aesthetic sense, with a reputation for hostility to interviewers. It's certainly true that he demands everything on his own terms, but once I got through the wall of suspicion and made it clear I was interested in his work, Danzig was easy to talk to. Contrary to the image portrayed by some journalists, he's a bright, well-read, serious, if wilfully-aggressive individual.

There's a lot of Satanism in your work – especially referring to the Miltonian Satan . . .
Yes. One of the better things written about me was that when other people sing about Satan it's like in a cartoon. When I sing about Him I give Him a soul and a character. He's not just this futile entity but someone you can see many aspects to. I've always felt like that. Some people don't see Satan as this guy with horns who's evil, they see Him as the first rebel. Then you can see why He's so attractive to many young people. He's someone who's standing up to the greatest power in the universe and saying, 'Fuck you!' If that 'evil' is of a rebellious nature, then I guess, in Christian terms, that evil is the Satan in you. I don't buy that. I believe in honesty, standing up for yourself. That's my 'good'.

I've read some interviews where you seemed to be distancing yourself from Satanism to an extent . . .
I've never said that. We don't just write about Satanism, as a matter of fact it may only figure in about ten-twenty per cent of the material, and even then it's not the classical portrayal of Satanism. There are so many different Satanists that there are so many different types of Satanism. There are all of these different organisations and they all contradict each other. It's almost like watching the Christians squabble, you get that same kind of thing going on in Satanism. Eventually, what happens is when Satanism mirrors organised religion it becomes hypocritical.

Would you disassociate yourself from characters like LaVey?
Obviously Anton LaVey is very smart. As far as *The Satanic Bible* goes, I don't put much credence in it, but there are a lot of people who do, and for them that's great. Whatever works for you. As far as I'm concerned, I have my own beliefs. I believe in myself, and I believe in some kind of higher power, but I have no need for it.

Is there a different Danzig persona on stage and in everyday life?
No, what you see here is the same person. I don't take this off, put it away in a closet, then put it back on. If the situation happened right here where I had to cut your throat, I would do it.

Well, thank you very much!
I think a lot of kids know that. I can be nice, but if I have to turn it on to save my own ass, it'd be on in a second.

Glenn Danzig.

Are you trying to portray Satan as a heroic figure?
Not at all. Most of the concepts I employ are taken from classical literature. If you look at the early tracts of *The Bible* there's really not much about Satan in there anyway. I'm just relating the facts, trying to bring a little common sense into this, a little logic. I think a lot of the Christian religions have tried to overblow and create a whole legend around Satan which isn't true to the actual scriptures we have. Am I trying to further the image of Satan? No. I'm just getting things straight.

If you're a Christian and believe in Jesus, He'd be rolling over in His grave at the way the Church is being run. The Vatican has an assassination bureau, and has had for centuries. That's not what Jesus taught, not the Jesus I learnt about. The Christians have had holy wars in which vast numbers of people have died, more than in any of the wars we've seen in our lifetime. This is in the name of someone who said, 'Turn the other cheek and please be a passive society.' To me, that's evil. That's more evil than even the most distorted account of Satan in the scriptures.

How would you describe your beliefs?
I empathise with all beliefs. Whatever I need to get my end result, I will use. Mine is a very logical and common-sense approach. I won't be blinded by something because I believe in it. If what I believe in turns on me, I turn on it. Because of that I can deal with life on a big, even level. I know how to deal with people. I programmed my songs 'How the Gods Kill' and 'Sistinas' back-to-back on my CD player and just sat in my room in the dark and listened to them over and over. Those two songs, back-to-back, create a mood for me, put my whole world on a very even plane. From that level I can deal with any situation. If I was sitting there in the darkness and someone just walked in, in a very smooth and serene manner I could destroy them, then sit right back down in my spot.

You can't help people from a position of weakness . . .
Exactly. You must first make yourself strong, you can then help others if you so desire. You should only help people who want help, a lot of times people don't really want your help. You tell most people what has to be done to change their lives, they won't listen.

You write very good lyrics, while few other bands seem to . . .
I don't think they care to. With a lot of other bands, I think they're more sensationalist – 'Death, murder, bluerghh' – especially with a lot of these thrash and death metal bands. If I decide in a song to sing about Satan or something with a Satanic slant, I try to approach it in a serious manner. It's like, look, this isn't a joke, it's not a comic book, it's something a lot of people are very serious about and I want to give it something that will last. Immediately someone else sees it, it's written off as drivel and shit because of these other cartoon, comic-book guys treating it like a joke with their 'Hail to Satan, eater of babies' shit. People wearing KISS make up. I've never met Satan, if He exists, but if He does I'm pretty sure He doesn't wear KISS make up.

You see Satan as a much more seductive character?
Sure. I've always said that if Satan were corporeal, He would not be something repulsive, He would be something seductive. He would want to win you over and gain your trust, and of course being repulsive or disgusting would not be the way to go. I'm not saying those aspects don't figure later on, but I'd imagine that this would be a seductive, beautiful creature.

A fallen angel?
Perhaps. In the Gnostic account of the fall of the angels, the angels were supposed to be watching over this flock of humans and all of a sudden they're perpetrating sexual acts with them. Eventually this created the Cyclops, the Minotaur, things of this nature. There are so many accounts of the fall of the angels, it's like a fantasy tale that you'd like to believe actually happened. It's kind of a cool history, and when you think it may actually have some basis in reality . . . it's cool.

NAKED BLASPHEMY

A conversation with Paul Ledney, founder of Profanatica and Havohej.

Paul Ledney, a lively young American, spoke to me over the phone in 1992 concerning both his collapsed project, Profanatica, and then-current band, Havohej. Despite the wilfully-provocative nature of his material, Ledney was polite and articulate, with a sincere interest in the peculiar territory he was exploring.

Would you consider yourself a Satanist?
I would, but a lot of other people wouldn't. I believe I am my own God and nobody can judge me and nobody is more powerful than me. I indulge in pleasurable perversion. People have so many different ways of looking at it, but I don't believe Satan is an actual entity. It's just a worship figure, but a lot of people do think of Satan as a real god. Maybe they're crazy, why should their 'Master' care about someone like them anyhow?

Where do you draw your Satanic belief from?
Mostly Crowley. His *Book of the Law* really opened my eyes. Satanism is anti-religion. I don't believe in any gods. I suppose it's good that some people gather for Black Masses with their corresponding dark beliefs, but I think everybody should think for themselves. If everyone thought the same way then that would be Hell on earth.

What do you feel about organised Satanic churches like the Church of Satan?
I don't agree with them. Take the Church of Satan's magazine, *The Black Flame*. On the back they had this ad, I can't remember the exact quote, but it said, 'Imagine your friends' delight as they drink coffee out of their Baphomet mug.' I can't remember how much it was – around $15.95 – but it was the most ridiculous thing I've ever seen. There were copies of *The Black Flame* being handed out at our gigs and there were some of our roadies, who were Satanists, who wanted that mug and couldn't appreciate what money-making junk it is. When that many people get together in a church

it's hard not to get involved with cheesy stuff like that ad. Satanic churches and so forth are just more organised religion. I believe in hate, because hate is the strongest emotion. On the other hand, I don't believe people can go on hating forever without lying to themselves because you'd no longer be able to function.

So are there positive aspects to your faith?

Definitely. Havohej is a way of getting out aggression but it has many hints of my personal beliefs – it's not just some fairy tale. The positive aspects of my faith don't all come out through Havohej. My philosophy helps me get as much money as I can, get as much pussy as I can, drink as much as I can. But I try and balance all of it out. Indulge and compete.

Does your faith involve violence?

Not at all. I believe if someone hits you in the face, hit him back twice as hard. There's lots of people that I hate, but I just let it come.

What do you think of love?

I don't know – I love sodomy.

What are you trying to do with Havohej?

I want it to be painful to listen to. I want people to feel different after listening to it – depressed, angry, charged, or whatever. I don't want to just get a reaction from somebody, I want them to have changed. You can go into some movies and forget about them afterwards, but some movies really affect you, I want my music to be like a really effective horror movie.

Paul Ledney, centre, in his flamboyantly perverse and profane project Profanatica.

What are all of the blasphemies about?

The lyrics are almost short stories, but they're not. I don't like to print or publish the lyrics, they're personal to me. But Havohej's lyrics are all blasphemies. Things

like 'Masturbate Upon God'. It's offensive, but true, inasmuch as I am saying what I mean or feel. It's not for shock value, but it is shocking.

Why is there so much nudity in your publicity shots?

We did these publicity shots at around the same time as this other band, Impaled Nazarene, covered in cow's blood. We came up with the idea of making the whole thing more black and perverse, because that is what the whole Profanatica project was about, the blood and nudity were symbols of that. If we play live with Havohej, then we will do it with the whole band totally naked. Havohej will be bathed in blood, urine and semen live. I want actual shit and worms gnawing at Bibles on stage.

PURE FUCKING ARMAGEDDON

An interview with Euronymous, head of Deathlike Silence Records/frontman of Mayhem.

I conducted this interview with Euronymous late in 1992, several months before his feud with Count Grishnackh erupted and ended his life. He was courteous and eager to talk about his odd ideas and nihilist philosophy, remaining curiously deadpan throughout the interview even when delivering his more extreme rants.

Is your music a form of worship?

No, it's more an expression of feelings. Technically, we're not just trying to be horrific, like a lot of the other bands, we're trying to create this atmospheric feeling.

Which Norwegian bands would you consider Satanic?

The only Satanic bands are Mayhem, Burzum and Dark Throne. Immortal are not Satanic, they just use a lot of dark imagery. Enslaved are into ancient Norse religion, only with a kind of negative aspect to it. Emperor are interested in dark ideas and violence, but they are not Satanists. There are of course tons of black metal bands all over the world. The problem is that they are calling themselves Satanists but they are actually into Christianity. This is because they think Christianity is corrupt and evil, it represses people. But we think this is great! When bands are talking about how all

Christianity is evil and should be stopped, these bands are preaching goodness and freedom and therefore I don't accept them as Satanic.

Could you tell me a little bit about the Black Metal Circle or Black Metal Militia?

There are two different things here. The Black Metal Circle is a kind of cult consisting of ourselves, Mayhem and Dark Throne. We discuss things and try to keep the

Rare early Mayhem shot, featuring (left to right) Euronymous, Manhiem, Dead and Necrobutcher. Both Euronymous and Dead subsequently died violently.

ideology clean and pure. We are kind of brothers. We do everything for each other – if one of us gets into trouble, the whole group can help.

Within this group, do you perform religious or magical ceremonies?

You could say that, but mostly we talk. I cannot speak too much about it because there is quite a lot about it which is illegal. But in the Black Metal Circle we don't just have black metal people, we also have brutal death metal people – people who worship death and destruction. We have no problem with this because they believe in the same things as us but they don't have any religion.

We think it's important to take care of our enemies in a certain way. These enemies are mostly Christians, but when I speak of Christians I don't mean extreme or fundamentalist Christians – we support them 100 per cent because they are spreading so much sorrow and oppression. They should get more money, they should get more power. We would like to see Christians going round to our houses with weapons, trying to kill us. It would be great, it would be total religious war. We think that when things

happen against the Church – churches are burning, graveyards desecrated – there will be more and more extreme Christians. We think they might become extreme because they think, 'Okay, we have an enemy.' Christians today think nothing's happening, so they don't take their religion so seriously. We think when something really dark happens these people will gather together, join forces and blow this cosmos apart. That's great.

What we hate is Christian moderates and those Christians who use their lives to help others, like Mother Teresa. That's the enemy, not the religious leaders who oppress others. Our hit list also includes organisations like the Red Cross. A lot of the death metal bands are also our enemies – without knowing it, they are allies of Mother Teresa and her kind. They should call themselves what they really are – '*life* metal'.

Do you have any aims beyond trying to bring about religious war?

Myself, I have no aims. I am commanded by Satan. We are all just servants of Satan and we don't expect anything in return. We don't expect to be rewarded with pleasure, riches or anything – it's just horror and Hell that we will receive. As to what happens to me, it doesn't matter – as long as I can take as many with me as I can.

Where do you take your Satanic beliefs from?

It's purely biblical. When we are leading our ordinary, everyday lives, we try as much as possible to avoid anything which God wishes. For example, when having sex: in *The Bible* it says, 'You must not spill your seed upon the ground.' It means you must not fuck except for trying to have children, otherwise it is blasphemy. What could be more blasphemous than sodomising a woman? We try to pervert what's written in *The Bible* as much as possible. I think if you carry on in a normal way, especially if you have children, then you are taking part in the ultimate life-rituals. By creating life you are obeying God's commands. I would like to prevent people from reproducing. People want to do it and it gives pleasure, therefore I have to prevent it. Imagine the sorrow you could spread if you chopped everybody's dicks off! It's impossible, but that doesn't matter – it's the idea behind it which is important.

Why don't you impose this sorrow on others within the Black Metal Circle?

I don't care what happens to them. For example, if Fenris from Dark Throne should die, I wouldn't cry. I wouldn't go to the funeral. I wouldn't care at all, except he is my ally and I need him. He'd say the same about me. Count Grishackh, for example, he wouldn't waste a minute killing me if I weren't an ally. He needs me and I need him. We have become very cynical. If I should have a girlfriend and she died, I wouldn't cry, I would probably screw the corpse. We try hard to avoid having human feelings. Clearly, I can't say I'm 100 per cent pure evil, that's impossible. But we try our hardest to achieve the ultimate evil in ourselves.

Is your Satanism linked to medieval beliefs?

Definitely. I think in a perverted way the tradition of Satanism is actually beautiful. The vision of a creature so evil that it is not possible for a human mind to comprehend is beautiful. Of course, if I saw Him, even I would probably die from fear. I hate to hear people saying, 'If I saw Satan I would laugh.' I tell them to fuck off. They don't know what they're talking about.

So do you express your Satanic beliefs through actions?

Some of us do, some of us don't. For example, the vocalist from Dark Throne has isolated himself around 150 kilometres from here. And he lives all by himself, as does the guitarist. I only see the drummer because of this Black Metal Circle. We have some members who are doing all sorts of things.

What kind of things?

I'm not sure how much I can tell you, because the telephone is probably bugged. I know the Count's phone was bugged, because our drummer tried to call him and he got through to the police! Have you heard about everything which has happened up here? If people think we have done all of the things we are accused of – let them think so. If they think we haven't done them – let them think that.

If we assume these accusations are true – someone has been burning down churches, someone has stabbed some Christians – would that be something which you'd approve of?

Yes. I support it 100 per cent. I think all kinds of action which are neccesary for spreading sorrow are great. Many people say, for example, that desecrating churchyards is just stupid because you don't harm the Christians. But I think it's great because it can depress so many people. You go to church and find the graves desecrated or destroyed, then you're thoroughly depressed – it's a tragedy. It spreads sorrow and I think that's very important.

What have you done, that you could tell me about, which would be the most extreme expression of your beliefs?

Myself, I don't do much. Within the Black Metal Circle we are broken up into smaller cells. One cell takes care of the economics – that's me. If I took part in a lot of action then I would probably be caught and the whole organisation would just fall apart. I can't afford to be involved, though there are a couple of things which I have done and cannot tell you about now. We have a kind of death squad or action group. They are taking care of action, and action only.

How many people would you say are in this 'action group'?

Up to ten people. Really dedicated people who don't care. They have no respect for human life at all, and they have done a lot of stuff. There's a lot of fuss about what's going on now – they're writing about us in *Kerrang!*, for example – which is great promotion. But I don't understand why, because what we have done so far is just a tiny little piece of what's about to happen.

Do you mean the battle predicted in 'Revelations'?

It's hard to say. 'Revelations' is a very difficult gospel to understand. We'll just have to wait and see what will happen, but I think it will happen very soon. Nostradamus predicted that the world would end at the end of this century, so it should be very interesting. I think that several catastrophes will occur, humankind will be wiped out, but some people will be left. There will be absolutely no law, it will be total anarchy, and I am looking forward to it. We conceal ourselves, we would survive, and we would be very strong. We would have armies, an old king – stuff like that. One great thing about Norway is that with the countryside you can hide out here forever.

Why do you reject Satanic churches?

I think they're bullshit. For example, the Church of Satan – I see them as greater enemies than the Christians. I would say that they are intelligent people – I don't want people to be intelligent, I want dumb slaves. I think that they know why Christianity is bad and they want to make sure Christians have no power. They say Christians are oppressing freedoms and all that shit, but I think that's great. We would love to destroy the Church of Satan because they are a power on the side of goodness. They see themselves as the good force and the Christians as the evil force, they engage in rituals trying to prove to themselves that they are not enslaved by religion and I think that's blasphemy. I hereby on behalf of the Norwegian Black Metal Circle declare total war on the Church of Satan. If they want to establish in Norway they are going to have problems.

STEALING AURAS

An interview with Count Grishnackh,
founder of Burzum/murderer of Euronymous.

I spoke to the Count early in 1993, while he was on
bail for the Norwegian church burnings – before the
international music press seized upon the story, or
the death of Euronymous. He spoke with an intense,
dour tone and seemed – as far as I could tell –
entirely serious about everything he said. It was also
clear that, like Euronymous, he'd thought about it all
in some detail and wasn't just ranting on the spur of
the moment.

How would you describe the music you play?
Dark and depressing. It's an expression of hate, cold
hate.

Are you a Satanic band?
People think of Satanism as individualism, like with the
Church of Satan. I don't want to be compared with
those people. I really don't like the Christians, so we are
Satanists of course, but I prefer to call it Devil-worship
when I talk to others. I don't like the word Satanism,
because we have a lot of stupid bands making it into a
stupid word. Bands like Bathory and Venom. I like
those bands, but they make fun of Satanism, all those
bands like Slayer who claim to be Satanic and turn out
being hard-core idiots. We are the way Venom and
Bathory claimed to be. We believe what they pretended
to believe.

*What do you believe? Do you believe Satan exists? In
what form?*
He exists in a spiritual form. Like a big black shape, too
black to be seen.

If you believe in Satan, do you then believe in God?
Of course – God is good, Satan is evil. They wage war
upon each other.

And you serve Satan in this war?
Yes.

Why, what does Satan offer you?
He offers me nothing. I wage war, that is why I am here.
You could call me Satan's slave.

Where do you draw your Satanic theology from?
Euronymous, he reads and takes his theories from *The
Bible*, right? I don't read *The Bible*, even though that is
the only book about Satan for real Satanists. I make up

my own realities. There's a lot of inspiration from
Mordor in the Tolkien stuff. I don't believe in Tolkien's
world, but it has a lot of connections with the real thing.
There are major parallels between Hell and Mordor.

So, in a way, you see yourself as fighting for Mordor?
I don't want to use words like Mordor because it could
be dismissed as a joke. Mordor is just one word for Hell.
Call it whatever you like. Like Satan, you can call Him
Sauron [sorcerous overlord of Mordor in *The Lord of the
Rings*] if you want. I don't care, He's still my Lord.

How do you know what He wants you to do?
I don't know, I do what I feel is right.

*Why do you and Euronymous have such a great
hatred of the Church of Satan?*

Varg Vikernes, aka Count Grishnackh, in Viking mode.

Satanism is supposed to be something forbidden,
something evil, something secret, something people
don't know anything of. You go to America and in the
telephone directory you can see 'Church of God',
'Church of Jesus' and 'Church of Satan'. You call, and a
woman answers: 'Church of Satan, may I help you?' You
think, 'This isn't Satanism! Some stupid fuck is trying to
ruin everything.' The superstitious part of it falls apart.
The Church of Satan deny Satan, they say He doesn't

exist, yet they act as if He did, they rebel against God. They call themselves Satanists because He also rebelled against God, but they're basically light and life-worshipping individualists.

And that's something you can't identify with at all?
Exactly.

You're a member of the Black Metal Circle?
Well, the phone is tapped, so I think you'd better write what you know.

Because you're under surveillance, that makes it difficult for you to talk about certain things?
Not really. I think we can talk about them – if they confront me with it I can tell them I was joking or saying it for publicity.

Could you tell me a little about recent events in Norway?
Eight churches have been burnt in 1992. Over a period of six months there have been eight churches ruined by fire. Some people have disappeared. And of course the normal grave desecration . . .

Who's disappeared?
Normal people just disappear and never show up again.

This could have a Satanic connection?
It does.

Why would these people have disappeared?
Every human is life, and we hate life, especially human life. That's the reason.

So you're saying that these people may have disappeared for some form of sacrifice?
Exactly.

Supposing that perhaps you knew what had happened to these people, what specifically would it be?
Something like what you would call a Satanic murder.

A ritualised sacrifice?
The murder is the ritual.

Would these murders gain power for whoever was responsible?
Of course. I have this belief in auras; everybody has their own aura. If I, for example, murdered a person, I could steal his aura and add it to mine, so I would get a more powerful aura. The same goes for church burning. A church has its own spirit – the church has been worshipped in for maybe hundreds of years and has thus gained a lot of spirit in that time. A person who

sacrifices that will gain a lot of power and grow stronger.
Is there anything someone could do in the name of Satan that you would disagree with?
A lot of things: anything which can bring happiness, goodness or light.

If something causes suffering to you, would that be an evil deed? If, for example, you went to gaol, that wouldn't be fun would it?
No, it wouldn't be fun, but I hate fun so I really wouldn't care too much. I was in prison for six weeks and I sometimes wish myself back in my cell because it's so happy out here. Everybody's so kind and loving and I hate that.

So if the trial goes against you, you don't care?
Well, of course there's a great symbolic value if I win. It will cause a lot more fear, so it's very important that I win.

Do you perform any rituals as part of your faith?
When people talk about rituals, they think of Anton LaVey appearing in his pyjamas with horns and fucking a girl on an altar or something like that. I don't take part in such rituals. But I study other things – tarot cards and things like that – which have nothing to do with Satanism. Astrology, psychology. Rituals – yes – but not in the same form as most people think.

If you were to perform a ritual, when would you do it, and why?
I would be likely to do it during the full moon, at night, because it has a lot of symbolic value. A lot of people believe in the full moon, a lot of people believe in virgins. That makes both the full moon and the virgin more powerful because of belief in them.

Is it possible that Satan and God are just creations of people's minds?
That's very possible. But I believe that God was first and He created the world. Of course, a lot of scientists would deny that. But I would attack their view because I believe God used evolution, which is why it took so long, which is why we have evidence like dinosaur bones.

Some Gnostic Christians have suggested Satan created the world, what do you think of that?
I think it's wrong, because God is more powerful than Satan. Much more powerful. But if I, for example, had to fight a much more powerful foe – a great white knight, say, weighing 300 pounds with his armour and sharp blade – I would lose. But I am evil, so I need not fight him – I hide in the shadows and shoot poisonous darts in his back. That's why I win – because I am the evil one. Satan is the evil one who will win, God is the strong knight who will be shot in the back.

Is there a right-wing element to Satanic belief?
Yes, because the strongest will survive, and stuff like that, which has parallels with the Nazis. When it comes to racial issues, I am a racist.

Could a black person or an oriental be a Satanist?
Of course, but I would not see him as my brother in any way. I am of the Northern race and I don't respect others who are not of the Northern race, like the French or Germans. The Germans have nothing to do with the Aryan race. The Saxons were Aryan, but there aren't many Saxons left in Germany. The Saxons I respect, but the rest can fuck off. They should be enslaved.

You're very much against freedom and free speech – what, ideally, would replace it?
A lot of Satanists talk about a 'victory' you're supposed to win. Of course I agree, but in a different way. I think the ideal situation is war. War between good and evil – like the situation in *The Lord of the Rings*. Everybody will be taken as slaves except the warlords.

The eternal war you talk about, has it anything to do with Ragnarok, the Nordic Apocalypse?
I believe in Ragnarok, because *The Bible* tells us it will be quite soon. In the next decade.

Do you think the Black Metal Circle could have been founded anywhere else? Is it something peculiarly Scandinavian?
I think Scandinavia has been the victim of 'kind propaganda' – like 'feed the Somalis and be kind to everybody'. It's very unnatural for the Vikings to save some fucking niggers down in Africa because they're hungry. We're supposed to go and butcher them.

Is Scandinavia a depressing place? You never get much sunlight, it's always cold . . .
Especially in my hometown. The Evil comes from the North. We are very far North.

Will Scandinavian evil spread?
Yes. It would be better if it was America, because everyone's so fucking stupid over there, so everybody would be drawn into it. In Scandinavia it will go much more slowly, because we are much more intelligent than anywhere else. I think it will begin here. The Church of Satan are our biggest enemies. They're the most brilliant, so we will fight and kill them before even the Christians. Hippies, peace-loving idiots, the Church of Satan, they are our biggest enemies.

How do you feel about the fundamentalist Christians?
That's the only Christianity I respect.

ILL MET BY CANDLELIGHT

Thoughts from Lee Barrett, owner of Candlelight Records.

At the time of the interview in late 1993, Lee Barrett ran the independent Candlelight label from his home, not far from where Sir Francis Dashwood's Hellfire Club once met. The label concentrated on extreme metal and occultic bands, mirroring Barrett's own interests, and signed many of the most controversial acts. Young, pragmatic, independent-minded and mischievous, Barrett courted trouble with a disarming grin.

Would you describe yourself as a practising occultist?
To an extent. There's a ritual element in what I do, but I don't take much from old books or other outside influences.

Euronymous makes the front page of a Norwegian tabloid by virtue of his August 1993 murder.

How did you become involved with the Norwegian black metal scene?
I'd been friends with Euronymous for some time. In 1986 I bought the Mayhem demo, *Pure Fucking*

Armageddon, then a year later bought the LP and started writing to the band. I kept up with the scene through fanzines and talking to Euronymous.

Did Euronymous' murder surprise you?
No. I think it was inevitable really, they were taking everything to such an extreme.

Why do you think it happened?
They're very full of national pride in Scandinavia. On the Norwegian scene they're very up on the ancient Norse religion – the true Viking warrior image is one they like to put over. The attacks on Christian churches come partially from that – they were a pagan country until the arrival of the Christian missionaries and as far as they're concerned the churches shouldn't be there, which is why they're burning them down. There's a lot of people who bowed down to everything the Black Metal Circle said. Read any black metal fanzines and you'll constantly hear Euronymous referred to as 'the Master'. He was setting himself up as a Charles Manson figure, where he wouldn't do much himself, but would get other people to do it. He was a big influence on a lot of black metal kids in Norway and they did more-or-less anything he said. It took someone like Grishnackh to take it one stage further.

What was your impression of Grishnackh?
Obviously quite insane, basically. He phoned me a couple of hours after he'd killed Euronymous and he was just laughing and joking, saying, 'Ha ha, Euronymous is dead, I'm going to dance and piss on his grave.' These are not the rantings of someone who's all there. He told me about the dynamite he had and how he was going to blow up churches and so forth. Basically, they were taking things to illogical extremes, but it all made sense in their own heads.

They're not scary, imposing people though, are they?
Oh no. Euronymous wasn't a very tall person. Grishnackh wasn't the most well-built bloke in the world. They created their own little world, basically. That's what they wanted to live in, that's how they wanted to live.

Does it bother you being associated with this kind of thing?
Not really, no. The whole point of the label is to wind up as many people as possible. Associating myself with this is working rather well. I like wearing T-shirts with swear words on them just to get a reaction. It's confrontational.

Kerrang! *magazine had some problems over the Norwegian scene, did not they?*
Kerrang! took the piss out of the band Emperor, who weren't at all amused. When a couple of kids from

Manchester wrote to some members of the Black Metal Circle and asked, 'How do we get into the "Inner Circle"?', the word is that they wrote back and said, 'Burn down a church and kill Jason Arnopp from *Kerrang!*' They promptly burnt down a church and started making threatening calls to *Kerrang!*, saying they were going to petrol-bomb the place. Arnopp had to move house.

How serious are the kids who are on the fringes of the black metal scene?
I get a lot of letters with things like 'stay black' written on them, but how serious these kids are is impossible to tell until you meet them. I think there will be a severe case of 'monkey see, monkey do' with this which can't be avoided. If people are stupid enough to do that, then that's their problem. If they have to follow people, they're missing the entire point.

AT THE EVIL EYE OF THE STORM

An interview with Vincent Crowley of Acheron.

Vincent Crowley, frontman of the band Acheron (named after the 'river of sorrows' which runs through Hell in classical Greek mythology), spoke to me from death metal's spiritual heartland in Florida during early 1993. Acheron are as close to an official Church of Satan black metal band as it's possible to be, evidenced by the heavy involvement of other CoS members. The gruff but likeable Crowley spoke about his band, the black metal scene and the Order of the Evil Eye, his unofficial sister organisation to the Church of Satan.

Could you tell me a little about the Order of the Evil Eye?
There's three parts to it really. There's an anti-Christian circle, which is a worldwide movement. The second part's a Satanic movement which follows the doctrines set down in *The Satanic Bible*, from which we supply Satanic literature and material on the Church of Satan. Lastly, there's an inner circle here in Florida, mostly composed of local people, which produces Satanic propaganda. It's definitely growing – we've over 3,000 members now.

Some established Satanists, LaVey included, seem very suspicious of Satanic metal music. How do you feel about that?
I agree with him. There's a lot of idiots at shows for foolish reasons – abusing drugs, behaving like a bunch of idiots under the pretence of rebellion. There's nothing wrong with rebellion, but if you just want to

use it as a scapegoat for your idiotic behaviour, then that's another story. There are a lot of fakes in the metal scene and I can understand why a lot of people can't take it seriously. You go all the way back to bands like KISS or Motley Crue or Black Sabbath and they were Satanic until the veil was ripped away and they were exposed. It's hard now for someone who's legitimately Satanic in this business to get themselves taken seriously.

Church of Satan-affiliated death metal band Acheron. The Reverend Vincent Crowley is wearing dark glasses.

What is the significance of the Black Mass to you?
We thought, for the first album, that we could actually perform it on stage as the psychodrama which is a blasphemy of the Catholic rite. If you get down to magic, what we performed in public was more for the sake of sucking up energy than getting people into the psychodrama. We don't do it very often, but we have the girl on the altar, the Satanic banners, the acolyte on stage brings me out the cross to smash – the whole atmosphere of the Black Mass.

What's 'Satanic music'?
It doesn't have to be all 'Hail Satan' or 'Fuck God' or whatever. Satanic music comes straight from the heart. If your music is emotional and affects you, it's Satanic. It can be classical, death metal, whatever. It's a matter of how you write it and why you write it.

Have the events in Norway had a negative effect on Satanic metal?
It's hard to get tours because a lot of clubs aren't booking shows with black metal bands now, distributors won't touch this kind of stuff, *Rock Hard* magazine in Germany aren't running any interviews with black metal bands. A lot of the black metal bands are getting a bad name for us – there's a lot of negativity involved. Several big labels were interested in us, but when they found out what we were into, it was 'Goodbye.' The whole thing's ridiculous. I don't care what's going on in the black

metal scene – if they want to kill each other, I'm not going to cry over it. But when they start throwing our name around, that's when fucking war starts.

Is radical Christianity on the wane in the US at the moment?
People are becoming more aware. A lot of priests are getting exposed for molesting children, evangelists are getting in trouble for pocketing funds or visiting prostitutes. These things are getting exposed and people are getting sick of it. The extreme Christian weirdoes are still out there, believe me. Since the beginning of the band we've been getting shit from people. I get death threats in the mail. People put shit on my P.O. box. They're supposed to love their neighbours but I get messages like, 'Die, you Satanic piece of shit!' It's ridiculous. They call us the bad guys, but they're the ones who behave in this fashion.

I did a show with the radio evangelist Bob Larson around a year ago. He came to town and was coming out with all this shit about how us and Deicide are hiding behind tombstones and would never confront him. So me, the guitarist and the bass player decided to meet him in his little church and debate with him. There were a thousand Christians in this church and he took his Bible out and started condemning our CD, so I took a Bible and ripped it up right there on the altar and threw it down to the audience. We had to leave by the side door.

ROCKING THE CRADLE OF FILTH

Communications with Andrea Meyer

The curious career of Andrea Meyer is, in some ways, emblematic of the whole black metal scene. When I spoke to this young German woman in London, in late 1993, she represented a meeting point between the occult world and the burgeoning black metal scene, having recorded with extreme metal bands Aghast and Cradle of Filth. (Cradle of Filth have gone on to become one of the foremost acts on the current black metal scene.)

Andrea subsequently met guitarist Samoth (Tomas Haugen) of the Norwegian band Emperor, who was gaoled at one point for burning down a church. The happy couple are now married, with a

child, living in Norway where the former Ms Meyer is now known as Andrea Haugen. Like many Norwegian black metallists, she has since abandoned her former Satanic beliefs in favour of Norse paganism – ideas which she communicates through her neo-folk music project Hagalaz' Runedance.

Why is ritual so central to your Satanism?

I find rituals quite important as they impress one's mind – you know you are dealing with 'serious stuff' – and that is how magic works. It comes from within: you release certain energies and draw in certain energies; therefore it is important that people can control their own minds. This takes a lot of effort to master. For example, I advise novices to throw themselves into situations they could not normally cope with, in order to learn to deal with them. A Satanist should suffer from no paranoias and master their fear.

Where do you draw your Satanic beliefs from?

My Satanic philosophy harmonises quite closely with Boyd Rice's and I like his musical work. But I also find Michael Aquino's ideas interesting. The Decadent movement of the late nineteenth century was quite Satanic, and the concept of the Decadent lifestyle is quite appealing. I am a great fan of the Decadent writers, such as Edgar Allan Poe, and enjoy stories about the macabre and unknown in general, like the work of H. P. Lovecraft. I agree with a lot of Nietzsche's philosophy on the will to power, morals, and the superman. I read the Marquis de Sade, who I find fascinating – Gilles de Rais was also a very interesting character.

Is Satanism a religion?

Satanism to me is a way of living. It's a philosophy and a magical path, not a religion.

What makes a Satanist?

I think to be a Satanist you have to have a dark, sinister side to you – you have to be born that way. You must be an extreme person, a strong-willed person – emotional but not controlled by emotions. You have to understand the darker aspects of human psychology and behaviour. You must be your own master, responsible for your own actions. A Satanist is an individual. A Satanist is usually also a misanthrope. He appreciates that most people are weak and foolish and follow the crowd, like sheep. Even *The Bible* refers to people as 'sheep'. I am not a happy person. Once you understand what life is about it's difficult to enjoy it, but this doesn't stop me making the most of my life. There is no afterlife. This is a difficult concept for many people – they can't imagine being gone forever one day.

Are there many female Satanists?

Satanism is quite masculine. It requires logical, cold thinking. Most orders have no women involved.

Women in general are more interested in Wicca and all that 'white light' stuff. I have heard of women in Satanic orders, but they were masochists with emotional disorders and weren't too bright, it has to be said.

What do you think of other magical schools?

I completely disagree with right-hand path magic. One cannot possibly work only positive magic. Most white magicians are too scared to step into the dark side because they know they couldn't handle it. How can they call themselves magicians if they can't handle 'demons'? It's pathetic. The real demon is their own fear.

Andrea Meyer, in her early Satanic incarnation, presides over a moonlit ritual for British black metal favourites Cradle of Filth. She also provided vocals on their debut album, The Principle of Evil Made Flesh.

Do you publish any material?

I am publishing a magazine called *Nothing*. It is a nihilist, Satanic, Thulian-inspired journal which also deals with the fall of humanity. I reckon the world is falling apart – sit back and enjoy it.

You have some connections with the black metal scene, don't you?

I am with a black metal band called Cradle of Filth and I advise them concerning Satanic theory and practice. A lot of black metal bands know nothing of Satanism. They like the image and claim to be 'evil'. What's 'evil'? How stupid. These boys give proper Satanists a bad name by claiming they indulge in sacrifices and drink blood or whatever. They don't even actually do it. I'd like to take them into a ritual chamber with me – they'd shit themselves! Look what happened in Norway – now those guys are in gaol. Are they strong, proud Satanists? I don't think so. Still, I liked Euronymous. He wasn't stupid – just too extreme. It's a shame that he's dead.

WAR IN HELL

The Death of Anton LaVey, and
Satanism in the 1990s

n 29 October 1997, Anton LaVey suffered a fatal heart attack. He was 67 years old, and had held the position of High Priest of the Church of Satan for just under half that span.

His closest intimates kept news of LaVey's death quiet for nearly two weeks, feeling that the Black Pope wouldn't have wanted to spoil Halloween – a favourite time of year for those who respected and revered him most. When made public in the second week of November, news of his death made the front pages of national newspapers on both sides of the Atlantic. Anton LaVey had provided the media with good copy for three decades, and did not disappoint from beyond the grave: the typically LaVeyan epitaph upon his memorial stone read, 'I only regret the times that I was too nice.'

While LaVey's death made a minor ripple in the mainstream, the reverberations within the Satanic community were far more dramatic. Despite the Black Pope's doctrines of individuality and self-rule, the question remained as to who was going to become the new High Priest of the Church of Satan. Detractors declared the CoS had only ever been an extension of LaVey's personality cult, and could not survive without him – while Blanche Barton, his partner and biographer, announced at a press conference, 'We will follow in his footsteps to keep the Church of Satan alive and strong.'

But this was to be no smooth succession. Immediately following LaVey's death, his youngest daughter Zeena announced on an evangelical Christian radio show that she'd placed a death curse upon her father. His elder daughter Karla initially lent moral support to LaVey's common-law widow, Blanche, but the alliance did not hold. In early 1998, Karla filed a petition seeking sole right to administer her father's estate – part of which was to be the Church of Satan. Barton disputed the claim, providing the courts with a handwritten will declaring Xerxes, her young son by LaVey, to be sole beneficiary. To raise the stakes further, the Black House, the very place where the movement began three decades previously, was repossessed and put up for sale. (LaVey lost control of his home in 1993, following a bitter and protracted divorce dispute with his second wife Diane.)

For many Church of Satan members, the sadness of LaVey's death was compounded by his recent revival of activity after more than a decade as a recluse. Though coronary problems had dogged him since 1990, the Black House appeared to be mobilising for action: *The Cloven Hoof*, official bulletin of the Church of Satan, resumed publication in 1995 after a long period in limbo; the grotto system of officially-sanctioned local branches, abandoned two decades before, was also revived, with LaVey appointing Satanic priests to act as public and media contacts.

Part of this new lease of life was doubtless inspired by the birth of his son in 1994. Xerxes' mother, Blanche Barton, who joined the Church of Satan in 1976 and became actively involved by 1984, had been LaVey's companion, confidante and consort for several years. As well as editing the revived *Cloven Hoof*, in 1990 she wrote *The Church of Satan*, a history of the organisation, as well as a biography of her high priest and lover-to-be, *The Secret Life of a Satanist*.

LaVey himself, now known by close associates as simply 'the Doctor', had started publishing again for the first time in twenty years. In 1992, *The Devil's Notebook*, a compendium of essays from *The Cloven Hoof*, appeared; days before he died, LaVey completed a second collection entitled *Satan Speaks!* In the foreword to *The Devil's Notebook*, he describes his 'brand of Satanism' as 'the ultimate conscious alternative to herd mentality and institutionalised thought. It is a studied and contrived set of principles and exercises designed to liberate individuals from a contagion of mindlessness that destroys innovation.'

Significantly, the jacket compares LaVey not only to the old circus showman P. T. Barnum, but also the outspoken Jewish playwright and screenwriter Ben Hecht and celebrated, cynical journalist H. L. Mencken. The Black Pope was staking a claim for himself as a social critic rather than a sorcerer, and LaVeyan Satanism as an anti-conformist lifestyle instead of a religion – whether in pieces celebrating the successful Satanic ritual as pure psychodrama, or extolling his fetish for watching pretty girls urinate. The sole unifying theme of these writings is LaVey's advocacy of isolation from the fads and foibles of modern society – where battles over the social agenda are waged between the servants of the old god, Jehovah, and the new god, Television.

Anton Szandor LaVey & Blanche Barton
proudly announce the birth of

Satan Xerxes Carnacki LaVey

shortly after midnight on
Halloween of XXVIII.

Please join us in wishing congratulations to
our High Priest & High Priestess
on this joyous occasion.
May Infernal blessings be upon their son and heir.

Hail Anton!
Hail Blanche!
Hail Xerxes!
Hail Satan!

The birth of Anton LaVey's son is celebrated in the Church of Satan magazine, The Black Flame.

Perhaps the most striking inclusions in *Satan Speaks!* are two essays on Judaism. Debate within the Church of Satan during the 1980s had polarised into those who embraced sinister Nazi-chic as a confrontational expression of individualism, and those who regarded Nazism as the repellent epitome of conformity. LaVey, fond of what he called 'the uncomfortable alternative', came up with a novel solution. The true Satanist should be a 'Nazi Jew', adopting the roles of both scapegoat and villain: 'The aesthetic of Nazism is grounded in black. The medieval black magician, usually a Jew, practised the "Black Arts". The new Satanic (conveniently described as "neo-Nazi") aesthetic is spearheaded by young people who favour black clothing, many of whom have partially Jewish backgrounds.'

And it wasn't only these young people who had 'partially Jewish backgrounds'. Acording to a profile by journalist Lawrence Wright for the September 1991 issue of *Rolling Stone* magazine, the Black Pope himself was of partly Jewish parentage – born Howard Stanton Levey, from which he'd adapted the more evocative 'Anton LaVey'. (This revelation is also a strange occultic coincidence. One of Satanic showman LaVey's sacred books was William Lindsay Gresham's carnival novel *Nightmare Alley* – telling the story of a ruthless carny, 'the Great Stanton', who builds a career as a phoney clairvoyant by telling people what they want to hear.) While Wright clearly liked LaVey – who he described as a 'bookish musician who took us all on a journey into the dark side of himself' – he paid little heed to the uncharacteristically naive request he claims the Satanist made in their final conversation: 'I don't want the legend to disappear.'

Wright's attempt to deconstruct the LaVey legend did not go unchallenged. Many claimed to have seen documentary evidence disproving Wright's suggestion that the Black Pope's early years weren't nearly as exotic as they were painted. In some ways, LaVey's career was all the more remarkable if stories of his early days were mere myth. If LaVey had not been a police photographer, reasoned his closest confederates, how did he cultivate such friendly links between the Church of Satan and the San Francisco Police Department? If he had never been employed in a circus, how did he learn to train big cats? Nonetheless, the *Rolling Stone* article became a touchstone for those who wished to see the Black Pope dethroned.

Among these were Michael Aquino – who included the article as an appendix to his lengthy, largely hostile history of the Church of Satan – and Zeena LaVey, who used it as the basis for a document entitled 'Anton LaVey: Legend and Reality'. This incendiary tract – a more sustained and vitriolic attack than either Aquino's or Wright's – was co-written with her partner Nikolas Schreck, and published after her father's death. The revelations of Jewish ancestry must have been particularly problematic for the Alpha Male and Female of the Werewolf Order, long immersed in the teachings of German racist mystics. Zeena has since taken to referring to herself as Zeena Schreck, and to her 'unfather' Howard Levey.

The Schrecks had not been idle in the years following their break with the Church of Satan. True, their plans for an ambitious haunted house and horror museum in LA had been ill-fated (though they recorded a commentary from their favourite actor, Christopher Lee), and the Werewolf Order was muted, if not permanently shelved.

In 1995, however, the pair became members of the Temple of Set, and two years later Nikolas was ordained as a priest – then recognised in 1998 as 'Master of the Order of Leviathan', one of the Temple's numerous internal orders. According to Schreck, he has become 'deeply involved with research into the fountainhead of the Leviathan myth, the Mesopotamian dragon goddess Tiamat and her connection to ageless existence and the feminine principle that is central to the Left Hand Path' – the strident Euro-pagan embracing the subtle, intuitive aspects of the occult which, with their focus in the irrational, are still rooted very firmly in the dark side.

Despite persistent predictions that it was on the wane, the Temple of Set has survived a quarter-of-a-century. (Michael Aquino passed the mantle to the present high priest, a well-respected writer on occult matters named Don Webb, in 1996.) However, increasing discomfort among its members is leading the Temple to gradually dispense with the label 'Satanist', with its various negative connotations – as in the Wiccan community, where there is now a growing movement to discard the term 'witch' and all its suggestions of dark mystery.

Others remain more than happy to adopt the role of the occult villain. The rise of the Internet has created a vital network whereby isolated individuals with unusual outlooks can find each other – allowing Satanism to thrive in cyberspace. Organisations like the First Church of Satan boast of '1,000 visitors a day' to their web-site, their priests as far apart as Australia and their HQ in (appropriately) Salem, Massachusetts.

Despite the presumption of calling themselves the First Church of Satan, when the original CoS is now more than three decades old, their High Priest Lord Egan claims to have been a member of LaVey's church in the early 1970s, and that the First Church is 'returning to the individualistic, self-empowering Satanism that is no longer alive in the organisation Anton LaVey started'. They list Nietzsche, philosopher of selfishness Ayn Rand, revisionist feminist Camille Paglia, euthanasia campaigner Dr Jack Kervorkian, H. L. Mencken, scientific heretic Nikola Tesla, foppish Victorian wit Oscar Wilde, pop icon Madonna and shock-jock Howard Stern among their canon of Satanic role models. Lord Egan boasts (with a level of irony, one trusts) of being 'known as the country's first televised evangelical Satanic preacher' and touts his church as 'the fastest growing religious organisation in the world today!' Despite all this, LaVey's *Satanic Bible* remains their central text, while many of the '1,000 visitors a day' to their site must surely be looking for LaVey's organisation.

Anton Szandor LaVey: 1930 – 1997. His influence lives on.

Another 1990s Satanic fraternity intent on 'taking up where established Satanic orders have left off' is the Ordo Templi Satanis (purposely redolent of both the Knights Templar and Crowley's Ordo Templi Orientis), a breakaway group from the Temple of Set. According to the Californian order's 1991 *Book of Darkness*, 'The OTS has been conceived to be a modern equivalent to an Order of knighthood, and is organised along lines similar to those used in medieval Europe. The ultimate goal of the Order is to bring this nation back to the Satanic principles upon which it was founded, and to ensure that the natural Satanic elite is no longer on the brink of destruction at the hands of the masses.' So far, these modern Templars have made little tangible progress in their noble quest.

Even more exotic, the Cult of Mastema (name based on an obscure alternative name for the Devil in early Christian texts) combines heretical biblical lore with the New Age fad for angels. 'Common angels look like human bundles of chainsaws with loads of tiny mirrors attached to them', explains their literature. 'Demons tend to be somewhat more independent than angels . . . When possession takes place, you won't get to see them at all.' Quite . . .

In the more earthbound realms of political extremism, small Satanic groups continue to appear who combine a dark spiritual stance with a white supremacist agenda. The Florida-based Luciferian Light Group (LLG) adopted the 'Watcher myth' of devils that were originally angels, sent to earth to guard mankind and cursed by God for screwing their charges. In the original myth the couplings produced monsters, but, according to the LLG, the actual result was the Aryan race: 'the true Children of Satan'.

Curiously enough, this mirrors the doctrines of the Christian Identity movement, the most powerful spiritual force in modern racist culture – though most 'good racists' would be horrified at any suggestion that (as black Islamic racists suggest) 'the White Man is the Devil'. According to Christian Identity doctrine, the 'mud people' (racist terminology for non-whites) are the children of Satan, while Aryans are the true tribe of Israel.

More sophisticated occult explorations of this cultural and political taboo are rare. However, Michael Moynihan became a rising star on the right-wing of the Church of Satan when, in 1988, he issued his own translation of Nietzsche's *The Antichrist* at age eighteen. He also began a creative partnership with Boyd Rice, sharing his apartment in Colorado and getting involved in both the musical project Non and the Abraxas Foundation. For a good while, Moynihan was commonly regarded as Rice's protégé, or even his apprentice, but the two would go their separate ways in the early 1990s after what Moynihan described as 'personal conflicts'. In 1989 Moynihan launched Blood Axis, primarily a musical project which served as a vehicle for an 'axis of ideas' – redolent though the name is of World War Two's Axis powers, Nazi Germany, Fascist Italy and Imperial Japan. Prominent influences included Norse paganism, Mithraism (a blood cult favoured by Roman legionaries), and the wacky philosophy of Charles Manson.

Moynihan's belief that Manson was not a loathsome criminal but a great thinker was shared by James N. Mason – a former associate of assassinated American Nazi Party leader George Lincoln Rockwell, Mason was expelled from the party for his vocal opinion that Charlie was the natural successor to Hitler. Mason's bizarre dogmatism in the face of near-universal hostility endeared him to prominent members of the Church of Satan. Most just cultivated him on a social level, visiting the racist demagogue to talk about their mutual admiration for old black and white horror movies, but Moynihan was less circumspect. In 1992 he published *Siege*, a compilation of Mason's writings cribbed from his newsletters. Ads proudly quoted reviews that described it as 'the *Mein Kampf* of the 90s' and 'the mind fuck of the century'. (Which response pleased Moynihan most is anyone's guess.)

While Charlie Manson remains a powerfully anti-social icon for many people, his potency has waned over the years, his public image becoming as much kitsch as killer. In 1998, *Lords of Chaos*, Moynihan's book on the murder of Norwegian black metal musician Oystein Aarseth by another black metallist named Varg Vikernes, was published by Feral House. On the surface an astute study of the crime's violent prelude and aftermath, the book often seems to be grooming Vikernes to become another Manson, an anti-social messiah for an alienated generation. As such, he's welcome to him.

Vikernes' appeal to Moynihan may lie in the racist politics and Viking quasi-mysticism that he spouts from his prison cell. Some modern European pagans – particularly those interested in ancient Germanic and Scandinavian myths – have associated their creed with a racialist political agenda. In an age that encourages Afro-Americans and other racial groups to take pride in their cultural roots, so the argument goes, why should the same concept not apply to Europeans? The argument cannot be countered by liberal sophistry, and so the ghosts of German völkisch occultists continue to be conjured by cultural mischief-makers.

This 'axis' between fascist paganism and Satanism remains an important faction within the Church of Satan, though its influence has waned since the late 1980s. LaVey was loath to make public pronouncements on the ongoing battle between the libertarian and right-wing camps, observing instead, in an essay in *Satan Speaks!*, that 'Odinism [Norse paganism] is an heroic and admirable form of Satanism, as is an affinity for Coyote [the American Indian trickster god] or Vlad Tepes [Vlad the Impaler, the historical inspiration for Dracula]. Just remember: things are not always what they seem.'

The role of cultural villain again proves to be a delicate balancing act – nothing can ever be condemned on purely moralistic grounds. Of late, Michael Moynihan has been inclined to define his stance as 'heretical', rather than fascistic, and emphasises that he also takes ideas from anarchistic or radical left-wing sources. In this relative sense, Satanism is not the worship of 'evil', but a creed where cultural taboos are tested and nothing is unspeakable. As LaVey puts it, in his essay 'A Plan': 'The only place a rational amalgam of proud, admitted, Zionist Odinist Bolshevik Nazi Imperialist Socialist Fascism will be found – and championed – will be in the Church of Satan.'

During the 1990s, the Church of Satan regained some of the colour that drained from it during the previous stark, authoritarian decade. While it could never go back to the playful indulgences of its early years, there was a growing feeling that the carnival was due back in town – even if the freak show had become a little weirder, and the rides a good deal scarier. This is born out by the affiliation of two sinful pop-culture luminaries: 'goth-rock' star Marilyn Manson and pop-artist Coop.

Manson in particular presented some interesting ideological questions for the Church of Satan. While prominent members had long condemned drug abuse, young Marilyn candidly confessed in print and song to a flamboyant record of drug usage. While the Church of Satan encouraged a dignified, predatory image and denounced the blurring of gender identities, Manson revelled in an outrageous evil-clown persona that centred on androgyny. In terms of LaVeyan doctrines of questioning orthodoxy, ignoring convention, ridiculing hypocrisy and pursuing individuality, however, the eccentric shock-rocker scored highly. LaVey invited him into the Church of Satan with open arms, conferring a priesthood on the eager Manson in 1994.

Any internal debates this may have sparked were overshadowed by LaVey's death, three years later. It split those closest to him into three broad factions: Those who, like his younger daughter Zeena, wanted to draw a line under the Black Pope's legacy, denounce it as a sham and present themselves as prophets of 'true' Satanism. Then there was Blanche Barton, and those who had been most prominent in the Church of Satan during the past decade, keen to build upon the 1990s revival. There were also peripheral figures who felt Barton's role had been a trivial, or even negative one, and challenged her right to the role of high priestess – notably Karla LaVey who felt, as the Black Pope's eldest child, that she had a right to the position.

Much of the internecine struggle manifested itself in cyberspace. Karla posted a message on the Internet commemorating her father which caused outrage in the Barton camp – not only for the implication that it was an official pronouncement from the High Priestess of the Church of Satan, but the barbed postscript which stated: '"The Black House" is no longer owned or occupied by anyone affiliated with the CoS or myself, and has not been for some time.'

Having recently stayed at the Black House during her short-lived camaraderie with Blanche, Karla went to collect some of her belongings. According to a friend, Satanic priest Rick Rinker, 'After discovering a voodoo doll on the altar with a spike through its heart it soon became apparent that someone in the house had some animosity for one of us. It isn't a great mystery who left the voodoo doll on the altar and what message they were attempting to send.' Rinker had been ordained in recognition of his work setting up the 600 Club – an Internet site named in deliberate mockery of the evangelical Christian 700 Club – which disseminated information on LaVeyan Satanism. After LaVey's death, he was one of a number of Internet Satanists excommunicated by Blanche Barton.

As far as Satanism is concerned, the Internet's strengths are also its weaknesses. While it allows immediate contact with the diverse Satanic community in a largely uncensored environment, ensuring that fringe groups are not issuing damaging or idiotic pronouncements – tagged as official Church of Satan communiqués –

The programme for the LaVey memorial concert, held in New York City in 1998.

has proven a full-time job for Barton. In trying to emphasise the need for a common party line to ensure cohesion, her perceived authoritarianism has resulted in a spate of resignations and excommunication.

The conflict between promoting individuality and presenting a united front plagues every serious Satanic organisation. LaVey's solution was typically perverse: an organisation dedicated to liberty, but run as a dictatorship. That LaVey's ideal – of a church for productive misfits, a club for non-joiners – hasn't been too contradictory to survive is remarkable in itself. Even if the present incarnation of the Church of Satan does not endure, the status of Anton LaVey as an icon of iconoclasm seems assured. The artist Coop, interviewed for a feature on the Church of Satan in San Francisco's *SF Weekly* newspaper, commented refreshingly, 'All that "Who's gonna take over?" Honestly, who cares? I really don't think that's important. It's a portable feast, man. All you have to do is go to B. Dalton's and buy *The Satanic Bible*. It's all there. If that loser Jesus could keep a church going for 2,000 years, I think the Doctor can certainly fucking compete with that!'

Or, as the Black Pope himself once reassured his flock, 'the first 99 years are always the toughest. Rege Satanas!'

A Compleat Witch

A conversation with Blanche Barton.

I spoke to Blanche Barton in early 1994, prior to the birth of Xerxes, her son by Anton LaVey.
While we chiefly corresponded by mail, this interview was conducted over the telephone. She was friendly, almost chatty, and passionately devoted to the doctrines of her lover and mentor. We spoke about Satanic witchcraft, the feminine role in the Church of Satan, and just what makes a Satanist . . .

When did you first decide you were a witch?
When I first encountered *The Satanic Witch*, or *Compleat Witch* as it was then known, I didn't understand a lot of it because I was only twelve or thirteen at the time. I wasn't really interested in the sexually-stimulating aspects of Satanism, but I was drawn to the dark side, and read a lot of horror novels and was attracted to the archetype of Satan in a prepubescent way. It had that tingle of pre-sexual excitement to it, which was fun. Then, as I got older, I found a lot of the power of the witch was in enchantment and mystery, which were both sexually and archetypically stimulating and, at the same time, dark, brooding and mysterious, promising all kinds of forbidden treats.

One of the criticisms levelled at Satanism, particularly within the pagan community, is that it is somehow anti-woman . . .
When *The Satanic Witch* was published, feminism was very young. *The Satanic Witch* is quite a pro-woman book – it celebrates feminine power. It's not about dressing like a man, competing with men on their level, wearing Daddy's clothes that never quite fit. It's about the power of women to enchant and manipulate, to be a true sorceress. Women have always been in league with the Devil, women have always been decried by the Church as too sexual or too tempting. It was Eve who accepted the apple from Satan. The Doctor makes the point in the opening chapter when he talks about how Satan's best allies have always been women. But women *as* women. That's what I don't understand about feminists saying Satanism is anti-female. The altar of the Church of Satan has always been a naked woman. How much more celebratory of the female can you get than that?

Paganism has only been articulated to the extent it is today in the past ten or fifteen years. The same is true of feminism. There were little bubblings and burpings, but it's only since the early eighties that paganism's become associated with feminism. I think that's been a boon to paganism. Feminists have realised that worshipping the Goddess can be empowering for them. I have no problem with that. The problem with paganism is that they seem to be bothered by us. People call up occult stores and ask if they carry *The Satanic Bible*, which is a reasonable question, and get given a lecture about Satanism being inverted Christianity, how LaVey is a charlatan, and how you shouldn't mess with this stuff. That fits with my thesis that paganism is just neo-Christianity: they cling to the same values, the same 'good-guy badge', the same victimology.

Pagans fabricate some figure – like nine million women – who, as one Wiccan put it, were 'genocided'. They generate this increasingly familiar victim mentality. Satanism is opposed to victimology and scapegoating. Maybe it's because Wicca has been taken over by feminism that it's become synonymous with victimology. Why should a woman compromise her power by casting herself as a victim? If I want to dress in high heels and stockings then walk down the street, I'm sure as Hell not going to be anybody's victim – I'll be carrying my weapon of choice. I won't dress in sackcloth and ashes for fear someone will attack or jeer at me.

Wiccans often claim their version of witchcraft is somehow more historically accurate. How do you respond to that?
Wicca and paganism have been rebuilding themselves since the mid-eighties, but when I first came across witchcraft in my early teens, 'witch' equalled nasty, spooky stuff. Anton LaVey changed that. All the texts I could find were about sacrificing cocks at sunrise, pouring pigeon's blood over knotted cords that you'd anointed in some ungodly concoction. All of which was rather nonsensical and silly. Historically, the Wiccans are rather off the mark: if there was any authentic historical witchcraft, it wasn't goddess-worship. There wasn't some idyllic pre-history where women were goddesses and everyone worshipped them and was in tune with nature. Witchcraft has always been blasphemy, it has always been heresy. If witches were out there, practising some of the old ways of the pre-Christian gods and goddesses, then they were still Satanic in the sense that they were heretical.

One side of the heretical and diabolical is the scientific aspect of Satanism. Copernicus and Galileo were regarded as practising sorcerers in as far as they dared to challenge the supremacy of God with their heresies – their scientific research. Anton LaVey codified modern Satanism. There's a rich heritage of heresy and blasphemy behind it, but as far as an aboveground religion that reveres Satan, there wasn't anything before the Church of Satan's foundation in 1966. There were

Black Masses that parodied the Catholic Church, and literary references in the works of Twain, Milton and others that used Satan as an archetype in a fictional sense. A lot of modern Satanism draws from that codification or personification of Satan.

Blanche Barton (far left), Anton LaVey and friend.

Wiccans seem to want to build on a peasant culture. It's regressive and pre-scientific. Satanists are more interested in power, and what was going on in the castles and courts of the time. The interactions of power and Machiavellian machinations interest a Satanist rather than going out and finding herbs to cure indigestion.

One of LaVey's more provocative comments was that all the true witches wouldn't have been burnt because they'd have been sleeping with the inquisitor!
That's the whole point of Satanic witchcraft in a nutshell. I think Wiccans are looking for a religion of the peasantry and Satanists are reaching for a religion of the aristocracy. We have all the aspects of that pride, that fire, that style, and hopefully those elevated standards. Aesthetic standards that are a little more discerning than the Mother Goddess-types in their shapeless robes.

Satanists regard themselves as pragmatists, don't they?
Anton LaVey has always emphasised that. That's why,

when people want to get involved in Satanism, he de-emphasises elaborate initiations, degrees, Satanic baptisms or whatever. He says, if you want to do that, fine, do it yourself. Your relationship with your personal Satanic archetype is yours alone. The only way I can see how effective you are as a practising black magician is how well you get on in the outside world. You're not going to put on some fancy apron or robe like the local lodge hall and be a big shot there, while having no effect outside, then try to tell me you're a powerful person.

To what extent is Satanism some kind of cultural counterbalance?
Satan has always represented and will always represent the adversary. He is a counterbalance to the unspoken injustice that prevails in the current society, whether that be overweening elitism or, going to the opposite extreme, mob rule. We always have to be in the minority that push hard in the other direction to get the pendulum swinging. Satanism will never be a religion of the people. It will never be populist beyond its current position. You see hundreds of thousands of kids making the sign of the horns, wearing black, getting devil tattoos, and listening to rock music they think is Satanic. They will take all the trappings and even grasp a few of the basic ideas, like Satan representing indulgence and independence of spirit. But, beyond that, we will always be a minority and that's how it should be.

Anton LaVey seems to preach that you should take your enemy's devils and use them . . .
Exactly! Why waste them?

THE DARK DOCTRINE

A correspondence with Kerry Bolton, founder of New Zealand's Order of the Left Hand Path.

After quarrelling with other members of the Temple of Set, New Zealand occultist Kerry Bolton left and formed his own organisation, the Order of the Left Hand Path (OLHP) in 1990. A dedicated and inventive, if highly unorthodox scholar, Bolton had a very multi-cultural approach to Satanism. He was active in combating the Satanic ritual abuse myth in his native country, and became well known and respected among the international Satanic community. I spoke to Bolton in 1993, communicating chiefly by mail. In 1994, he handed control over to his deputy, Harri Baynes, who renamed the organisation the Ordo Sinistra Vivendi and took the Order to the political Right. At present, it appears to be largely inactive.

Is the OLHP a philosophy or a religion?
OLHP is a philosophy of life and a magical order. The emphasis is on the former, of living according to one's real nature. The basis of what one truly is is instinctual – genetic. One can, of course, rebel against oneself or repress it, as demanded by many dogmas, from Christianity to Marxism.

The OLHP contains many references to other cultures (particularly oriental) – what is the basis of this cross-cultural approach?
Satanism is a reflection of nature, of the laws of the cosmos, therefore it is as universally applicable as any law of nature – gravity, genetics, etc. Every culture has its Devil or Satan archetype. We are not oriental per se philosophically. Satan derives from Sat and Tan – Sanskrit. It therefore predates both Judaism and Christianity. OLHP harks back to the pre-Christian pagan past and its traditions, which were kept alive in places in which one doesn't usually look for Satanism, such as within the Rosicrucian and masonic societies which inspired the Renaissance. Satanism as a cosmological philosophy can be principally traced back to the Turanians, who have influenced many races and civilisations including the occidental, levantine (or Moorish), and oriental. The real dark doctrine can be found in many unexpected places including Taoism and Cabalism. Because Satanism is a reflection of nature, it is universal in scope, but particularist in application, since it recognises nature as 'ordaining' the different races and cultures. Therefore Satanism stands opposed to all dogmas which seek to level man in the dead weight of equality, in some version of a world state, whether done in the name of a religion, like Christianity, or an ideology like capitalism or communism.

What do you think of 'established' Satanists like LaVey or Aquino?
LaVey merits respect for making the basics of Satanism (i.e. 'the carnal doctrine' and 'the dark force in nature') readily accessible to those who are instinctively attuned to it. Aquino – a pompous, hypocritical jackass, misusing the symbols and terminology of Satanism under the pretext of representing a 'higher development of Satanism' (sic).

What type of individual joins the OLHP, and for what reasons?
Those who join or otherwise support the OLHP tend to be creative types . . . Some indication may be had from the background of some of our 'priests': a psychiatrist and sociologist presently working in TV production; a graduate in English; a graduate in anthropology; a psychiatric worker; a 'generational Satanist' born into a Satanic community (i.e. a pythagorean/masonic community). As can be deduced from our magazine, *The Heretic*, we have a good share of talent: artists, writers, researchers. As to why people join – I don't believe people are converted to a particular religion, ideology or whatever. They instinctively identify with it when they come across it, as though it's part of themselves waiting to be realised. This again has relevance to the principle that people are what they are genetically.

Is the OLHP a 'magical order', and if so what type of rituals are undertaken?
I would expect that most OLHPers are too busy getting on with living to waste a great many hours poncing about in darkened rooms performing rituals. Most Satanists I know who have a deeper understanding of the subject rarely perform rituals, some never. Magic takes many forms – some not so obvious, and seemingly quite mundane.

Is there any danger involved in belonging to, or opposing the OLHP?
There is no physical danger in being involved in the OLHP, although one's ego might take a bashing if one tries to misuse the Order or deceive it (such as the paedophile who started citing *The Bible* and Jehovah after being rejected), such persons being exposed for what they are. Those who oppose us are dealt with defensively, by using their own weaknesses against them (which is the genuine definition of 'Left Hand Path' – what Ninja uses on the physical level). One reaps what one sows, karma without mysticism (or, 'don't spit in the wind or you'll get your own back').

Examples of this are: (a) the Order's counter campaign against Christian child abuse (particularly paedophiliac priests) when the Christians tried to import the 'Satanic ritual abuse' scam from the USA. We've been totally vindicated by the amount of attention the media has been focusing on Christian child abuse, and we said it first in New Zealand. (b) Our successful action against the anti-Satanist campaigners and their mouthpieces in the tabloid press. (c) Our complaint against the zealous policeman who tried to intimidate us at the behest of some Christian. These are all practical measures which succeeded on the mundane level, without a single recourse to the ritual chamber, which are nevertheless examples of genuine 'Left Hand Path' magic in operation.

An OLHP ritual featuring Kerry Bolton (far left) and Harri Baynes (holding chalice), with younger members of their families. Bolton, a confirmed family man, has stated he will kill to protect kith and kin when civilisation finally collapses.

How did you first become involved with Satanism and how did the OLHP come about?

I became involved with Satanism due to an inclination to examine the unorthodox and the 'hidden' (occult) whether in history, religion, politics or esoterica. I have since an early age also had a strong sense of individuality, opposed to herd conformity, and a recognition that people are not born equal. I came to like the anti-egalitarian philosophy of Nietzsche. I eventually found that the doctrines of Crowley and LaVey had a Nietzschean basis and explored these subjects further, deciding that Satanism is a practical manifestation of my views. Seeing that there was no obviously readily-accessible Satanic group in New Zealand for those of a like-minded inclination, the OLHP was established in 1990 and *The Watcher* (now *The Heretic*) was published in January 1990.

Does Satanic crime – ritual child abuse, human sacrifice, for example – take place and, if so, is it ever justified?

Satanic child abuse exists to the extent that a few paedophiles sometimes use the Church-derived stereotype as a control mechanism. For this we can thank Christians. However, even this has been greatly exaggerated by the Christians and reached the proportions of mass hysteria in the USA, receiving impetus from con-men, psychotic women 'survivors' (sic) and attention seekers. No, there's no instance where child abuse is justified. Most ritual abuse takes place within the Christian context. This much at least has been proven in the law courts. Human sacrifice was historically a part of virtually all religions including Judaism and Christianity (the latter being based in Jesus' One Big Sacrifice). Some psychotics might get added thrills by killing in the name of 'Satan', but again we can thank Christians for providing the appropriate stereotype.

On another level, Satanism is not pacifistic, and there are some present-day Satanic groups which openly advocate 'human sacrifice', principally the Order of the Nine Angles in Great Britain. They do so as a method of 'population culling', which is really a call for vigilante action or retribution; no worse than that being glamorised in the mass-entertainment industry, or even by children's comic book heroes. Additionally, if we recognise that history is cyclic, we can expect this Western civilisation to face its own Ragnarok. The resulting collapse of the social order will take the Western societies back to a survivalist ethos. There'll be 'Satanic sacrifices' aplenty then, as anyone with the will to survive will throw off any vestige of Christian or liberal brotherly love, and 'turn the other cheek' idiocy, and defend themselves and their kin with whatever bloodletting necessary.

ARYAN ANGELS?

A correspondence with Draeon Undomiel of the Luciferian Light Group.

The Luciferian Light Group, based in Florida and headed by the forthright and forceful Draegon Undomiel, is an example of the organisations that flourish in the grey area between the radical Right and the darker fringes of the occult. The LLG's magazine, *Onslaught*, features more white supremacist material than features of Satanic interest. I corresponded with their leader in late 1992.

What are the connections between Satanism and right-wing – particularly racial – politics?
We speak only for ourselves, for there are many visions of reality. We have encountered many 'Satanic' orders who just love everybody, and who believe that we are all 'equal'. We are 'right-wing', we are not Nazis, ours is the religion of the Nazis, the path of the warrior. We are their priests.

Would it be possible, for example, for a black or oriental to be a true Satanist? If not, why not?
No, not within our framework. As mentioned above, our path is Aryan Satanism. Real religious, white boy shit. Dedicated to race and nation. The sub-races have their own paths and pantheons, let them pursue them.

How do you feel about established Satanic figures like LaVey and Aquino?
These men, priests of His Majesty, were (are) pioneers. They were able to break through the walls of stagnation and bring before the world its first vision of the new Aeon. While some may vary in opinion to their methods, they must always be held in the highest respect.

How large is your order?
Our Inner Circle now stands at seven. The Outer Circle, Associate Members International, is around 300. We receive thousands of requests and enquiries yearly.

What would you consider the positive and negative aspects of Satanism?
Positive, that one may know the absolute magnitude of their being. Negative, it's better to burn out than fade away.

Is there any danger inherent in being involved with the LLG, or openly opposing it?
There is no danger with the Luciferian Light Group, other than that from the agents of a pompous and crumbling empire. We are a lawful, licensed, tax-paying entity, just spreading the Devil's word, in accordance with Amendment One to the Constitution of the United States, and protected by the Second Amendment.

How did you become involved with Satanism and when did the LLG form?
I looked into the heavens one night and prayed to whatever powers that be to show me the truth. And I saw Lucifer as a star fall from Heaven, and from Him came to me the light

THE LUCIFERIAN LIGHT GROUP
PO BOX 7207 • Tampa, Florida 33673

An Open Letter To His Majesty's Legions

July 4, 1992 ev

My Friends,

That which has long been prophesied now comes to pass. Oh, what a great and magical time it is to live, for now we stand at the very changing of the age. The communist bloc has crumbled for stagnant governments cannot stand. Monumental disaster lurks as the western United States trembles underfoot. The city of angels was almost burnt to the ground by its own people. Don't say I didn't tell you so. And this is only the preview. Yes, friends it will all get much worse before His Majesty's throne on earth is rightfully reclaimed.

Yes, my friends, these are troubled times. This is an election year and things aren't getting any better. Southeastern Europe is in flames and American democracy and personal liberty are constantly under threat. Case in point: Congressman Major Owens (D-N.Y.) is pushing for a Constitutional amendment to repeal the Second Amendment of the United States, that being the right to keep and bear arms. That would leave only the government, the police and criminals armed. Imagine what a great place this would be.

Prohibition, the 18th amendment is a clear example of the kind of disaster that results from screwing around with the U.S. Constitution. Always keep in mind that the Constitution does not grant liberties and rights (or take them away), rather it protects our rights from government intrusion. Any attempt to take away the rights of the American people constitutes treason. Any politician who would do so should be considered guilty thereof.

Why would government entities be so intent on disarming the American people? To protect us? No, I think not. I smell a Zionist occupational plot somewhere, I just can't quite put my finger on it. But I'll let you know when I do. In the meantime, just sit back, watch the news, and keep it cocked and locked.

AVE SATANIS,

Draegon Undomiel
Imperial Dragon,
Church of Luciferian Light

This 1992 anti-gun control editorial, from the Luciferian Light Group's Onslaught *magazine, gives some idea of their social agenda. Note the reference to an unspecified 'Zionist plot'.*

of true salvation. And behold, I was made whole by His infernal wisdom. My chains lifted off, I was made free.

There seems to have been some friction between your group and some other Satanic organisations – what was its source, and what do you object to about your rivals?
Yes, we pissed off some factions of His Majesty's legions. Mainly because of our political position (Nazism, elitist

Recruitment ad from the Luciferian Light Group's Onslaught *magazine.*

asshole positions on our place in the world, etc.). While many claim to be Satanic, a lot of practitioners/groups, etc. cannot get past their Christian upbringing. White lighters (Wiccans) too despise us, for they too choose to ignore the truth. They claim that we are not even pagan. Weak dick assholes, they suck up to the very people who would burn them at the stake!

Do you feel any of the Satanic black metal bands are authentic? Which bands or artists truly represent the Satanic aesthetic?
They all promote the cause. While there are many great bands out there, cutting heads in the Devil's orchestra, I still prefer Wagner. Now that really was some Satanist stuff.

THE FAUSTIAN SPIRIT OF FASCISM

Words with Michael Moynihan

I spoke with the young, cultured, earnest-but-likeable Michael Moynihan by phone in late 1993. He made no secret at the time of his controversial views, some of which have attracted unwelcome attention over the years. It may just be co-incidence, but after corresponding with Moynihan much of my international mail was opened before I received it.

Are you still a member of the Abraxas Foundation?
Abraxas is a loose-knit thing. It's not an organisation; it's more like a clearing-house for ideas. At one time I was working on the propaganda, if you want to call it that, with Boyd Rice. We decided he'd concentrate on that and I'd concentrate on other things – Blood Axis primarily, and running a mail order company. Blood Axis is mainly a musical project. I came up with the name as a title for the propaganda I'm engaged in. I like the concept of an axis of ideas, which is how I look at everything – it's a magical concept. Ever since I was a kid I thought the people with the ideas which had power would eventually cross my path. It's meant to be.

That's how it happened with LaVey and the Church of Satan. I read *The Satanic Bible* when I was thirteen or fourteen, and I felt like it was repeating things I already knew. That's where you get the LaVeyan idea of Satanists being born and not made. To me Satanism is a symbolic thing – I don't see it as worshipping some cloven-hoofed deity that actually exists. It represents certain things which I agree with and identify with. To me, it symbolises strength, being in touch with natural instincts, and purity. Being true to your natural self.

So Satan doesn't exist?
It does as a force that you're either part of, or you're not. You can accept it and let it exist within yourself, or, as in the case of a Christian, you can try and force it out of your system. Then you become one of these confused, schizophrenic personages, like these Christian preachers who preach something but can't uphold it in their personal lives.

Satan seldom appears in your art and writing, why is that?
I see in the pagan elements I employ some very Satanic messages. I see Satanism in a broad way – there are a lot of people I see as Satanic who would never call themselves Satanists. I couldn't care less about some kid on the street who says he worships Satan – that doesn't make him a Satanist. He's got his ideas from Christian propaganda, and I'm not interested in anything based

on Christianity. Satanism isn't some byproduct of Christianity; it's something which has always been opposed to Christianity. That's why I see it in paganism.

You're quite interested in Nazism, aren't you?
I don't think National Socialism exists anymore. It existed for a certain time, it played its role, now it's

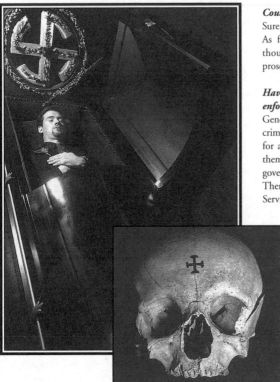

Michael Moynihan rests beneath 'an ancient European religious symbol'. Insert: a Blood Axis ritual skull.

over. I wouldn't want to go and meet any Nazis. But there's a power in what happened, in those symbols, and it still affects history now. I'm definitely interested in that. I don't subscribe to the whole ideology – parts of it give me problems. But there are certain people in it, aspects of it that again reflect things which I already believe. There's definitely a Satanic spirit, a pagan spirit, to a lot of what happened. I don't have an interest in the 'wholesome goodness' ideas of Nazi morality, or this idea of leading the masses.

I think it would be absurd to deny that race plays a part in things, however, and I view things in racial terms a lot of the time. It doesn't mean I wouldn't speak to someone, or would treat them differently, because of their race, let alone want to do away with them. But

anyone who's intelligent has to consider the issue – anybody who ignores it is shying away from reality. As far as other races go, besides the Europeans, I don't feel much of a connection to them. I want to associate with and interact with the culture I feel a part of. I don't want to blow Africa off the map or something, it just doesn't interest me.

Could there not be black or Jewish Satanists?
Sure, I just wouldn't have much in common with them. As far as the Church of Satan proper is concerned though, there's certainly never been any racial proscription.

Have you had any problems from the law enforcement agencies?
Generally, the Satanists I would know certainly aren't criminals. If anything, the police would come to them for advice on a weird crime rather than to interrogate them about it. On the other hand, in terms of the government, there's definitely been an interest in us. There was a pretty strange thing – we had three Secret Service guys at my apartment door, claiming I had 'witnessed the murder of a black man' and wanting to talk to me about it. It turns out that George Bush would be in town in a few days and they thought I was in a plot with the Manson girls to assassinate him! At one point, one of these men asked, 'Why did you put a swastika on one of your letters you wrote to Charles Manson?' Of course, Manson's always held the swastika as a mystic symbol. So I said, 'That's an ancient European religious symbol.' 'No it's not, it's a symbol of Satanism!' he said – at this point I just rolled my eyes. I don't know what he'd been reading. They'd told the landlady of the apartments that I was a Nazi terrorist and wanted to see any records she had of my background and renting record.

Why did you correspond with Charles Manson?
He's a symbol. He has a definite Satanic spirit running through him, he's definitely anti-Christian, despite this image he had of calling himself Christ. Manson once had this quote that 'the cross of iron is stronger than the cross of wood'. There's a fascistic element to him, and his whole philosophy of nature fits in with what I believe. He's another of these symbols where a whole lot of different ideas meet.

What are your opinions on magic?
I would pretty much agree with Crowley's definition of it – forcing things to happen in accordance with your will. If that's a science, as I believe it is, then you should be able to refine techniques. I don't think the old medieval techniques are relevant anymore, chanting in robes with twelve other people. What I do is a matter of

figuring out what you want to do, concentrating on it, reinforcing the idea of it happening, and then doing it. With this I've achieved pretty much everything I've wanted. Meeting inaccessible people I've wanted to meet. Meeting some woman I was interested in. If the way I go about things is magical and ritualistic, then it's natural that things should happen.

You write a lot about Satanic metal – what's you opinion of it?

Obviously, the imagery is present in tons of this stuff, a lot of which is irrelevant. I think it's good that it's out there – just in the terms of this incredibly violent, angry music that offers an alternative to the other extreme of loving everybody. So, the phenomenon is good, but most of the music is of little consequence. But there are a few bands that go beyond just inverting the Christian imagery, and I would say that Morbid Angel is one of those. If you ask some kid in the average death metal band why they're a Satanist then you'll probably just get some confused gibberish. I can appreciate the fact that they're obsessed with this stuff, but a lot of them don't understand it. I can respect it as an instinctual thing though. If I was at that level and I had to choose between Christianity, and all that it represents, or the Satanic side – I would certainly pick the Satanic side. It's far more stimulating.

Lighting the Black Flame

The modern Satanic doctrine of the Reverend Gilmore.

Musician, publisher and writer Peter Gilmore and his wife Peggy Nadramia have been among the most prominent figures in the Church of Satan for two decades. Together since their high school years – when, according to Gilmore, 'my lectures as well as my surrealist paintings . . . defining my infernal allegiance' attracted Peggy to him – they became official members of the Church of Satan in the early 1980s, and were later recognised into the CoS priesthood, appointed to the Magistry and included in the exclusive Council of Nine. As administrators, media contacts and editors of *The Black Flame* – the Church of Satan's International Forum – the couple have become the backbone of the modern CoS. More recently, they have stood firmly behind Blanche Barton in her efforts to stabilise the Church of Satan

following the death of Anton LaVey. I've known Peter, a spirited and friendly fellow, for some years, and conducted this interview via e-mail in early 1999.

What is the Church of Satan – a cult, a creed, a cabal, or what?

The organisation is a cabal, a shadowy, underground network of like-minded individuals who work to lever against the inertia of the world, towards ends favourable to Satanism. Dr LaVey used Orwell's *1984* as a model for a cell-system in which each member didn't have awareness of exactly who else might be involved. This

Magister Peter Gilmore (centre), with the Reverend André Schlesinger and Rosemary of New York City's Maninblack Grotto.

allows for those who are famous to express their allegiance, but then not be the target of lesser members seeking a short-cut to stardom. It also protects us from being pigeonholed by the media, who tend to think they can tame things through quantification. Information is always on a need-to-know basis, but we use this network to link-up those who are working with similar means to our ends, so that they can be more effective in the pursuit of individual goals.

What was the nature of the public schism between Zeena LaVey and her father?

Zeena, along with her companion Barry 'Nikolas Schreck' Dubin, wanted to ease Dr LaVey into retirement so that they could assume his position. Neither was suited for this role, and Dr LaVey was quite firmly in control. So when their efforts failed, they made a big show out of departing the 'corrupt' Church of Satan and leaving the United States behind for 'Fortress Europa'.

The Church of Satan appeared to go through a rather grim, fascistic phase during the 1980s. The 1990s seem to be seeing a resurgence of the 'carnival element'. What's your take on this?

The core of the Church of Satan has never been altered;

the premises on which it is based remain the guiding principles. However, we really are Devil's advocates and take our role of counter-balancing societal trends quite seriously. During the eighties, when it looked like society was perishing amidst an orgy of Political Correctness and ultra-mediocritisation (anything, no

generation of dedicated Satanists. We laid the groundwork for the current resurgence of 'Lounge Culture'. Books like Feral House's *Cad: A Handbook for Heels*, the ever-more prevalent imagery of Coop, Boyd Rice's preservation of overlooked cultural pleasures (Martin Denny, Scopitones, girl bands, 'thrift store art', and so many other things – the man is a dynamo at ferreting out forgotten orthodoxies that have evocative power). All of this has helped to prepare the way for what can be seen as a Carnival – a celebration of fleshly things all across the cultural landscape.

How do you see the Church of Satan progressing in the new millennium?

I see it still growing along the vectors established by Dr LaVey. The membership continues to grow, and those who are joining now seem even more talented and accomplished than at any previous time in our history. They come to us not out of curiosity, as we have ample literature in print, audio and video media to satisfy that, but out of commitment to forwarding the ideals embodied in our literature. These fellow pack members share our vision of a world where the natural balance has been restored. They are capable of moving things forward on all fronts. It is an exciting time – Satanism is for the living, and we are all living our lives to the fullest, and building the structure that we trust will have a lasting influence during the new millennium. Today and tomorrow belong to us.

Church of Satan luminaries in the CasaBonita Mexican theme restaurant jail (left to right): Shauna, Thomas Thorn of the Electric Hellfire Club, Peter Gilmore, Boyd Rice, Desirée Partridge and Diabolus Rex.

matter how shabby, was extolled, while talent was felt to be an insult to the less-gifted), some of our members decided to use fascist imagery as shock tactics to redress the cultural imbalance. Slovenliness was what the herd cherished; we wore black uniforms. The herd felt everyone must be made equal; we spoke for real stratification and natural selection.

Our values never changed, but our presentation did, and we always are aware of the power of showmanship. It was effective, and got some real opposition principles out there that influenced our current younger

LUCIFER RISING

Satanic Culture in the New Millennium

very few years a book is published on Satan – or some affiliated gothic topic – based upon the premise that the Devil is dead, or dying. This has been used as a starting point for authors ever since the sixteenth century, but reports of Satan's demise have been much exaggerated.

Modern culture treats the Prince of Darkness light-heartedly: Satan appears on Valentine cards, in comedy sketches, and advertising campaigns. The fact that we can laugh at Him is no indication of His waning powers. Satan encourages satire and scorn, thrives on laughter and irreverence – it's the Christian tradition that demands we approach the world with straight-faced, pompous sincerity.

Popular ambivalence about the Devil has plagued Christianity throughout its history. The Church needs Satan as its ultimate cosmic scapegoat, but His omnipresent threat is that His playful, charismatic evil can seem so much more attractive than Christian doctrine. (As my editor once asked – why are so many Satanists such nice, polite people, while so many Christians are malignant, neurotic bigots?) Thus, every infernal manifestation in modern popular culture, whatever its apparent intent, has Satanic significance. But are we, as Anton LaVey claimed, entering an 'Age of Satan'? Is Lucifer rising?

On a political level, the battle for hearts and minds continues to rage in the most powerful nation on earth, the USA. During the1980s, the forces of radical Christianity were among those who helped Ronald Reagan sweep to power. Folksy, reactionary and evidently no intellectual, this firm friend of the religious Right possessed a genius for appealing to the lowest common denominator. After a brief interlude with the colourless George Bush – who some believe fell from power because he could not secure the trust of the radical Christian lobby – the pragmatic 1990s were personified in the form of Bill Clinton.

Though ostensibly a Christian (still mandatory for everyone seeking political power in the USA), Clinton was no friend to the Bible-bashers – once intimating to a writer friend that his only true enemies were religious fundamentalists. Emblematically, his enemies tried to bring him down by drawing attention to his carnal sins. With devilish verve, the man in the White House hung onto political power and his popularity ratings. Despite working his way up the ladder behind a facade of liberalism, Clinton is a cynical operator with sinful tastes and a seemingly self-serving agenda. He's also a pretty sharp president.

One of the most unexpected supporters of President Clinton within the entertainment industry is the musical performer Marilyn Manson. The androgynous Ms Manson (a.k.a. the six foot six Brian Warner) is one of those rare creatures who cross the boundaries of being a mere entertainer to become a cultural phenomenon. His recipe for success displayed a grounding in LaVeyan Satanism: even his stage name is notably Satanic, a combination of Marilyn Monroe – the buxom sex symbol LaVey claimed to have had a brief affair with in the late 1940s – and modern Satanic icon Charlie Manson.

A dark carnivalesque aesthetic is prominent in Manson's work, as are images of childhood bogeymen and ritualised sexual deviance. Electronic and industrial elements collide with black metal and glam-rock to create a venomous cocktail that sacrifices musical purity for visceral impact. As a depraved harlequin, Manson tries, like the medieval witch, to turn the whole world upside down. Ugliness becomes beauty, notoriety becomes fame, pain becomes pleasure, the victim becomes the oppressor, and vice becomes virtue.

Above all, Manson epitomises the self-conscious scapegoat turned predator. When sanctimonious politicians railed against him, concerned parents' groups lobbied to ban his concerts and outraged evangelists filled their websites with apocryphal stories of blasphemous (and exaggeratedly criminal) excess, none seemed even dimly aware they were acting as the best publicity agents the divine Ms Manson could hope for.

Unlike the many rock performers who have employed demonic imagery, Marilyn Manson seems to understand it, and even endorses it. In his best-selling autobiography, *The Long Hard Road Out of Hell*, he devotes an entire chapter to his audience with Anton LaVey. Taking a break on his 1994 tour supporting Trent Reznor's Nine Inch Nails, Manson visited the Black House where he was ordained as a priest: 'As I left, LaVey put a bony hand on my shoulder, and, as it lay there coldly, he said, "You're gonna make a big dent. You're gonna make an impression on the world."'

One principle of LaVeyan magic is that in disowning the demonic, the former Satanist will lose all it has gained for him or her. To date, Manson has remained true to his roots (despite the pressures caused by his acceptance of the villain role, of which more later). If his music has been less overtly infernal since his big breakthrough, the 1996 concept album *Antichrist Superstar*, then his support for the philosophy of LaVey hasn't wavered. In *Satan Speaks!*, the posthumous 1998 collection of the Black Pope's essays, Manson provides a foreword which opens 'Anton LaVey was the most righteous man I've ever known' – recognition both of LaVey's status as, in outlaw-biker slang, a 'righteous dude', and of his perverse but stringent personal moral code.

In Manson's pigeonholing as a 'goth-rock star', he is the only performer to bring authentic Satanic credentials to that gloomily romantic musical genre. However, his ability to surf the Satanic *zeitgeist* has a perverse origin, as related in an interview for *The Black Flame*, the official Church of Satan magazine, just before the release of *Antichrist Superstar*:

'After ten years in a private Christian school, I was inundated and told about things like Armageddon, the Rapture, taking the Mark of the Beast, etc. When I realised it wasn't going to happen I felt fortunate, but at the same time I felt cheated. For me, the things that had tormented me as a kid, I have become. What I set my mind on was, if Armageddon wasn't going to happen, I was going to bring it upon the world myself. I felt the obligation to be exactly what they had told me to be afraid of. So on this record, I take on the role of the Anti-Christ. This record is me asserting myself in that position. It is the tale of how things are going to happen in the future. It will scare America, and rightfully so.'

Ironically, Marilyn Manson identifies the real engine behind the recent growth in Satanic culture: the Christians brought it upon it themselves. Adopting the role of your enemy's demons and scapegoats is a fundamental Satanic principle. In blasting youth subcultures and forms of entertainment as tools of Satan, Christian fundamentalists have only managed to highlight the vibrancy and excitement of infernal culture compared to the barren neurosis of their Church.

Marilyn Manson's spectacular Antichrist Superstar *stageshow featured a parody of a fascist rally.*

One consistent target has been role-playing games – often known generically by the name of the first innovator in that field, *Dungeons and Dragons*. Originating in 1974, *Dungeons and Dragons* offered players an imaginary world wherein they took the role of self-invented characters interacting with plots created by the referee, or 'gamesmaster', while conflicts were resolved using dice and a predetermined set of rules. It quickly became popular, particularly among adolescent males, selling over ten million games over the past 25 years.

Many schools and parents encouraged the activity, which fostered literacy and numeracy while encouraging young imaginations, but not everybody was happy with these innovative new games. The same accusations aimed at heavy metal music – that it encouraged suicide, violence and general delinquency – were levelled at role-playing games by evangelical Christian campaigners. (Research conducted by sociologists and behavioural psychologists – such as Daniel Martin and Gary Alan Fine in 1991 – has determined that, if anything, role-playing games improved social skills and emotional stability in the young.)

American fundamentalist Pat Pulling, who blamed the 1982 suicide of her son on *Dungeons and Dragons*, has become one of the most tireless campaigners against role-playing games. To her, role-playing rulebooks are recruiting pamphlets for the Devil. In 1986, during one of her anti-occult seminars, she asked, 'Where is the fantasy in this fantasy role-playing game if all the characters, deities, gods, spells, incantations, skills, and traditions are firmly embedded in actual occultism, demonology, sorcery, necromancy and magic? What *D&D* actually comprises is a crash course in sorcery which equips the avid player with the skills necessary to . . . perform satanic rituals.' (Once again, the manufacturers should have carried her endorsement on the packaging.)

Dungeons and Dragons, in common with many role-playing games, used a 'sword and sorcery' setting wherein knights battled dragons, and dwarves and elves roamed a quasi-medieval world, borrowing heavily from numerous historical and mythological traditions. Anyone hoping for 'a crash course in sorcery' would be justified in demanding their money back. It's no surprise that Christian fundamentalists perceived the game with a bizarre literal-mindedness – after all, their creed insists that everything in *The Bible* must be accepted at face value. More depressingly, law enforcement officers have attended 'occult crime' seminars where they were warned of the dangers of *Dungeons and Dragons*, schools were pressurised into banning it on site, and parents encouraged to see the game as a gateway to delinquency and death.

By the early 1990s, the tide turned as a new breed of role-playing enthusiasts began to surface from the counterculture. Previously regarded as the province of nerds, this new breed of black leather-clad gamers were determined not to be policed by self-appointed religious censors, and to subvert the slanders against them.

White Wolf, the most successful new company on the role-playing market, made their imaginary milieu a nihilistic modern setting they call 'Gothic Punk' – where monsters lurk just beneath the crumbling surface of the mundane world. While *Dungeons and Dragons* and its imitators had encouraged a simplistic, vaguely Christian 'good versus evil' morality, the universe created by White Wolf is far more murky and ambivalent.

In White Wolf's first and most successful game, 1992's *Vampire: the Masquerade*, the author quotes at length from

Computer games, the largest growth area in the entertainment industry, have shown a consistent fascination with the infernal. Requiem, a recent example, pits homicidal angels against nihilistic demons.

Adam Parfrey's *Apocalypse Culture*, in endnotes entitled 'Nature Red in Tooth and Claw' – where once the 'gaming' worlds of wizards and trolls were inspired by Tolkien, now they subscribe to a more ferocious, Nietzschean perspective. The designer, Mark Rein-Hagen, also explains: '*Vampire* was written in order to discover the nature of Evil. Evil most certainly does exist, but it is not as cut and dried as some would have us believe. The age-old dichotomy of good and evil, black and white, is false. *Vampire* is an exploration of evil, and as such, it is unsafe. You are digging deep when you play this game. This game was not meant to be comfortable – it was designed to provoke and inspire.'

The boldest publication to-date is the popular and critically-acclaimed 1997 game *In Nomine*, by the US company Steve Jackson Games. The back cover features the following warning: 'This book is intended for mature readers. It contains interpretations of religious themes which some readers may find unsettling.' This is the only concession to religious sensibilities in a game based around the conflict between angels and demons in a modern setting. Both God and Lucifer feature in a well-crafted product re-evaluating the mythical conflict between Heaven and Hell, from a cultured and witty perspective – here, the angels are just as brutal and merciless as their infernal counterparts. Currently a best-seller, it's inconceivable that such a cleverly controversial product could have enjoyed success in the USA as recently as ten years ago.

The rise of the demonic anti-hero in youth culture is also reflected in, of all places, the toy market. Toys like the moveable, voluptuous devil-babe Purgatori, or the rubber demon named Violator. Both characters originate in comic books: *Purgatori* belongs to a growing sub-genre of independent comics featuring well-endowed, demonic women in sordid sagas of breasts, blood and blasphemy. Glenn Danzig's *Satanika* is a prime example of this thriving cottage industry, while the current connoisseur's choice is Trevlin Lee Utz's Donna Mia – a demoness who conceals her infernal nature by sticking her tail up her arse.

The Master and Monica? The title is actually Devil Girl *by Coop, pop-culture's premier Satanic visual artist.*

Violator originates in the phenomenally-successful *Spawn* comic, whose creator, Todd MacFarlane, has featured on the cover of US business magazines hailing his success story. (Interestingly, MacFarlane also makes moveable figurines of traditional Christian-fundamentalist hate figures like KISS and Ozzy Osbourne. Maybe the evangelists should invest in a few and try sticking pins in them.) First published in 1992, *Spawn* is short for 'Hellspawn' – once an assassin working as a dirty tricks operative for the CIA, the lead character is betrayed and killed by his employers. Offered a second chance by the Devil, he sells his soul and returns as Spawn, a demonic creature possessed of terrifying infernal powers. Grim, violent and cynical, *Spawn* spins its story against the backdrop of an ugly world where the government, and even Heaven itself, are run by merciless, amoral forces. An implicit attack on conventional religious morality, *Spawn* regularly sells around a million copies an issue.

While the cynical tone, anti-Christian subtext, and explicit violence of *Spawn* have set precedents in the mainstream, other more adult titles have pioneered darker territories still. During the late 1980s and early 1990s, two comics surfaced that challenged both the limits of the medium and those of 'good' and 'bad' taste: Howard Chaykin's *Black Kiss*, a psycho-sexual *noir* thriller, featured kinky high-society Satanists; Faust, by Tim Vigil, was a saga of almost surreallistically graphic sex, violence and black magic that became a minor legend for its exuberant offensiveness.

Influenced by their success, market leader DC launched their adult imprint, Vertigo, in 1992 – with all of its most successful titles reinterpreting Christian mythology. *The Sandman*, a thoughtful metaphysical fantasy, included Lucifer among its characters. (He even got a comic to Himself, as hero of a three-issue spin-off published in 1999.) *Hellblazer* is a gritty, contemporary psychological horror comic with a hero – a roguish occultist named John Constantine – who frequently finds himself battling devils and demons. Constantine, however, also remains resolutely cynical towards the servants of Heaven. *Preacher* – a coarse but clever stylistic hybrid of road movie, western and occult thriller – features a Texan reverend imbued with a voice that cannot be disobeyed, the progeny of forbidden copulation between an angel and a demon. With his new-found power, he resolves to hunt down God Himself to make Him answer for the terrible state the world has fallen into. All these current titles tackle religious themes with a level of sophistication and explicitness unthinkable twenty years ago. Blasphemy is a regular component, while the most innovative creators in this maturing medium show increasing 'sympathy for the Devil'.

Indeed, it's not only comic-book art that wears its infernal colours with pride. Prominent American fine artists who claim inspiration from Old Nick include Church of Satan member Timothy Patrick Butler, whose distinctive work hangs somewhere between the Renaissance woodcuts of Albrecht Durer and a pornographic Dr Seuss. Self-described 'holy terror' Stephen Kasner depicts a morbid, dreamlike world of ominous shadows and maudlin dread. CoS Magister Diabolus Rex describes his work as 'necro-erotic', exploring the realms where the organic and mechanical meet, as first pioneered by the influential Swiss surrealist H. R. Giger. Coop is best known for the buxom female devils that inhabit his pop-art images of sleaze and seduction. All of these artists occupy the Satanic fringes of popular culture, their work more likely to appear on a T-shirt or tattoo than on the wall of some trendy gallery. While they may lack the approval of society's cultural arbiters, at least they're not dependent on government grants.

Images from the surreal world of Satanic artist Timothy Patrick Butler.

This dependency was the weak point in the artistic community's defences when, in the late 1980s, it came under attack from Christian elements in the US Government. Two photographers who had used their work to challenge or mock Christianity – Robert Mapplethorpe and Andres Serrano – had both received government funding via the National Endowment for the Arts, and subsequently became whipping boys for conservative and religious lobbyists. Serrano is best known for his 1987 photograph *Piss Christ*, depicting a crucifix suspended in a tank of the artist's own urine. Subtle it ain't – as with much of Serrano's work, it contrasts sacred and profane imagery while making heavy use of the aforesaid bodily fluids. As such, Serrano's mockery of the Christian Church is oddly reminiscent of the traditional Black Mass, wherein sexualising holy iconography and throwing shit, piss, blood and semen around were very much the order of the day.

While Serrano's images often border on the Satanic, many of the late Robert Mapplethorpe's photographs positively revel in it. This facet of his work is usually downplayed by both supporters and opponents – while conservatives were keen to attack him for his most explicitly gay material (frankly pornographic, though this is no bad thing), his sado-masochistic, homosexual erotica made him the type of outlaw the liberal establishment could applaud. For Mapplethorpe himself, however, the Devil was central to his life and work.

Mapplethorpe's best self-portrait, taken in 1988, shows the photographer in demonic

Images from the surreal world of Satanic artist Timothy Patrick Butler.

mode, complete with horns. As an art student, he used to keep a monkey named Scratch (after 'skrat', a medieval colloquialism meaning 'satyr', also a nickname for Satan), which he jokingly claimed was possessed. When Scratch died, Mapplethorpe beheaded him, boiled his skull dry, then made it the focus of a black altar in his apartment. (The young Mapplethorpe had even bought a goat's head from a butcher and surrounded it with candles in an effort to conjure Satan.) The pentagram, most potent of all Satanic symbols, was also a recurring motif in his pictures and sculptures. 'Whenever you make love with someone,' he once told a sexual conquest, 'there should be three people involved – you, the other person, and the Devil.' As Mapplethorpe's sex life and work became increasingly entangled, the artist would encourage a photographic model to indulge his most perverse sexual fantasies by whispering the mantra, 'Do it for Satan.'

While Mapplethorpe and Serrano were at the front line of the battle against censorship in the USA, in the UK a visual artist named Nigel Wingrove became a reluctant champion of sacrilegious freedom. In 1989, Wingrove submitted a short film he'd directed entitled *Visions of Ecstasy* for approval by the British Board of Film Classification. This atmospheric piece climaxes with its lead character – Saint Teresa, an obscure canonised nun – writhing erotically on a crucified Christ. Wingrove expected his modest art film to be certificated without comment. Instead, the censors unofficially banned it on the grounds that it might possibly (or possibly not) be illegal under British blasphemy laws. Wingrove, incensed, began a legal war with the authorities that dragged on for most of a decade.

Wingrove lost the battle over *Visions of Ecstasy* – but, with a middle-finger thrust at middle-class concepts of decency, he began an influential project named Redemption (later Salvation) Films. Basically a video distribution and publishing company, Redemption/Salvation's stylishly-lurid visual aesthetic originates with designer Wingrove's multiple obsessions of sex, nuns, lesbianism and blasphemy.

Despite the obvious demonic elements in his work – not least his compulsive sexual subversion of Christianity – Wingrove doesn't regard himself as a Satanist. This calls to mind

LaVey's dictum that you can't use Satanic images without promoting Satanism, as Wingrove's projects in recent years include the imagery that helped propel Cradle of Filth to the forefront of the black metal movement, and, at time of writing, a photographic series of *Satanic Apostles*.

If Nigel Wingrove is uncomfortable with the Satanic label, he's less circumspect about being associated with the modern fetish scene. With sexual fetishism a recurring theme in his work, Wingrove was instrumental in designing the glossy British magazine *Skin Two* – regarded by many as the unofficial bible for today's trendiest perverts. In the US and Europe, the final years of the second millennium have seen a huge increase of interest in sado-masochism, bondage and leather-and-rubber fetishism. What was once the object of derision and disgust is now the height of fashion. As ever with the promotion of deviancy into the mainstream, Satanism must take some of the credit.

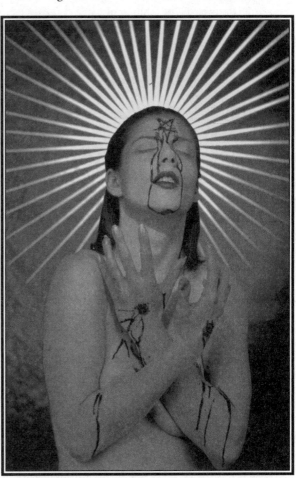

In April 1998, the Torture Garden – London's leading fetish club – held a 'Requiem for Anton LaVey'. 'We the participants are serious Magickians [sic],' announced the organisers, 'and we are performing this important ritual with real intent. At this time, near the end of the second millennium of Christian oppression, it is time . . . to throw off the shackles of religion and break its power. WE HAVE NO GODS BUT OUR OWN TRUE SELVES. The Black Mass is a great celebration of the Flesh, Ecstasy and Sexual Freedom. Our intent:- It is our Will, to summon Satan – FOR FUN!!!'

The event was entertaining, with four floors of self-conscious exhibitionism, though, sadly, Satan never put in an appearance. Perhaps this is because fetishism is almost conformist today, unlike the days when LaVey was an enthusiastic

One of Nigel Wingrove's Satanic nuns.

advocate of sexual perversity. As a popular speaker with the Sexual Freedom League, the Black Pope did not advocate universal promiscuity but indulgence of whatever appetites an individual might possess. Images of sado-masochism figured prominently in his descriptive language, on a personal, sexual and social level: one early Church of Satan rite, entitled the Strengthening Ritual, involved a member ('the Vessel of Pain') being symbolically whipped by the others to catharsise the masochistic tendencies of Christian morality.

In an interview with his younger daughter, Zeena LaVey recalled, 'I remember, as a very young child in the 1960s and early seventies, knowing the Dutch Madam Monique Van Cleef, who operated the most infamous Whip and Rod House (as they were then called). She was also one of the early members of the Church of Satan. Our house boy, Rudy, would only do his job if my mother demanded he wear a French maid's outfit and spanked him, earning him the nickname "Spanky" . . . In the realm of the pop culture Satanism of the sixties, there was a thin line between the supposed Satanic religion and a glorified sex club. Apparently many of the underground spanking clubs and brown wrapper peddlers of gags and whips thought there was a crossover, as the Church of Satan regularly received catalogues and newsletters on this then-secretive scene. It should be remembered that what has now become the fashionable S/M milieu was then illegal.'

Gotherotica is an archive of authentic satanic erotica maintained by the Reverend BJ, a Church of Satan member and editor in the adult entertainment industry.

Many have seen the increasing prominence of fetishism as evidence of the influence of Aids, a disease that makes unconventional, non-penetrative sex more attractive. This is only part of the picture. Fetishism is also an effort to make sex exciting again. The experiments in 'free love' of the 1960s and 1970s may have made promiscuity fashionable, in certain circles – but they also demonstrated that, to a person of any sophistication, anything in endless, monotonous supply could become dull. The secret of sexual satisfaction is aesthetic, not simply quantitative. In many ways, recent sexual developments have been a Satanic progression. Christianity preaches that sex is merely a procreative act, devoid of pleasure – sexual activity wherein proceation is avoided, or is near impossible, is therefore one of the most pleasurable blasphemies. Truly Satanic sex is where the individual indulges their own true personal proclivities – rather than aping the latest fad for PVC bondage-wear, or whatever the hip deviant is wearing this season.

The other major development in Western sexual mores (perhaps also connected to fear of Aids) is the rising prominence and respectability of pornography. Porn chic, which enjoyed a brief popularity during the 1970s, is back with a vengeance. Porn is inherently Satanic as an art form: it has no other role beside self-indulgence in its most basic form; it glorifies man's carnal nature, blending the most beautiful aspects of the human animal with the most debased.

Even today, much that is hidden about people could be exposed through their personal tastes in pornography (which is a relative term, given that that which titillates is in the eye of the beholder). Early coverage of the Church of Satan appeared most regularly in American porn magazines of the late 1960s and early 1970s (one prominent early member was also the USA's leading manufacturer of dildoes). The tradition is continued today when men's magazines publish explicit features on Satanism that other journals might avoid, while Satanists occupy prominent positions in what is deliciously termed the 'vice trade'.

Despite opposition from hard-line feminists and fundamentalist Christians (the same unlikely bedfellows who promoted the Satanic ritual abuse myth), the largest growth area in porn over the past decade has been the Internet – where devotees of the most exotic fetishes imaginable can find kindred spirits. As with all new information media, the Internet has been the subject of numerous scare stories, not least because it's difficult, or sometimes impossible, to monitor or censor. Ultimately, the fact that the Internet is nothing more than an efficient avenue of communication is no less worrying to those who would limit and control all information.

During the completion of this book there was an horrific massacre at the suburban Columbine High School, just outside Denver, USA. Two students – eighteen-year-old Eric Harris and seventeen-year-old Dylan Klebold – shot dead a dozen fellow pupils and one teacher, before turning their guns on each other in an act of suicide. It was a shocking crime by anyone's standards, but answers to the question 'Why?' were depressingly prosaic. Too prosaic, as it turned out, for a self-righteous world media that required a motive as grotesque as the crime itself.

In reality, two emotionally-disturbed teenagers had decided to take revenge on those they felt had persecuted them over the previous year. They even left a note stating, 'Don't blame anyone else for our actions. This is the way we want to go out.' But while the media so often preaches the gospel of individual responsibility, it rarely applies that philosophy. The usual suspects were dragged out – the Internet, neo-Nazism, computer games, Hollywood

Evilspeak, *a 1981 movie which dealt prophetically with Satan in cyberspace, was lauded by Anton LaVey.*

films. Finally the mob dragged another scapegoat to the forefront: Marilyn Manson – 'Antichrist Superstar' and self-proclaimed Satanist – whose photograph ran with news of the massacre in newspapers across the Western world, with no real explanation of the assumed connection.

In many ways, the whole episode confirmed Manson's main message: modern America is a dark and scary place, largely inhabited by deeply ignorant people with an aching desire to crucify anything they regard as deviant. By this point, however, the shock-rock star's smartest career move – his willingness to adopt the role of scapegoat for a sanctimonious society – must have weighed heavily. Much of the media smugly asserted that the boys' criminal motivation could be identified by studying their CD collections. Indeed, so adamant were the assertions that Marilyn Manson was somehow to blame that – if the newspapers took their own hypothesis of murder-by-influence seriously – the print media could stand accused of endangering his life by making him a target for unstable Christians.

As Anton LaVey was wont to observe, a crime scene where *The Satanic Bible* is found is immediately labelled a 'Satanic crime' – whereas a crime scene where *The Holy Bible* is found is not automatically identified as a 'Christian crime'. Just as the ignorant like to maintain they were made in the image of God, they also prefer to believe the Devil was fashioned from the likeness of that weird family down the street.

The ritual of driving the scapegoat out into the desert, stemming from biblical times, persists into the new millennium. Professor Carl Raschke – who, by way of co-incidence, teaches at Denver University – is the author of *Painted Black*, a woefully inaccurate and hysterical 'exposé' of modern Satanism. After the Columbine High School massacre, Raschke was interviewed for liberal British newspaper *The Observer*, which described his book as 'seminal' (presumably meaning that fundamentalist Christians tend to glue its pages together with excitement). This is in direct contradiction of ex-cop and criminal justice analyst Robert D. Hicks, whose 1991 book *In Pursuit of Satan* is an admirably sober and well-researched look at 'Satanic crime'. In his introduction, Hicks describes Raschke as 'an exemplar of all that I argue against in this book', who 'doesn't understand what he criticises'.

For all this, Raschke is revealing. He blames the Columbine massacre on 'a mix of Nazi chic with Anton LaVey's Church of Satan. It's a pop outgrowth of the decadent and occult movements of the last century in France, Germany and England, which formed the basis for Nazism. Same nihilism, same sordid fantasies.' (If Raschke knew anything about that which he feels able to pontificate on, he'd know that Nazism arose partly as a reaction against the decadence of Weimar Berlin – like the Professor, the Nazis saw themselves as opponents of decadence and evil.) 'The problem with American democracy,' he concludes, 'is that we just don't like setting limits to unacceptable behaviour – even when it's playing with political and spiritual nitro-glycerine.' To Professor Raschke, this 'unacceptable behaviour' is comprised of non-conformist ideas and symbols – in short, the most dangerous behaviour of all equates as freedom of expression and thought.

Satanists will continue to play with 'spiritual nitro-glycerine', while taking responsibility for our own actions and insisting that others accept responsibility for theirs. In embracing perennial Christian taboos, rejecting both the tradition of scapegoating and the 'victim culture', we intend to prevent present-day idiocies from dragging the next millennium into another miserable Dark Age. If a New Satanic Age is born, it will be born from the ideals of curiosity, independence and pleasure. From a Satanic perspective, there's room for optimism. The Devil is winning.

HATESVILLE

More words with Boyd Rice.

When I met Boyd Rice in the spring of 1999, he was performing in London. It seems like controversy dogs Rice wherever he goes: over the previous three weekends, nail-bombs had gone off in the capital. With the arrest of a single young man for the crimes, conventional wisdom suggested it was the work of a lone right-wing nut.

Despite the apparent arrest of the bomber, the concert, which featured acts – including Rice himself, appearing as 'Non' – with a following among the Far Right, had stringent security. Newspaper interviews with neighbours of the young suspect had already made an inferred connection with the recent Columbine shootings in the USA, when he and his friends were described as dressing in 'gothic clothes'. Only two weeks before, at the Columbine High School in Littleton, Colorado, near the Rocky Mountain foothills just outside Boyd's hometown of Denver, a violent massacre had been committed by two teenagers who, the media claimed, were inspired variously by fascism, Satanism and the Internet. Rice, used to the role of media villain and having performances cancelled due to protests, was unruffled.

You're something of a media villain, aren't you?
Yes.

Were you born a villain, did you achieve villainy, or did you have villainy thrust upon you?
I've always been this way. When I was two-years-old in the sandbox, I had a really specific view of the world. I've always followed that vision, and whenever I've strayed from it it's created problems. I try to be as frank as I can. When I tell people something, they know I'm not just bullshitting them because I have no reason to misrepresent myself. I think some of this has been thrust upon me because people want, or even need, villains. They can't be the good guys without having a bad guy to point at. In the absence of a real bad guy, they choose the next best thing, and find someone and say, 'You're promoting ideas that lead to massacres and bombings and stuff.'

How do you react when people say that?
There are supposed to be protesters here tonight. The anti-Nazi woman I was talking to earlier today said, 'Someone like you toys around with imagery which creates an atmosphere in which people with proclivities to violence are emboldened to pursue activities of violence.' I think it's bullshit. I've just been adapting

Boyd Rice (and friend), in characteristically stark, melodramatic pose.

Shakespeare's *Titus Andronicus* as a screenplay. It's the most violent thing you've ever read in your life – people's hands lopped off, their tongues cut out, beheaded, baked into a casserole. You have something like this being performed hundreds of years ago, but people didn't see Titus Andronicus and then go home and chop off somebody's hands or head.

You can't legislate sanity. There are always going to be people who have a screw loose or have been abused by somebody, and their reaction to that abuse may be overkill. You can't blame it on guns, music, or whatever it is people are trying to blame it on now. I don't know what someone who's planting nail-bombs thinks he's going to accomplish. Is everybody who dislikes homosexuals or Asians going to say, 'Oh yeah, well done, we're going to support this guy and his ideas'? What reasonable person's going to say that? Any reasonable person's going to say, 'This is totally inappropriate.'

What's your reaction to the recent massacre near your hometown? What do you feel about the way the media have scapegoated Satanism, and Marilyn Manson?
They blamed him. He was supposed to come on Walpurgisnacht [30 April] and play in Denver. One of

the kids, the shooters, the FBI went into his bedroom and found a copy of *The Industrial Culture Handbook*, and they went to San Francisco to see the publisher. I'm sure the publisher said, 'Boyd Rice is probably involved in this. He lives in Denver . . . ' So I expected them to come, but so far nothing. The only thing is that the last issue of *Der Spiegel*, in Germany, had an article about me saying I was a 'Goth superstar' into social Darwinism, and I created the atmosphere that led to this. So people in some places are blaming me.

There was a thing in Tasmania where some guy walked into a restaurant and killed all these people. He was some weird guy who'd just visited Disneyland, and I had a song about Disneyland on the album *Music, Martinis and Misanthropy*. This guy had asked the girl sitting next to him on the aeroplane to marry him. She said, 'Well, where do you live?' He said he lived in Disneyland. Someone put two and two together there and blamed me for that. Then there was a group of kids who planned to go to Disneyland and dress up as characters and shoot all these people.

Do you think people are finally getting sick of all this scapegoating?

Not at all. I think it gives people a platform for trotting out whatever their agenda is – guns are responsible, music's responsible, the way people dress. The initial coverage of the school massacre interested me for like a day. Then, after that, everybody in Denver got an opportunity to be a hero for a day, because they're the good guys compared to these kids who committed the violence. It seemed to me to be scapegoating at an unprecedented level.

Doors to Outer Gateways

Reflections and speculations from Diabolus Rex

Diabolus Rex is a Magister and long-time member of the Church of Satan, an increasingly popular cult artist who also created the cover painting of this book. We spoke in early 1999, communicating chiefly by e-mail, about how he combined his art and beliefs. His early introduction to the Church of Satan makes him as close to a 'generational Satanist' as one is likely to find in the real world.

What first drew you to Satanism?

I was always a Satanist, even from the time I was very young, and held a great fascination for all that was dark, forbidden, and feared. I considered the Devil my personal God even before Dr LaVey's *Satanic Bible*

found its way into our house. My parents attended a few of the very early lectures at what would later become Church of Satan central, and introduced *The Satanic Bible* into the home library, which was unusual to say the least at that time. This was late in 1969. I was born in 1960, so it was just the beginning of the 'Age of Fire'.

Diabolus Rex with his personal interpretation of Abraxas, the Gnostic demon who provided the name of Boyd Rice's 'fascist think tank'.

How does Satanism influence your art?

Satanism and my art are inseparable, and therefore should be seen as a whole. One could just as well ask, 'How has my art influenced Satanism?', and the answer would be as cogent. My daily routine reflects the importance Ritual and Magic play in my life. Painting everyday in my studio is a sojourn to my infernal keep, each new piece a doom released upon the world, a door to outer gateways smashed open to let the Dark Ones march through.

H. R. Giger is an obvious influence – why has he had such an impact on the darker fringes of culture?

Giger's impact has for the most part been in the influencing of the common man. Making the grotesque, the perverted, and the forbidden more acceptable for the masses, as they have been his greatest champions. I was first made aware of Giger's work in the late sixties when I was in Europe with my father, and immediately recognised the influence of external forces on his psyche.

His first books were the best, but have lost much of their initial impact no doubt to the overexposure of the style in the 'hipster' lexicon of so called 'extreme' culture.

Your work has a very sinister feel – is there any unifying theme/philosophy running through it?
My work has had so little exposure to the mainstream art mafia, as my reputation as a Satanist has always preceded it. My paintings do not represent a cleansing of my psyche, but an exercising of my WILL upon my surroundings. In this manner they share a similarity to the work of Austin Osman Spare, only I do not evade the origins of the work's imagery. The paintings can function as sigils [occult symbols], and create change in accordance with the Magician's desires, and ultimately this is the fashioning of a new Dark Aesthetic, and the creation of a Universal Satanic Necropolis.

Some occultic artists talk about curious effects, either involved in the creation of their art or as a result of their art. Have you had any such experiences?
Yes, and I was the first Satanic artist to relate these almost *X-Files*-style events that have taken place at my exhibitions and in my studio, and have made this known in interviews dating back over twenty years ago. I have stated in the past that 'my artwork was fuelled by the powers of Satan', and my prediction that it would soon become popular for artists to say 'the Devil made them do it' has come to pass. Events, ranging from fires and weird illnesses to earthquakes and ritual murders, have been blamed on my art and this is why gallery and museum curators have cancelled some shows, or taken out extra insurance policies when they have gotten wind of past exhibitions.

VISIONS OF BLASPHEMY

Words with Nigel Wingrove.

I'd known Nigel for several years when we spoke in early 1999, as he was about to undertake his most Satanic project to date: photographing a series of 'Satanic nuns'. A friendly but determined maverick, occupying the no-man's-land between the art world and lurid populism, Nigel brings a mischievous enthusiasm to his work that's decidedly contagious.

Why are you attracted to blasphemy?
I don't have an attraction to blasphemy, what I have an attraction to – and I couldn't tell you why – is

interpreting religion, particularly Christianity, visually. It's not that I set out to blaspheme, it's just that the images I create tend to be potentially blasphemous. The only analogy I can put is that I'm a bit like a kid with a chemistry set – I pinch and plunder different aspects and mix them all together and every now and then it might blow up.

I have no formal religious education or religious training, so my knowledge of Christianity is fairly simplistic, a layman's knowledge. So, if I hear a story or a biblical reading, I tend to think I'll put it in visually. The areas of Christianity tend to be those that pertain to women or blood, both of which appear in my work a lot. I know when I'm being blasphemous, or at least I know when I'm potentially causing offence. I thought I was safe on *Visions of Ecstasy* but I was wrong. I've worked on a series of images in my sketchbook to see how far we could go with provocative images for a series of T-shirts. But I didn't think there was any depth to them – a vampire Christ, a 'spunk Christ' – and I don't think it's that difficult to make an image that's going to offend.

I've been working for the past eighteen months on a series of big paintings I'm doing on computer. They're called *Seeing Heaven* and I've mixed images from pornography with the Old Masters, painters like the medieval Italian artist Giotto. I blend these very orthodox depictions of Christ, Mary and all these icons from Christianity with pornographic imagery, and then take the texture from the Old Master so when the picture's finished it's mixed so well it becomes an 'Old Master'-work itself. They are probably going to be profoundly offensive because that period of art defined how most people see God, Heaven, Christ and so forth. For me to dabble in that seems more shocking, because even though that's just an artist's view of Christ from the thirteenth century, it's become how most people see Him.

Do you belong to that loose infernal tradition in the art world, of blasphemous characters like the Decadent artist Felicien Rops or the flagellant poet Algernon Swinburne?
I'm a great admirer of Swinburne, but I have no agenda. It's not something I do deliberately, but I am very drawn to it. When I made *Visions of Ecstasy* I'd read dozens of books about Saint Teresa and I had no desire to hurt her memory. When the British Board of Film Censors said they thought it was blasphemous, to me it wasn't at all. It's quite gentle, and no-one from the Christian faith I know of ever found it blasphemous. 'Offensive' is the most anyone ever said.

What did you learn from the response to Visions of Ecstasy?
There was little response from the public because they were denied the right to see the film. What was

interesting at the time of the ban was that the support was from writers not film-makers, the main reason for that being that it was within months of the fatwa on Salman Rushdie. The only support I received from the film community was from Michael Winner. It was an unusual time in my life.

What was the British Board of Film Classification's official ruling on Visions . . . ?

The BBFC said they had a criteria which gave them the power to refuse a certificate on the grounds that, in their opinion, it broke criminal law. My lawyers said the BBFC had no right to interpret criminal law, that should be done by a court, and that they were exceeding their authority. It took seven years for the case to reach the European Court, where I lost the case in November '96.

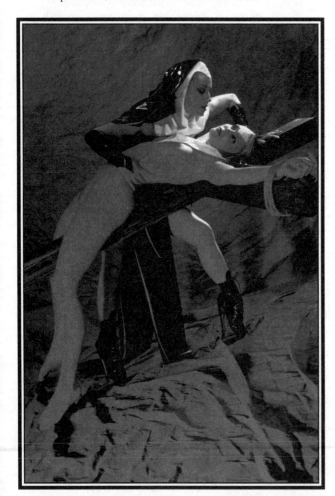

Nigel Wingrove's distinctive blend of sacred imagery and polished erotica has become a trademark style during the 1990s.

Do you think the fuss over your film had anything to do with the case of Rushdie's The Satanic Verses?

I do. In the twelve months previous to *Visions . . .* there had been *The Last Temptation of Christ*, Madonna's 'Like a Prayer' video and then the Rushdie thing, so blasphemy was very much flavour of the month. The BBFC hadn't done anything about *Last Temptation . . .* – which is a very good film, so obviously I wouldn't want them to – but a lot of people thought it was blasphemous. The Vatican had actually declared 'Like a Prayer' to be blasphemous. Yet my thing was a complete unknown, and if they hadn't have banned it I would have been lucky to sell 5,000. They thought they could make an end of it. I wasn't expecting the amount of publicity it got and the way it went, and I don't think they were either.

Can you see a broad Satanic artistic, or even cultural, movement developing?

Yes and no. I think, without question, it's getting much bigger, though I'm mildly sceptical. To give you an example, one of the images I shot, which was used by the band Cradle of Filth on one of their T-shirts, is a model with a crown of thorns all covered in blood. Of all papers, the *Daily Sport* used that shot. The *Daily Star* recently used some vampire pictures, and *The Sun* might be doing something with them. Five years ago, I could never have envisaged work of mine with these girls covered in blood being used in a national paper. I could never have imagined imagery like that being, if not mainstreamed, then not used in a shock-horror way. I'm doing a big still shoot of Satanic nuns with girls strapped to crosses, bathed in blood, suckling devil babies and all this stuff. *The Express* are covering that, as are London Weekend Television.

I'm not sure I can push this stuff much further. I think what's happened with people like the members of bands like Cradle of Filth, doing their pop columns, is that they're losing their credibility. I think there's a danger that as it gets more popular, enters the mainstream, it becomes diluted. It loses its power and becomes rather camp. One of the things I'm conscious of – particularly with the new stuff I'm working on, like the religious-pornographic images – is that they're still potentially very shocking. I think I broke a little ground in the early nineties, and there are more people doing it now, but a lot of that kind of imagery is now rather formularised – camp and non-threatening.

What's your take on Satanism? You use Satanic imagery but refuse to adopt the label . . .

I'm just as happy blaspheming Satanism as I am blaspheming Christianity, creating an image that'll rub Satanists up the wrong way as easily as Christians. I'm indiscriminate, if you like.

JUST A HORNY LI'L DEVIL

Coop's reflections on the world

Coop is the best known artist in the Church of Satan. His 'lowbrow art' features busty babes, dandy devils and high-octane hot rods. It appears on posters, album covers and T-shirts for a roll-call of the hippest rock bands: from Green Day and Nirvana to White Zombie and the Sex Pistols. The antithesis of the suffering-artist cliché, Coop is clearly having a blast and it's difficult not to share his enthusiasm for life. I spoke to him in person during his first UK exhibition in the spring of 1999, and by phone shortly afterwards.

When did you first become involved with the Church of Satan?

My friend Nick Bougas is a member of the Church and was one of the Doctor's closest friends in the last years of his life. Nick liked my art, thought it was Satanic, and took it upon himself to send some to Dr LaVey. The Doctor really liked it and seemed to think I was doing things the right way. He invited my partner Ruth and I to visit the Black House. I wasn't sure what to expect. I'd read *The Satanic Bible* and I agreed with the philosophy – it was pretty much how I lived my life anyway. Still, meeting Anton LaVey in person – I wasn't sure what to expect. I didn't know whether he'd be a kook, or a pervert, or a boring person. I was very happily surprised. We had a great time. We ended up spending the evening and well into the next morning talking to the Doctor and Blanche. He was an amazing person. We were very lucky, because we quickly became part of their small circle of people that they actually spent time with. After one of our visits, as we were leaving at around three or four in the morning to go home he passed an envelope over to us. As we were driving home we opened it up, and it was two certificates conferring priesthood in the Church of Satan.

Next time we were up there we talked to him about it, because we weren't really sure what was expected of us. Were we supposed to run around town in capes, scaring people? The Doctor said the obvious: 'Just keep doing what you're doing – you're more than fulfilling your obligations by just being who you are.'

How has the Church of Satan developed during the 1990s?

I can't speak for anyone else, but my interest in the Church always reflected my interests in my own life. I'm fascinated by all kinds of things, but the thing all my interests have in common is a Satanic undercurrent, philosophically. I've always been attracted to the odd little things in life. I think part of the reason the Doctor and I got along so well were these shared interests.

The first time we visited the Black House we spent a good portion of the evening talking about country and western music. The Doctor loved it because classic country and western is incredibly Satanic, it's so bombastic and sentimental. Its goal is to grab you by the balls, and that's pretty much the definition of Satanic music. I remember one night we were all in the kitchen listening to the Doctor playing the keyboard, and he started playing a medley of old hymns and gospel songs. His rendition sounded like the drunken organist at some rundown church. It was wonderful – hilarious, entertaining, and ultimately very touching. The mere fact that he was performing that kind of music would probably be a horrible surprise for many people. He had, among his many positive traits, a wicked sense of humour.

Part of the reason interest in the Church of Satan has revived is because of high-profile people like Marilyn Manson talking about it. But also I think, because the Church has been around for 33 years now, there's a whole generation of people like me born in the Satanic Age, if you will. There are a lot more people today living their lives outside the expectations of society. While some people can never get past the shock value of being a Satanist, that isn't the reason a lot of people are interested in the Church of Satan. It's just an outgrowth of who they are and it's not something they need to do to attract attention to themselves. It's just their philosophy, and it reflects the way they desire to live.

There's definitely been an attempt with my work, as I get further into it, to present these archetypal images, predominantly the Devil, and present them not as an object of menace or evil, but as a personification of what the Church of Satan's philosophy is about. This personification of the Devil is just a guy inviting you to experience for yourself the things you've been told are bad or wrong or evil, and make your own decision about them. That's why I typically depict the Devil as somewhere between a carnival barker and a used car salesman. I don't depict some drooling monster with fangs leaping out of the pits of Hell to rip your head off, because I don't find that interesting.

To an extent, while Marilyn Manson does use some of the shock tactics of rock and roll, he also manages to present what he's doing with a sense of humour and showmanship. He has fun with the audience and also at the audience's expense. This, of course, is also part of

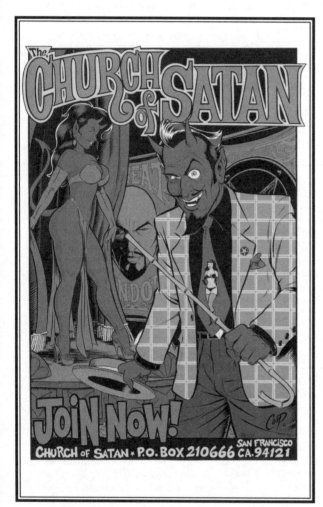

Coop's recruitment poster for the Church of Satan won approval from Anton LaVey – whose image dominates the design – for its distinctly carnivalesque elements.

Satanic philosophy. Anton LaVey played organ in a carnival and a burlesque house. He understood showmanship. That's what it's all about – wowing the suckers. That's what I try to do, and I perceive that in what Marilyn Manson tries to do.

There are a lot of people here in Hollywood who,

if they're not card-carrying members of the Church of Satan, they're certainly fellow travellers. They're aware of LaVey's writing and interested in the same areas we are. They help to promote our agenda, whether consciously or otherwise. In fact, when I've dealt with people in the entertainment industry, I've yet to meet one who was offended or horrified by my membership of the Church of Satan. I would imagine I'd get more static if I went around proclaiming myself a born-again Christian.

You've described your work as black magic – what do you mean by that?
On the simplest definition, all art is essentially creating something from nothing, and that's the definition of magic as far as I'm concerned. As an artist, if you're producing art that's affecting other people and resonates with them emotionally, intellectually, or just makes them horny, that fits with a Satanic definition of magic. Magic is getting people to do what you want, whether they want to or not. Unenlightened people tend to look for the more archetypal, obvious methods. Mixing love potions or rubbing crystals on each other's asses. That's bullshit, it doesn't fucking work.

On the other hand, there are people in the popular media who are able to make people think what they want them to think. If you couch what it is you want to say in the framework of something as innocuous as mainstream entertainment, that just makes the message more powerful. It's able to sneak under the radar so much more easily than if it has a big neon sign saying, 'This is the message.' That's what our culture has become. The only things that affect people's lives and make them do things are symbols. The people who have the most power in our society today are the people who can best wield these symbols. An understanding of Satanic magic is useful not only for changing things yourself, but also for seeing how other people are trying to manipulate you.

You've also said that painting the kind of women that you do almost seems to conjure them . . .
A lot of people, when they meet my girl, their first reaction is, 'You must model for his art.' The kind of women I draw, I drew before I met her, and to an extent that's why she showed up when she did. Certainly, she's not the only woman that's come into my life who looks

like I drew her. Other artists with an obsession with the female form have described how women start appearing who look like the women they draw. I think that's got to be a pretty damn wonderful side-effect of being a successful artist.

An appreciation of the more voluptuous figure seems to be a common feature among members of the Church of Satan. It's a modern heresy, in a way . . .
I think it's less of a heresy than the mainstream media would have you believe. Once you start talking to guys about what they like about women, I think I've only met a couple of guys who've been really emphatic about loving skinny women. Every other guy, whether they're in the Church of Satan or are completely unaware of it, naturally prefer women to have – to give an example – big asses. There are extremes, chubby chasers, men who are not interested in a woman who weighs less than 300 pounds. I'm not a member of that camp – I don't want a woman I'm afraid of being crushed by. But, as a general rule, many women in America could stand to gain ten pounds. This obsession among women with starving themselves until they look like concentration camp victims disturbs me. Men like women with a little meat on them. That is a Satanic stance, but certainly not an exclusively Satanic stance.

Women should look like women, and men should look like men. There's a reason that we have evolved into this state, and I can't see why we should throw that out of the window after it's worked for so many thousands of years. I think the image of the voluptuous woman is firmly planted in the darkest, least evolved parts of our brains. If you look at stone-age fetish figurines – like the famous Venus of Willendorf – they were just basically little statues of fat chicks that cavemen jerked off to. Really, this whole obsession with skinny women has only come into our culture recently. Before around 1964-65 skinny women were not considered attractive, with the one exception of the flapper era [the 1920s].

Women are appreciating the way they look is the way they're supposed to look, and maybe they should accentuate that. This is something I come back to a lot when I think about the way things are today. We're mere months away from the end of the millennium and everybody's running around like chickens with their heads cut off. Just recently we had this thing in Denver, where these kids went wild in their school and shot up a bunch of jocks or whatever. Everybody's running around like Chicken Little waiting for the sky to cave in. But, if you take a couple of steps back, and really look at what's going on in the world, I think things are getting better. There's no major thing I can point at to prove my point, but I see it in lots of little things. Granted we're going through a lot of cultural and social upheaval, but I think in many cases it's changing for the better. We're getting a little closer to a less fucked-up world. I bring this up because I think this argument about women reflects that. People are gradually shrugging off the media template of what we're supposed to look like. That's a good thing and also, in a way, a very Satanic thing.

BIBLIOGRAPHY

General Works on Satanism
Ashe, Geoffrey *Do What You Will* (W. H. Allen, UK, 1974).
Cavendish, Richard *The Black Arts* (Pan, UK, 1967).
Cavendish, Richard *The Powers of Evil* (Routledge and Kegan Paul, UK, 1975).
Lyons, Arthur *Satan Wants You* (Mysterious Press, US, 1988).
Nugent, Christopher *Masks of Satan* (Sheed and Ward, UK, 1983).
O'Grady, Joan *The Prince of Darkness* (Element, UK, 1989).
Rhodes, H. T. F. *The Satanic Mass* (Arrow, UK, 1965).
Zacharias, Gerhard *The Satanic Cult* (George Allen and Unwin, UK, 1980).

Historical Background
Bataille, Georges *The Trial of Gilles de Rais* (Amok, US, 1991).
Butler, E. M. *The Myth of the Magus* (Cambridge University, UK, 1993).
Clifton, Chas S. *Encyclopaedia of Heresies and Heretics* (ABC-Clio, US, 1992).
Pagels, Elaine *The Origin of Satan* (Penguin, UK, 1997).
Rose, Elliot *A Razor for a Goat* (University of Toronto, Canada, 1989).
Russell, Jeffrey Burton *Witchcraft in the Middle Ages* (Cornell University, US, 1972).
Russell, Jeffrey Burton *The Devil: Perceptions of Evil From Antiquity to Primitive Christianity* (Cornell University, US, 1977).
Russell, Jeffrey Burton *Satan: The Early Christian Tradition* (Cornell University, US, 1981).
Russell, Jeffrey Burton *Lucifer: The Devil in the Middle Ages* (Cornell University, US, 1984).
Russell, Jeffrey Burton *Mephistopheles: The Devil in the Modern World* (Cornell University, US, 1986).

Crowley, Summers, and Wheatley
Ahmed, Rollo *The Black Art* (Arrow, UK, 1987).
d'Arch Smith, Timothy *The Books of the Beast* (Mandrake, UK, 1991).
Summers, Montague *Witchcraft and Black Magic* (Rider, UK, 1946).
Suster, Gerald *Legacy of the Beast* (WH Allen, UK, 1988).
Symonds, John and Kenneth Grant (Eds.) *The Confessions of Aleister Crowley* (Routledge and Kegan Paul, UK, 1979).
Symonds, John *King of the Shadow Realm* (Duckworth, UK, 1989).
Wheatley, Dennis *The Devil and All His Works* (Arrow, UK, 1973).

The Third Reich
Brennan, J. H. *Occult Reich* (Futura, UK, 1976).
Goodrick-Clarke, Nicholas *The Occult Roots of Nazism* (I. B. Taurus, UK, 1992).
King, Francis *Satan and Swastika* (Mayflower, UK, 1976).
Suster, Gerald *Hitler Black Magician* (Skoob, UK, 1996).

The 1960s and Psychedelic Satanism
Atkins, Susan *Child of Satan, Child of God* (Hodder and Stoughton, UK, 1978).
Bainbridge, William Sims *Satan's Power* (University of California, US, 1978).
Bugliosi, Vincent with Curt Gentry *Helter Skelter* (Bantam, US, 1974).
Faithfull, Marianne and David Dalton, *Faithfull* (Michael Joseph, UK, 1994).

Landis, Bill *Anger: The Unauthorised Biography of Kenneth Anger* (Harper Collins, US, 1995).
Manson, Charles with Nuel Emmons *Without Conscience: Manson in His Own Words* (Grafton, UK, 1987).
Pilling, Jane and Mike O'Pray (Eds.) *Into the Pleasure Dome: The Films of Kenneth Anger* (BFI, UK, 1989)
Sanchez, Tony with John Blake *Up and Down with the Rolling Stones* (Blake, UK, 1991).
Sanders, Ed *The Family* (Nemesis, UK, 1993).
Satan, Johnny *Death Trip* (Death Valley, US, 1994).
Schreck, Nikolas *The Manson File* (Amok, US, 1988).
Sennitt, Stephen *The Process* (Nox Press, UK, 1989).
Process magazine.

The Church of Satan
Barton, Blanche *The Church of Satan* (Hells Kitchen, US, 1990).
Barton, Blanche *The Secret Life of a Satanist* (Mondo, UK, 1992).
LaVey, Anton Szandor *The Satanic Bible* (Avon, US, 1969).
LaVey, Anton Szandor *The Satanic Rituals* (Avon, US, 1972).
LaVey, Anton Szandor *The Satanic Witch* (Feral House, US, 1989).
LaVey, Anton Szandor *The Devil's Notebook* (Feral House, US, 1992).
LaVey, Anton Szandor *Satan Speaks!* (Feral House 1998).

Satanic Cinema
Clarens, Carlos *An Illustrated History of Horror and Science Fiction Films* (Da Capo, US, 1997).
Hardy, Phil (Ed.) *The Aurum Film Encyclopedia of Horror* (Aurum, UK, 1985).
Miller, Frank *Censored Hollywood* (Turner, US, 1994).
Newman, Kim *Nightmare Movies* (Bloomsbury, UK, 1990).

Modern Satanism
Abrahamsson, Carl (Ed.) *Fenris Wolf* volumes 1-3 (Psychic Release, Sweden).
Aquino, Michael, *The Crystal Tablet of Set* (The Temple of Set, US, 1983-93).
Drury, Nevill *The Occult Experience* (Robert Hale, UK, 1987).
Haining, Peter *Anatomy of Witchcraft* (Tandem, UK, 1972).
Harms, Daniel and John Wisdom Gonce III (Eds.) *The Necronomicon Files* (Nightshade, US, 1998).
Johns, June *King of the Witches* (Pan, UK, 1971).
Sennitt, Stephen (Ed.) *Nox: The Black Book Volume One - Infernal Texts* (Logos, UK, 1998).
Sennitt, Stephen and Gareth Hewitson-May (Eds.) *The Nox Anthology: Dark Doctrines* (New World, UK, 1991).
Smyth, Frank *Modern Witchcraft* (MacDonald Unit 75, UK, 1970).

Journals of the various groups under discussion were often consulted, including *The Cloven Hoof* and *The Black Flame* (Church of Satan), *Onslaught* (Luciferian Light Group), *Dark Lily* and *Fenrir* (Order of the Nine Angles) and *The Watcher* and *The Heretic* (Order of the

Left Hand Path).

Satanic Crime
Cawthorne, Nigel *Satanic Murder* (True Crime, UK, 1995).
Hicks, Robert D. *In Pursuit of Satan* (Prometheus, US, 1991).
Murray, Gary *Enemies of the State* (Simon and Schuster, UK, 1994).
Paisnel, Joan *The Beast of Jersey* (Pan, UK, 1972).
Richardson, James T. with Joel Best and David G. Bromley (Eds.) *The Satanism Scare* (Aldine de Gruyter, US, 1991).
St Clair, David *Say You Love Satan* (Corgi, UK, 1990).
Victor, Jeffrey S. *Satanic Panic* (Open Court, US, 1993).

Heavy Metal and The Moral Majority
Bashe, Phil *Heavy Metal Thunder* (Omnibus, UK, 1986).
Brothers, Fletcher A. *The Rock Report* (Starburst, US, 1987).
Davis, Stephen *Hammer of the Gods* (Sidgwick and Jackson, UK, 1985).
Godwin, Jeff *Devil's Disciples* (Chick, US, 1985).
Jasper, Tony and Derek Oliver, *The International Encyclopaedia of Hard Rock and Heavy Metal* (Sidgwick and Jackson, UK, 1991).
Jeffries, Neil (Ed.) *The Kerrang! Directory of Heavy Metal* (Virgin, UK, 1993).
Larkin, Colin (Ed.) *The Guinness Who's Who of Heavy Metal* (Guinness, UK, 1995).
Marsh, Dave *For the Record: An Oral History of Black Sabbath* (Avon, US, 1998).
Popoff, Martin *The Collector's Guide to Heavy Metal* (CG, US, 1997).

Rock magazines were consulted extensively, most notably the UK journals *Kerrang!*, *Metal Hammer* and *Terrorizer*.

Satanic Culture
Manson, Marilyn with Neil Strauss *The Long Hard Road Out of Hell* (Plexus, UK, 1998).
Morrisroe, Patricia *Mapplethorpe* (Macmillan, UK, 1995).
Moynihan, Michael and Didrik Soderlind *Lords of Chaos* (Feral House, US, 1998).
Parfrey, Adam (Ed.) *Apocalypse Culture* (Feral House, US, 1990).
Walter, Nicolas *Blasphemy Ancient and Modern* (Rationalist Press, UK, 1990).

INDEX